FORTRAN IV, 2ND ED.

JEHOSUA FRIEDMANN
Jerusalem College of Technology, Israel

PHILIP GREENBERG
Kingsborough Community College, New York

ALAN M. HOFFBERG
Information Resource Management, Inc., New York

JOHN WILEY & SONS
New York • Chichester • Brisbane • Toronto • Singapore

Publisher: Judy V. Wilson
Editors: Dianne Littwin and Martha Jewett
Production Supervisor: Rachel In
Composition and Make-up: Susan S. L. Ramirez

We dedicate this book to our families, whom we've tried not to neglect as we worked on this manuscript:

To Fanny Friedmann
To Rita Greenberg, Michael, Andrew, and Matthew Greenberg
To Janet Hoffberg, Amy Sue, Donna Lori, and Wendy Michelle Hoffberg

Acknowledgments

We thank Judy Vantrease Wilson, Publisher, Self-Teaching Guides, and Irene Franck Brownstone, Editor, Programmed Instruction, for their perceptive insight, imagination, good humor, and advice during our preparation of the manuscript.

Library of Congress Cataloging in Publication Data

Friedmann, Jehosua, 1938–
    FORTRAN IV, 2ND ED.

    (Wiley self-teaching guides)
    Includes index.
    1. FORTRAN (Computer program language)--
Programmed instruction. I. Greenberg, Philip J.,
joint author. II. Hoffberg, Alan, 1940– joint
author. III. Title.
QA76.73. F25F75 1980   001.64'24   80-21709
ISBN 0-471-07771-2

Printed in the United States of America

81   10 9 8 7 6

Foreword to the Second Edition

In the past five years since the first edition of FORTRAN IV was published there have been some major changes in the philosophy of teaching programming and programming style. From these have evolved the concepts of structured programming and hierarchial program design. The use of structured programming enables the programmer to create programs using standard structures (IF-THEN-ELSE, DO-WHILE) which make it easier to document, test, and prove the accuracy of a program. Hierarchial program design allows the programmer to sub-divide a program into functional modules which are called by a main module when required.

The FORTRAN language has also changed with the publication of FORTRAN 77 (officially called American National Standard Programming Language FORTRAN, X3.9-1978). This new version of the FORTRAN language has new input/output operations (including new FORTRAN codes), a new IF-THEN-ELSE statement, and an enhanced DO statement. The new enchancements in FORTRAN 77 will make the language easier to use by both scientific and commercial users.

The forthcoming FORTRAN 77 compilers from major hardware vendors will, no doubt, contain enhancements of the new FORTRAN language and make this first "high level" language easier to use and up-to-date for the 80's. Users of FORTRAN 5 compilers will find many of those features in this book.

Users who do not yet have a FORTRAN 77 compiler will find illustrations of the major enhancements employing the 1966 FORTRAN language. Thus, one can write structured programs without being concerned with the level of the compiler. When a FORTRAN 77 compiler becomes available on their computer, the program can be easily upgraded (modified) to use the more powerful FORTRAN 77 statements.

Another major change since the time of the first edition is the shift away from punched-card oriented batch processing mainframes to real-time disk oriented systems running on all size computers from mainframe down to micro-computers. Many programs and much data are now entered into a computer system by using CRT terminals and hard-copy terminals. Thus, we have included in this new edition a discussion of data terminals and also the use of various magnetic peripherals (disk, diskette, tape) in our illustrative programs.

Alan Hoffberg prepared a supplement on FORTRAN 77 for the APPLE II mini-computer. This compiler, available since late 1980, was one of the first implemented on a mini-computer. You may purchase this supplement directly from the publisher, whose address is at the bottom of page vii. The cost of the supplement is $4.50 postpaid.

Jehosua Friedmann moved to Israel since publication of the first edition. The other authors take full responsibility (and kudos) for errors of omission and commission.

We wish to thank Judy Wilson, Dianne Littwin, and Doreen Jasquith of John Wiley & Sons for their continuing high-level assistance with this new edition.

Philip Greenberg
Alan M. Hoffberg

New York
August 1980

To the Reader

Although FORTRAN stands for FORmula TRANslation, it's no longer true that FORTRAN is a programming language solely for scientific programming applications. More and more business firms are recognizing how simply and efficiently an application can be programmed in FORTRAN. In this Self-Teaching Guide, we present a well-rounded variety of problems to suit the varied tastes of those interested in FORTRAN.

Because some of you will have had no previous background in data processing, we've provided Chapter Zero—a brief introduction to the world of data processing: its terms and concepts—so that the jargon used in the subsequent chapters will not seem strange.

We expect that you'll want to begin writing FORTRAN programs as soon as possible, so we've placed all of the basic essentials within the next three chapters. Chapter One familiarizes you with a FORTRAN program and the coding form, along with how to flowchart a simple computer solution to a problem. In Chapter Two we show you how to perform arithmetic calculations and move data around inside the computer's memory. After you've completed Chapter Three on the elementary concepts of input and output, you'll be writing simple but complete FORTRAN programs.

At this point, though, you won't be satisfied because you will want to control the execution of your program, that is, repeat certain instructions or skip others, depnding upon various conditions tested within the program. So we present elementary control statements in Chapter Four.

Then we give you more working tools: intermediate level input and output is presented in Chapter Five, with advanced input and output covered later in Chapter Nine. But don't skip ahead because the material from the intervening chapters will be required.

Chapter Six presents additional control statements which will allow you to write powerful programs, in which a few statements can activate a large amount of data processing. These control statements are then used with the multi-dimensional variables presented in Chapter Seven. Chapter Eight presents explanations and illustrations of other types of variables.

Chapter Nine covers advanced features of input and output, drawing upon the resources presented in the earlier chapters.

After you've written a number of FORTRAN programs, you'll realize that an identical sequence of FORTRAN statements may appear repeatedly within a program or series of programs. It's at this point you will then appreciate the contents of Chapter Ten: functions and subprograms which provide you with the ability to modularize and "reuse" FORTRAN coding without constantly rewriting it.

Chapter Eleven is like the frosting on the cake—not really necessary, but it does make the difference between one programmer and another. There we present introductory material on specialized input and output using magnetic tape and disk devices, as well as other interesting FORTRAN programming techniques.

The Appendixes contain valuable reference information, including the resulting precision of arithmetic operations, descriptions of the built-in FORTRAN library functions (reusable FORTRAN coding), and some ideas for writing more efficient programs.

How to Use This Book

To learn FORTRAN, you need only this book, a pencil, lots of scratch paper and FORTRAN coding forms, and a quiet place to work. You do not need any previous data processing background nor do you need access to a computer. However, if you will be using a particular computer installation, find out where the FORTRAN manuals are, so you can see what specific features your computer system offers.

The material is presented in short numbered sections called frames. Each frame teaches something new about FORTRAN and then asks you to answer a question or write a program segment. After you have completed the question or program, you should compare your answer with the answer given following the dashed line. We urge you to keep the book's answer covered with an index card or piece of paper until you have written your own answer. We've carefully designed the questions to call your attention to important points in the examples and explanations, and to help you learn to apply the material being explained or demonstrated. If your answer is correct, you understand the material and are ready to go on the next frame. If your answer does not agree with the book's, you should review the previous frames to be sure you understand the material before you go on.

At the end of each chapter is a Self-Test which helps you to evaluate how well you learned the material in the chapter. Answers are given at the end of the test, along with frame references if you wish to review the frames on a particular question. You may test yourself immediately after reading each chapter. Or you might do a chapter, take a break, and save the Self-Test as a review before you begin the next chapter.

Each chapter begins with a list of objectives—what you will be able to do after completing the chapter. If you have had some previous experience using FORTRAN and these objectives look familiar, you can use the Self-Test as both a review and a guide showing where you should start following the text. Try the Self-Test before reading the chapter. If you do well, study only the frames indicated for the questions you missed. If you miss many questions, start at the beginning of the chapter.

Because of the length of the manuscript, we were unable to include a Final Test in the published book. However, a draft copy of the Final Test is available on request from:

Editor, Self-Teaching Guides
John Wiley & Sons, Inc.
605 Third Avenue
New York, New York 10016

Authors and publisher would welcome comments on the use of this book. Please send any comments or data for revision to the above address.

Contents

CHAPTER ZERO
Introduction to Computer Concepts

In this chapter we will introduce you to the computer and give you an idea of how one operates. You will learn some basic terminology required for proper understanding of this Self-Teaching Guide. When you have finished this chapter you will be familiar with:

- a general purpose digital computer;

- a computer system;

- input and output units;

- machine language;

- high-level programming languages;

- programming syntax and semantics;

- the FORTRAN language;

- . . . and other technical computer jargon.

If you already understand how a computer system operates, you may skip the first part of the chapter and start with the introduction to the FORTRAN language in frame **17, on page 16.**

What is a Computer?

1. A computer is an electronic machine that is capable of processing incoming information (data or instructions), and creating from it outgoing information or data. Whereas a bulldozer manipulates dirt and rocks, we can think of a computer as a high speed symbol manipulator; that is, a computer is capable of doing arithmetic calculations, reading, writing, storing information, and even making decisions.

A computer is a "dumb machine"—it can do only what we have told it to do through our <u>instructions</u>. The process of writing those instructions is called <u>coding</u> or <u>programming</u>. The instructions we code to solve a particular problem form a <u>program</u>. We call the person who codes the instructions a <u>programmer</u>. <u>Data</u> is any fact that can be manipulated by the computer following a recipe (program) provided by the programmer. Finally, a program is a set of instructions read into a computer which operates on data, or information.

There are two types of computers: analog and digital. A digital computer (which represents data by a counting process) can do anything an analog computer (which represents measurements in continuous form) can do—but the reverse is not true. Moreover, the digital computer can yield more accurate results. This Guide deals only with digital computers.

A general purpose digital computer can accept many different kinds of programs and therefore is capable of solving one type of problem after another whenever a new program is supplied. However, a special purpose digital computer is designed to use a program built into it to perform special operations repeatedly. Whenever we use the term "computer" in this Guide, we mean a general purpose digital computer.

Answer true or false.

_____ (a) A missile-guidance computer is a special purpose computer.

_____ (b) A computer that can calculate payroll, keep track of inventory, and diagnose a patient is a general purpose digital computer.

_____ (c) An analog computer is generally more accurate than a digital computer.

- - - - - - - - - - - - - - - - - -

(a) true; (b) true; (c) false

2.   A typical computer system has six basic components:

Control unit;

Central or main storage unit;

Arithmetic and Logical Unit (ALU);

Auxiliary storage unit;

Input units;

Output units.

The first three are often combined into one machine called the CPU (Central Processing Unit). The CPU is directly involved in processing information (data).

Information entering the computer system is called input. This information, once entered, is then processed by the computer program, and the information produced as a result of the processing is called output. The last three components of a computer system, as indicated above, are involved in the input process of feeding information into storage and the output process of creating information from data in storage. Input and/or output is referred to as I/O. The following photographs show a typical large computer system, the IBM 4331, as-well as a typical personal computer system, the TRS-80.

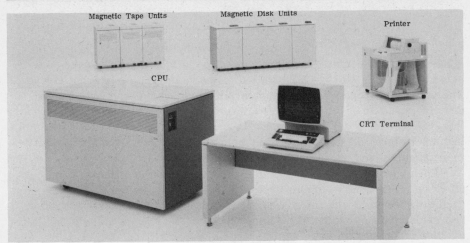

IBM 4300 Series Computer with CRT and Printer.   Courtesy IBM Corporation

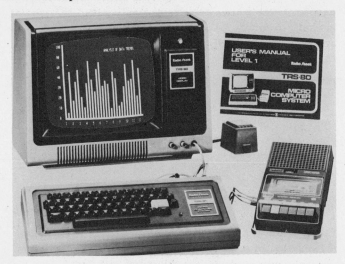

Radio Shack TRS-80 Microcomputer System

(a) Information which enters a computer system is called_____.
(b) The computer processes the inputted information to produce_____.

- - - - - - - - - - - - - - - - - -

(a) input; (b) output

  The next few frames refer to the binary, hexadecimal, and octal number systems. If you are not familiar with these systems, don't worry—just read on. You won't really need to know them to understand the rest of the book. But if you want to learn more about them, two other Self-Teaching Guides, Ruth Ashley's Background Math for a Computer World, second edition, or Introduction to Data Processing, second edition by Martin Harris, would provide these prerequisites, as would many other introductory books in data processing or computer science.

Main Storage

3.   The computer manipulates data by following instructions. These instructions and associated data are stored in the memory unit of the computer called <u>main storage</u> (also called <u>primary storage</u> or <u>internal storage</u>). The internal storage in most computers is composed of semi-conductor devices (made up of integrated circuits) which are extremely small. Today's integrated circuits are technologically equivalent to thousands of transistors and other electrical components. A typical chip might measure five milli-meters square and would cost under $100.00.

Each position in memory, called a bit, can assume either of two states; off or on. The binary number system which has two digits, 0 and 1, is often used to represent these two states. For example, 0 represents off and 1 represents on. For this reason, each memory position is called a <u>bit,</u> a contraction for <u>binary digit.</u>

Prior to the 1980's, a frequently used memory technology was the use of small magnetic cores which were very small (about the size of a pinhead) and could be easily magnetized into two possible states, that is, magnetized clockwise or counterclockwise. The two magnetized states could represent the on and off states.

Answer true or false.

_____   (a)   A bit can be either of two possible states: <u>off</u> or <u>on</u>.

_____   (b)   The state of a bit can be represented by the binary digits 0 or 1.

_____   (c)   A bit is a small chunk of plastic material.

- - - - - - - - - - - - - - - - - - -

(a) true (b) true (c) false

4.   Just as the Morse telegraph code combines dots and slashes into groups to represent symbols, bits are organized in groups for the same purpose. In many computers main storage is segmented into groups of eight adjacent bits, often called a byte. Eight consecutive bits (one byte) can have 256 <u>different</u> combinations of 1's and 0's. Therefore we may assign up to 256 different meanings to a byte depending on the combination used. So the computer is given the ability to associate a particular combination of bits with a specific symbol. For example, some computers associate 11000010 with the letter B. The various combinations of 1's and 0's in a byte are known as the EBCDIC code (Extended <u>B</u>inary <u>C</u>oded <u>D</u>ecimal <u>I</u>nterchange <u>C</u>ode). In this code the letter B is represented as

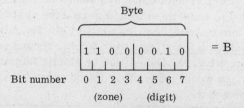

It is convenient to divide a byte in two halves, the <u>zone</u> portion and the <u>digit</u> portion.

Four binary digits correspond to <u>one</u> hexadecimal digit, so a byte can also be represented as two hexadecimal digits. The example below shows one set of codes.

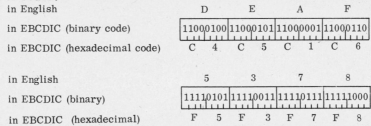

	D	E	A	F
in English	D	E	A	F
in EBCDIC (binary code)	11000100	11000101	11000001	11000110
in EBCDIC (hexadecimal code)	C 4	C 5	C 1	C 6

	5	3	7	8
in English	5	3	7	8
in EBCDIC (binary)	11110101	11110011	11110111	11111000
in EBCDIC (hexadecimal)	F 5	F 3	F 7	F 8

Other codes are common, too. In the BCD (<u>B</u>inary <u>C</u>oded <u>D</u>ecimal) six consecutive bits represent 64 different characters, alphabetic upper case, numeric, and special characters. ASCII (<u>A</u>merican <u>S</u>tandard <u>C</u>ode for <u>I</u>nformation <u>I</u>nterchange) code uses seven consecutive bits to represent symbols. Up to 128 different symbols may be represented. The ASCII-8 code is an eight-bit version of the ASCII code used by computers that use the eight-bit code. The ASCII code was introduced by the communications and data processing industry to enable efficient communication between different types of computers and other peripheral equipment. The ASCII code is used in microcomputers and minicomputers.

(a) What is a byte?_____

(b) How many different combinations of 0's and 1's can a byte have?
_____

- -

(a) A byte is a group of eight adjacent bits that may represent a symbol.

(b) 256 bit combinations

5. We can compare computer storage with mailboxes in a post office where each box is identified by a number. We hope you agree that the contents of a mailbox are separate from, and not the same as, its address (number). In the same way the computer allocates a <u>unique address</u> (a number) to each memory location, separate from the numbers or alphabetic letters contained in that location. When writing a program the programmer assigns a <u>symbolic name</u> (or address) to each storage location. The computer uses a <u>cross reference table</u> to associate this name to a unique numerical address, thus relieving the programmer of this arduous task. (We'll discuss later how to select names.) Remember, a symbolic location name is the same as a location address (number) and therefore <u>not</u> the same as the content in that storage location.

Main storage

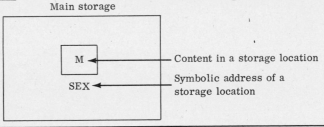

M ← Content in a storage location

SEX ← Symbolic address of a storage location

It is customary to use the letter K to denote a group of 1,000 addressable storage positions (to be precise, $K = 1,024 = 2^{10}$). A typical computer might have 64K storage locations. Most computers have storage capacity from 32K to over 1,000K.

Answer true or false.

_____ (a) A storage location may contain digits, letters, or any other recognizable symbols.

_____ (b) Each storage location is identified by an individual storage location called an address.

_____ (c) The computer assigns a symbolic address to each storage location.

_____ (d) A symbolic address is the same as the contents of that address.

- - - - - - - - - - - - - - - - - - - -
(a) true (b) true; (c) false (d) false

6. A computer is equipped with electronic circuits to read and write information in and out of the main storage. When we enter information into a storage location, it replaces the information previously contained in that location. When information is retrieved from a memory location, the contents in that location remain unchanged. In fact we obtain a duplicate of that information. Therefore, once we enter information in storage it can be reused many times. In this respect the information is similar to music or voice stored on a tape for playback on a tape recorder. Below we illustrate these ideas.

Main storage

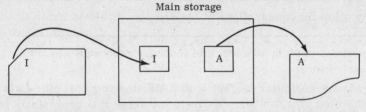

Answer true or false.

_____ (a) Once magnetized, a memory location is capable of retaining its magnetism.

_____ (b) When we input information into a memory location the previous content of that particular location remains unchanged.

_____ (c) Many computers can input and output (I/O) information to and from storage in one millionth of a second or less. (Take a guess; we didn't tell you about this!)

- - - - - - - - - - - - - - - - - - - -
(a) true (c) true; (b) false

7. Some computers use one byte (with its own address) as the basic unit of information. Each byte is generally used to represent a unit of information. A unit of information is called a <u>character</u>, and generally consists of a letter, digit, or special symbol such as $. Characters are generally grouped into

words, which are stored in consecutive bytes. Such units generally represent one number. The size (number of bits) of the computer word will determine the magnitude of the number that can be represented in storage.

Word size usually ranges from 8 bits to 32 or more bits, depending on the intended application of the computer. However, any given computer has only one word size--such as a 16 bit word length. Computers intended for heavy computational use might have 32 bit or larger words. On the other hand, commercial business applications oriented towards character processing typically have 8 to 16 bit word lengths.

A word has a single address, that is, the address of the first byte. FORTRAN language uses variables (that is, symbolic names) to define addresses, so when we reference a symbolic address (variable) in a FORTRAN instruction, the computer automatically stores and retrieves a word. For example, the variable name AMT may refer to a specific area or address in storage which contains a word, or unit of information. To store a larger number we may use a double word, also addressed as a unit. (We'll elaborate on this in Chapter Eight.)

Suppose a computer uses eight bits in a byte and four bytes in a word; match one letter entry in column A to one number entry in column B.

	A		B
_____	(a) byte	(1)	64 bits
_____	(b) half word	(2)	8 bits
		(3)	16 bits
_____	(c) word	(4)	32 bits
_____	(d) double word		

- - - - - - - - - - - - - - - - - - -

(a) 2; (b) 3; (c) 4; (d) 1

Auxiliary Storage

8.   Oops, we almost forgot—there are two kinds of storage, main storage and auxiliary storage.

Main storage is used to place or store input information and to remove output information as needed. This information can be:

> data (for input, computer processing, or output);
>
> instructions to direct computer operations;
>
> reference data needed during execution of a computer program (tables, codes, and constants).

All information handled by a computer must pass through main storage, so main storage must have the capacity to retain the instructions and data needed during processing of a program. Many applications exceed the capacity of main storage and require additional storage which is supplied by auxiliary storage.

Auxiliary storage (also called secondary storage) is of two types:
(1) Sequential access, which includes all kinds of magnetic tape storage

media. To locate a record we must read sequentially all the records preceding the record we desire (hence the name sequential access), just as with a home tape recorder we must "run through" the beginning of a tape to reach the part we want to hear.

(2) <u>Direct access</u>, which includes drum, data cell, disk storage media, bubble memory, and non-rotating solid state "disk." On these media any record can be accessed directly (hence the name direct access), just as we can move a phonograph needle directly to the location of the music we want to hear without having to hear the music from the beginning of a record.

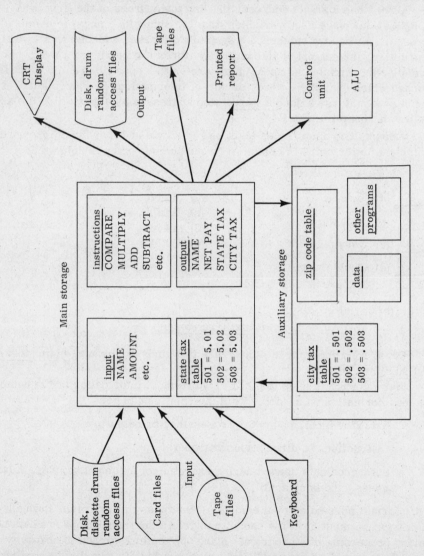

Main storage is much more expensive than auxiliary storage but it is also much faster, so it is used to store the instructions and some data required during program execution.

Match one letter entry in column A to one or more numeric entries in column B.

A	B
_____ (a) Main storage	(1) Secondary storage
	(2) Magnetic core storage
_____ (b) Auxiliary storage	(3) Magnetic disk
	(4) Magnetic tape
	(5) Magnetic drum

Answer true or false.

_____ (c)   Auxiliary storage is used to hold the data and the instructions
needed during program execution.

_____ (d)   Main storage is used for storing mainly data not immediately required during program execution.

- - - - - - - - - - - - - - - - - - -

(a) 2; (b) 1, 3, 4, 5; (c) false   (d) false

Virtual Memory

9.   A computer functions properly only when the program and instructions
are in main storage. Therefore, the programmer must be sure that his program and the required data fit into available storage. In situations where
memory is too small to fit a complete computer program we use a technique
called segmentation. This technique requires a main segment of the program
to reside in main storage at all times. The rest of the program is segmented
into small parts. The first segment is placed into main storage along with
the main segment; the rest is placed into auxiliary storage. After the first
segment is executed, another segment is brought into main storage by program command, thus replacing the first segment. This process is repeated
for the other segments in auxiliary storage.

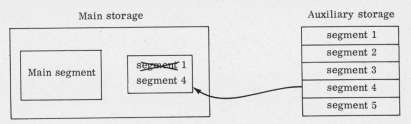

Most of today's computers implement a concept called virtual memory.
The basic idea is that the computer, rather than the programmer, automatically segments the program. These segments are scattered throughout main and auxiliary storage. The computer uses tables and indexes to
keep track of each segment and to move a segment into main storage when-

ever required.   Because there appears to be no limit to the amount of storage available, the programmer does not have to be concerned with storage management.   Hence the name virtual memory.

And now, what is virtual memory?_____

_____

_____

- - - - - - - - - - - - - - - - - - -

Virtual memory is a technique used by the computer to manage the location of a program by segmentation so that the computer seems to provide the programmer with an almost unlimited amount of storage.

Input and Output Units

10.   Card input and output units are often combined into one unit.   A card reader is an example of a popular input unit.   Often information is punched into cards by a keypunch machine (which greatly resembles a typewriter). On the next page is a typical 80-column punched card with a standard set of punched symbols.

A 96-column punched card, shown below, is also common.

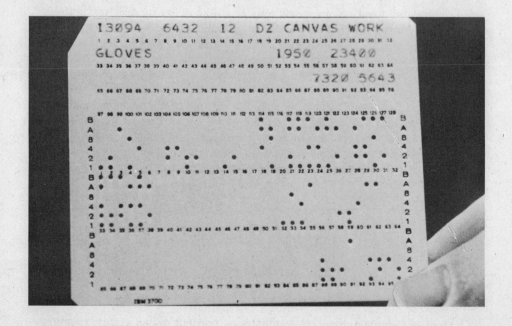

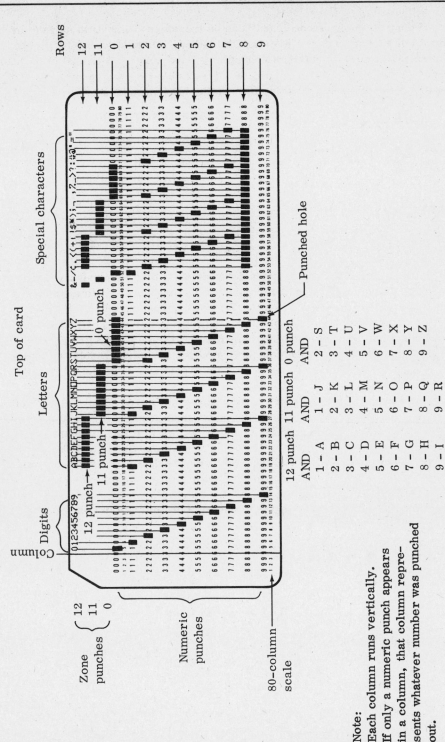

Information on punched cards can be transferred (input) to storage by means of a card reader. In a similar fashion, information can be punched (output) from the computer into cards by a card punch. A typical card reader can process 1,000 cards per minute. This is very slow compared to a computer which can execute instructions in the microsecond (μ sec) range.

Match one entry in column A to one or more entries in column B.

Column A

_____ (a) card reader

_____ (b) card punch

_____ (c) keypunch machine

Column B

(1) output unit
(2) puches holes into cards
(3) input unit

- - - - - - - - - - - - - - - - - - - -

(a) 3;   (b) 1, 2, 3;   (c) 2

11. A keyboard terminal (either a CRT terminal or a teletypewriter) is frequently used to enter instructions and data into the computer storage. A keyboard terminal resembles an electric typewriter with additional keys that perform some special functions. A programmer can key in a program and data, and then command the computer to execute the program. The programmer's input and the computer's output are either displayed on a CRT terminal or printed on paper in a teletypewriter (also called a hard-copy terminal).

If you have such a terminal available, by all means use it. A FORTRAN program and the resulting output can be communicated with a terminal. A terminal is a relatively slow device but it serves well for communicating directly with the computer. Most computer systems use a keyboard terminal called a console, to communicate with the data processing staff and vice versa. Generally, the console is not used for extensive Input/Output, or I/O.

Match one entry in column A to one or more entries in column B.

Column A

_____ (a) hard-copy terminal

_____ (b) card reader

_____ (c) CRT terminal

Column B

(1) is a relatively slow I/O device
(2) operates only as an input device
(3) resembles an electric typewriter
(4) displays output on a screen

- - - - - - - - - - - - - - - - - - - -

(a) 1, 3;   (b) 2   (c) 1, 4

12.   There are some advantages in using a CRT terminal over a hard-copy terminal for data entry and retrieval purposes. A programmer can print a form on the screen of a CRT terminal. The user of the program can then enter information onto the "form" since the cursor (pointing to where information will be written) can be controlled by the program. The user can easily correct data entry errors on the screen before the information is

transmitted to the CPU for processing. A CRT terminal can transmit and receive information faster than a hard-copy terminal. The user is also able to get a "hard-copy" of the information on the screen by printing it into a small printer which is attached to the terminal.

Another advantage of a CRT terminal over a hard-copy terminal is for entry of programming code. A program can be completely entered, and then a "clean" copy of the program can be printed on a line printer. This eliminates a lot of paper usually produced during program entry with deletions, corrections, and so on.

You would want to use a CRT terminal rather than a hard-copy terminal for:
a) data entry and retrieval
b) program entry
c) to save paper
d) all of the above

- - - - - - - - - - - - - - - - - - -

d) all of the above

CRT TERMINAL. Courtesy of Data General Corporation.

13. The most popular output device is the <u>printer.</u> Much output from a computer center needs to be in the form of a printed document to be read by non-data processing personnel and/or high-level management—hence the popularity of the printer. A typical printer can produce 1,100 lines of print per minute, but some printers can achieve speeds in excess of 20,000 lines per minute. Fifty lines per page at 20,000 lines per minute can produce 400 pages per minute.

Printers have two main disadvantages. They are relatively slow devices when compared to the speed that the computer processes data. They produce huge quantities of paper which can create a severe handling and storage problem.

Answer true or false.

_____ (a)   A printer is an input device.

_____ (b)   A printer is a relatively slow output device.

_____ (c)   A printer can produce huge quantities of paper.

- - - - - - - - - - - - - - - - - - - -

(a) false;   (b) true;   (c) true

I/O Media Coding Systems

14. Two people speaking different languages need a translator to communicate. The translator transforms the conversation of the first into a language form understood by the other. Similarly, information which is recorded in a form understandable to humans is generally not in a form understandable to a computer, and vice versa. This communication problem is resolved by using I/O units as mediators between us and the computer. We already discussed the card reader which is used for input, the card punch and printer that are used for output, and the CRT terminal and teletypewriter that are used for I/O. Magnetic tape and magnetic disk, two other I/O devices, will be discussed in Chapter Eleven.

Because of technological limitations, each I/O unit requires a unique medium to communicate with it. The card reader and the card punch units use punch cards, the printer uses continuous paper, the teletypewriter uses continuous paper and paper tape, the tape unit uses magnetic tape, and the disk unit uses magnetic disk.

Match one letter in column A to one or more numeric entries in column B.

A	B
_____ (a) card reader unit	(1) magnetic tape
_____ (b) card punch unit	(2) punched card
	(3) paper tape
_____ (c) teletypewriter	(4) magnetic disk
_____ (d) magnetic tape unit	(5) continuous paper
_____ (e) disk unit	

- - - - - - - - - - - - - - - - - - -

(a) 2;   (b) 2;   (c) 3, 5;   (d) 1;   (e) 4

The ALU (Arithmetic and Logical Unit)

15. The ALU consists of a series of small storage units (called registers) and other electronic circuits capable of performing arithmetic and logical operations. These operations include addition, subtraction, comparison of two values to determine which is the larger, and the determination of whether an expression is true or false.

Which unit of the CPU is responsible for carrying out arithmetic operations and making logical decisions? _____

- - - - - - - - - - - - - - - - - -

ALU (Arithmetic and Logical Unit)

The Control Unit

16. Finally, the control unit in the CPU (Central Processing Unit) acts as an overall coordinator of the computer system. It controls the various input/output devices and the ALU. Below are some of the functions it performs.

> fetches instructions from storage;
>
> interprets instructions given it by the programmer;
>
> initiates I/O device instructions and transmits information in and out of main storage;
>
> initiates execution of the computer program.

Here is a schematic diagram of a computer system broken down into six functional parts. The arrows show information flow within the computer system.

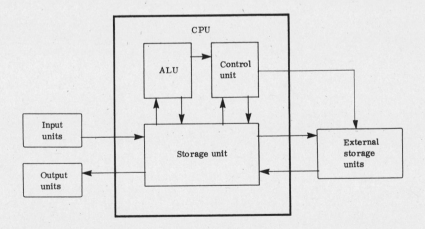

In summary, the control unit interprets the program instructions and directs the actions of other units, ensuring that everything is done in proper sequence and time. This is similar to the manner by which our nervous system guides the actions of our bodies or a traffic patrolman directs traffic at a busy intersection. There are many computer devices and storage media. In this Guide only the most common ones have been discussed.

See if you can put the chips together. Match one letter entry in column A to one or more numerical entries in column B.

A	B
_____ (a) input unit	(1) control unit
	(2) disk unit
_____ (b) output unit	(3) printer unit
	(4) teletype unit
_____ (c) I/O unit	(5) main storage
	(6) ALU
	(7) card reader unit

Name the components of the CPU. _____

_____

- - - - - - - - - - - - - - - - - - -

(a) 2, 4, 7; (b) 2, 3, 4; (c) 2, 4
The components of the CPU are: main storage unit, control unit, and ALU (arithmetic and logical unit).

Computer Languages

17. We humans use "natural" languages to communicate with each other. The English language, for example, consists of symbols (A-Z, 0-9, and special characters) and rules of grammar (called <u>syntax</u>). By using these symbols and grammatical rules we can come up with legitimate words and sentences. A computer understands only one language—called <u>machine language</u>. This language consists of strings of binary digits (0 or 1) because, as we noted earlier, instructions which the computer follows must be stored in the memory and only the binary digits 0 and 1 can be stored. Using the machine language grammar and the digits 0 and 1, we can design words which are combined to form instructions immediately obeyed by the computer without translation.

Those <u>machine instructions</u> are built into the machine as a part of the computer circuitry. Each such instruction is designed to perform a specific function. A typical instruction might be: Read a ten-digit number into storage location (address) 5001. An instruction might look like (in binary notation):

Branch and link	Reg. 14	Reg. 15	Value "8"
01000	1011	1000	0011110000000001000

Add content of register 15 to value 8 and store result in register 14. Branch to <u>address</u> found in register 14.

A typical computer can have 100 or more such instructions (sometimes called the instruction repertoire). The repertoire differs from computer to computer since their circuitry differs. Thus, you cannot generally take a machine language program written for one computer and expect another computer to understand it. But, although instruction codes may differ, these are common functions all computers can perform. Indeed, it is amazing that with such a limited instruction set a computer is so powerful.

Match one letter entry in A to one numeric entry in B.

A	B
_____ (a) machine language instruction	(1) a set of instructions a particular computer understands
_____ (b) syntax	(2) 011000100001100100
_____ (c) instruction repertoire	(3) grammar

- - - - - - - - - - - - - - - - - -

(a) 2; (b) 3; (c) 1

18. In the early 1950's, program instructions were prepared in machine language. Programmers found the language difficult to learn and to understand. In addition, the coding was tedious and errors were hard to locate and correct. Over the last thirty years, programming languages have been developed which are a compromise between the English language and machine language, since they contain many English words and other familiar symbols that make it much easier to write computer programs. Two general types of languages were developed: assembly languages and high-level languages.

Programming in an assembly language is not easy. You must have a fairly good idea of a computer's operation and design characteristics. For this reason, assembly languages are called machine dependent languages. That is, each computer has its own assembly language. An assembly language instruction is generally equivalent to one machine language instruction. Such languages are only infrequently used for general business functions; their use is more specialized.

High-level languages require little knowledge of how a computer works. These languages are easier to learn and are usually machine independent. That is, you can write a program for one manufacturer's computer and with little or no change execute this program on a different manufacturer's computer. Generally, one high-level language instruction is equivalent to many machine language instructions. Translation of a high-level program into machine language is a more complex and sophisticated process than the translation of low-level languages.

Four of the best known high-level (or problem-oriented) languages are COBOL, PL/I, BASIC, the FORTRAN (FORmula TRANslation) language. The FORTRAN language first implemented in 1956, was designed for solution of mathematical problems. It is now also widely used in business applications. COBOL (COmmon Business Oriented Language) is primarily used to solve business problems. This language was first implemented in 1960. The PL/I (Programming Language version I) is a general purpose language first implemented in 1965, designed to solve both commercial and scientific problems. BASIC, a language similar to FORTRAN, is popular on mini- and microcomputers. Other high-level languages include RPG, SNOBOL, LISP, and PASCAL.

Match one letter entry in A to one or more entries in B.

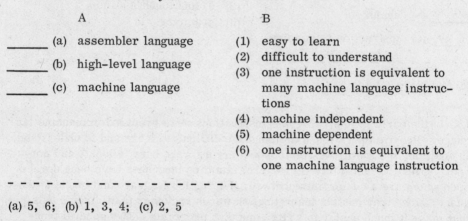

A

_____ (a) assembler language

_____ (b) high-level language

_____ (c) machine language

B

(1) easy to learn
(2) difficult to understand
(3) one instruction is equivalent to many machine language instructions
(4) machine independent
(5) machine dependent
(6) one instruction is equivalent to one machine language instruction

- - - - - - - - - - - - - - - - - -

(a) 5, 6; (b) 1, 3, 4; (c) 2, 5

19. But if you try to communicate with the computer in a language that closely resembles the English language, the computer would be very unhappy, because it only understands instructions given in its own machine language. This situation is resolved by providing compilers (translators).

A compiler is a relatively large computer program. The compiler translates a high-level language program, called the source program, or source code, into an equivalent machine language program, called the object program, or object code. If the high-level language is punched on cards (which form a deck), we obtain a source deck. The source code may also be located on a magnetic tape, disk, or diskette. The object program can either be stored on tape, disk, diskette or punched cards. If we request a translation from a high-level language to a machine language to be punched onto cards, we obtain an object deck.

The process of translation is called compilation. Below is a graphic representation of this process.

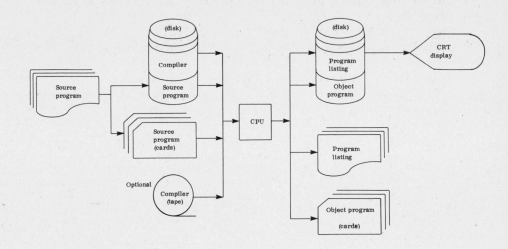

Each computer requires a compiler for each high-level language used. Whenever you desire to run your program on a different computer system you generally must recompile your program for that system. Since compilers differ, some small modification of your source deck may be necessary before recompilation is attempted. Don't forget to check the manufacturer's computer language manual.

Match column B to column A.

A

_____ (a) compilation

_____ (b) compiler

_____ (c) source program

_____ (d) object program

_____ (e) execute

_____ (f) source code

_____ (g) object code

B

(1) high-level language program
(2) run
(3) a translated machine language instruction
(4) translator
(5) an instruction in the high-level language
(6) a process of translation
(7) an equivalent machine language program

- - - - - - - - - - - - - - - - - -

(a) 6; (b) 4; (c) 1; (d) 7; (e) 2; (f) 5; (g) 3

20. FORTRAN is a language and has some basic elements common to all languages; it has a set of characters, a small English vocabulary, and syntax. Syntax refers to the rules of grammar which tell you which character combinations are allowed and which are prohibited. If you know the syntax of the

FORTRAN language you will be able to write correct instructions. However, if you disobey the rules of grammar your computer might refuse to execute your program.

Semantics explains the meaning of each FORTRAN statement. The manual provided by the computer manufacturer along with the compiler explains how the compiler interprets your source language instructions. Thus, when the computer executes your instructions it does what the compiler says it should do. In this Guide we will discuss the syntax and semantics of the FORTRAN language.

Match one entry in A to one entry in B.

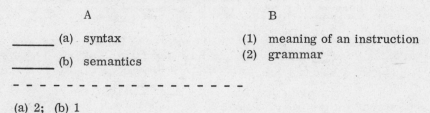

	A		B
_____	(a) syntax	(1)	meaning of an instruction
_____	(b) semantics	(2)	grammar

- - - - - - - - - - - - - - - - - - -

(a) 2;   (b) 1

21. Several versions of FORTRAN have been developed. Each version includes enhancements (extra programming goodies) over an earlier version. Each version also is designed so a program written in an earlier version will continue to compile and execute correctly using the new version compiler.

The first version, FORTRAN I (or FORTRAN), was implemented in 1957. An improved version, FORTRAN II, was implemented in 1958. FORTRAN III was restricted by some manufacturers for their internal use. Finally, FORTRAN IV was released in 1962. A new version, FORTRAN V and FORTRAN VI (extensions of FORTRAN IV) are currently being implemented by some computer manufacturers. The FORTRAN language has become very popular and today almost all computer manufacturers can provide their customers with a FORTRAN compiler.

The American National Standards Institute standardized the FORTRAN language in 1966. Two versions were standardized: BASIC FORTRAN, called USA STANDARD BASIC FORTRAN, intended for small computers; and USA STANDARD FORTRAN, henceforth called FORTRAN, intended for medium sized and large computers. BASIC FORTRAN is a subset of FORTRAN. That is, all BASIC FORTRAN commands are found in FORTRAN. This means if you write a program in BASIC FORTRAN you can also execute it on a larger computer by using the FORTRAN compiler. However, the converse is not true.

The standard was again revised in 1977. However, most of the mini- and microprocessors implement the 1966 standard, plus enhancements which either include part of or go beyond the 1977 standard. Furthermore, they usually include special statements for use by terminal devices.

In this Guide we discuss STANDARD FORTRAN. As a result of customer demand, manufacturers have added features (called extensions) which are not included in BASIC FORTRAN. Many of these features are widely used, and

so we will discuss them in this Guide. Whenever we mention them, we identify them clearly as extensions. In Chapters One through Seven we cover most
of the features of BASIC FORTRAN, and in Chapters Eight through Eleven we
primarily cover STANDARD FORTRAN.

Answer true or false.

_____ (a) USA STANDARD FORTRAN cannot be used in a BASIC FORTRAN
             compiler.

_____ (b) USA STANDARD BASIC FORTRAN is a subset of USA STANDARD
             FORTRAN.

- - - - - - - - - - - - - - - - - -

(a) true; The BASIC FORTRAN language is a subset of the USA standard
FORTRAN. This means that some of the statements in USA standard FOR-
TRAN will not work in BASIC FORTRAN; (b) true

22. Compilation and execution of a FORTRAN program requires the following
steps.

1. Write the instructions on a piece of paper (called a <u>coding sheet</u>)
    to obtain a source program.

2. Either:
    (a) Punch the instructions on punch cards (as explained in
         Chapter One) to create a source deck, or
    (b) Type the program into a keyboard terminal to be stored
         on either a tape, disk, or diskette.

3. Feed the FORTRAN compiler into storage (this is usually done for
    you).

4. Feed the source program into storage.

5. The source deck is translated into an object deck (if the
    compiler finds no errors).

6. Store the object program and data in memory.

7. Start program execution.

The compiler checks only for syntax errors. For all statements whose
syntax is incorrect, the compiler generates error messages on a printer or
terminal in addition to a complete <u>listing</u> of the source program. The programmer must correct all errors indicated by the compiler and then he can
recompile his program. This process must be repeated until the compiler
prints no error messages. Only then is an object program obtained and the
last two steps performed. Semantics errors—that is, errors in program
logic—are not checked by the compiler. They manifest themselves when you
execute your program and get no results, unexpected results, or incorrect
results. For example, if you intended to subtract the value in the variable A

from the value in the variable B, but by mistake you instructed the computer to add the content of the variable A to the content of the variable B, the computer would obey your order even though you intended otherwise. It is the responsibility of the programmer to find these errors, called bugs, and correct them in the source program, then repeat steps 3 through 7 (called debugging) until the program is free of error, or debugged.

Often we eliminate the object deck. That is, when a program is compiled successfully we transfer the object program into another portion of main storage and proceed to execute the program immediately, eliminating the need for an object deck.

When debugging his program, a programmer sometimes wants to examine the content of storage. Some compilers have provisions for a memory dump. That is, you may request a printed record of the content of storage. The memory dump represents the status of storage at the time the dump is printed. By examining this dump a programmer might find it easier to locate the area of difficulty.

Data Organization—Files, Records, Fields

23. Information is handled more effectively if it is organized properly. A set of characters used together is called a field or item. For example, a name field contains characters representing a particular name; the item net pay contains numbers representing an employee's pay. In FORTRAN, a field roughly corresponds to a variable.

A collection of related items (fields) is called a record. In FORTRAN, we may regard all items transmitted into main storage or out of main storage in one I/O operation as a record.

Here are two examples of records and the items (fields) they might consist of.

Master record	Detail record
employee name	employee number
address	hours worked
city	gross pay
state	
zip code	
employee number	
hourly pay rate	

Related records can be further organized into a file. In the above example, all master records can be organized into a master file, and all detail records can be organized into a detail file. Files are usually classified into two types: the master file which contains permanent records; and the detail file or transaction file which contains records which are used to keep up to date (update) the records in the master file. For example, a large department store would store each customer name, address, and other relevant information on a master purchasing file, and place the details of purchases, returns, cash payment, and other relevant information on the purchasing transaction file. The resulting detail records would be used daily, weekly, or monthly to update each record in the master file.

It is common practice to store large files on tape or disk. However, we may store files on punched cards or any other media we find convenient for that application.

Below is an example of a tape file. Records are stored on the tape in a sequential order leaving a <u>gap</u> (an unrecorded space) to separate the records from each other.

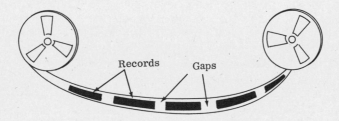

In your own words, what is an item or field? What is a record? What is a file? _____

_____

_____

– – – – – – – – – – – – – – – – – – –

Your answer should have been something like: A field is a set of characters used together. A record is an organized set of related fields. A file is an organized set of related records.

Now that you have acquired some general computer concepts, you are ready to learn FORTRAN programming.

CHAPTER ONE
And Now, FORTRAN Programming

This chapter will present some easy to understand examples of FORTRAN programs. When you complete this chapter, you should be able to:

- relate FORTRAN program statements with the computer functions of input, processing, and output;

- use standard flowcharting symbols to diagram the flow of your FORTRAN programs;

- properly enter statements on a FORTRAN coding sheet.

1. In Chapter Zero, we briefly introduced the various computer functions and how we direct and control them through a program. Now let's take a look at a relatively simple, but nonsense, program.

1	5	6	7	10	15	20	25	30	35	40	45	50
			WRITE (6, 10001)									
10001			FORMAT (' BØØ! WHØ ARE YØU? ')									
			STØP									
			END									

If we compile and run (execute) the above program, it would print the message "BOO! WHO ARE YOU?" and the computer would stop (halt). Our short program example illustrates that FORTRAN programming uses words which are familiar to you. Which of the following computer functions did the program specify? (Place a check mark beside the correct answer.)

_____ (a) input   _____ (b) calculation   _____ (c) output

- -

The program specified (c) output. The program did not read (or input) data, nor did it calculate any result. The program merely printed a message and stopped.

Flowchart Symbols: Start and Stop

2.   People in the computer field have established a standard set of symbols to represent the various computer functions for diagramming the flow of operations in a computer program. We will introduce you to these symbols as you need them.

Refer back to the nonsense program in frame 1. The program has three basic parts: start, output, stop (or termination). The symbol (⎯⎯) represents either the start or termination of a program. You can specify the symbol's function by writing either "Start" or "Stop" inside the symbol.

(a)   Write the symbol for the beginning of a program.   _____

(b)   How do we indicate the end of the program flow?   _____

- - - - - - - - - - - - - - - - - - -

(a) (Start) ; (b) (Stop)

Flowchart Symbols: Input and Output

3.   The symbol /⎯⎯/ represents either operation of input or output.

(a)   You can indicate this symbol's function by writing inside the symbol

either "Input" or _____ .

(b)   What is the flowcharting symbol to indicate output?   _____

(c)   What is the symbol that specifies input?   _____

- - - - - - - - - - - - - - - - - - -

(a) Output; (b) / Output / ; (c) / Input /

4.   The standard method of drawing a flowchart is to draw the appropriate symbols beginning at the top of your chart and work downwards to the bottom, connecting each symbol to the next in sequence with a line. Try drawing a flowchart of the program in frame 1. (Hint: Remember the three basic parts of the program?)

- - - - - - - - - - - - - - - - - -

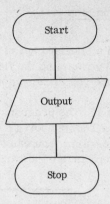

If you got this right, GO TO frame 6.

5.   The flowchart from the previous frame shows this sequence of program operations: start, output, and stop. Draw a flowchart to indicate the operations of a program which inputs data and then outputs the data.

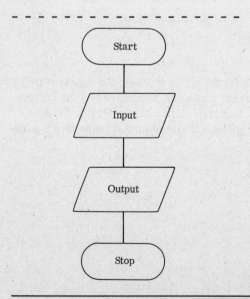

Flowchart Symbol: Processing or Calculation

6.   The symbol ☐ represents the computer operations of

arithmetic, such as addition, subtraction, multiplication, and division. You may write inside the symbol either the word "Processing"—to indicate generally some processing operation(s) take(s) place—or the specific operation(s). The purpose of your flowchart will determine how much detail you include inside the flowchart symbol. This concept applies to <u>all</u> flowchart symbols.
     Compare the detail of the two flowcharts below.

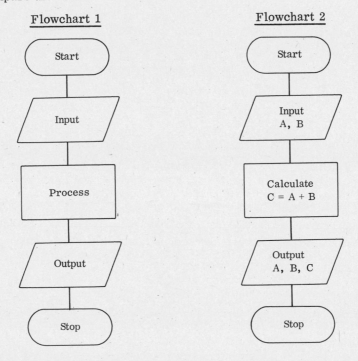

Flowchart 1

Start

Input

Process

Output

Stop

Flowchart 2

Start

Input
A, B

Calculate
C = A + B

Output
A, B, C

Stop

(a)   Which of the above flowcharts describes a programming application in a very general way? _____

(b)   If you were to program the application, which flowchart would you want to use when writing the program code? _____ Why? _____

- - - - - - - - - - - - - - - - - - -

(a) Flowchart 1 describes the general system.   (b) We would use flowchart 2 to help us code the actual program because it contains more detail about what the program is to accomplish.

The flowchart symbols may be hand-drawn or drawn with a template. You may purchase a flowcharting template from a computer vendor, or from any art supply house. Also, the flowchart may be drawn on a regular sheet of paper or you may purchase special forms, designed for this purpose, from the computer manufacturer. If you wish to gain more facility with flowcharting you may refer to other Self-Teaching Guides, <u>Introduction to Data Processing,</u> Second Edition, by Martin Harris and <u>Flowcharting</u> by Nancy B. Stern.

<u>FORTRAN Character Set</u>

7. Forty-six characters constitute the set of characters acceptable by all FORTRAN compilers. These characters include the 26 letters of the alphabet, 10 decimal digits from 0 to 9, and the special characters listed below.

<u>Special characters</u>

printed text	handwritten	
+	+	plus sign
-	—	minus sign
*	✳	asterisk
/	/	slash
=	=	equal sign
.	•	decimal
,	)	comma
	ƀ or △	blank
(	(	left parenthesis
)	)	right parenthesis

Most computer manufacturers have extended the character set which their FORTRAN compiler will accept. Such extended sets include ' (apostrophe mark) and $. Check your computer installation's FORTRAN manual to determine its acceptable FORTRAN character set. We will use the ' in this study guide. But don't worry; we will show you how to avoid using a ' if you can't use one at your installation.

Which of the following characters are accepted in FORTRAN statements by <u>all</u> FORTRAN compilers?

Character	Yes or No
%	
/	
;	
:	
$	
.	

- - - - - - - - - - - - - - - - - - - -

The only characters in this list accepted by all compilers are the / (slash), $ (dollar sign), and the . (decimal).

Handwritten FORTRAN Coding

8. Certain characters, when handwritten, are easy to confuse with other handwritten characters. For this reason, when writing FORTRAN code we write some of the characters differently.

Printed text	Handwritten	Not to be confused with
letter I	I	number 1
letter O	$\emptyset$	number 0
letter Z	$\overline{Z}$	number 2
letter U	u	letter V

We will use the above lettering conventions throughout our text. When you submit your programs for keypunching, you must instruct the keypunch operator as to these conventions. We'll show you how to do this near the end of this chapter.

Look back at frame 1. Notice how we slashed the letter O to differentiate it from the number 0 (zero). Notice also that the letter I has little tails, or serifs, but the number 1 is a simple figure.

The FORTRAN compiler does not generally accept small or lowercase letters (although some of the newer keypunches have the capability of punching upper- and lowercase characters). To be safe, always use capital letters when coding your program.

Print (in capital letters using appropriate lettering conventions) the words and expressions below.

(a) WRITE _____   (d) ZERO _____

(b) PROD1 _____   (e) C = XU + 10 _____

(c) INPUT2 _____

- - - - - - - - - - - - - - - - - - -

(a) *WRITE* ; (b) *PRØD1*; (c) *INPUT2*; (d) *ZERØ*; (e) *C = XU + 10*

9. Using flowchart 2 from frame 6, we wrote the FORTRAN program on the following page.

```
1      5 6 7    10     15     20     25     30     35     40     45     50
        READ (5, 11) A, B
11      FØRMAT (F6.0, F6.0)
        C = A + B
        WRITE (6, 31) A, B, C
31      FØRMAT ('b', F6.0, 'bPLUSb', F6.0,
       -   'bEQUALb', F7.0)
        STØP
        END
```

Note the numbers written in columns 1 through 5; we call these numbers statement numbers. A statement requires a number only if another statement in the program refers to this statement; otherwise, a statement number is optional. In subsequent frames and chapters you will learn which statements require statement numbers.

Sometimes a FORTRAN statement may require more than one line; that is, it must be continued on one or more lines. We indicate a continuation line by placing any acceptable FORTRAN character except blank or zero in column 6. Notice in the continuation line for statement number 31 we used a hyphen in column 6.

The actual FORTRAN statement is written within columns 7 through 72 of the coding form. Although our examples show only a portion of the form, you could extend your program statements to column 72.

From the program above, copy the applicable FORTRAN statements requested below. If you are not sure, guess!

(a) Input statements. (Hint: Include the statement which you think describes the format or arrangement of the input data.)

(b) Processing (or calculation).

(c) Output statements.

(d) The END statement instructs the compiler that there are no further program statements to be compiled for this program. In contrast, the STOP statement instructs the computer to cease executing the program. Write the END and STOP statements in their proper sequence.

(e) What do you think is the purpose of the statement numbered 31 in the program? _____

(f) In our program, the READ statement instructs the computer to input data values for the variables A and B. For what variables does the WRITE statement output data values? _____

- - - - - - - - - - - - - - - - - - -

(a)
```
      READ (5,11) A, B
11    FØRMAT (F6.0, F6.0)
```

(b)
```
      C = A + B
```

(c)
```
      WRITE (6,31) A, B, C
31    FØRMAT ('Ø', F6.0, 'ØPLUSØ', F6.0,
     -      'ØEQUALØ', F7.0)
```

(d)
```
      STØP
      END
```

(e) The FORMAT statement numbered 31 describes to the computer how the data is to be arranged or formatted when output.
(f) The WRITE statement outputs values for the variables A, B, and C.

Flowchart Symbol: Collector

10. Another useful flowcharting symbol is $\bigcirc$ called a <u>collector</u>. The collector represents an <u>exit to</u> or an <u>entry from</u> another part of the flowchart. This requires some explanation. Now if we were to flowchart a lengthy program, unless our flowchart paper was unusually long, we would soon reach the bottom of the paper, requiring us to continue drawing the flowchart, say, perhaps to the right and at the top of our paper. If we did not have adequate room to the right, we would continue our flowchart on another sheet of paper.

So we use the $\bigcirc$ to link one "string" of flowchart symbols to another. On the next page is an illustration.

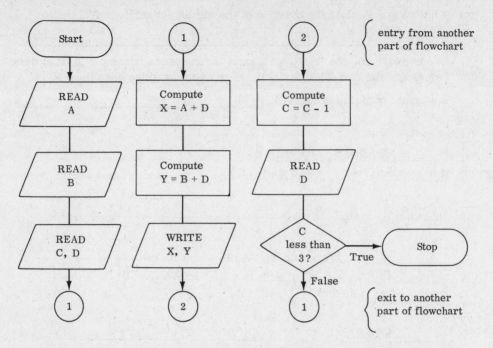

After reading values for the variables C and D. the collector ① tells us to look for another collector having ①. Also notice the arrows. Feel free to use arrows wherever they convey better understanding of the flow-chart.

(a) In your own words, describe the purpose of the connector symbol.

(b) Look at the above flowchart. What will happen if the value of the variable C is less than the value 3? Guess on this one if you don't know already.

— — — — — — — — — — — — — — — — —

(a) You are correct if you said something to the effect that the collector symbol ◯ serves to indicate an exit to or an entry from another part of the flowchart. Reference information, such as a unique number or letter, may appear inside each collector for identification, if required.

(b) The statement will cause the computer to stop execution if C has a value less than 3.

Flowchart Symbol: Decision Point

11. Our flowchart in frame 10 also used this symbol ⬦ to specify a decision point in the program. FORTRAN permits us to write statements that make decisions, statements which, in effect, change the general sequence of instruction execution. These statements which change the instruction sequence are also called <u>control</u> statements. These control statements give the computer much of its "thinking" power.

From the flowchart in frame 10, what do you think is the purpose of the decision point?

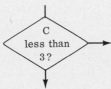

If you said that the decision point causes the program to cease execution if C has a value less than 3, you are correct. Just imagine what would happen if the value of C was never less than 3—the program would continue to run until someone shut down the computer.

12. Draw the appropriate flowchart symbols for the functions indicated.

(a) Start

(b) Input: age, rank, serial

(c) Decision: age less than 21

(d) Computation: $a = x + y - z^2$

(e) Output: hours, pay

(f) Collector: 1

(g) Stop

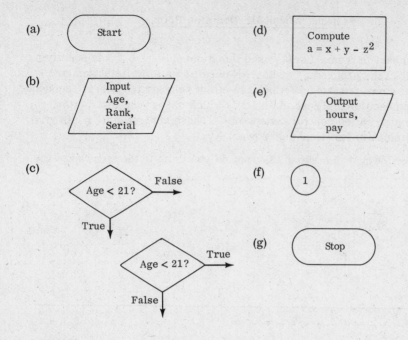

(a) Start

(d) Compute
$a = x + y - z^2$

(b) Input
Age,
Rank,
Serial

(e) Output
hours,
pay

(c) Age < 21? False
True
Age < 21? True
False

(f) 1

(g) Stop

13. Draw a detailed flowchart for the following program steps.

(a) Start
(b) Compute KOUNT = 0
(c) Input values for QTY and COST
(d) If QTY less than 1 branch to step (j) below (Hint: use collectors)
(e) Compute TOTAL = COST x QTY
(f) Compute KOUNT = KOUNT + 1
(g) Output values for QTY, COST, and TOTAL
(h) Input values for QTY and COST
(i) Goto to step (d) above
(j) Output value of KOUNT
(k) Stop

If we have not left you enough room, use a separate piece of paper.

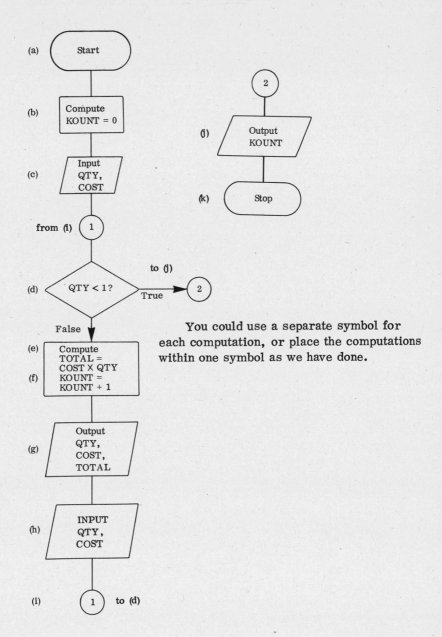

(a) Start

(b) Compute KOUNT = 0

(c) Input QTY, COST

from (i) 1

(d) QTY < 1?

to (j)

True 2

False

(e) Compute TOTAL = COST X QTY

(f) KOUNT = KOUNT + 1

(g) Output QTY, COST, TOTAL

(h) INPUT QTY, COST

(i) 1 to (d)

(j) Output KOUNT

(k) Stop

You could use a separate symbol for each computation, or place the computations within one symbol as we have done.

Structured Flowcharting

Using the process, decision, and collector symbols, we can form two other flowchart structures or constructs. These are the IF-THEN-ELSE and DO-WHILE structures. The combination of the IF-THEN-ELSE, DO-WHILE, and process structures form the foundation of a structured program. It can be shown (but not in our limited space) that all programs can be designed using these three structures.

The advantages of using structures are multi-fold. Programs written using structured programming concepts are usually coded in a uniform manner, making it easier to test for logical correctness and errors.

IF-THEN-ELSE Structure

14. Suppose our employee records contain information about each employee's sex, that is, gender ... not frequency. This information is coded as
     0 for female, and
     1 for male.
If our program is to tally the number of employees by sex, we could illustrate the program logic with this flowchart:

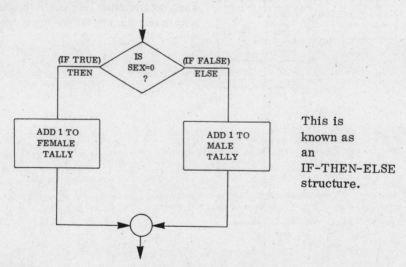

This is known as an IF-THEN-ELSE structure.

We could also represent the above structure in summary form by using a single process:

Using the IF-THEN-ELSE and process structures, draw a structured flow-chart which illustrates these three steps:

    1.   Read a record, including sex, name and address.

    2.   If sex = male,

         THEN print "MR. ", NAME AND ADDRESS;

         ELSE print "MS. ", NAME AND ADDRESS.

    3.   ADD 1 to person counter.

– – – – – – – – – – – – – – – – – – – –

Here's a possible solution:

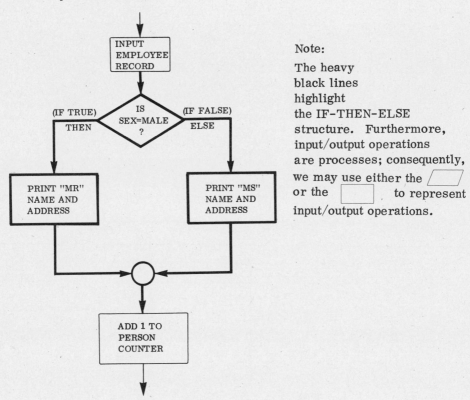

Note:

The heavy black lines highlight the IF-THEN-ELSE structure. Furthermore, input/output operations are processes; consequently, we may use either the ⟋ ⟋ or the ☐ to represent input/output operations.

or if you don't need a lot of detail in your flowchart:

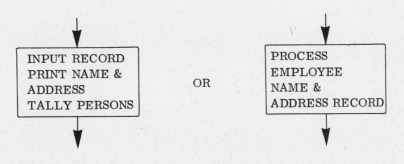

DO-WHILE Structure

15. Another common structure is called the DO-WHILE. It gets its name from the fact that as long as some condition exists, a process will occur. If the condition does not exist, the process is not performed. Here's a simple illustration:

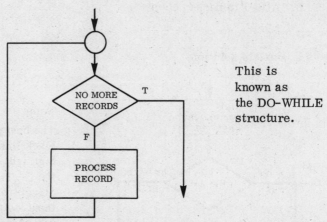

This is
known as
the DO-WHILE
structure.

Just as in Frame 14, we could use a single process box to present the above structure in summary form.

Using the DO-WHILE and process structures, draw a structured flowchart which illustrates these steps:
1. Read NUMBER
2. While NUMBER is less than 1000,
    a. Double NUMBER
    b. Add 1 to COUNT
3. Print COUNT and NUMBER

- -

Your answer should be similar to this structure:

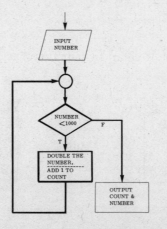

NOTE:
The heavy
black lines
highlight the
DO-WHILE
structure.

In very summary form, we could also represent the above structure as a single process:

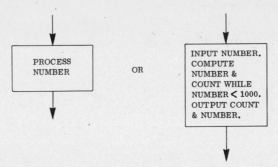

16. Now let's combine the use of the IF-THEN-ELSE and DO-WHILE structures. If the "process record" step in Frame 15 actually consists of the solution to Frame 14, we would have the following composite structured flowchart:

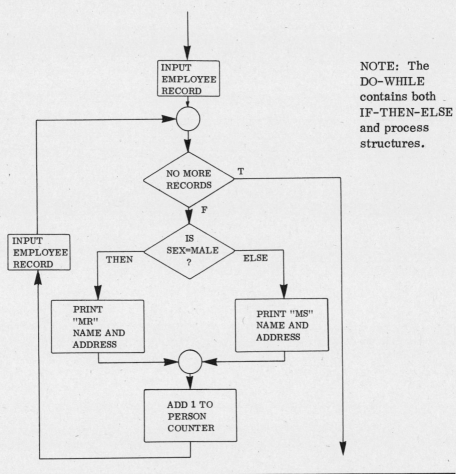

NOTE: The DO-WHILE contains both IF-THEN-ELSE and process structures.

Chart the following steps using structured flowchart concepts:
  1. Input Inventory Record, if any.
  2. For each inventory record,
      a.   IF quantity on hand $>$ economic order quantity,
           THEN continue:
           ELSE print purchase order for item.
      b.   PRINT inventory status of item on inventory report.

You might have it done this way:
        (SEE NOTE)

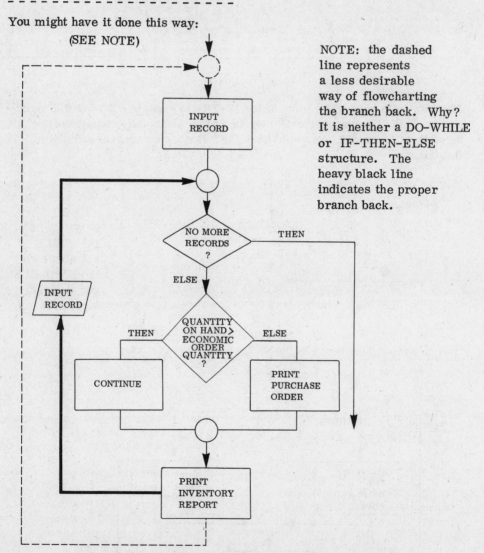

NOTE: the dashed
line represents
a less desirable
way of flowcharting
the branch back. Why?
It is neither a DO-WHILE
or IF-THEN-ELSE
structure. The
heavy black line
indicates the proper
branch back.

Identifying the Operations within a FORTRAN Program

17. The following is a short program which will cause the computer to print
a multiplication table for the numbers 1 through 9. Next to the program,
we've labeled the purpose of the program statements.

			Statement type
	DØ 301, NUMBER = 1, 9		control
	NUM2 = 1		assignment
298	MULT = NUMBER * NUM2		calculation
	WRITE (6, 299) NUMBER, NUM2, MULT		output
299	FØRMAT (' ', I1, ' TIMES ', I1,		output specification
	- ' EQUALS ', I2)		continuation
	NUM2 = NUM2 + 1		calculation
	IF (NUM2 .LT. 10) GØ TØ 298		decision and control
301	CØNTINUE		control
	STØP		control
	END		compiler instruction

At execution time, the computer will print the following results.

1 TIMES 1 EQUALS 1
1 TIMES 2 EQUALS 2
1 TIMES 3 EQUALS 3
⋮

4 TIMES 5 EQUALS 20
4 TIMES 6 EQUALS 24
⋮

9 TIMES 9 EQUALS 81

Which of the following computer operations did the program perform?

_____ (a) input   _____ (d) output

_____ (b) calculation   _____ (e) control

_____ (c) decisionmaking

- -

The program performed all except (a), input. In our example, the program generated its own data and did not require input.

18. The program in frame 17 also contains some control statements. A control statement is a computer instruction that changes the normal sequence in which the computer executes instructions. The instructions are usually stored in sequence within the computer; the computer will execute the instructions in that same sequence unless it is directed to do otherwise by a control instruction.

Which of the FORTRAN statements on the following page do you think are control type instructions? (Check the ones which are.)

_____ (a)	. . . .	IF (NUMBER .EQ. -2) GØ TØ 15
_____ (b)	. . . .	QUICK = JACK + BEE - NIMBLE
_____ (c)	. . . .	JACK = BQUICK + 1
_____ (d)	. . . .	WRITE (6,21) THIS, IS, ØUTPUT
_____ (e)	21 . . .	FØRMAT (' ', A4, 2X, I6, 1X, F7.3)

- - - - - - - - - - - - - - - - - - -

Choice (a) is a control statement. The GO TO is one common form of control statement. It is also a decision statement, as we'll see later. Choices (b) and (c) perform calculations, whereas (d) gives us output and (e) describes the format.

DOCUMENTATION WITHIN THE PROGRAM

19. Suppose we obtained a bank loan of $1,000 which we had to repay at $350 per month with an annual rate of interest of 13 percent (on a monthly basis that would be 1.08 percent). After reading this book, you will be able to write a program (as we have done) to calculate how much of each monthly payment represents interest and how much is to be applied toward repayment of the loan. This program also provides us with some totals at the end of the report so we can see how much interest we actually paid. We have even written the program so that we can enter the amount of loan, interest rate, and monthly payment. Look over the program, and you might find that you understand many of the program statements. If you do not understand some or all program statements, don't worry, as in subsequent chapters we will discuss each type of statement in greater detail. The program appears on pages 43-46.

In our sample program that follows, we have shaded those statements which the FORTRAN compiler will compile. The remaining statements are for you, the programmer or analyst, to read and understand the program and its logical flow. Notice that the number of statements compiled is significantly less than the actual size of the program itself.

```
LOAN      FORTRAN  P      02/05/80      08.47.36        PAGE 1

C   PROGRAM: LOAN.
C
C   PURPOSE: CALCULATE THE MONTHLY REPAYMENT OF A LOAN.
C
C   VARIABLES:
C       AMOUNT - AMOUNT OF LOAN.
C       RATE - RATE OF ANNUAL INTEREST EXPRESSED AS PERCENT.
C       PAYMNT - AMOUNT OF EACH MONTHLY PAYMENT.
C       TOT PAY - TOTAL OF THE MONTHLY PAYMENTS.
C       AMT INT - PORTION OF MONTHLY PAYMENT APPLIED TO INTEREST.
C       TOT INT - TOTAL INTEREST PAID ON LOAN.
C       PRIN - PORTION OF MONTHLY PAYMENT APPLIED TO REPAY LOAN.
C       TOT PRN - TOTAL PAYMENTS AGAINST LOAN AMOUNT.
C       ROUND - FUNCTION TO ROUND RESULTS TO NEAREST CENT.
C
C   SPECIFICATION STATEMENTS.
C
      DOUBLE PRECISION TOT PAY, TOT INT, TAMNT, TOT PRN, PRIN, AMOUNT,
     -                 TPYMNT,PAYMNT, AMT INT, ROUND, WORK
C
C   PROGRAM STATEMENTS.
C
C   READ AMOUNT OF LOAN, ANNUAL INTEREST RATE, AND MONTHLY PAYMENT.
C
      WRITE (6,10000)
10000 FORMAT ('0ENTER LOAN AMOUNT, RATE OF %, AND MONTHLY PAYMENT',
     -        ' IN THE FORMAT XXXXXXX. XX.XX% XXXXXX.')
      READ (5, 10001) TAMNT, TRATE, TPYMNT
10001 FORMAT (F8.0, 1X, 2PF5.0, 2X, 0PF7.0)
C
C   WRITE REPORT HEADING.
C
      WRITE (8, 10002) TAMNT, TRATE, TPYMNT
10002 FORMAT ('1AMORTIZATION OF ',F8.2,' LOAN AT ',2PF6.3,'%'/
     -        ' PAYABLE ',0PF7.2,' MONTHLY.'/
     -        '0MONTH  PAYMENT  INTEREST  PRINCIPLE  BALANCE'/
     -        ' _____  _____  _____  _____  _____')
C
C   CONVERT INTEREST RATE FROM ANNUAL TO MONTHLY.
C
      RATE = TRATE / 12.
C
C   INITIALIZE LOAN  AND PAYMENT AMOUNT
C
      AMOUNT = TAMNT
      PAYMNT = TPYMNT
C
C   INITIALIZE TOTALS TO ZERO.
C
      TOT PAY = 0.D0
      TOT PRN = 0.D0
      TOT INT = 0.D0
      MONTH = 0
      LINE = 0
C
C   PROCESS EACH PAYMENT.
C
C       DETERMINE IF LOAN IS FULLY PAID.
C
10003    IF (.NOT.(AMOUNT .GE. 0.01D0)) GOTO 10006
C
C       CALCULATE INTEREST ON LOAN BALANCE.
```

```
C
          WORK = RATE * AMOUNT
          AMT INT = ROUND (WORK)
          TOT INT = TOT INT + AMT INT
C
C     DETERMINE IF PAYMENT IS GREATER THAN AMOUNT DUE AND
C     ADJUST DOWNWARDS IF REQUIRED
C
          WORK = AMOUNT + AMT INT
          IF (PAYMNT .GT. WORK) PAYMNT = WORK
          TOT PAY = TOT PAY + PAYMNT
C
C     CALCULATE AMOUNT OF PRINCIPLE PAID.
C
          PRIN = PAYMNT - AMT INT
          TOT PRN = TOT PRN + PRIN
C
C     CALCULATE UNPAID LOAN BALANCE.
C
          AMOUNT = AMOUNT - PRIN
C
C     INCREMENT MONTH COUNTER.
          MONTH = MONTH + 1
C
C     INCREMENT LINE COUNTER.
          LINE = LINE + 1
C
C  CHECK LINE COUNT AND WRITE HEADING IF REQUIRED.
C
          IF (LINE .LT. 26) GOTO 10004
             LINE = 0
             WRITE (8, 10002) TAMNT, TRATE, TPYMNT
C
C  WRITE PAYMENT INFORMATION.
C
10004     WRITE (8, 10005) MONTH, PAYMNT, AMT INT, PRIN, AMOUNT
10005     FORMAT ('0',I5,F9.2,F10.2,F11.2,F9.2)
          GOTO 10003
C
C  WRITE END OF REPORT TOTALS.
C
10006 WRITE (8, 10007) MONTH, TOT PAY, TOT INT, TOT PRN
10007 FORMAT ('0=====   --------   ---------   ----------'/
     -         '0',I5,F9.2,F10.2,F11.2/
     -         ' =====  =======  ========  ========')
      STOP
      END
C
C  PROGRAM: DOUBLE PRECISION FUNCTION ROUND.
C
C  PURPOSE: ROUND DOLLAR AMOUNT TO NEAREST CENT.
C
C  VARIABLES:
C     VALUE - AMOUNT TO BE ROUNDED TO NEAREST CENT.
C     ROUND - AMOUNT THAT HAS BEEN ROUNDED TO NEAREST CENT.
C
      DOUBLE PRECISION FUNCTION ROUND (VALUE)
      DOUBLE PRECISION VALUE
C
C  MULTIPLY VALUE BY 100, ADD 1/2, AND TRUNCATE DECIMAL PORTION.
C
      NUMBER = VALUE * 100.DO + .5DO
C
C  CONVERT TO REAL NUMBER AND DIVIDE BY 100.
C
      VALUE = NUMBER
      ROUND = VALUE/100.DO
      RETURN
      END
```

The computer only compiles these program lines.

```
          DOUBLE PRECISION TOT PAY, TOT INT, TAMNT, TOT PRN, PRIN, AMOUNT,
       -               TPYMNT,PAYMNT, AMT INT, ROUND, WORK
          WRITE (6,10000)
10000 FORMAT ('0ENTER LOAN AMOUNT, RATE OF %, AND MONTHLY PAYMENT',
       -          ' IN THE FORMAT XXXXXXX. XX.XX% XXXXXX.')
          READ (5, 10001) TAMNT, TRATE, TPYMNT
10001 FORMAT (F8.0, 1X, 2PF5.0, 2X, 0PF7.0)
          WRITE (8, 10002) TAMNT, TRATE, TPYMNT
10002 FORMAT ('1AMORTIZATION OF ',F8.2,' LOAN AT ',2PF6.3,'%'/
       -          ' PAYABLE ',0PF7.2,' MONTHLY.'/
       -          '0MONTH  PAYMENT  INTEREST  PRINCIPLE  BALANCE'/
       -          '  -----  -------  --------  ---------  -------')
          RATE = TRATE / 12.
          AMOUNT = TAMNT
          PAYMNT = TPYMNT
          TOT PAY = 0.D0
          TOT PRN = 0.D0
          TOT INT = 0.D0
          MONTH = 0
          LINE = 0
10003     IF (.NOT.(AMOUNT .GE. 0.01D0)) GOTO 10006
          WORK = RATE * AMOUNT
          AMT INT = ROUND (WORK)
          TOT INT = TOT INT + AMT INT
          WORK = AMOUNT + AMT INT
          IF (PAYMNT .GT. WORK) PAYMNT = WORK
          TOT PAY = TOT PAY + PAYMNT
          PRIN = PAYMNT - AMT INT
          TOT PRN = TOT PRN + PRIN
          AMOUNT = AMOUNT - PRIN
          MONTH = MONTH + 1
          LINE = LINE + 1
          IF (LINE .LT. 26) GOTO 10004
              LINE = 0
              WRITE (8, 10002) TAMNT, TRATE, TPYMNT
10004     WRITE (8, 10005) MONTH, PAYMNT, AMT INT, PRIN, AMOUNT
10005     FORMAT ('0',I5,F9.2,F10.2,F11.2,F9.2)
          GOTO 10003
10006 WRITE (8, 10007) MONTH, TOT PAY, TOT INT, TOT PRN
10007 FORMAT ('0=====  -------  --------  ---------'/
       -          '0',I5,F9.2,F10.2,F11.2/
       -          ' =====  =======  ========  =========')
      STOP
      END
      DOUBLE PRECISION FUNCTION ROUND (VALUE)
      DOUBLE PRECISION VALUE
      NUMBER = VALUE * 100.D0 + .5D0
      VALUE = NUMBER
      ROUND = VALUE/100.D0
      RETURN
      END
```

The FORTRAN program on pages 43-45 produces the following report.

```
AMORTIZATION OF 10000.00 LOAN AT 13.000%
PAYABLE  350.00 MONTHLY.
```

MONTH	PAYMENT	INTEREST	PRINCIPLE	BALANCE
1	350.00	108.33	241.67	9758.33
2	350.00	105.72	244.28	9514.05
3	350.00	103.07	246.93	9267.12
4	350.00	100.39	249.61	9017.51
5	350.00	97.69	252.31	8765.20
6	350.00	94.96	255.04	8510.16
7	350.00	92.19	257.81	8252.35
8	350.00	89.40	260.60	7991.75
9	350.00	86.58	263.42	7728.33
10	350.00	83.72	266.28	7462.05
11	350.00	80.84	269.16	7192.89
12	350.00	77.92	272.08	6920.81
13	350.00	74.98	275.02	6645.79
14	350.00	72.00	278.00	6367.79
15	350.00	68.98	281.02	6086.77
16	350.00	65.94	284.06	5802.71
17	350.00	62.86	287.14	5515.57
18	350.00	59.75	290.25	5225.32
19	350.00	56.61	293.39	4931.93
20	350.00	53.43	296.57	4635.36
21	350.00	50.22	299.78	4335.58
22	350.00	46.97	303.03	4032.55
23	350.00	43.69	306.31	3726.24
24	350.00	40.37	309.63	3416.61
25	350.00	37.01	312.99	3103.62
26	350.00	33.62	316.38	2787.24
27	350.00	30.20	319.80	2467.44
28	350.00	26.73	323.27	2144.17
29	350.00	23.23	326.77	1817.40
30	350.00	19.69	330.31	1487.09
31	350.00	16.11	333.89	1153.20
32	350.00	12.49	337.51	815.69
33	350.00	8.84	341.16	474.53
34	350.00	5.14	344.86	129.67
35	131.07	1.40	129.67	0.00
=====	--------	--------	---------	
35	12031.07	2031.07	10000.00	
=====	========	========	=========	

Now, which of the following operations did the program specify?

_____ (a) input   _____ (c) output

_____ (b) calculation   _____ (d) control

- - - - - - - - - - - - - - - - - - - -

All the functions listed.   Here are a few examples.

(a) input   READ (5, 10001) AMOUNT, RATE, PAYMNT
                            10001 FORMAT (F8. 0, 1X, 2PF5. 0, 2X, 0PF7. 0)

(b) calculation   WORK = RATE * AMOUNT
                                   AMTINT = ROUND (WORK)

(c) output   WRITE (8, 10005) MONTH, PAYMNT, AMTINT,
                            -      PRIN, AMOUNT
                            10005 FORMAT ('0', I5, F9. 2, F10. 2, F11. 2, F9. 2)

(d) control   IF (AMOUNT . GT. 0.) GO TO 10004

20. You have probably noticed that many of the program statements (lines) in
our program example began with the letter "C" in the first position on the
line. These statements are called <u>comment statements.</u> The FORTRAN
compiler does not process a statement that contains a "C" in column 1—comment statements are simply listed on the printer, but do not cause any other
compiler action.

   We consider it a very good habit to document your FORTRAN programs
with comment statements. The comments will make it easier for you (and
any other programmer) to understand what your program is trying to do, especially after a number of days, months, or years have gone by. Comment
statements are part of what we call program documentation.

   In your own words, why should you document a program?

- - - - - - - - - - - - - - - - - - -

You are right if you mentioned that comments make it easier to understand
the program. In our opinion, documentation takes time when developing and
writing a program, but it saves even more time later when we have to review
our program—whether it be for correction, modification, or just to find out
how the program works.

Preparing the FORTRAN Coding Form

21. The process of writing a FORTRAN program is called coding. When you begin to write your FORTRAN programs, you might write them on a scrap of paper, notebook paper, or whatever is handy—or you could use what is called a FORTRAN coding form. (See reduced sample which follows.) The end result of coding a program is called a source program.

An operator usually keys in the characters of the source program; the source program itself is stored either on magnetic disks, punchcards, or magnetic tape. As you read in Chapter 0, we enter the source program into the computer through the terminal keyboard, or the medium of a punchcard, tape or disk.

The FORTRAN compiler will work only if the program statements are written in a certain way—correctly. FORTRAN statements must be written in a certain format or arrangement; otherwise, the compiler will not consider it FORTRAN. Here are a few of the rules regarding the preparation of a coding sheet.

Place the letter C in column 1 and the compiler will treat the entire line as a comment. If you put any other letter, number, or even a blank in column 1, the FORTRAN compiler will try to compile the line as a statement. Comments can extend from columns 2 through 80, but for readability we start the comment in column 4 (with a C in column 1). Some computers have an upper limit on the number of continuation lines they will accept, which varies from compiler to compiler. Statement numbers, which we will discuss in Chapter Three, belong in columns 1 through 5. For style, we position them starting in column 1. You should check your computer installation FORTRAN manual, however, since compilers differ in the maximum size of this number they will accept.

Columns 7 through 72 contain your FORTRAN program statements.

Finally, columns 73 through 80 can contain optional entries; the program will still execute correctly if these entries are omitted. Generally, an ascending sequence number is placed in these columns for the purpose of helping you sort the cards back into sequence if you accidentally drop the program (source) deck on the floor. Or you might use the first eight characters of the program name as an optional identifier in columns 73-80. There are other uses for these columns which may be determined as the need arises.

The actual size of FORTRAN coding paper is usually $8\frac{1}{2}$ inches by 11 inches. You may obtain these forms from either your school bookstore or from a computer vendor (see your telephone book) through its publications division.

Each line on the FORTRAN coding form represents the 80 positions of a punched card. It may also represent an 80 position (byte) record on a disk or tape. When entering the FORTRAN source code through a keyboard, whether it be a key punch or terminal, the statement must be entered in exactly the same way as it appears on the coding form.

FORTRAN CODING FORM

Program

Programmer

Date

Punching Instructions

Graphic

Punch

Card Form #

Page   of

Identification

73   80

C FOR COMMENT

STATEMENT NUMBER

FORTRAN STATEMENT

1   5 6 7   10   15   20   25   30   35   40   45   50   55   60   65   70 72

Now, to explain more fully the idea we mentioned in frame 9—column 6. Sometimes you will want to write a program statement that requires more than one line.

1	5	6	7	10	15	20	25	30	35	40	45	50

```
10000  FORMAT ('OENTER LOAN AMOUNT, RATE OF %, AND ',
       -    'MONTHLY PAYMENT'/' IN THE FORMAT F7.0,
       -    2PF5.0, OPF6.0)'')
```

The FORTRAN language provides that you may continue the statement on the next line, beginning in column 7 or indented for readability (whichever you prefer), if you put some nonblank or nonzero character in column 6 of the continuation line. A statement may be written on two or more lines. While you have a choice of characters to use in column 6 of a continuation line, many programmers use a minus sign (hyphen) to indicate each continuation line. Every computer has an upper limit on the number of continuation lines it will accept. This limit can be found in your installation's FORTRAN manual. Comment statements may not be continued in this manner. Simply punch a C in column 1 of the next line.

Match each item in the left column with its mate on the right.

	Content		Column positions
_____	(a)	FORTRAN instruction	(1) 1
_____	(b)	Statement number	(2) 2 to 80
			(3) 1 to 5
_____	(c)	Sequence number	(4) 6
_____	(d)	Letter C indicates comment line	(5) 7 to 72
			(6) 73 to 80
_____	(e)	Compiler does not compile this if the line is a comment	
_____	(f)	Continuation character to indicate continuation line	

- - - - - - - - - - - - - - - - - - - -

(a) 5; (b) 3; (c) 6; (d) 1; (e) 2; (f) 4

22. Study this FORTRAN statement.

```
       IF (NUM2 .LT. 10) GO TO 298
```

Note how it fits on one coding line.

(a) Rewrite the above statement so that it requires a continuation line. On the first line, write the part of the statement that includes the word IF

and the expression contained within parentheses. On the continuation
line, write the remainder of the IF statement.

```
|    |  |    |    |    |    |    |    |    |    |    |    |    |    |
|    |  |    |    |    |    |    |    |    |    |    |    |    |    |
```

(b) A FORTRAN program might have a WRITE statement which causes the
computer to output a long list of variables. We've supplied part of a
WRITE statement below, including a list of variables which you are to
use in completing the WRITE statement. Use as many continuation lines
as necessary. If you need help as to what a WRITE statement looks like,
refer back to frame 12. For now, ignore the FORMAT statement. Here's
the list of variables: PROD1, PROD2, PROD3, PROD4, PROD5, PROD6,
PROD7, PROD8, QTY1, QTY2, QTY3, QTY4, QTY5, QTY6, QTY7, and
QTY8.

```
|      | WRITE (6,30011)                              |
|      |                                              |
|      |                                              |
|      |                                              |
```

- - - - - - - - - - - - - - - - - -

(a)
```
|      | IF (NUM2 .LT. 10)                     |
|    - |                  GØ TØ 298            |
```

(We could have placed GO TO 298 anywhere in columns 7-72.)
(b) Here's one possible answer (note how we lined up the variables).

```
|      | WRITE (6,30011) PRØD1,  PRØD2,  PRØD3,  PRØD4, |
|    - |                 PRØD5,  PRØD6,  PRØD7,  PRØD8, |
|    - |                 QTY1,  QTY2,  QTY3,  QTY4,     |
|    - |                 QTY5,  QTY6,  QTY7,  QTY8      |
```

If you need help as to what a WRITE statement looks like, refer back to
Frame 14.

23. A continuation line is indicated by a nonblank or nonzero character in
column 6 with the actual continued statement in columns 7 through 72. Something is wrong with the continuation statements which follow. Write a correct
statement for each one of them.

(a)
```
|1 3 7 00| SAMSØN = PILLAR + ØF + STØNE * WHICH ** HE-|
|1 3 7 01|X PUSHED - ØVER / WITH + EFFØRT ** AND * HELP|
```

(b) `201` `WRITE (6,202) NAME1, NAME2, NAME3, STRET1,`
`OSTRET2, STRET3, CITY1, CITY2, CITY3`

- - - - - - - - - - - - - - - - - - -

(a) A continuation line cannot have a statement number.

`13700` `SAMSØN = PILLAR + ØF + STØNE * WHICH ** HE -`
`XPUSHED - ØVER / WITH + EFFØRT ** AND * HELP`

(b) The continuation character must be other than a blank or zero.

`201` `WRITE (6,202) NAME1, NAME2, NAME3, STRET1,`
`-STRET2, STRET3, CITY1, CITY2, CITY3`

24. If you are unable to obtain the preprinted FORTRAN coding sheets like the one illustrated in frame 21, you can easily make your own. Let's do it together. On a blank (or horizontally ruled) sheet of paper, draw three vertical lines as illustrated below and insert the numbers at the top to represent the column boundaries. The numbers on our coding sheet below correspond to card columns or positions in which data is to be punched or keyed.

We've written some lines of coding on a FORTRAN coding form. Look at these statements carefully (on the next page), and then copy them onto your homemade coding sheet. Use all capital letters (to make the keypunch operator's job easier) because that's what the compiler will accept.

Page		of	
		Identification	
		TEST 18	
73			80

```
1       5 6 7   10      15      20      25      30      35      40      45      50
C  PRØGRAM:  TEST 18
C
10001  DØ 10009 MYSTEP = 4, 25, 7
       PEN = 1.0
       DØ 10008 MYFØØT = 1, 9, 2
       PENCIL = PEN * 2. - PENCIL
       FEET = 2. ** MYFØØT
       PEN = PEN + FEET
10008  CØNTINUE
10009  CØNTINUE
       STØP
C  THIS PRØGRAM IS NØNSENSE
       END
```

- - - - - - - - - - - - - - - - - - -

Your answer should look something like this.

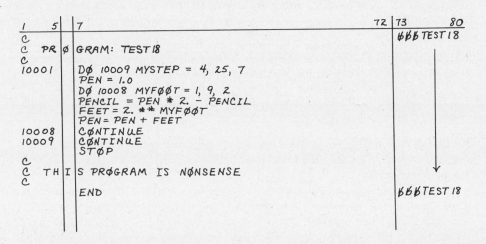

```
1     5 | 7                                              72|73          80
C                                                          | bbb TEST 18
C   PR Ø | GRAM: TEST 18                                   |
C         |                                                |
10001    | DØ 10009 MYSTEP = 4, 25, 7                      |
         | PEN = 1.0                                       |
         | DØ 10008 MYFØØT = 1, 9, 2                       |
         | PENCIL = PEN * 2. - PENCIL                      |
         | FEET = 2. ** MYFØØT                             |
         | PEN = PEN + FEET                                |
10008    | CØNTINUE                                        |
10009    | CØNTINUE                                        |
         | STØP                                            |
C         |                                                |
C   TH I | S PRØGRAM IS NØNSENSE                           |      ↓
C         |                                                |
         | END                                             | bbb TEST 18
```

25. Frames 25 through 29 refer to the FORTRAN coding form. You may refer back to frames 21 through 23. What does the letter C mean if it is written in column 1 of the coding sheet? _____

- - - - - - - - - - - - - - - - - - -

The letter C in column 1 indicates that the remainder of the line is to be treated as a comment by the compiler.

26. Other than part of a comment statement, what information or characters can be written in columns 1 through 5? _____

- - - - - - - - - - - - - - - - - - - -

Columns 1 through 5 are for statement numbers, consisting of from one to five digits, depending upon your compiler.

27. Sometimes a FORTRAN statement may require more than one line. How do you indicate a continuation line on a coding sheet? _____

_____

- - - - - - - - - - - - - - - - - - - -

A character other than a blank or zero in column 6 indicates to the compiler that the information contained in columns 7 through 72 is a continuation of the previous line.

28. What information is written in columns 7 through 72 of the coding sheet?

_____

- - - - - - - - - - - - - - - - - - - -

FORTRAN statements (or commands) are written in columns 7 through 72. If there is a C in column 1, comment information may be contained in columns 7 through 72.

29. Where would a program identifier or sequence number be indicated on the coding sheet? In what card columns would this information be punched?

_____

- - - - - - - - - - - - - - - - - - - -

An optional identifier or sequence number may be indicated in columns 73 through 80 of the coding sheet and is punched into columns 73 through 80 of the punched cards.
    The coding sheet will provide for either an identifier (like ours in frame 18) or a sequence number. Note that the homemade coding sheet has provision for a sequence number. It is a good idea to number each card in increments of 10; for example, the first would be 00000010, the second 00000020, and so on. Later, if you have to modify your program, you can then use the intermediate numbers such as 00000011, 00000012, and so on. We've illustrated this concept on the next page.

Original program deck   Additional program cards

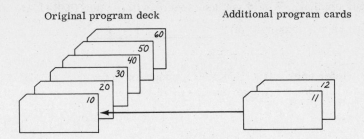

30. It is most important that you communicate to the keypunch operator which of the lookalike characters are numbers and which are letters. The preprinted FORTRAN coding sheet (see page 42) has provided for this; we've filled out that section below.

Punching Instructions							
Graphic	I	l	Ø	O	Z	2	u	Card Form #
Punch	A	N	A	N	A	N	A	

The entries in the chart specify which of the characters are to be treated as alphabetic (letter A) or numeric (letter N). Look at the chart again. The character written as I is to be punched as an alphabetic character, but the character l is to be punched as a _____.

- - - - - - - - - - - - - - - - - - -

numeric character

31. Copy the table in frame 27 into our blank chart below. Notice how many of the characters look alike were it not for the method we have used to differentiate them.

Punching Instructions							
Graphic								Card Form #
Punch								

- - - - - - - - - - - - - - - - - - -

Your chart should look the same as the one in frame 27.

32. Depending upon your FORTRAN compiler, you may be able to use spaces freely without confusing the compiler. This feature provides you with another method of making your program more readable by humans.

Which of the following statements are more readable?

_____ (a) TOT AMT = TOT PRN + TOT INT

_____ (b) TOTAMT = TOTPRN + TOTINT

What is your opinion? Would you use spaces within your FORTRAN statements as we have in example (a)? _____

- - - - - - - - - - - - - - - - - - -

We would. Refer back to the FORTRAN program in frame 19. Notice how many of the variables were expressed as "two words."

Self-Test

1. Copy the following FORTRAN statements from our homemade coding sheet onto the preprinted one.

```
  1     5  7                                                      72
    C   SP E CIFICATIØN  STATEMENTS
            DIMENSIØN CUMQTY (100)
            INTEGER CUMQTY/100 * 0/, PRØDNØ,  QTY
    C   RE A D TRANSACTIØN
    1       READ (1, 2) PRØDNØ,  QTY
    2       FØRMAT (I3,  I4)
    C   TE S T FØR LAST TRANSACTIØN
            IF (PRØDNØ .GT.  100)  GØ TØ 3
```

FORTRAN CODING FORM

		Punching Instructi
Program	Graphic	
Programmer	Date	Punch

C FOR COMMENT

STATEMENT NUMBER		FORTRAN STATEMENT
1 5	6 7 10 15 20 25 30 35 40 45	

line
1
2
3
4
5
6
7
8

2.   For each description below give the line number of the applicable program statement as shown in question 1.

_____   (a)   Comment statement

_____   (b)   Control statement

_____   (c)   Input statement

3.   Draw the appropriate flowchart symbols for the functions indicated.

(a)   Start

(b)   Decision point: A greater than B

(c)   Addition: X = A + B + C

(d)   Input: name, street, city, state

(e)   Multiplication: $e = mc^2$

(f)   Output: matrix

(g)   Collector: 5

(h)   Stop

4.   Draw a detailed flowchart for the following program steps: (a) Start; (b) input values of X and Y; (c) compute A = X + Y; (d) compute B = X - Y; (e) WRITE values of A, B, X, and Y; (f) IF A is less than 0, Stop; (g) else repeat steps (b) through (f).

5.   You have been selected to be the lead programmer/analyst for the secret "Goldilocks" robot project. Your current assignment is to create the algoithm (procedure) to permit Goldilocks to eat her porridge. You are to follow the logic set forth below. In other words, draw a flowchart.
     a) Get a bowl of porridge.
     b) Read the temperature.
     c) If the temperature is greater than 150° F, then "cool it";
         else continue
     d) Eat the porridge.

6.   Continuing with our assignment on the Goldilocks project from question 5 above, expand the "cool it" procedure by using the logic below.
     e) If the temperature is greater than 150° F, then continue with
         step (f) below; else continue with step (d) above.
     f) Count to 100.
     g) Read the temperature.
     h) Repeat step (e) above.

Answers to Self-Test

1.

| Program | | | Graphic | | | | | | | | Ca |
| Programmer | | Date | Punch | | | | | | | | |

C FOR COMMENT

STATEMENT NUMBER	Cont	FORTRAN STATEMENT
1 5	6	7 10 15 20 25 30 35 40 45 50

```
C   SPECIFICATION STATEMENTS
        DIMENSION CUMQTY(100)
        INTEGER CUMQTY/100*0/, PRØDNØ, QTY
C   READ TRANSACTION
1       READ (1,2) PRØDNØ, QTY
2       FØRMAT (I3, I4)
C   TEST FOR LAST TRANSACTION
        IF (PRØDNØ .GT. 100) GØ TØ 3
```

(frame 24)

2.   (a) 1, 4, 7; (b) 8; (c) 5   (frames 1, 11)

3.   (a) Start

(b) A > B? — False
True

(c) Compute
X = A + B + C

(d) Input
name,
street,
city,
state

(e) Compute
$e = mc^2$

(f) Output
matrix

(g) 5

(h) Stop

(frames 2-6, 10-14)

4.

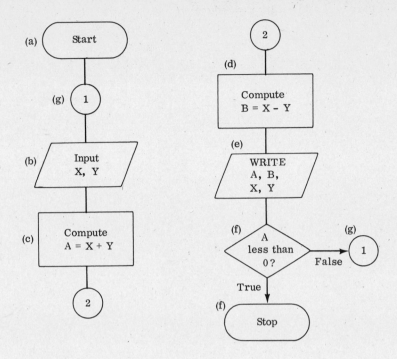

(a) Start

(g) 1

(b) Input X, Y

(c) Compute A = X + Y

2

2

(d) Compute B = X − Y

(e) WRITE A, B, X, Y

(f) A less than 0 ?

(g) 1   False

True

(f) Stop

(frames 2–6, 10–14)

5. Here's Goldilocks unmasked:

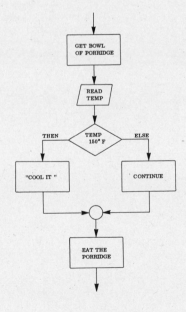

GET BOWL OF PORRIDGE

READ TEMP

THEN   TEMP 150° F   ELSE

"COOL IT "   CONTINUE

EAT THE PORRIDGE

(frame 14)

6.   This is the "cool it" procedure:

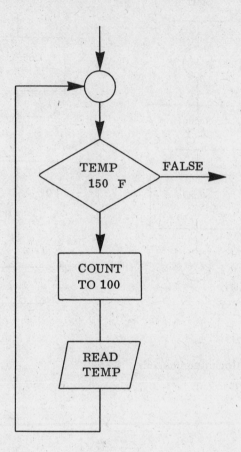

(frame 15)

CHAPTER TWO
Numerical Variables and Arithmatic Statements

In Chapter One, you saw some complete FORTRAN programs, each containing many program statements that would cause the computer to perform various operations. Chapter Two covers in greater detail those FORTRAN statements for performing arithmetic operations. You will learn input, output, and control statements in the three chapters that follow.

Although the computer stores data in specific memory locations, the FORTRAN programmer is usually not concerned with where the data is stored because he refers to the data by either value or variable name.

Upon completing Chapter Two, you should be able to:

- distinguish between numerical variables and constants, both real (with a decimal point) and integer (without a decimal point);

- assign appropriate names to stored data;

- write FORTRAN statements that will cause the computer to perform the arithmetic operations of addition, subtraction, multiplication, division, and exponentiation (if you don't know what this is, you probably won't use it).

Variables and Constants

1.   Because the computer can perform mathematical operations so rapidly, we sometimes refer to a computer program that does a lot of arithmetic as a "number cruncher."

In elementary algebra the statement $y = 5x + 1$ is made up of constants (the digits 5 and 1) and variables (the letters y and x). The mathematician likes to call an unchanging magnitude a constant. A variable is a quantity that may assume a succession of changing magnitudes. FORTRAN was constructed to contain constants and variables. For efficiency, FORTRAN provides one type of computer storage for integer constants or variables and another type of storage for real constants or variables. We will first examine the two types of constants, followed by the variable types, and finally the associated arithmetic modes.

Speed and efficiency are critical for a computer. Therefore, FORTRAN provides for two <u>distinct</u> types or modes of arithmetic: integer and real (often called <u>floating point</u>). The deliberately emphasized word <u>distinct</u> is meant as an early warning that the computer becomes somewhat disobedient if you attempt to mix the two types. Until you reach the frame where we discuss this point in more detail we pledge to stick to one mode of arithmetic at a time.

Take a deep breath and answer the questions below.

(a) How many types of arithmetic does FORTRAN provide? Name them.

_____

(b) What is a constant? _____

(c) What is a variable? _____

- - - - - - - - - - - - - - - - - - -

(a) two types—integer mode and real mode; (b) an unchanging magnitude;
(c) a quantity that may assume a succession of changing magnitudes

2. We define an <u>integer</u> constant as a number written without a decimal point. For example, 985 is an integer constant. An integer constant may be either positive, zero, or negative. FORTRAN assumes that a number is positive if it has no sign (plus or minus). However, if you wish to sign a value, the appropriate sign must be placed to the left of the constant as the examples show.

$$-312 \qquad\qquad +15 \qquad\qquad -87$$

• Warning: Computers vary in the maximum number of digits you can use. Check your computer installation's FORTRAN manual for the maximum number of digits. Appendix A indicates the plus and minus ranges for one, two and four byte integer variables.

(a) The number 537 is an integer constant. Is the number 62.4 an integer

constant? _____

(b) Which of the following are <u>improperly</u> signed?

_____ 55 _____ 55+ _____ -55

- - - - - - - - - - - - - - - - - - -

(a) No, because it contains a decimal point. In fact, we call 62.4 a <u>real</u>
value, which we'll formally cover in frame 4.
(b) 55+ is incorrect. It should be written as +55 or 55. The number 55 is
assumed to be positive because it has no sign.

3. FORTRAN does not use numbers which contain embedded commas. Although 6,324,517 is more readable than 6324517, FORTRAN will only store the latter as a numeric data value.

Which of the following are not valid integer values, and why?

(a) −204 _____

(b) +7,305 _____

(c) 2417. _____

- -

Choices (b) and (c) are not valid integer values. Since +7,305 has an embedded comma, it is invalid. It should be written as either +7305 or 7305 (without the sign). Because it contains a decimal point, 2417. is not an integer value.

4. We call the second type of number which FORTRAN uses real. A real number looks somewhat like an integer number, except that it contains one decimal point. For example, the following are real numbers.

$$+32.87 \qquad .5324 \qquad -240.$$

Although the numbers 240 and 240. have identical numeric values, FORTRAN considers them as two distinct types.

What we stated in frames 2 and 3 about signed values and embedded commas also applies to real numbers. Again, each computer has a limitation to the size of a real number it can accommodate.

Which of the following are invalid real values? Why?

(a) −3,732.4 _____

(b) 67.245 _____

(c) 32 _____

- -

(a) −3,732.4 is not a valid real value because it contains an embedded comma.
(b) 67.245 is a valid real value which we could also write as +67.245.
(c) 32 is not a valid real value; it is an integer value.

5. In Chapter Zero you learned that data and instructions must be stored in a computer's memory. Each item is stored in a storage location labeled with a unique number so we can refer to that location whenever we want. However, a computer language requires many thousands of such storage positions to be allocated before and during program execution. This type of activity could make our job very difficult. Fortunately, in FORTRAN we need not be concerned with the actual addresses of the memory locations in which data is stored; instead, we can refer to data by either name or value. The compiler (language translator) assumes the responsibility of assigning to each name or value an actual storage address. To keep track of various storage addresses, a table (which associates each name with an actual storage address) is kept in storage. In this way, the computer knows the location of each item of data named in the computer program.

If we refer to data by name, we call that name a variable. A variable is a name that refers to a storage location inside the computer. That storage location is to contain a value which is represented by the variable name. The value of a variable may either remain the same (constant) or change during execution of a program, but that's up to you.

We can create a variable name only by following certain rules:

- The name must be unique (two or more variables cannot have the same name).

- It may contain any combination of from one to six capital alphabetic (A to Z) or numeric (0 to 9) characters, and with some compilers the dollar sign ($).

- The first character must not be numeric, for good reason. Since a FORTRAN variable name can consist of only one character, the compiler would be unable to distinguish between a variable name 6 and a constant 6.

Here are some valid variable names.

SOME1   GOGO   A12345

But NEVERMORE (which has more than six characters), 123HUP (first character is numeric), and NO-GO (dash is not permitted) are invalid variable names.

Which of the following do you think are valid or invalid, and why?

Name	Valid	Invalid and reason
X+RAY		
ZOOM		
TERRIBLE		
SMART		
ALEC69		
650IMB		

- -

ZOOM, SMART, and ALEC69 are valid FORTRAN variable names. X+RAY has an invalid character; TERRIBLE has more than six characters; and 650IMB begins with a numeric character.

6.   Don't become confused. A variable name means either a particular storage location or the value stored in that location; think of them as one and the same. For instance, if we say "The value of PUTUP is 5," we mean that the memory location established by the FORTRAN compiler and computer will contain the value 5. If you said, "Seventeen is stored as the value of the variable SHUTUP," you would mean the value _____ is stored in the memory

location assigned by the compiler and computer for the variable _____.

- - - - - - - - - - - - - - - - - -

17; SHUTUP

7. There are advantages and disadvantages to using real or integer mode. For example, it is useful to know that a real mode designation relieves the programmer of the responsibility for keeping track of the decimal point during computations. The computer takes care of lining up decimal points before arithmetic computations. For this reason, real mode computation often takes longer to execute. Therefore, whenever speed is important and the values are integers, use integer mode. Another consideration is that integer arithmetic is often more accurate than real. However, the allowable range of real numbers is much greater than the allowable range for integers.

An integer variable is one that may take on any of the values permitted for an integer constant—namely, zero or any positive or negative integer in the range permitted for the particular computer used.

The first character in a variable name indicates whether the variable is integer or real. An integer variable name must start with one of these alphabetic characters: I, J, K, L, M, or N. For example, these are acceptable integer variable names:

IMA   MIDGET   KZR

If a variable name begins with any other alphabetic character, the compiler assumes the variable is real and establishes storage for a real value. Here is an easy way to remember this FORTRAN convention: The range of letters for INteger variable names is I through N.

(a) Will the variable WHAT store a real or integer value? _____

(b) What will the variable ISIT store? _____

- - - - - - - - - - - - - - - - - -

(a) a real value; (b) an integer value

8. Here's a practical suggestion: You may use a large variety of names limited only by your imagination. However, we advise you to name variables in some organized or logical fashion so that you can easily keep track of them in your program. One way is to select names that help you remember the function they serve. For example, to calculate gross wages, we could use the real variables HOURS, TIME, and GROSS rather than H, T, and G, or X, Y, and Z. However, if these values are integer, we could precede these variable names with any of the letters I, J, K, L, M, or N to change the mode. In our example, the variables would then be IHOURS, ITIME, and IGROSS.

The variables on the next page are to contain only integer values. How would you correct these names written by a careless programmer?

Real mode	Integer mode
AVER	(a) _____
SPEED	(b) _____
TIME	(c) _____
DIST	(d) _____

- - - - - - - - - - - - - - - - - - -

Any answer which precedes the name with one of the letters I, J, K, L, M, or N is correct.   Two possible sets of answers are:

(a) IAVER   KDAVER
(b) JSPEED   ISPEED
(c) KTIME   ITIME
(d) LDIST   IDIST

9.   For each variable name, identify its mode by writing an appropriate value under the proper column heading.   We've done the first one for you.

Variable name	Integer mode	Real mode
HOURS	(a) _____	24.0
MINUTE	(b) _____	_____
A49872	(c) _____	_____
LQQQQ	(d) _____	_____
DC9	(e) _____	_____
MOUTH	(f) _____	_____
TONGUE	(g) _____	_____

- - - - - - - - - - - - - - - - - - -

Many answers are possible.   We've selected these:

	Integer	Real
(b)	59	
(c)		+49.872
(d)	-9999	
(e)		1000.1
(f)	+6	
(g)		-25.

Remember, each integer value must not have a decimal point.   And each real value must have a decimal point.

10. For each constant on the next page, identify its mode by writing an appropriate variable name under the proper column heading.   We've done the first one for you.

Constant		Integer	Real
−307	(a)	IH	_____
+15.49	(b)	_____	_____
98.6	(c)	_____	_____
0	(d)	_____	_____
−.01	(e)	_____	_____
98765	(f)	_____	_____
+95	(g)	_____	_____

- - - - - - - - - - - - - - - - - -

Again, many answers are possible. We thought these appropriate:

	Integer	Real
(b)		F1549
(c)		TEMP
(d)	IZERO	
(e)		BIT
(f)	NINE25	
(g)	NORMAL	

The integer name must begin with either I, J, K, L, M, or N. The real name must begin with a letter other than those. And all variable names must consist of one to six characters (letters and numbers).

Summary of Variables and Constants

Constant: A constant is a numerical value which is either positive, zero, or negative. A constant is one of two modes:

An integer constant contains no decimal point.

$$+300 \qquad 10 \qquad -409$$

A real constant contains one decimal point.

$$+300. \qquad 1.04 \qquad -409.65$$

A sign is optional; if there is no sign, the computer assumes the constant is positive. The symbol + indicates positive and the − means negative. The symbol must appear to the left of the constant.

positive:	+300	+300.	10	1.04
negative:	−409	−409.65		

Variable: A variable is a one- to six-character name that represents (refers to a storage location inside the computer memory that is to contain) a value. The first character of the variable name must be one of the 26 letters of the alphabet. The remaining characters of the name, if any, may be any combination of the 26 letters and 10 digits of the decimal number system. The initial letter of the variable name indicates its mode:

An integer variable has as its first letter either I, J, K, L, M, or N, and the value contains no decimal point.

J   K2R   NUMBER

A real variable has a first letter other than I, J, K, L, M, or N, and the value contains one decimal point.

Z   A1235   FOWL

Arithmetic Operators

11. FORTRAN provides five basic arithmetic operations. You will notice that most are very similar to the ones you used in highschool mathematics.

Operation	Highschool style symbol	example	FORTRAN style symbol	example
addition	+	a + b	+	A + B
subtraction	–	c – d	–	C – D
multiplication	x	e x f	*	E * F
division	÷	g ÷ h	/	G / H
exponentiation	none	i^j	**	I**J

These arithmetic "operators" are used with variables and constants to form FORTRAN expressions. FORTRAN expressions can consist of a single constant, a single variable, or of two or more of these elements combined by the use of arithmetic operators and parentheses to form various types of FORTRAN expressions. More precisely, an expression is a rule to compute a numerical value. Examples:

Expression	Meaning (value of expression)
A	the value of the real variable A
B * C	the product of the values of B and C
PRETTY + UGLY	the sum of the values of PRETTY and UGLY
(A+B)/(C+D)	the sum of the values A and B divided by the sum of the values C and D

Up to this point, we have used addition and subtraction in our examples because the symbols are already familiar to you. Now look at this algebraic expression:

$$ay + b - \frac{c}{2}$$

In FORTRAN, we would write it as:

A * Y + B - C/2.   or   (A * Y) + B - (C/2.)

Note that we used a real constant in an expression containing real variables. Some compilers prohibit the mixing of modes in an expression. We will discuss this further in frame 33.

Try writing the following expressions in FORTRAN.

(a) abc + d/e _____

(b) db/c - 3. (b) _____

- - - - - - - - - - - - - - - - - - -

(a) A*B*C + D/E, or (A*B*C) + (D/E)
(b) (D*B/C) - (3.*B)
We like to use parentheses because they make expressions easier to read. As you can see, FORTRAN expressions can be very similar in form and construction to algebraic expressions.

12. The fifth FORTRAN arithmetic operator is for exponentiation (or raising a number to a power). If you're not interested in exponentiation, skip to frame 13 (but some problems later in this chapter will use exponentiation, so don't say we didn't warn you).

The algebraic expression a^4 is a shorthand notation for a x a x a x a. This expression is an exponentiation. This example of exponentiation would be expressed in FORTRAN as:

A**4

Rewrite the following algebraic expressions in FORTRAN.

(a) $3^k + 4m$ _____

(b) $(1/2)\ gt^2$ _____

- - - - - - - - - - - - - - - - - - -

(a) 3**K + 4*M
(b) G * (T**2) / 2., or (G * (T**2)) / 2., or (1./2.) * G * T**2, or something similar

Parentheses

13. You may use parentheses to write FORTRAN expressions that are equivalent to various algebraic expressions. In FORTRAN, as in algebra, expressions contained within the innermost set of parentheses are computed (evaluated) first. As an example, in the FORTRAN expression

(WISDOM * (RICH + FOLKS))

the expression in the innermost set of parentheses, (RICH + FOLKS), will be evaluated first. The expression (WISDOM * (RICH + FOLKS)) will then be evaluated. For the FORTRAN expression

$$TRY * (BASE ** (NUMBER + 2)) - 3. * (BAD + TRIP)$$

what is evaluated first? _____

- - - - - - - - - - - - - - - - - - - -

(NUMBER + 2) is evaluated first. After this, the exponentiation operation will be performed. Generally, use parentheses if you want to be assured that a computation will be evaluated in a specific manner.

14. As parentheses are used in algebraic expressions to imply a grouping of terms, we can use parentheses in FORTRAN expressions for the same purpose. Thus, the FORTRAN expression

$$A + C * (F + G)$$

is equivalent to the algebraic expression $a + c(f + g)$.

Write FORTRAN expressions for each of the following algebraic expressions.

(a) $3.5a - 2.7(c - 13.2f)$ _____

(b) $\dfrac{2.6a + b}{c}$ _____

(c) $\dfrac{a + b}{c + d}$ _____

(d) $(a + b)^3$ _____

(e) $c^{k + 3}$ _____

- - - - - - - - - - - - - - - - - - -

(a) 3.5 * A - 2.7 * (C - (13.2 * F)), or 3.5 * A - 2.7 * (C - 13.2 * F)
(b) ((2.6 * A) + B) / C, or (2.6 * A + B) / C
(c) (A + B) / (C + D) (Not A + B / C + D, which is the same as $a + \dfrac{b}{c} + d$)

Did you get this one correct? Yes? Fine. As you see, it is sometimes necessary to insert parentheses in a FORTRAN expression even though the algebraic equivalent of the expression had none. Parentheses were implied in expressions (b) and (c).
(d) (A + B) ** 3 (The FORTRAN expression A + B ** 3 is a valid expression but is equivalent to the algebraic expression $a + b^3$.)
(e) C ** (K + 3) is correct. The expression C ** K + 3 would be equivalent to $c^k + 3$, which is not what you want. This point will be further clarified in frame 17.

15. To see the difference the use of parentheses makes in evaluation of an arithmetic expression, let us look at the two following examples.

1. D + (B/E) where the values of D, B, and E are 4., 8., and 2. respectively. Substituting these values in this expression gives 4. + (8./2.) = 4. + 4. = 8.

2. (D + B)/E. Using the same values as above gives (4. + 8.)/2. = 12./2. = 6.

Now, if you saw an expression D + B/E, you could ask, "How should I evaluate this expression, as in the first or second example?" Since the answers in the two cases were different, this is a very good question.

While you are pondering this question, how about evaluating two expressions using the values of 2. and 4. for A and B respectively.

(a) (A + B) ** 3 _____

(b) A + (B**3) _____

- - - - - - - - - - - - - - - - - - -

(a) 216., since (2. + 4.) ** 3 = 6. ** 3 = 6. * 6. * 6. = 216.
(b) 66., because 2. + (4.**3) = 2. + (4. * 4. * 4.) = 2. + 64. = 66.

16. FORTRAN does not allow you to place two operator signs next to each other. If you want to write the FORTRAN expression equivalent to the algebraic expression a + -b, you must write either A + (-B) or -B + A. It's okay to use ** to indicate an exponentiation, because two adjacent * symbols do not mean two multiplications, but instead imply the special operator of exponentiation. We freely use parentheses to indicate grouping of terms. However, unlike their use in algebra, they do not imply multiplication. Thus (OOPS + WHOA) (STOP + THINK) is not a valid FORTRAN expression. It should be written as (OOPS + WHOA) * (STOP + THINK).

Now you work a bit. Which of the following are valid FORTRAN expressions?

Expression	Valid	Invalid and reason
(a) (STEADY + - AS) * SHE + GOES		
(b) HARD - WRITING * 3BOOKS		
(c) WATCH (YOUR + SELF)		
(d) (SHOULD * GET - THIS) * ONE - RIGHT		

- - - - - - - - - - - - - - - - - - -

Only (d) is valid. Hurrah for you if you did these correctly. In choice (a), although the operator combination + - is not allowed, (STEADY + (-AS)) * SHE + GOES is okay. In (b), WRITING and 3BOOKS are not valid FORTRAN variables. WRITING has more than six characters and 3BOOKS starts with a numeric character. In (c), FORTRAN does not have implied multiplication. WATCH * (YOUR + SELF) is the correct answer.

17. The FORTRAN language was designed to perform computations in a manner very similar to the one you would use in evaluating algebraic expressions. You would probably compute the algebraic expression ab + c as follows: First, compute the product of a and b; then add the product value to c.

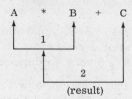

(result)

Formally, FORTRAN evaluates expressions using a hierarchy or sequence of arithmetic operators. Although you may not understand these terms, you will be familiar with what follows:

Arithmetic operation	Evaluation sequence
parentheses	first
exponentiations	second
multiplications and divisions	third
additions and subtractions	fourth

Thus, in the expression

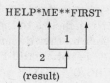

(result)

ME ** FIRST is computed first, and then the resulting value is multiplied by the value of HELP.

(a) In the expression (SON + OF) * A ** NUT, what will be computed first?

_____

(b) In the expression LOTS - OF ** LUCK, what will be computed first?

_____

(c) What is the evaluation sequence of the expression A + B/C - D?

_____

- - - - - - - - - - - - - - - - - - -

(a) Moving from left to right, the expression contained within the first complete set of parentheses is evaluated.

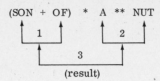

(result)

(b) Exponentiation ranks higher than addition and subtraction, so it is performed first.

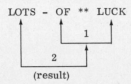

(result)

(c) The operations of multiplication and division rank higher than addition and subtraction.

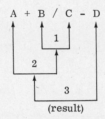

(result)

18. Now that you have learned the hierarchy of operations, we will show you how the computer evaluates expressions in order of priority. Operations having the same priority (hierarchy) are executed in order of appearance from left to right. This means that all multiplications and divisions are performed from left to right as they appear, and then all additions and subtractions are performed from left to right as they appear. However, some compilers perform adjacent exponentiations—such as L**M**N—from right to left. That is, M**N is computed first and then this value is used to compute L**(M**N). Check your computer's FORTRAN language manual as to how your computer will compute such an expression.

For this reason your problems will not require parentheses unless the normal evaluation sequence is contrary to what you want to occur. One safe rule to follow is <u>when in doubt, use parentheses</u> to indicate the evaluation sequence.

In our subsequent examples, we will assume that the operations are performed from left to right, as in the following one on the next page.

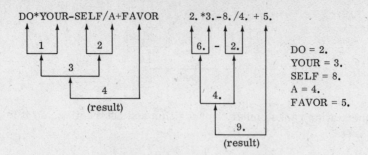

DO = 2.
YOUR = 3.
SELF = 8.
A = 4.
FAVOR = 5.

(1) Calculate the value of DO * YOUR and store it.

(2) Calculate the value of SELF / A and store it, too.

(3) Subtract the results of the first two computations and store this result.

(4) Add the result of the last computation from (3) and the value of FAVOR.

That's simple. Remember that you can rely upon the hierarchy of operations to cut down the number of "unnecessary" parentheses.

Now it's your turn. In what order would FORTRAN evaluate this expression?

HOPE ** (WE * DO) / THIS * RIGHT

- - - - - - - - - - - - - - - - -

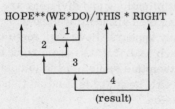

Here goes:
    (1) First compute WE * DO since they are contained in parentheses.
    (2) Perform HOPE ** (WE * DO).
    (3) Divide the product in (2) by THIS.
    (4) Finally, multiply the value in (3) by RIGHT.
By the way, this FORTRAN expression is equivalent to the algebraic expression

$$\frac{(HOPE)^{(WE*DO)}\,(RIGHT)}{THIS}$$

19. Write the following mathematical expressions in FORTRAN. We've completed the first one for you.

Mathematical expression		FORTRAN expression
$ax + b$	(a)	A * X + B
$jklm$	(b)	_____
$b^2 - 4ac$	(c)	_____
$\dfrac{ab}{cd}$	(d)	_____
$\dfrac{1}{b^4}\left(\dfrac{c}{a}\right)^{x-1}$	(e)	_____

- - - - - - - - - - - - - - - - - - - -

(b) J * K * L * M
(c) B**2 - 4. * A * C
(d) (A * B)/(C * D), or A * B / C * D
(e) ((C/A) ** (X - 1.)) / B**4, or (C/A)**(X-1.)/B**4

20. Write these FORTRAN expressions as mathematical expressions. As an example, we've done the first one for you.

FORTRAN expression		Mathematical expression
(-B+B**2-4.*A*C)/(2.*A)	(a)	$\dfrac{-b + b^2 - 4ac}{2a}$
X**A - 3.	(b)	_____
A/B - C**D + E/F	(c)	_____
(A**2-B**2+C**2)/P	(d)	_____
(A+B)**1.6	(e)	_____

- - - - - - - - - - - - - - - - - - - -

(b) $x^a - 3$

(c) $\dfrac{a}{b} - c^d + \dfrac{e}{f}$

(d) $\dfrac{a^2 - b^2 + c^2}{p}$

(e) $(a + b)^{1.6}$

21. Parentheses are used to clarify the order of computation in an expression. However, each left parenthesis "(" must have a matching right parenthesis ")". A simple test to see if there is a matching number of parentheses is as follows: Starting with a count of zero, add one for each left parenthesis and subtract one for each right parenthesis. At the end of the expression, the count should be zero. An example is shown on the next page.

$$X*(X*(X*(X*(X*(X*A6+A5)+A4)+A3)+A2)+A1)+A0$$

```
      +1 +1 +1  +1 +1          -1  -1  -1  -1  -1

  0    +1 +2 +3 +4 +5          +4  +3  +2  +1   0
```

However, even though the parenthesis count of an expression is zero, it does not follow that the expression is correct, since

$$ERROR = (A + B)\ (C + D)$$

```
              +1      -1 +1     -1

          0   +1       0 +1      0
```

has a parenthesis count of zero, but is an incorrect expression.

Which of the following have the correct amount of matching parentheses and are valid expressions?

(a)   (A+B)**R-(P-(Q*(R-B)))   _____

(b)   INK-(DINKA-4*(DOO+SCOTT)**JOPLIN-RAGS   _____

(c)   (A-B)/C-D/(E-F)G   _____

- - - - - - - - - - - - - - - - - - - -

(a) Correct count.   (A+B)**R-(P-(Q*(R-B)))
```
                    0  +1  0    +1 +2 +3   +2+1 0
```
This is also a correct expression.

(b) Incorrect parenthesis count.

INK-(DINKA-4*(DOO+SCOTT)**JOPLIN-RAGS
```
  0  +1          +2            +1
```

(c) Correct parenthesis count. (A-B)/C-D/(E-F)G
```
                              0 +1  0     +1   0
```

But this expression is invalid since (E-F)G is not a valid FORTRAN expression.

Summary of Arithmetic Operators

FORTRAN provides six symbols for arithmetic operations:

Evaluation sequence	Type	Symbol	Example
1	parentheses	( )	B * (A + 24.3)
2	exponentiation	**	I ** J
3	multiplication	*	E * F
3	division	/	G / H
4	addition	+	A + B
4	subtraction	–	C – D

The operators + and – may precede a constant or variable to indicate its sign. However, if another operator is to appear to its left, parentheses must be used to separate the operators.

$$-B * C \qquad\qquad A * (-1.)$$

The compiler evaluates arithmetic expressions from left to right, evaluating the expression according to the sequence indicated above when more than one operator is present.

Assignment Statements

22. The FORTRAN assignment statement consists of two basic parts:

$$VERY = SPEC * AL - FORT / RAN ** STAT + EMENT$$

single   any FORTRAN expression
variable

Notice that the assignment statement looks like a mathematical equation, but it is not. The computer treats the assignment statement like this: First, it evaluates the expression to the right of the equal sign; second, it stores (assigns) the result as the value of the variable to the left of the equal sign. Here's a simple illustration: If JANET has the value 30, execution of the statement JANET = JANET + 1 will cause JANET to now have a value of 31.

Similarly, the statement BABY = RITA * PHIL multiplies the values of the variables RITA and PHIL and stores the product (result of a multiplication) as the value of BABY. The previous value of BABY is replaced.

The assignment statement also enables you to move values within your program, from a constant or another variable:

$$DOCTOR = 400.$$
$$WALLET = BILL$$

DOCTOR has the value 400. and the variables WALLET and BILL both have identical values.

(a) If A has the value of 3.6 and B is .2, in the statement C = A/B what is the value of C? _____

(b) Each variable has an initial value:

Variable	Value
HOURS	37.5
RATE	3.75
PAY	125.25
TXRATE	.2

The following assignment statement is executed: PAY = (HOURS * RATE) - TXRATE * (HOURS * RATE). After execution, what is the value of PAY? _____

(c) Using the value of PAY above, when the statement NEWPAY = PAY + .5 is executed, what is the value of NEWPAY? _____

- - - - - - - - - - - - - - - - - -

(a) 18.   (Don't forget the decimal point.)

(b) 112.5 Here's how:

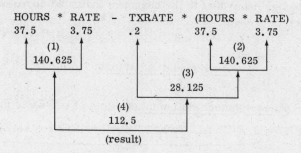

(result)

(c) 113 (No decimal because NEWPAY is an integer variable.)

23. A <u>real</u> number or value consists of two parts: the <u>integer</u> portion and the <u>fractional</u> portion. Let's analyze the number +237.145:

$$\underbrace{+237}_{\text{integer}} \quad \underbrace{.145}_{\text{fractional}}$$

Indicate the integer and fractional parts for each of the numbers below.

		Component	
Number		integer	fractional
−18.5	(a)	_____	_____
+904.3	(b)	_____	_____
108.46	(c)	_____	_____
33	(d)	_____	_____

- - - - - - - - - - - - - - - - - - - -

	integer	fractional
(a)	−18	−.5
(b)	+904	.3
(c)	108	.46
(d)	33	none

24. You may also use the assignment statement to convert an integer value to a real value, or a real value to an integer value. If WIDTH has the value of 3.8, the expression LENGTH = WIDTH takes the value of WIDTH (3.8) and converts it to an integer value (3) by truncating (chopping off) the fractional portion, and stores the result as the value of LENGTH. As you can see, LENGTH does not really equal WIDTH; in fact, there is a difference in value of 0.8. The value of WIDTH remains unchanged.

The following simple assignment statements on the next page illustrate the conversion process.

M = 13.6	The value of 13 is stored as the integer value of the variable M.
M = 13.6 + R	If R has the value of 0.5, then the value 14.1 will be truncated to 14, which is the value stored for M.
M = A + .5	If A has the value 601.73, then 602 will be stored for M. Note: In these two examples we've shown you how to round a number to a whole number. The next statement will convert the value back to real.
A = M	If M has the integer value 602, then A will have the value 602. because of the conversion to real mode.

(a)   A = 15.4.   What is the value of A? _____

(b)   Using the value of A from above, M = A + .5.   What is the value of M?

_____

(c)   Using the value of M above, A = M.   What is the value of A? _____

- - - - - - - - - - - - - - - - - - -

(a) 15.4;   (b) 15;   (c) 15., or 15.0

25.   Which of the following assignment statements are incorrect and why?

Assignment statement	Valid	Invalid and reason
(a) ALPHA = BETA ** ZETA		
(b) 38 = IOTA		
(c) FRONT + BACK = SIDE * REAR		

- - - - - - - - - - - - - - - - - - -

Choice (a) is correct.   Choice (b) is incorrect because an assignment statement can have only a single variable to the left of the equal sign; the number 38 is a constant.   The statement in (c) violates the rule that just one variable can be to the left of the equal sign, not two or more.

26.   Let's write some assignment statements.

(a)   Increase by 4 the value stored in the variable INCHES.

_____

(b)   Reduce the value of WEIGHT by 10%. _____

(c)   Round the value stored in the variable PRICE to the nearest whole decimal number.   Store the result in PRICE.   (Hint: Use two assignment statements.) _____

- - - - - - - - - - - - - - - - - - -

(a) INCHES = INCHES + 4
(b) WEIGHT = WEIGHT * .9, or WEIGHT = WEIGHT – (.1 * WEIGHT)
(c) One possible solution is:
IPRICE = PRICE + .5
PRICE = IPRICE

Summary of the Assignment Statement

Up to this point you have learned that the assignment statement works like
this:

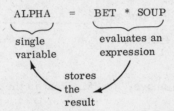

Operation: The assignment statement
  (1) evaluates the expression to the right of the equal sign;
  (2) if required, converts the mode of the value obtained in (1) to the
       mode of the variable to the left of the equal sign;
  (3) stores the result as the value of the variable to the left of the
       equal sign.

Purposes: You can use a single assignment statement for the following purposes:
  (1) **to evaluate an expression consisting of two or more variables**
       and/or constants and store the result in a single variable:
       $$A = ((37.3 * A) - A**17)/B$$
  (2) to convert the mode of a constant or the value of a variable:
         INTVAL = RLVAL
         MEN = 13.6   (MEN has the value 13)
         RLVAL = INTVAL
         AGE = 33   (AGE has the value 33.)
  (3) to store a single value in a variable:
         $$X = 16.4$$
         $$Y = B$$

27. These next frames focus on the finer points of FORTRAN assignment
statements. You should remember that <u>integer</u> arithmetic always produces
<u>integer</u> results; that is, there is no fractional part to the answer. Even
though you might attempt to convert the result to <u>real</u> mode, you will not re-
cover the "lost" fractional part.

To illustrate, what is the value of N?

L = 2
M = 5
N = M/L   _____

- - - - - - - - - - - - - - - - - - -

N has the value of 2, not 2.5 or 2.0.

28. If we change the variable name N to REALN, what is the value of REALN?

L = 2
M = 5
REALN = M/L   _____

- - - - - - - - - - - - - - - - - - -

2.0 is the value of REALN.

29. What is the value of C in this program segment?

A = 2
B = 5
C = B/A   _____

- - - - - - - - - - - - - - - - - - -

2.5 is the value of C, and here's how the computer arrived at that answer:
   (1)   The value 2 is converted to real mode and stored as the value of
         variable A.

$$A\ =\ 2 \qquad \curvearrowright 2.$$

   (2)   The value 5 is also converted to real mode and stored as the
         value of B.

$$B\ =\ 5 \qquad \curvearrowright 5.$$

   (3)   The division is performed in real mode, causing the result to be
         in real mode.

$$C\ =\ B\ /\ A$$
$$2.5 \leftarrow 5.\ /\ \ 2.$$

30. Write an assignment statement to convert the value stored in the variable
MODEL from integer to real mode. _____

- - - - - - - - - - - - - - - - - -

One possible answer is: $\underbrace{\text{AMODEL}}_{\substack{\text{real} \\ \text{variable}}}$ = $\underbrace{\text{MODEL}}_{\substack{\text{integer} \\ \text{variable}}}$

Your answer will be correct if the name of the variable to the left of the equal sign started with any letter other than I, J, K, L, M, or N.

31. Now let's write a program segment to calculate a unit price. Using the following variables, write a program segment to calculate the average cost of each bolt in inventory. Store the final result in COST. Do not mix modes in your arithmetic expression. (Hint: Use an assignment statement to convert the mode of the integer value.)

Variable name	Stored value	Explanation of variable
INVTRY	2009	represents how many bolts are in the stock bin
TOTCST	276.08	total number of dollars that the bolts cost us
COST	to be calculated	average cost of each bolt in dollars

- - - - - - - - - - - - - - - - - -

Here's one possible answer:

$\left.\begin{array}{l}\text{any real} \\ \text{variable}\end{array}\right\}\longrightarrow$ QTY = INVTRY
COST = TOTCST / QTY

32. Write a program segment to calculate the total number of hours (including fractional parts) given the values of elapsed hours, minutes, and seconds. Use the following variables.

Variable name	Stored value	Explanation of variable
IHOURS	5	number of whole hours elapsed
MINS	25	number of minutes elapsed (not included in IHOURS)
ISECS	51	number of seconds elapsed (not included in MINS)
TIME	to be calculated	decimal number of elapsed hours

- - - - - - - - - - - - - - - - - - -

There are two basic approaches to writing this program segment.

(1) Convert all the times to seconds and store the result as a real value; then convert the seconds to hours, expressed as a real value.

TIME = IHOURS * 3600 + MINS * 60 + ISECS
TIME = TIME / 3600

(2) Convert each of the integer values to real; then calculate the number of hours.

HOURS = IHOURS
TMINS = MINS
SECS = ISECS
TIME = HOURS + TMINS / 60. + SECS / 3600.

Take your choice. The first approach is more efficient because it uses only four variables and three constants. The second approach requires seven variables and two constants. Furthermore, a computer will perform multiplication more rapidly than division in most instances. Whatever method you used, the computer should calculate 5.43083 as the answer.

33. Up to this point, we have been careful not to mix modes; that is, we have used only one mode of variables and/or constants on the right side of an assignment statement. Using statements from the last frame:

TIME = IHOURS * 3600 + MINS * 60 + ISECS

variables and constants are all integer

TIME = HOURS + TMINS / 60. + SECS / 3600.

variables and constants are all real

The American National Standards Institute published Standards for FORTRAN in 1966 (hence the name ANS FORTRAN). ANS FORTRAN did not permit mixed mode in expressions. Consequently, we have been careful not to violate this rule thus far. Furthermore, ANS FORTRAN permits the following forms of exponentiation.

Algebraic form	FORTRAN expression	
19^2	19 ** 2 integer	Although our examples use constants, you may substitute appropriate variables.
2.6^3	2.6 ** 3 real integer	
$6.32^{.5}$	6.32 ** .5 real real	

ANS FORTRAN is not so restrictive as it may seem. For example, back in frame 31 we developed the solution

QTY = INVTRY
COST = TOTCST / QTY

because we did not want to mix modes. What would happen if we used COST = TOTCST / INVTRY? That all depends upon your FORTRAN compiler. With the advances in compiler design, many compilers allow mixing of modes in expressions ("thank goodness," you sigh). This certainly removes much of the burden from you, the programmer. In effect, whatever you don't do, the compiler will do for you. Specifically, the compiler will generate machine instructions to convert the data values from integer to real if your expression contains mixed modes.

In 1977, the American National Standards Institute again developed revised standards for FORTRAN, commonly known as FORTRAN 77. FORTRAN 77 permits various forms of mixed modes expression, whereas 1966 FORTRAN does not.

Of the compilers that permit mixed mode, many follow this rule: If any variable or constant in the expression is real, convert and process all other integer values as real. Refer to your computer installation's FORTRAN manual to see how your compiler handles mixed modes.

For each type of compiler, write suitable program segments to perform the algebraic calculations below. To assist you, we've worked out the first problem for you.

Algebraic statement

(a) $a = b/2 + 21$
(b) $f = i(j - zeta)$
(c) $m = k^5 + 35.89$
(d) $L = n^{.5} + .51$
(e) $dist = \dfrac{mph}{60}(mins + \dfrac{secs}{60})$

Suppose your compiler does not accept mixed mode. Write your segments.

(a)   A = B/2. + 21.   (d)

(b)   (e)

(c)

Now suppose that your compiler does accept mixed mode.

(a)   A = B/2 + 21   (d)

(b)

                                       (e)

(c)

- - - - - - - - - - - - - - - - - - -

First, for the compiler which does not accept mixed mode:
(b)   FI = I
      FJ = J
      F = FI * (FJ - ZETA), or something similar.
(c)   M = K ** 5 + 35   (The .89 is not relevant because the result of K**5 and
M are both integer.)
(d)   RN = N
      L = RN ** .5 + .51
(e)   RMPH = MPH
      RMINS = MINS
      DIST = RMPH * ((RMINS + SECS/60.) / 60.)
Then, for the compiler which accepts mixed mode:
(b)   F = I * (J - ZETA)
(c)   M = K ** 5 + 35.89
(d)   L = N ** .5 + .51
(e)   DIST = MPH * ((MINS + SECS/60.) / 60.)   (Note that we've saved the
compiler the job of converting 60 to a real value.)

Self-Test

1.   Matching test.   Match each numbered entry from Column B to a lettered
entry from Column A.

Column A	Column B
_____ (a) 3,141,569.32	(1) valid integer variable name
	(2) invalid variable name
_____ (b) 432,347	(3) mixed mode assignment statement
_____ (c) -6731524	(4) invalid operator expression
	(5) valid integer constant
_____ (d) 3COINS	(6) invalid real constant
_____ (e) NUTS	(7) invalid integer constant
	(8) valid real variable name
_____ (f) WISDOM	
_____ (g) -A * -B	
_____ (h) GOO = MUD * SLIME	

2.   Identify which of these variable names are valid and which are invalid and why.

To store real values	Valid	Invalid and reason
(a) 38D		
(b) MATRIX		
(c) 4		
(d) 4.		
(e) B4		
(f) J123456		
(g) H123456		
To store integer values		
(h) 38D		
(i) MATRIX		
(j) 4		
(k) J123456		
(l) I		
(m) NUMBER		
(n) B26		

3.   Write FORTRAN expressions equivalent to the following mathematical expressions.

(a) $a^p - d(n + w)$ _____

(b) $\dfrac{a + p}{r + 4d}$ _____

(c) $3ap^s - r^2$ _____

4.   Let the values 32, 4, and 2 be stored in variables L, M, and N, respectively. What value will be stored in the variable K by the assignment statement K = L/M/N? _____

5.   By using the values of L, M, and N from problem 4, determine whether the values of K1 and K2 (computed using the following statements) will be the same.

        K1 = (L/M)/N
        K2 = L/(M/N)

6. Determine the values stored by the assignment statements. For all problems assume A = 3, B = -13, C = 27, K = -2, L = 3, and M = -1.

(a) SUM = A ** 3. - C _____

(b) LOOK = -L/K**2 _____

(c) LOOKE = -L/K * K _____

(d) M = C/A - B**2.

Answers to Self-Test

1. (a) 6 (frame 4); (b) 7 (frame 3); (c) 5 (frame 2); (d) 2 (frame 5);
(e) 1 (frame 7); (f) 8 (frame 7); (g) 4 (frame 16); (h) 3 (frames 11 and 33)

2. | | Valid | Invalid and reason |
|---|---|---|
| (a) | | Any variable name must start with a letter, not a number. |
| (b) | | Real variables start with a letter other than I through N. |
| (c) | | Any variable name must start with a letter, not a number. |
| (d) | | Variable names must start with a letter and cannot contain a period. |
| (e) | Okay | |
| (f) | | Real variables start with a letter other than I through N and cannot be more than six characters long. |
| (g) | | Variables must be one to six characters long. |
| (h) | | Variable names must begin with a letter. |
| (i) | Okay | |
| (j) | | Variable names must begin with a letter. |
| (k) | | Variable names cannot exceed six characters. |
| (l) | Okay | |
| (m) | Okay | |
| (n) | | Integer variable names begin with any letter from I through N. |

(frames 5-10)

3. (a) A ** P - D * (N + W) (If the compiler does not permit mixed mode, you would have to convert the integer value stored in N to a real value and then use the real value in the expression.) (frames 11-13)
(b) (A + P) / (R + 4. * D) (frames 13-19)
(c) 3. * A * P**S - R**2 is correct; even better is 3. * A * P**S - R * R, since a computer can perform R * R faster than R**2. (frames 12 and 19)

4. 4 (Evaluation is from left to right, so 32 is divided by 4 giving 8. Then 8 is divided by 2 giving 4, which is stored in K.) (frame 18)

5. No! They are not equal. The statement K1 = (L/M)/N gives K1 = (32/4)/2 = 4 (as in problem 4). The statement K2 = L/(M/N) gives K2 = 32/(4/2) = 32/2 = 16. In this case, parentheses will be necessary to clarify the meaning of the expression L/M/N if you want the computation to proceed as L/(M/N). (frame 18)

6. (a) SUM = 3^3 - 27. = 0. (frame 17)
(b) LOOK = -(3/(-2)-2) = -(3/4) = 0 (integer division) (frame 17)

(c) LOOKE = -3/(-2) * (-2) = -(3/-2)(-2) = -(-1)(-2) = -2 "What?" you
say in rage, "You just told me (question 3) that I should write K * K instead of K**2 for computer speed.   But now that's wrong because (b) and
(c) aren't equal.   What's happening?" Well, since expression evaluation
is always from left to right you would need to enclose the K * K term in
parentheses to make it equivalent to K**2 at that point.   Hah, maybe we
got you? (frame 18)

(d) 27./3. - (-13)(-13) = 9. - 169. = -160., but this must be stored in M,
thus the value of M is -160 (an integer value).   (frame 24)

CHAPTER THREE
Elementary Input and Output

This chapter introduces to you the elementary FORTRAN input and output (I/O) statements. The I/O statements will enable you to prepare programs which produce (hopefully useful) reports for both business and science applications.

In this chapter you will learn the function and the arrangement of the READ, WRITE, and FORMAT statements. When you have finished this chapter you should be able to:

- write programs which transfer numerical data items to and from external media such as punched cards, magnetic tape, or disk to variables stored in the computer memory by use of the WRITE and READ statements;

- write simple FORMAT statements using the symbols I, F, and X;

- use the STOP and END statements to prepare simple complete programs which can be compiled and executed on a computer.

1.   You will probably agree with us that it is wasteful to spend millions of dollars on a computer system with which we are unable to communicate. There are computers that can perform more than 1,000,000 additions in one second, but this computation is useless to us if we wanted the result but could not get it out of the computer. The communication of results, such as the total of the computation, is accomplished by means of peripheral devices, referred to as input or output, or simply I/O devices.

In Chapter Zero, we briefly covered computers in a general way. Do you remember at least two of the devices which we could use to input numbers into the computer? _____ and _____ Name at least two devices that we could use to output the numbers from the computer. _____ and _____

- -

If you remembered (or looked up the answer), you might have mentioned any of the following:

For input	For output
card reader	card punch
magnetic tape unit	CRT
terminal keyboard	magnetic tape unit
disk unit	terminal printer
paper tape reader	disk unit
optical character reader	paper tape punch
	high-speed printer

...and there are many more possible answers.

READ Statement

2.   We will explore in this chapter those input statements which relate to a card reader or terminal keyboard and those output statements which relate to a lineprinter, terminal printer, or CRT screen.   In Chapter Eleven you will learn about I/O statements for some of the other peripheral devices.

The FORTRAN language uses a READ statement for all input into the computer.   Here is an example of a READ statement.

```
READ (5, 128) LEARN, INPUT, STATE, MENTS
```

This statement tells the computer to read four items from an input device (which has a code number of 5), and transfer the data read to the variables LEARN, INPUT, STATE, and MENTS.

Now complete the READ statement below to input values to the storage positions (variables) I, KNOW, and THIS.

```
READ (5, 128) I, KNOW, THIS
```

3.   Let's look at our example of the READ statement again.

READ (5, 128) LEARN, INPUT, STATE, MENTS

1   2   3   4

For identification, we have labeled its parts:

1.   The word READ commands the computer to read or obtain information from some input device.

2.   Either an unsigned constant or integer variable (which has a positive value) represents the particular input device from which the input data is to be read; examples include card reader, paper

tape reader, disk drive, tape drive, or terminal keyboard.

3. The FORMAT statement number refers to a FORTRAN <u>FORMAT</u> statement that "describes" where and how the input information is represented on the input medium (card, disk, tape, etc.); in effect, the format of the input data. We'll discuss this in greater detail later.

4. The input list of variables directs the computer to read data and store the values for the variables listed.

If you changed the order of the parts in the READ statement, the compiler would become quite nervous; in fact, it would reject the statement. Look at the following READ statement. If you think it is wrong, correct it.

```
READ LEARN, INPUT, STATE, MENTS (5, 128)
```

- - - - - - - - - - - - - - - - - -

```
READ (5, 128) LEARN, INPUT, STATE, MENTS
```

4. In our last example, the device number is _____, and 128 is the _____. The input list of variables consists of _____.

- - - - - - - - - - - - - - - - - -

5; FORMAT statement number; LEARN, INPUT, STATE, and MENTS

5. The fourth part of the READ statement is a list of variable names.

```
READ (5, 128) LEARN, INPUT, STATE, MENTS
```

Each variable is separated from the next by a comma. Look carefully at the punctuation. Wrong punctuation confuses the computer.

Here are some other READ statements that we dreamed up. Which ones are nightmares, and why?

(a)
```
READ 5, 128) I, J, X
```
(b)
```
READ (5, 128) A, B, C, D, E,
```
(c)
```
READ (5, 128), A, X, Y, Z
```

- - - - - - - - - - - - - - - - - -

We had a very restless night. In (a) the left parenthesis is missing. In (b) the comma after the E in the list does not belong there since it causes the computer to look for another item in the list, but there is none. In (c) there should not be a comma between the parenthesis and the first item in the list.

Remember, the computer is very fussy and nothing less than a correctly punctuated statement is acceptable.

6. Now, let's focus on the device number—the first number that appears within the parentheses following the word READ. In this new example, which is the device number? _____

READ (1, 128), I, KNØW, MØRE, NØW

- - - - - - - - - - - - - - - - - - -

The device number is 1 (not 128).

7. In frame 2, we said that our examples will use the card reader for a terminal keyboard as an input device. However, in a large computer installation there may be many peripheral devices used for input, so you can understand why each peripheral device is assigned a number. The device number can be an integer or it can be stored in an integer variable, which we will discuss later; in either case it must be unsigned. A typical list of devices and their corresponding numbers appears in the table below.

Device	Device Number	Function
Tape drive	1	input/output
Terminal keyboard	5	input
Terminal printer or CRT	6	output
Card reader	7	input
Line printer	8	output
Card punch	9	output
Disk drive	11	input/output

Some compilers, such as Microsoft FORTRAN, assume certain device numbers for the keyboard, printer (or CRT), and disk drive. Consequently, always consult your compiler manual for this information.

Throughout our text, we will assume the values in the above chart unless we tell you otherwise.

Now you write a statement to read from a tape into five variables: HEY, THIS, IS, A, and TAPE. (Use 128 as the FORMAT statement number.)

- - - - - - - - - - - - - - - - - - -

```
      READ (1,128), HEY, THIS, IS, A, TAPE
```

8.   Maybe you are allergic to the device number 1. Don't worry, since FORTRAN permits you to select almost any unsigned integer—but there is a catch. You may have to use the device assignments specified in the FORTRAN manual for your computer. Could we use -13 as a device number in the following statement? _____

```
      READ (-13,128) A, B, C
```

- - - - - - - - - - - - - - - - - -

No! We'll have to use 13 because the device number must be unsigned.

9.   Earlier we stated that the device number in your READ statement could be either an unsigned integer constant or an integer variable which has a positive value. Do you think the sequence of statements below will work? _____ If not, why? _____

```
      NDEVIC = 5
      READ (NDEVIC,128), THIS, IS, SNEAKY
```

- - - - - - - - - - - - - - - - - -

The sequence is satisfactory. The integer variable NDEVIC is assigned the value 5; consequently our use of a variable in place of the device number in the READ statement satisfies the rule we stated above.

Summary of the READ Statement

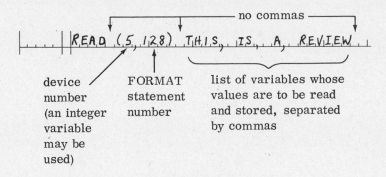

device
number
(an integer
variable
may be
used)

FORMAT
statement
number

list of variables whose
values are to be read
and stored, separated
by commas

Statement Numbers

10. The FORTRAN language makes provision for you to assign, if you wish, a unique number—an unsigned integer from one to five digits—to each program statement. We call this a FORTRAN statement number. This number

may appear anywhere within columns 1 through 5 of a FORTRAN statement. This number serves as a label for a FORTRAN statement. It doesn't change the order of execution of the program statements.

Even though a statement number may appear anywhere within columns 1 through 5, this Guide will start all statement numbers in column 1. Statement numbers in columns 1 through 5 should not contain any embedded blanks (one or more blanks between two digits) and they should be assigned in an ascending manner so that the numbers are easy to find. You cannot use an integer variable for a statement number—only an integer constant from 1 to 99999.

Which of the following are valid statement numbers? _____

(a) `735`
(b) `    57`
(c) `735245678`
(d) `NSTAT`
(e) `-17`
(f) `83 62`

- - - - - - - - - - - - - - - - - -

Only (a) is valid. Since 57 does not lie within columns 1 through 5, (b) is invalid. 735245678 is larger than 99999, thus (c) is invalid. NSTAT is an integer variable; since only constants are allowed, (d) is invalid. Choice (e) is invalid since statement numbers must be unsigned. Choice (f) is invalid because it contains an embedded blank; depending upon the compiler, it may be interpreted as 83062 or 8362.

WRITE Statement

11. A WRITE statement transfers data stored in a computer memory to an output media. The form of the WRITE statement is very similar to that of the READ statement.

Following the pattern you used with READ statements, complete the WRITE statement below to command the computer to print out the values contained in the variables LET, US, and OUT.

`      WRITE (6,101)`

- - - - - - - - - - - - - - - -

`      WRITE (6,101) LET, US, OUT`

The WRITE statement closely resembles the READ statement. We are using the number 6 to represent an output device, such as a terminal printer or CRT.

12. The WRITE statement in the answer to frame 11 referred to device number 6 (discussed in frame 7), representing a terminal printer. If you try to read from an output print device or write on an input device the program will stop executing. The computer may or may not print a message stating the reason that program execution stopped; this depends on the operating system of your computer.

In this and all subsequent examples and questions, assume that 5 represents the card reader. Which of the following statements are incorrect?

(a) `WRITE (6,281), STUDY, HARD`
(b) `READ (6,251), EASY, AS, PI`
(c) `WRITE (5,242), ONA, DEVICE`

- - - - - - - - - - - - - - - - - -

Choice (b) is incorrect (you cannot read from a print device). Also (c) is incorrect (you cannot write on a card reader).

13. Look carefully at this WRITE statement.

`WRITE (6,302), I, KNOW, THIS, COLD`

      1   2   3

The first part, the word WRITE, instructs the computer to output information. The second part, (6, 302), tells the computer what device will receive the output and refers to the FORMAT statement which specifies how the data is to appear on the output media. The third part is a list of variable names which tells the computer where to fetch the information it is to write. Just as in the READ statement, the arrangement of the parts in the WRITE statement is quite important.

Are the following statements correct? If they are not, correct them.

(a) `WRITE 6 1234570 SLY, ERROR`
(b) `THIS, IS, SLICK (6,16), WRIT`
(c) `WRITE (5,21), NO, MORE, COMEON`

- - - - - - - - - - - - - - - - - - -

All are incorrect.   (It figures, huh?)

(a)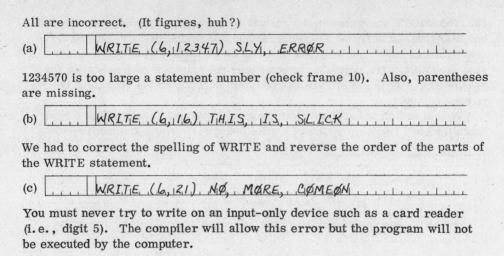

WRITE (6,1234570), SLY, ERRØR

1234570 is too large a statement number (check frame 10).   Also, parentheses are missing.

(b)

WRITE (6,16), THIS, IS, SLICK

We had to correct the spelling of WRITE and reverse the order of the parts of the WRITE statement.

(c)

WRITE (6,21), NØ, MØRE, CØMEØN

You must never try to write on an input-only device such as a card reader (i.e., digit 5).   The compiler will allow this error but the program will not be executed by the computer.

Summary of the WRITE Statement

WRITE (6, 103), A, REF, FRES, HER

list of variables where values are to be written from storage, separated by commas

statement number of the FORMAT statement according to which the data is to be written out

number (sometimes an integer variable) that identifies the output device being used

the FORTRAN command to initiate transfer of information from memory to output device

FORMAT Statement

14. Here is a pair of READ and FORMAT statements.

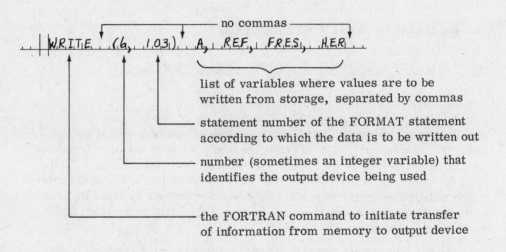

```
        READ (5,128), LEARN, MØRE, NØW
128     FØRMAT (I5, I2, I8)
```

The first statement causes the computer to read a card from card reader (device 5). This card is expected to contain three values which are to be moved to storage areas LEARN, MORE, and NOW. However, a punched card usually has eighty columns and the computer is puzzled as to which column(s) contain the value (or data) to be transferred to each variable. For this reason a second number, in this instance 128, follows the device number in the

READ statement.   This number refers to a special kind of statement called a FORMAT statement.   When the computer processes (executes) the READ statement it refers to its FORMAT statement to determine:

> from which columns the computer will read the data for each variable in the list;

> into which form (variable type) the computer will store the data.

In this sense, the FORMAT statement is a nonexecutable statement.   It only serves as a reference source for the READ statement.

In this pair of statements

```
       READ (5, 111), I, J, K
111    FORMAT (I5, I6, I10)
```

the READ statement refers to statement number _____ for format information.

- - - - - - - - - - - - - - - - - -

111

15.   Look carefully at this FORMAT statement.

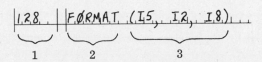

```
128.   FORMAT (I5, I2, I8)
```
```
  1        2        3
```

For identification we have labeled its three parts.   The first part, 128, is merely a statement number used by the READ statement to identify the associated FORMAT statement.   The second part, FORMAT, indicates to the computer that this is a FORMAT statement.   The third part, (I5, I2, I8), contains a series of specifications enclosed in parentheses and separated by commas, one specification for each variable in the READ statement.

Which of the following statements are incorrect and why? _____

```
(a)  171    FORMAT (I5, I3, I7
(b)  312    FORMT (I10, I2, I7)
(c)  301    FORMAT (I7, I6, I5)
(d)  405    (I7, I3, I5) FORMAT
```

- - - - - - - - - - - - - - - - - -

All except (c) are incorrect.   Here's why.

In (a) the right parenthesis is missing.

```
171    FØRMAT (I5, I3, I7)
```

Choice (b) has an incorrect spelling of FORMAT.

```
312    FØRMAT (I10, I2, I7)
```

In (d) there is an incorrect sequence of parts of the FORMAT statement.

```
405    FØRMAT (I7, I3, I5)
```

Summary of the FORMAT Statement

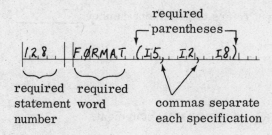

required
┌─parentheses─┐

```
128    FØRMAT (I5, I2, I8)
```

required   required   commas separate
statement   word   each specification
number

16. Generally, FORMAT statements may appear anywhere in your program; that is, before or after the corresponding READ statement or WRITE statement, but before the END statement. Most programmers place the FORMAT statement immediately following the first READ statement to which it refers, even though there may be more than one READ statement using the same FORMAT statement; likewise, each FORMAT statement must have its own unique statement number.

Below, we've conceptualized two programs; notice the placement of the FORMAT statements. Identify which FORMAT statements are improperly placed or numbered.

Program 1

```
        READ (5, 10411) IA, IB
        ⋮
        READ (5, 10412) IC, ID
        ⋮
10411   FØRMAT (4I3)
10412   FØRMAT (2X, I3, 4X, I2)
        END
```

Program 2

```
        READ (5, 10441) J1
10441   FØRMAT (16X, I1)
        ⋮
        READ (5, 10441) J7, J8, J9
10441   FØRMAT (3I2)
        ⋮
        READ (5, 10443) K
        ⋮
        END
10443   FØRMAT (I2)
```

- - - - - - - - - - - - - - - - - - -

In Program 1, even though the FORMAT statements do not immediately precede or follow their respective READ statements, they do appear before the END statement, so this program is correct.

Program 2, however, has a number of errors. Two or more FORMAT statements cannot have identical statement numbers (two are numbered 10441); all FORMAT statements must appear before the END statement, but 10443 appears after the END statement.

I Format Code

17.

	READ (5, 128), LEARN, MØRE, NØW
128	FØRMAT (I5, I2, I8)

The first format specification, I5, contains two parts. The letter I tells the computer that the input data is to be stored as an integer form. The digit 5 tells the computer that the data occupies five card columns (that is, the field length is 5). As a result, the computer would interpret and move the contents of five columns into the storage area labeled LEARN. But you might ask, "How do we know in which column to start the transfer of data?" Since I5 is the first specification in the FORMAT statement, the transfer begins in column 1 and ends in column 5. Remember, I5 means five columns are to be interpreted as the value for an integer variable.

The comma following the I5 indicates that another field specification is to follow. The next data on the card to be interpreted by the computer is an integer value and occupies the next two columns on the card (columns 6-7). This data is interpreted and moved to storage area MORE.

The last data item is found in columns _____; it is interpreted and moved to the storage area labeled _____. No comma is placed after the I8 format field specification because no other specification follows.

- - - - - - - - - - - - - - - - - -

8-15; NOW

18. A punched card or other input record contains four fields as follows.

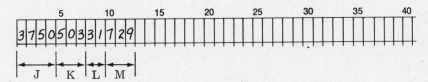

On the next page, write a pair of statements which would read the values and store them as variables J, K, L, and M, respectively.

```
|      ||                                              |
|      ||                                              |
|      ||                                              |
```

```
      READ (5, 301), J, K, L, M
301.  FORMAT (I4, I3, I2, I3)
```

The I4 specification indicates a four-digit integer (i.e., 3750) is to be moved to a storage area labeled J. The I3 specification causes the number located in columns 5 through 7 (i.e., 503) to be moved to the storage area of K. The storage area L receives the number 31 found in the next two columns and storage area M receives the number 729 found in the next three columns—columns 10 through 12.

19. It is important to keep in mind that the list of variables in a READ statement corresponds with the format specifications in a FORMAT statement. This implies two things. First, each variable must have a format specification. Second, the specification code (the letter part of a format specification) must correspond to the type of the variable in which the data will be stored. Otherwise, the result will be unpredictable.

In this case

```
      READ (5, 128) LEARN, MORE, NOW
128.  FORMAT (I5, I2, I8)
```

I5 corresponds to the variable _____ , I2 to the variable _____ , and _____ to the variable NOW.

- - - - - - - - - - - - - - - - - -

LEARN; MORE; I8

20. The I specification tells the computer that the number in the input record is to be interpreted as an integer value. As a result, the computer interprets the input data and stores it in the form of an integer constant.

For the example shown below, the first field of five columns in length would be converted to an integer constant and moved to an area labeled_____ .

```
      READ (5, 128) J, K, L
128.  FORMAT (I5, I2, I8)
```

- - - - - - - - - - - - - - - - - -

J

21. We have mentioned that a field specification in a FORMAT statement defines a field. In this example I5 defines a field of five card columns.

121	FØRMAT (I5, I2)

From this field we can input a number with a maximum of five digits. I2 defines a field of two (card) columns or digits.

FORTRAN allows blanks (no punches) within an input (card) field. However, in this case FORTRAN interprets a blank as a zero. Therefore, the meaning of a number depends upon its position within the field. Here are some examples using a punched card.

	Punched numbers	Stored value
Card columns	1 2 3 4 5	
(b̸ means	b̸ b̸ b̸ 3 3	3 3
blank or	b̸ b̸ 3 3 b̸	3 3 0
no punch)	3 3 b̸ b̸ b̸	3 3 0 0 0

What values would be placed in storage for this pair of statements?

	READ (5, 141) IPART
141	FØRMAT (I5)

	Punched numbers	Stored value
Card columns	1 2 3 4 5	
	b̸ b̸ 4 3 b̸	(a) _____
	b̸ 3 7 5 b̸	(b) _____
	b̸ b̸ b̸ 9 9	(c) _____
	1 b̸ b̸ b̸ b̸	(d) _____

- - - - - - - - - - - - - - - - - - - -

(a) 430; (b) 3750; (c) 99; (d) 10000

22. A result of frame 21 is that the FORTRAN language illustrates the general rule: number values be located in the rightmost position of their fields. We say that the number is right justified in its field.

Look at these statements.

	READ (5, 13) IPART, IQTY
13	FØRMAT (I6, I4)

If we had input the value for IPART in columns 1 through 6 as shown below, the computer would consider the value to be 3405.

5	10	15	20	25	30	35	40	45

3 4 5

However, if we entered in error the same number ƀ ƀ 3 4 ƀ 5 in columns 2

through 7 the computer would consider the value to be _____ .

- - - - - - - - - - - - - - - - - - -

3 4 0. Columns 1, 2, and 3 would have blanks and would be interpreted as
000. Columns 4 and 5 would contain 34, and column 6 would be considered 0.
Putting the digits together, we obtain 000340, which is not the same as 003405.
The digit 5 in column 7 would become part of the data value for IQTY.

23. You can read into storage a negative value by punching a minus sign to
the left of the value. However, in the format specification you must allow
one extra column for the minus sign.

   If you wanted to read in the value 972, you would have to allow at least

_____ columns; but to read in the value -972 you would need at least

_____ columns.

- - - - - - - - - - - - - - - - - - -

3; 4

24. We are confident that by now you can design simple FORMAT statements
to read into storage positive and negative numbers. Let's pretend that we
are writing a FORTRAN program for a manufacturing application. Suppose
that our program needs information about each part that we are to manufac-
ture. Below are the types of descriptions we will provide and the variable
names we will use.

Part number identification	IDPART
Length of part	LENGTH
Positive tolerance	IPOSTL
Negative tolerance	NEGTOL

Here is a picture of a card that contains the values.

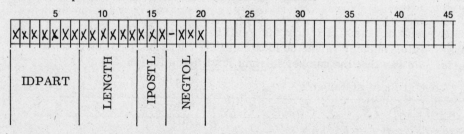

The X's indicate in which columns the data values will be punched. Write

both the READ and FORMAT statements, reading from the device 5.
Use any format statement number you desire. (You can write your
statements in the blank coding form lines below.)

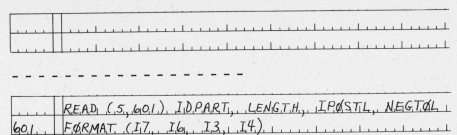

```
       READ (5,601), ID,PART, LENGTH, IPOSTL, NEGTOL
601    FORMAT (I7, I6, I3, I4)
```

Did you remember to allow one column for the minus sign? Also you could
have used a format statement number other than 601, but it must be at least
one digit and no greater than five digits.

25. FORTRAN is somewhat free-form, depending upon your compiler. Except for blanks contained between apostrophes (which we'll cover later), most
compilers will eliminate the blanks when compiling your FORTRAN statements. For example, these statements will compile identically.

    SOUP = A LPH A +   BE   T
    SO UP =   ALPHA+BET
    SOUP=ALPHA+BET

Applying the general rule that FORTRAN eliminates blanks, will the

FORMAT statements below compile identically? _____

    12345 FORMAT   (16X, I3)
    12345 FORMAT(1 6X , I 3)
    12345   FOR MAT (16 X, I3)

- - - - - - - - - - - - - - - - -

Yes, which is expecially helpful if you continually hit the space bar by acci-
dent when entering data.

26. The WRITE statement differs from the READ statement principally in
the use of the FORMAT statement. If you are wondering why there should
be different FORMAT statements for output, the next example illustrates
the reason.

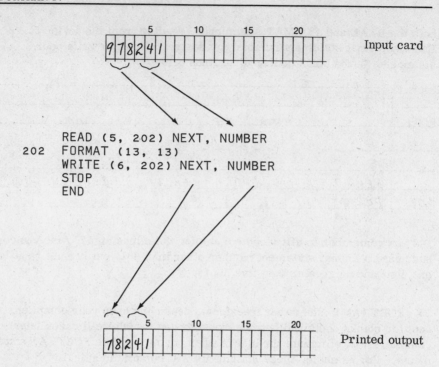

READ (5, 202) NEXT, NUMBER
202   FORMAT (I3, I3)
       WRITE (6, 202) NEXT, NUMBER
       STOP
       END

Look at the printed output. What value was fetched from the variable

NUMBER? _____ The value 78 was fetched from what variable?

_____

- - - - - - - - - - - - - - - - - - -

241; NEXT—if you ignore the fact that the digit 9 is missing. What? "9" is missing? Where did it go? Tune in to the following frame for the next episode in the case of the vanishing "9."

27. The Case of the Vanishing "9," continued: If you were a computer printer, printing out lines of reports, once in a while you might want to go to the next page, or skip a line or two before printing. To enable the printer to "know" when to write on a new line, a new page, and so on, the computer "interprets" the first character of the output record to be typed on the printer. This first character is called a <u>carriage (or output) control character</u>. The carriage control character is never printed, but simply conveys information to the printer about how the line spacing mechanism should position the paper. Output control can be used to position the cursor on the face of a CRT terminal or even to change the color of the display on a color CRT terminal. This explanation should indicate why the 9 disappeared from the variable NEXT which contains the value 978, as described in the last frame. When it arrived at the printer the record to be printed looked as follows.

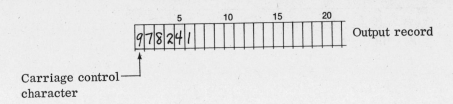

Carriage control —
character

The printer "understood" the first character (the 9) to be the carriage control character, which served only for reference purposes, and typed the rest of the record as output.

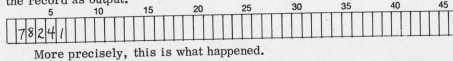

More precisely, this is what happened.

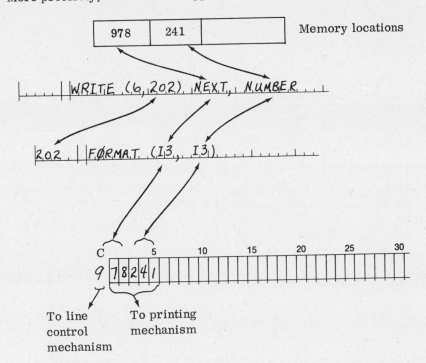

To line
control
mechanism

To printing
mechanism

When an output record arrives at the printer, which character of the record is split off and interpreted for carriage control? _____

- - - - - - - - - - - - - - - -

the first character (The Case of the Vanishing "9" is closed.)

28. Now, what should we do to avoid chopping off numbers which the printer considers carriage control characters? One technique is to avoid putting any output characters to be printed in the first position of an output record. For example, avoid statements such as the ones which follow.

```
      WRITE (6,101), I,1, J2, K3
101   FORMAT (I3, I3, I4)
```

It follows, generally, that you should not use a FORMAT statement corresponding to a READ statement for a WRITE statement (such as in the example of frame 27) unless you assure yourself that you will not do "bad" things. Things can be bad, by the way, as you will soon see.

As a post-mortem to the vanishing "9" problem, in order to avoid chopping off numbers, we must rewrite the program statements of frame 26.

```
      READ (5,202), NEXT, NUMBER
202   FORMAT (I3, I3)
      WRITE (6,301), NEXT, NUMBER
301   FORMAT (1X, I3, I3)
```

The 1X code inserts a blank in the first position of the output record. The values of NEXT and NUMBER follow, occupying positions 2 through 4 and 5 through 7 respectively. Schematically:

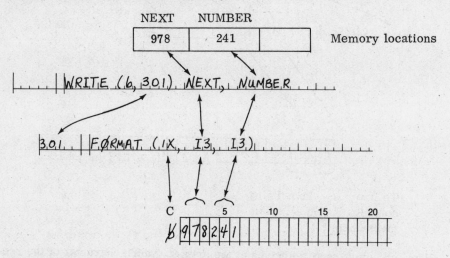

Thus, the output record sent to the printer will appear like this.

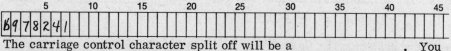

The carriage control character split off will be a _____. You should therefore make a mental note that the output record contains the same information as the printed record plus one extra position. This carriage control position immediately precedes the first item printed.

blank (created by the 1X format code in statement number 301). Slick, yes?

29. Integer values are printed in their allotted fields "right justified." That is, the last digit of the integer value is placed in the extreme right-hand position of the allotted field. You should remember that in input of integer values, the user was expected to position the integer value right adjusted in the allotted field. This rule has some very important consequences best illustrated by examples.

Leading zeros (zeros before the first nonzero digit) are suppressed, a + sign will not be printed, and a – sign is positioned just to the left of the printed integer value.

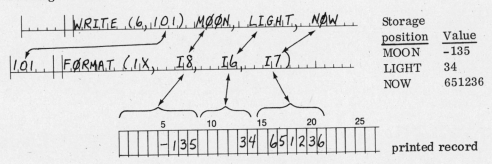

Storage position	Value
MOON	−135
LIGHT	34
NOW	651236

The generous format codes I6 and I7 separate the printed values of MOON, LIGHT, and NOW.

What would be the printed line for the following FORTRAN statements?

Storage position	Value
JIM	−00315
KIM	34
LYN	517624

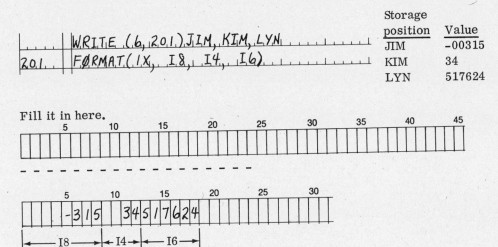

30. What happens if you try to print an integer value of −417352 using the format code I3? This value requires seven printing positions (six digits and a sign), but you have only allotted three (I3) positions. The result in this case depends on the computer used.

-417352	I3 ⟶	*	*	*

The computer will fill the entire output field with an asterisk (*).

Maybe the safest way is to overspecify. That is, specify a field width for the largest number (including the sign) you anticipate.

(a) To print the data value -6342 you should use a format code of _____.

(b) A format code of I6 will allow the printing of all integer constants from _____ to _____.

- - - - - - - - - - - - - - - - - - - -

(a) I5 or larger; (b) -99999 to 999999

31. Specify minimum field widths for the following ranges of integer constants.

Range		Specification
-99 to 9999	(a)	_____
-99999 to 999	(b)	_____
-999 to 999	(c)	_____

- - - - - - - - - - - - - - - - - -

(a) I4; (b) I6; (c) I4

STOP and END—A Quick Visit

32. You almost know enough at this point to write a program. However, there are two statements which you will need to complete your programs.

```
     STOP

     END
```

For now, it is sufficient to add these two statements (in this order) after all the other statements in your program. We will discuss these statements in more detail in Chapter Four. Can the order of the statements be reversed, like this?

```
     END
     STOP
```

Yes or no? _____ (You may cheat if you wish.)

- - - - - - - - - - - - - - - - - - -

No. The END statement must go after the STOP statement.

A Simple Complete Program

33. Let's look at a complete program.
Program objective: This program will read
an integer constant (N) punched in the first
four columns of a card; square the number
(NSQUAR); print the number and its square;
and then stop. A flowchart for this program
is shown to the right. Here is the program.

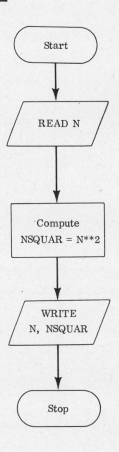

```
C
C   READ IN AN INTEGER-N
C
        READ (5,101) N
101     FORMAT (I4)
C
C   COMPUTE N**2
C
        NSQUAR = N**2
C
C   PRINT N AND NSQUAR
C
        WRITE (6,201) N, NSQUAR
201     FORMAT (1X, I4, I10)
        STOP
        END
```

You are going to write a program now. Don't get nervous; it resembles
the program above. Program objective: This program will read an integer
constant (call it N) from the first three columns of a card; square the number (call it NSQUAR) and cube the number (call it NCUBE); print the number,
its square, and cube; and then stop. (Hint: N cubed is written algebraically
as N^3. Translate that into FORTRAN.) Use a separate sheet of paper for
your answer.

- - - - - - - - - - - - - - - - - - -

Our answer:

```
C
C   READ AN INTEGER-N
C
        READ (5,101) N
101     FORMAT (I3)
C
C   COMPUTE NSQUAR=N*N AND NCUBE=N**3
C
        NSQUAR = N*N
        NCUBE = N**3

C
C   PRINT N, NSQUAR AND NCUBE
C
        WRITE (6,201) N, NSQUAR, NCUBE
201     FORMAT (1X, I3, I7, I11)
        STOP
        END
```

34. A FORTRAN compiler uses your FORTRAN program as input (called source code) and converts it to computer executable instructions (called object code). Many different FORTRAN compilers are available.

Because all computers are not designed alike, each may require its own FORTRAN compiler. Futhermore, there are different kinds of FOR-TRAN compilers. One kind analyzes your source code with the purpose of creating highly efficient and fast executing object code. We call this category of compilers optimizing compilers.

Other FORTRAN compilers may not optimize the object code, but, instead, they produce comprehensive diagnostics of your source code during the compilation (and even execution phase) of your program. We call these check-out compilers.

The sample FORTRAN program below contains many errors. See if you can identify some of them.

```
C       THIS PROGRAM READS IN THE AMOUNT OF RECORDS (N) , THEN READS
C            EACH OF THE RECORDS TO FIND THE AVERAGE OF THE VALUE IN
C            POSITIONS 6 THRU 9
        I=1
        READ(9,100) N
100     FORMAT(I4)
C       READ IN RECORDS
        REED(9,120) 1A
120     FORMAAT(5X,F4.1)
130     IF(I-N) 130,130,200
130     SUM=SUM + A1
        I = I + 1
        GO TOO 130
C       PRINT AVERAGE
        WRITE(6, 210) SUM/N
210 FORMAT(1X,F7.3)
        STOP
END
```

Now that you've desk checked (manually reviewed and checked) the above program, let's see what a compiler will find. A compiler may have many user options available. If we select the one which causes listing of the bad source code, we get the following listing.

```
F0000080        REED(9,120) 1A
                             $
01)   IGI011I UNDIMENSIONED
F0000090120     FORMAAT(5X,F4.1)
                             $$
01)   IGI003I NAME LENGTH
02)   IGI011I UNDIMENSIONED
F0000110130     SUM=SUM + A1
                   $
01)   IGI006I DUPLICATE LABEL
F0000130        GO TOO 130
                             $
01)   IGI001I ILLEGAL TYPE
02)   IGI013I SYNTAX
F0000150        WRITE(6, 210) SUM/N
                                  $
01)   IGI013I SYNTAX
F0000180END
       $
01)   IGI013I SYNTAX
01)   IGI015I * NO END STA.
IGI022I     UNDEFINED LABEL
       200
```

At the extreme left of the source line the compiler has printed what, if anything appears in card columns 72 through 80 of that statement. On the next line, a $ appears below each error the compiler detected in the source code line. Then each error is further described, one line per error. The diagnostic message includes a compiler reference error code as well as a human readable description—which may or may not be understandable to you.

If we select the option for a complete listing of the program source code, both good as well as bad lines, we would get the following listing.

```
        C          THIS PROGRAM READS IN THE AMOUNT OF RECORDS (N) , THEN READS
        C          EACH OF THE RECORDS TO FIND THE AVERAGE OF THE VALUE IN
        C          POSITIONS 6 THRU 9
0001               I=1
0002    100        READ(9,100) N
0003               FORMAT(I4)
        C          READ IN RECORDS
0004               REED(9,120) 1A
                              $
********     01)   IGIO11I UNDIMENSIONED
0005    120        FORMAAT(5X,F4.1)
                         $$
********     01)   IGIO03I NAME LENGTH          02)  IGIO11I UNDIMENSIONED
0006    130        IF(I-N) 130,130,200
0007    130        SUM=SUM + A1
                      $
********     01)   IGIO06I DUPLICATE LABEL
0008               I = I + 1
0009               GO TOO 130
                       $
********     01)   IGIO01I ILLEGAL TYPE         02)  IGIO13I SYNTAX
        C          PRINT AVERAGE
0010               WRITE(6, 210) SUM/N
                                 $
********     01)   IGIO13I SYNTAX
0011    210        FORMAT(1X,F7.3)
0012               STOP
                   END
                    $
********     01)   IGIO13I SYNTAX
********     01)   IGIO15I * NO END STA.
```

A check-out compiler gives us more complete diagnostics—sometimes too many, because one error may cause the compiler a problem with interpreting the remainder of the line or lines which immediately follow. A check-out compiler produced the following listing when it compiled the sample program. Note the extensive messages, including statements of probable cause.

```
    4    REED(9,120) 1A
***ERROR***  UNDECODEABLE STATEMENT
    5  120 FORMAT(5X,F4.1)
***ERROR***  UNDECODEABLE STATEMENT
    6  130 IF(I-N) 130,130,200
***ERROR***  THIS STATEMENT COULD TRANSFER TO ITSELF
***ERROR***  THIS STATEMENT COULD TRANSFER TO ITSELF
    7  130 SUM=SUM + A1
***ERROR***  STATEMENT NUMBER   130 HAS ALREADY BEEN DEFINED
    8      I = I + 1
**WARNING**  UNNUMBERED EXECUTABLE STATEMENT FOLLOWS A TRANSFER
       C     PRINT AVERAGE
***ERROR***  EXPECTING SIMPLE INTEGER VARIABLE OR CONSTANT,BUT 0130 WAS FOUND
***ERROR***  EXPECTING OPERATOR BUT END-OF-STATEMENT WAS FOUND
***ERROR***  EXPECTING OPERATOR BUT END-OF-STATEMENT WAS FOUND
***ERROR***  EXPECTING STATEMENT NUMBER,BUT END-OF-STATEMENT WAS FOUND
***ERROR***  EXPECTING OPERATOR BUT END-OF-STATEMENT WAS FOUND
   210 FORMAT(1X,F7.3)
**WARNING**  UNNUMBERED EXECUTABLE STATEMENT FOLLOWS A TRANSFER
**WARNING**  COLUMNS 1-5 OF CONTINUATION CARD NOT BLANK.
             PROBABLE CAUSE:STATEMENT PUNCHED TO LEFT OF COLUMN 7
***ERROR***  MISSING OPERATOR.UNEXPECTED X
***ERROR***  ILLEGAL USE OF DECIMAL POINT.UNEXPECTED . BEFORE 3
   12 END
**WARNING**  BLANK CARD ENCOUNTERED
***ERROR***  INVALID CHARACTERS IN COL 1-5. STATEMENT NUMBER IGNORED.
             PROBABLE CAUSE:STATEMENT PUNCHED TO LEFT OF COLUMN
**WARNING**  MISSING END STATEMENT;END STATEMENT GENERATED
***ERROR***  MISSING STATEMENT NUMBER   200 USED IN LINE   6
***ERROR***  MISSING FORMAT STATEMENT   210 USED IN LINE   10
***ERROR***  SUBPROGRAM NRMAT USED IN LINE   10 IS MISSING
```

Because there is no single FORTRAN compiler, we won't attempt to describe the operation of any of those here. Instead, refer to your computer installation's FORTRAN reference manuals. If you have an opportunity, try compiling the sample program and compare your listing with the ones above.

What is the difference between a check-out compiler and an optimizing compiler?

- - - - - - - - - - - - - - - - - -

The check-out compiler performs more extensive checking of the source code and produces extensive diagnostic listings. The optimizing compiler creates highly efficient and fast executing object code.

X Format Code

35. You have already seen an X when working with FORMAT statements for output—to indicate that a print position should be skipped. You can also use the letter X in a format specification to indicate that an **input (card) column** should be skipped.

If you want to skip four columns (or print positions), write 4X. If you want to skip ten columns, write _____.

- - - - - - - - - - - - - - - - - -

10X

36. To skip one column (or print position) we have used a 1X specification. Some compilers accept an X to mean a 1X; check yours. To skip one print position, would we use an X1 specification? Yes or no? _____

- - - - - - - - - - - - - - - - - -

No! 1X or X is correct.

37. Study these statements.

```
      READ (5,128) LEARN, MORE, NOW
128   FORMAT (I5, 1X, I2, 2X, I8)
```

(a) From which columns will the variable MORE be read? _____

(b) How many digits will be transferred to the variable MORE?
_____

(c) What does the 2X mean? _____

(d) In what card column will the next value, to be stored in variable NOW, start? _____

- - - - - - - - - - - - - - - - - -

(a) Columns 7-8. The value for the first variable, LEARN, was in columns 1-5 (I5) and column 6 was skipped. The value to be stored in the variable MORE will be read from columns 7 and 8.
(b) Two digits as specified by I2.
(c) 2X means ignore the next two columns which will be columns 9-10.
(d) Column 11. NOW starts there because the second value, MORE, ended in column 8 and columns 9-10 were skipped.

38. Here is a punched card with two values separated by spaces.

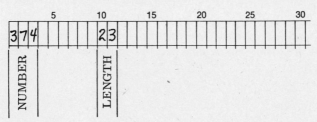

Just to be nice to you we supply the READ statement.

| | | READ (5, 131) NUMBER, LENGTH |

However, we ask you to write a FORMAT statement to go with our READ statement.

| | | |

- - - - - - - - - - - - - - - - - -

| 131 | | FORMAT (I3, 6X, I2) |

The first three columns contain the number 374 (I3 format). The next six columns are skipped (6X). The last two columns contain the number 23 (I2 format).

39. The following incident took place one day. A programmer wrote this FORMAT statement

| 131 | | FORMAT (X5, 3I, 6X, I7) |

and showed it to a fellow programmer. This second programmer looked at it for awhile, trying to figure out just what seemed wrong with the statement. Can you help the second programmer find the problem? _____

_____

- - - - - - - - - - - - - - - - -

X5 and 3I are incorrect. The FORMAT statement should be written

| 131 | | FORMAT (5X, I3, 6X, I7) |

Remember, X means to skip or ignore a column; the digit preceding the X is a repetition factor indicating how many columns to skip. In our example, 5X means the next five print positions are skipped. The repetition factor always precedes the specification. However, the digit 3 in I3 indicates the field width or how many columns are occupied by a number and it always follows the letter code of the specification.

40. Look at these two FORMAT statements—they're identical when compiled.

        12346   FORMAT (I4, 3X, 2X, I7)
        12346   FORMAT (I4, 5X, I7)

Consecutive X format codes can be summarized by adding the number of positions to be skipped. Rewrite the following FORMAT statement by summarizing the X code where possible.

        98765   FORMAT (6I4, 17X, 3X, I4, 1X, 8X, I2)

98765 FORMAT (6I4, 20X, I4, 9X, I2)

41. You may have noticed that the X format code for output has somewhat of a different meaning than for input. That is, for output 5X means skip five spaces or insert five consecutive spaces in the output record. For example,

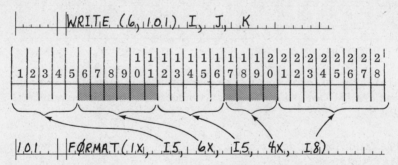

Now you have available two methods for horizontal spacing. You may use the X code or increase the integer field width much beyond your anticipated need. The unused portions of the fields will be automatically blank, as we explained in frame 29.

        Given this statement,

WRITE (6, 541) MORE, LOVE, NOW

write an associated FORMAT statement to print as follows:

        Print the integer value of the variables MORE, LOVE, and NOW start-
        int in positions 30, 44, and 73 respectively. Assume the values of
        MORE, LOVE, and NOW are 345, -700, and 1350, respectively.

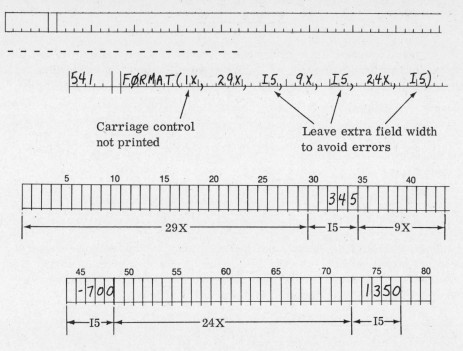

Carriage control not printed

Leave extra field width to avoid errors

42. Rewrite your program of frame 33 so the output values N, NSQUAR, and NCUBE start in print positions 10, 20, and 40, respectively. Use a separate sheet of paper for your answer.

- - - - - - - - - - - - - - - - - -

```
C
C   READ AN INTEGER
C
        READ (5,101) N
101     FORMAT (I3)
C
C   COMPUTE NSQUAR=N*N AND NCUBE=N**3
C
        NSQUAR = N*N
        NCUBE = N**3
C
C   PRINT N, NSQUAR, NCUBE
C
        WRITE (6,201) N, NSQUAR, NCUBE
201     FORMAT (1X, 9X, I3, 7X, I7, 13X, I11)
        STOP
        END
```

F Format Code

43. To read in a value for a real variable (variable name begins with any letter except I through N) we use the F format specification, the F standing for
floating point (or decimal point). For example, if an input record contains

column   1 2 3

9 8 6

and the storage area labeled REAL is to contain 98.6, we could use this pair
of statements.

. . . .	READ (5, 171) REAL
171	FORMAT (F3.1)

In the FORMAT statement, the specification F instructs the computer to
store, as a real number, the data read from the punched card. The digit(s)
between the letter F and the decimal point indicate the field width (or length
specification). The specification F3.1 indicates a field width of

_____ positions (or columns).

- - - - - - - - - - - - - - - - - -

three

44. If no decimal point appears in the input data value, the digit(s) to the
right of the decimal point in the format specification indicates the number of
positions the computer should consider to the right of an assumed decimal
point in the data (that is, the fractional portion of the number). For example,
say we had an input data value that was entered as ƀ31416 and we used the
format specification F6.4. The computer would read the value from six
positions and consider the four rightmost digits as if they were to the right
of the assumed decimal point—thus 03.1416.

Using input data of 986, the format specification F3.2 will store the value

as _____.

- - - - - - - - - - - - - - - - - -

9.86 (The .2 in the format specification F3.2 means the three-digit number
986 has two fractional digits to the right of the decimal point.)

45. If we entered a decimal point in the input field, that decimal point will
override the decimal specification of the F format specification. If an input
record contained 98.6 which we read in using the F4.2 format specification,
the value would be stored as 98.6 and the .2 part of the specification would
be ignored.

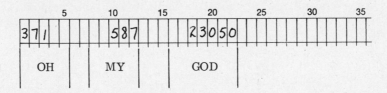

What would be the values read and stored if we used a F10.4 format specification to read these input values?

(a) ⌀⌀⌀⌀⌀⌀12345 _____

(b) ⌀⌀⌀.⌀12345 _____

- - - - - - - - - - - - - - - - -

(a) 000001.2345 (There is no decimal point in the input record, thus the computer would place it just before the four rightmost digits. The 10 tells the computer that the field has 10 digits, of which the leading blanks are con- sidered as zeros. Therefore, we have 0000012345. However, the 4 in F10.4 tells the computer to place a decimal point four digits from the right, so it stores the value 000001.2345.)

(b) 0.012345 (The input data contains a decimal point. Thus, the 4 in F10.4 is ignored and the computer merely stores the data in the 10 record positions as the value 0.012345. The blanks are treated as zeros, as is the case when using I, F, D, or E format codes. D and E format codes are discussed in Chapter Nine.)

46. If a decimal point is not included in the input data field, we must right- adjust the data (unless chaos is strongly desired!). For example, sup- pose that corresponding to this pair of statements,

```
        READ (5, 181), ØH, MY, GØD
181     FORMAT (F5.2, 2X, I5, 3X, F7.4)
```

we have this data card.

The values assigned to the variables are:

OH = 371.00 (The computer treats blanks as zeros, therefore we have 37100 which F5.2 transfers as 371.00.)

MY = 587

GOD = 002.3050 = 2.305

But suppose you really wanted the variables to contain:

OH = 3.71

MY = 587

GOD = .2305

Then the data should be entered as:

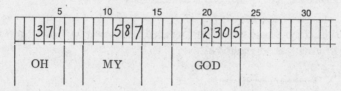

	OH			MY				GOD		

How about an exercise?

Input specification	Data		Stored value
F5.3	ᵇᵇ32ᵇ	(a)	_____
F3.1	ᵇᵇ3	(b)	_____
F6.1	ᵇᵇ301ᵇ	(c)	_____

- - - - - - - - - - - - - - - - - -

(a) .320; (b) .3; (c) 301.0

47. When should a decimal point be punched on a data card? Since the decimal point occupies one column on the punched card, one less column is available for data. The F specification allows us to enter data without punching the decimal point. However, the data must be properly entered to avoid errors.

If we include a decimal point in the data field when using the F specification, we do not have to right-adjust the data on the punched card. Generally, to minimize keystrokes, decimal points are omitted and numbers are punched right-justified. Thus, the habit of specifying where the decimal is to appear in an F format is a good one.

Negative values of real numbers are indicated by punching a minus sign to the left of the value on the data card just as you would for an integer value.

Look at the examples below and fill in the last two stored values.

Input specification	Data		Stored value
F6.3	ᵇ-37.2		-37.2
F6.3	37.2ᵇᵇ		37.2
F6.3	-37.2ᵇ		-37.2
F7.1	ᵇ-12.2ᵇ	(a)	_____
F5.2	-3.257	(b)	_____

- - - - - - - - - - - - - - - - -

(a) −12.2; (b) −3.25 (Note: the digit 7 will be picked up by the next FORMAT specification, if any.)

48. In writing a program for a school, we might want to use the student grade point averages along with other information. Write appropriate READ and FORMAT statements using the information below.

Description	Variable name	
card code number	ICARD	column 1
student identification	IDNUM	columns 3–11
cumulative grade point average	AVERAG	columns 17–20

```
    5      10      15      20      25      30      35      40      45
X  XXXXXXXXX          X.XX
```

- - - - - - - - - - - - - - - - -

```
        READ (5, 1001), ICARD, IDNUM, AVERAG
1001    FØRMAT (I1, 1X, I9, 5X, F4.2)
```

We could have specified F4.0 instead of F4.2, if the decimal were punched in the input data.

49. Let's look at the effect of these statements,

```
        READ (5, 241) CHANGE
241     FØRMAT (F4.0)
```

which will read and interpret this data.

```
    5      10      15      20      25      30      35      40      45
3251
```

The real value (3251.) is stored in CHANGE. The effect of the .0 part of the F4.0 code is to store the integer constant 3251 as a real constant. You can use this technique when such integer data values are used in expressions which will be evaluated as real.

Here's an example of such a case. Suppose you have four test grades (integer constants) punched on a data card and you want to compute the mean (average). The mean will be computed as:

```
        AMEAN = (GRADE1 + GRADE2 + GRADE3 +
       -    GRADE4) / 4.
```

This computation should be done in the real mode since the answer (in all fairness to the student) should be rounded to a whole number.

If the data card contains four integer constants punched in columns 1–12 of a data card with three columns for each constant, the statements

```
        READ (5, 201) GRADE1, GRADE2, GRADE3, GRADE4
201     FORMAT (F3.0, F3.0, F3.0, F3.0)
```

will input and store the data values in real type variables. Here's a piece of the program.

```
C
C   READ DATA CARD
C
        READ (5, 201) GRADE1, GRADE2, GRADE3, GRADE4
201     FORMAT (F3.0, F3.0, F3.0, F3.0)
C
C   COMPUTE UNROUNDED MEAN, STORE IN AMEAN
C
        AMEAN = (GRADE1 + GRADE2 + GRADE3 + GRADE4)/4.
C
C   ROUND AMEAN TO A WHOLE NUMBER--MEAN
C
        MEAN = AMEAN + .5
        :
        :
```

On the right is the flowchart for our program above.

Write a READ and FORMAT statement to store the following integer data values as real constants.

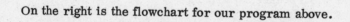

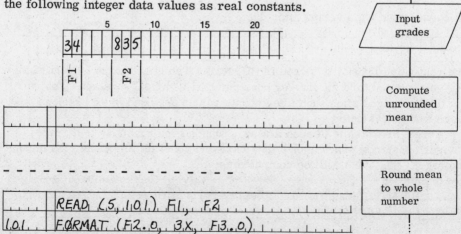

```
        READ (5, 101) F1, F2
101     FORMAT (F2.0, 3X, F3.0)
```

50. In FORTRAN the decimal point is always printed on the output, even though it can be implied for input. Although an extra position for a sign should be included, only the minus sign will be printed. The following examples illustrate how FORTRAN aligns the data on output.

Data value	Format code	Printed output	Some print this
32.	F6.2	ƀ32.00	
3.2	F6.2	ƀƀ3.20	
-.32	F6.2	ƀƀ-.32	ƀ-0.32
.032	F6.2	ƀƀƀ.03	ƀƀ0.03
.0032	F6.2	ƀƀƀ.00	ƀƀ0.00

Now, complete the printed output for the data values and format codes below.

Data value	Format code		Printed output
-36.37	F7.3	(a)	_____
-36.37	F10.5	(b)	_____
356.3	F6.2	(c)	_____
3.6	F6.2	(d)	_____

- - - - - - - - - - - - - - - - - -

(a) -36.370; (b) ƀ-36.37000; (c) 356.30; (d) ƀƀ3.60

51. Just to make sure you understand the rules for using the F format code to print real variables, here are some problems for you to complete.

Variable		Minimal F format code
-346.23	(a)	_____
XXX.	(b)	_____
XX.XXX	(c)	_____
XXX.X	(d)	_____

- - - - - - - - - - - - - - - - - -

(a) F7.2; (b) F5.0; (c) F7.3; (d) F6.1 (For (b) through (d), did you remember a position for a possible sign?)

52. The F format code, like the I format code, may truncate digits or fill the printer field with asterisks or other characters if the number of digits to be printed to the left of the decimal point exceeds the width provided for the field. Thus the printed output from this program segment

```
      EXCESS = 1325.247
      WRITE (6,350) EXCESS
350   FORMAT (1X, F7.3)
```

will be either _____ or _____ .

- - - - - - - - - - - - - - - - - - -

******* or 325.247 (truncated at the <u>left</u>)

53. What happens if the fractional part of an F code is insufficient to print
the entire fractional part of a number? As an example, this program segment will print 73.22.

```
      CUTOFF = 73.2157
      WRITE (6,100) CUTOFF
100   FORMAT (1X, F6.2)
```

A printed value of 73.22 is a rounded value at the second fractional digit.
This comes from the .2 part of the F6.2 format code.

On output, real variables will be rounded to the number of digits indicated
by this part of the F format code:

$$F \quad w \quad . \quad \overset{\downarrow}{d}$$

Your computer system rounds according to the rules with which you are familiar, as outlined below.

Given the number 12345.6789, suppose you want to round to the nearest
two digits to the right of the decimal. Therefore you would count two digits
to the right of the decimal point and round that digit according to the digit to
its immediate right.

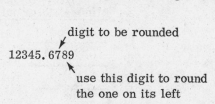

If the digit that determines the rounding is any digit 0 through 4, the digit to
the left remains the same. If the digit has any value 5 through 9, the digit
to the left is incremented by 1. So in the example above, our rounded number
is 12345.68 (7 was rounded to 8 since the digit on the right, 8, was greater
than 4).

In the general form Fw.d, the d indicates how many digits are to appear
to the right of the decimal. If the stored value has a greater number of digits
to the right of the decimal, the value is rounded to the specified number of
digits.

As a matter of interest, the format specification F8.2 would cause the
value 12345.6789 to be output as 12345.68.

(a) Round 341.67142 to two fractional digits (two digits to the right of the decimal point). _____

(b) How would the following be rounded for printing?

Data value	Format code	Printed output
-27.384	F5.1	_____
100.01619	F7.3	_____

- - - - - - - - - - - - - - - - - -

(a) 341.67; (b) -27.4, 100.016

54. Suppose you wanted to write FORTRAN statement(s) to round a real value to a specified number of places according to the rule given in the previous frame. Let REALNO be the number being rounded to N places, and this program segment will do the job.

```
100     INTNO = REALNO*10**N+.5
200     REALNO = INTNO
300     REALNO = REALNO/10.**N
```

Let's see why. We will use this procedure to round 3.1762 to two decimal places (N). (Mentally assign the value 2 to the variable N.)

The first statement (100) "moves" the decimal point two places to the right to "create" 317.62 to which .5 is added; thus 317.62 + .5 = 318.42, which is truncated to 318 and stored in INTNO (since INTNO is an integer variable). Statement 200 simply changes the mode of the value 318 to a real value (318.). The last statement (300) "moves" the decimal point back to where it really belongs, resulting in the value 3.18.

Statements 200 and 300 could be omitted, however, if we substituted statement numbered 301, as shown below, which is a mixed mode expression (your computer may not accept these).

```
301     REALNO = INTNO/10.**N
```

On the other hand, if your computer will handle mixed mode expressions, then by all means use the statement numbered 301.

Using the statements numbered 100, 200, and 300, explain how the computer could round 83.217415 to four decimal places.

- - - - - - - - - - - - - - - - - -

Statement 100 moves the decimal point four places to the right, giving 832174.15. Adding 832174.15 + .5 yields 832174.65, which is stored as 832174 in INTNO. Statement 200 converts 832174 to 832174., and the last statement moves the decimal point back to its "correct" position, giving 83.2174.

55. And now, we pick your mind with this question. What will be printed on a line by the following program segment?

```
      NAGE = 16
      HEIGHT = -5.8
      HAGE = HEIGHT * NAGE
      WRITE (6, 200) HEIGHT, NAGE, HAGE
200   FORMAT (1X, 4X, F6.2, 2X, I5, 3X, F6.2)
```

```
      -5.80      16   -92.80
```

This is an example of how spacing between fields can also be accomplished by using field widths larger than the minimum required.

Self-Test

For these problems, use device number 5 as an 80-column card reader and device number 6 as a 132 print-position printer.

1.   What is wrong with the following statements?

(a)
```
      READ A, I, L
```

(b)
```
      REED (5, 12) 0, K
```

(c)
```
      READ (5, 12) 0, K
```

(d)
```
15    FORMAT (-I5, F7.3)
```

(e)
```
      FORMAT (X5, 3I)
```

(f)

```
      WRITE (6,146), S,, I,, C,, K,,
```

(g)

```
24    FORMAT (I3,, F4.7)
```

(h)

```
      WRITE (6.200) DONOT,, KNOW,, WHY
```

2. What numbers can be used as device numbers? _____

3. Given the READ and FORMAT statements and their corresponding cards:

```
      READ (5, 24) I,, KAN,, NOW
24    FORMAT (I6,, I4,, 3X,, I9,)
```

and the data card

```
          1111111111222
          1234567890123456789012
          ₿₿3415123₿516826169596
```

(a) What will be stored in the following storage areas: I _____,

KAN _____, NOW _____.

Given

```
      READ (5, 23) I,, CAN,, MAYBE
23    FORMAT (I6,, F7.3,, 3X,, I4)
```

and the data card

```
          11111111112
          12345678901234567890
          ₿456₿6. 1₿₿₿₿₿35₿456₿
```

(b) What will be stored in the following storage areas: I _____,

CAN _____, MAYBE _____.

4. What will be printed by the following set of statements?

```
      K = -37
      WRITE (6, 200), K
200   FORMAT (/ X,, F10.7,)
```

5.   If you were a computer, what would you think of the programmer who wrote the following statements?

```
      READ (5,31) A, B, C, D, F, G
31    FØRMAT (F8.2, 10X, F10.6, 30X, F6.5, 20X, F16.2)
```

6.   Write a set of READ and FORMAT statements to read the values of the variables J, K, and L, respectively. J is in the range of -99 to +99, K is in the range of -999 to 999, and L is in the range of 0 to 99999. All the values are punched on one data card and no spaces are to appear between the data fields.

7.   Write a set of READ and FORMAT statements to read the values of THIS, TEST, IS, and OVER. THIS is in the range -999.99 to 0.0, TEST is in the range 0.0 to 100.00, IS ranges from -35 to 9999, and OVER is in the range -99.9999 to 9999.999. Assume all data values are on the same card with no spaces between the data fields. Decimal points are not punched on the card.

8.   Write a set of WRITE and FORMAT statements to print values stored in the variables LEMON, CRUSH, and SODA. LEMON is in the range -999 to 999, CRUSH is in the range -99.999 to 9999.9, and SODA is in the range -99.9 to 99999.999. Assume there are to be no spaces between printed data values.

9.   Using the variables and their respective ranges in problem 8, print the data values with a 6 print position space between the values of LEMON and CRUSH and a 25 print position space between the values of CRUSH and SODA.

10. Write a program to convert Fahrenheit temperature to Celsius temperature by using the formula $C = \dfrac{5}{9} (F - 32)$.

(1) This program will read in a Fahrenheit temperature punched in columns 5 through 8 of a card (right adjusted). This integer value can range from −465 to 500 degrees.

(2) The temperature value read in (1) is now converted to a Celsius temperature by the formula and rounded to one decimal place.

(3) The Fahrenheit and Celsius temperatures are printed out, in this order, with at least 10 print positions between the data values.

(4) Stop.

Answers to Self-Test

1. (a) The statement is missing a device and statement number. (frame 4)
        READ (5, 567) A, I, L
   (b) The word REED is an incorrect spelling. (frame 3)
        READ (5, 12) O, K
   (c) No comma should follow the word READ and the variables. (frame 5)
        READ (5, 12) O, K
   (d) First, there should not be a minus sign before the I5 specification.
(frame 17) Second, a comma belongs before the F7.3 format specification. (frame 13)
        15   FORMAT (I5, F7.3)
   (e) First, the format statement has no statement number. (frame 14)
Second, the X5 specification should be written as 5X. (frame 35) Finally,
the 3I specification should be written as I3. (frame 17)
        12345 FORMAT (5X, I3)
   (f) No comma should be placed after the last item in the WRITE list.
(frame 13)
   (g) The format code F4.7 is incorrect since it specifies a field width of
four positions with seven fractional digits and a decimal point. (frame 44)
   (h) There should be a comma between the numbers 6 and 200—not a period. (frame 13)
2. Any unsigned number—provided of course that it follows your computer
installation specifications. (frame 2)
3. (a) I = 003415; KAN = 1230; NOW = 826169596 (frames 18, 35)
   (b) I = 45606; CAN = .100000 = .1; MAYBE = 04560 = 4560 (frames
18, 35, and 47)
4. Unpredictable. Depending upon your compiler, it may issue a warning
(or error) message that you are attempting to write an integer value using
the F format code. (frame 21)

5. Not too much. The programmer must confine himself to 80 columns per card. (See instructions at beginning of Self-Test.)
6.   READ (5, 3524) J, K, L
   3524 FORMAT (I3, I4, I5) (frames 22-23)
7.   READ (5, 100) THIS, TEST, IS, OVER
    100 FORMAT (F6.2, F5.2, I4, F9.4) (frame 44)
8.   WRITE (6, 101) LEMON, CRUSH, SODA
    101 FORMAT (1X, I4, F8.3, F9.3) (frames 50-51)
        Note: SODA requires a maximum of five positions to the left of the decimal point, a maximum of three to the right, and the decimal point itself—a total of nine positions.
9.   WRITE (6, 201) LEMON, CRUSH, SODA
    201 FORMAT (1X, I4, 6X, F8.3, 25X, F9.3) (frame 41)
10. The program follows. (frames 49, 53)

```
C
C   F REPRESENTS FAHRENHEIT TEMPERATURE READ IN AS REAL
C   C REPRESENTS CELSIUS TEMPERATURE
C   READ IN FAHRENHEIT TEMPERATURE
C
        READ (5,101) F
101     FORMAT (4X, F4.0)
C
C   COMPUTE CELSIUS TEMPERATURE AND ROUND TO ONE
C     DECIMAL PLACE
C
        C = 5./9. * (F - 32.) + .5
C
C   WRITE FAHRENHEIT AND CELSIUS TEMPERATURES
C
        WRITE (6,201) F, C
201     FORMAT (1X, F5.0, 10X, F6.1)
C
C   STOP
C
        STOP
        END
```

CHAPTER FOUR
Elementary Control Statements

In this chapter, you will learn to use elementary control statements. When you complete this chapter, you will be able to write program statements that will:

- make an unconditional change in the execution sequence of the program statements (using the GO TO statement and a statement number);

- make a decision, the result of which can change the execution sequence of the program statements (using the IF statement and statement numbers);

- cease execution of the program statements, either temporarily (using a PAUSE statement with execution resuming at the command of the computer operator) or forever (using the STOP statement).

You will also learn the use of the END statement which signals the FORTRAN compiler that the physical end of the program has been reached, and that any subsequent statements are not part of this program.

Unconditional GO TO Statement

1.   In Chapter One, we mentioned that the computer executes instructions sequentially (the order in which the instructions are entered into the computer). However, in most computer applications you would not want this to occur. For instance, if your program were designed to calculate gross pay for each employee, you might want to use the following program segment for processing each employee's wages.

```
GRØSS = REGHRS * RATE
PREM = ØTHRS * ØTRATE
```

We can reuse these statements by simply using a GO TO statement following the last line of the group to be repeated.

```
1,0,0,0 | READ (5, 1,0,0,1,) IDNUM, RATE, ØTRATE,
       -  |    ØTHRS, REGHRS
           |  ⋮
           | GRØSS = REGHRS * RATE
           | PREM = ØTHRS * ØTRATE
           |  ⋮
           | GØ TØ 1,0,0,0
2,0,0,0 | TALLY = TALLY + 1
           |  ⋮
```

The GO TO command can also be written as GOTO—one word, on some computers. The GO TO statement merely transfers the execution (or branches) to the program statement number indicated. The GO TO can only branch to an integer—not to an integer variable.

In the last example, GO TO 1000 transfers execution to which statement?

_____ (a)   1000   _____ (c)   3000

_____ (b)   2000   _____ (d)   (1000 + 2000)

- - - - - - - - - - - - - - - - - - -

(a).   If you think you know all about GO TO statements, GO TO frame 3.

2.   Here's a pictorial diagram of what the GO TO statement accomplishes.

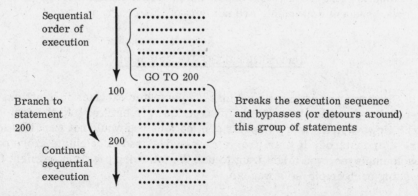

Somewhere in the program, you will branch to the sequence of statements beginning with statement 100 in our picture above. (It would make no sense to include those statements in the program in the first place if they served no purpose.)

Write a statement that will branch to statement 100. (Use your FORTRAN Coding Form. At this point we assume you have bought or prepared some blank FORTRAN Coding Forms to work on. We will no longer provide the blanks for you.)

- - - - - - - - - - - - - - - - - -

GO TO 100, or GOTO 100

3. The GO TO statement is often called an unconditional branch. We like to think of it as an "offer that the computer cannot refuse," but sometimes the consequences may not be desired. For example, what's wrong with the following sequence of statements?

	:	
	LENGTH = 10	
	IWIDTH = 30	
310	GØ TØ 310	
320	AREA = LENGTH * IWIDTH	
	:	

- - - - - - - - - - - - - - - - - -

If you said something to the effect that the GO TO 310 statement branches back to itself, you're correct. What will occur is that the computer will continue executing this statement over and over and over....

4. By the way, is there anything superfluous about the following set of statements?_____ If so, what?_____

120	GØ TØ 130	
130	:	
	:	

- - - - - - - - - - - - - - - - - -

Yes, there certainly is, since if the statement numbered 120 were deleted, execution would pass to the next sequential statement (numbered 130) anyway. Everyone does something like this when they start programming. You'll soon learn when GO TO is unnecessary.

5. The statement referred to in a GO TO statement must be an executable statement; that is, a statement which commands the computer to do something.

Examples of executable statements are assignment statements, READ and WRITE statements, the STOP statement, and the IF statement. The FORMAT and END statements are not executable since they only supply information for the compiler but do not affect program execution.

Are the following sets of statements correct?

(a)

	GØ TØ 50	
	:	
50	WRITE (6,52) A, B, F	

(b)

	GØ TØ 205	
	:	
	READ (5,205) AK, AL	
205	FORMAT (F5.1, F8.3)	

- - - - - - - - - - - - - - - - - -

(a) Yes, the WRITE statement is an executable statement;   (b) No, a FORMAT is not executable

Summary

As a summary of these last frames, let us look at the program of frame 33 of Chapter Three, which read an integer, computed its square, and printed the number and its square. However, this time we will modify this program so that many integers can be read in. This is done simply by using a GO TO statement before the STOP statement. The program and its flowchart are on the next page. To the right, you can see how the GO TO statement is flow-charted. When execution reaches A (at the bottom), it will return to the A at the top.

Notice the STOP statement, in the flowchart, is not connected to the rest of the program. This, of course, means that the program will never stop by itself. This is not a good thing to do; after all, how many numbers do you want to square? To find how to get rid of the "never stopping" problem, read on, as we introduce you to the arithmetic IF statement.

```
┌─ C FOR COMMENT
│ STATEMENT │C│
│  NUMBER   │O│
│1        5│6│7   10      15      20      25      30
C  READ IN AN INTEGER-N
C
100    READ (5,101) N
101    FORMAT (I4)
C
C  COMPUTE N**2
C
       NSQUAR = N**2
C
C  PRINT N AND NSQUAR
C
       WRITE (6,201) N, NSQUAR
201    FORMAT (1X, I4, I10)
C
C  BRANCH TO READ NEXT NUMBER
C
       GØ TØ 100
       STØP
       END
```

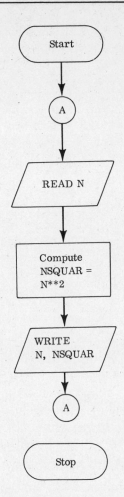

Arithmetic IF Statement

6.   The FORTRAN language provides a conditional instruction called an arithmetic IF statement, which will cause a branch to one of three possible statements. It looks like this.

$$\underbrace{\text{IF}}_{1} \quad \underbrace{\text{(MYAGE} - 65)}_{2} \quad \overset{\text{1st}}{\overbrace{123,}} \overset{\text{2nd}}{\overbrace{120,}} \overset{\text{3rd}}{\underbrace{\overbrace{129}}_{3}}$$

For identification, we've labeled its three parts.

1.   The word IF is the first part. This signals to the FORTRAN compiler to evaluate the expression that follows.

2. The second part is the arithmetic expression within a pair of parentheses. The computer will evaluate this expression and determine whether it is negative, zero, or positive.

3. The third part follows and consists of exactly three statement numbers, each separated by a comma from the other. Note that no comma appears before the first statement number or after the third statement number. Some of these numbers may be the same. But at least two statement numbers should be different.

A branch will then occur to one of the three statement numbers as indicated:

Value of computed arithmetic expression	Branch to statement
less than zero (or negative)	the first statement number
equal to zero	the second statement number
greater than zero (or positive)	the third statement number

All three parts of the arithmetic IF statement must be in this order. If they are not, the FORTRAN compiler will not compile the statement (properly).

Correctly rewrite those IF statements below that the proofreader did not catch. (Use your coding form to write the corrected statements.)

130	IF 5, 10, 15 (DESKS - CHAIRS
131	IF FLOOR - 5.) 15, 16, 17
132	IFF (100. - PROOF), 35, 45, 55,
133	IF (BATMAN - ROBIN) 5, 10, 5
134	IF (VALUE) 3, 4 9
135	IF (X**2) 3, 4, 5, 6, 7
136	((X+A)*(B-1.)) IF 130, 133, 136

- - - - - - - - - - - - - - - - - - -

Here are the corrected arithmetic IF statements.

130   IF (DESKS - CHAIRS) 5, 10, 15

131   IF (FLOOR - 5.) 15, 16, 17

132   IF (100. - PROOF) 35, 45, 55

Yes, 133 is correct.

134   IF (VALUE) 3, 4, 9 (Notice that it is not necessary to have arithmetic operators in the expression.)

135   IF (X**2) 3, 4, 5 (Any three statement numbers, but no more or less than three, are correct.)

136   IF ((X + A) * (B - 1.)) 130, 133, 135 (None of the three statement numbers should cause the IF statement to branch to itself.)

7.   For the following values of TOTHRS, to which statement will execution branch?

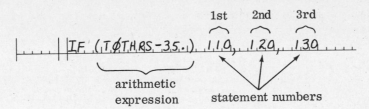

		Evaluated expression	Branch to statement number
Value of TOTHRS			
25.2	(a)	_____	_____
34.5	(b)	_____	_____
35.0	(c)	_____	_____
35.5	(d)	_____	_____
75.0	(e)	_____	_____

- - - - - - - - - - - - - - - - -

	Evaluated expression	Branch to statement number
(a)	-9.8 (25.2 $-$ 35.)	110
(b)	$-.5$	110
(c)	.0	120
(d)	.5 (or $+.5$)	130
(e)	40.0	130

Hmmm, that's a lot of overtime for (e)—so (e) buys the drinks this week.

8.   It is important that you don't confuse the statement numbers of an IF statement with the values of variables in the expression part of the statement. As an example, the statement

|......||IF (ØWED - 40.) 40, 30, 45 .... | . . . . | . . . . | . . . . |

will branch to the statement numbered 40 if the value of OWED is 30 because (OWED - 40.) = (30. - 40.) = -10. is negative. In the same manner, if OWED has any value greater than 40 the IF statement will branch to the statement numbered 45.

(a)   If the value of OWED is 40, the IF statement will cause a branch to the statement numbered _____ .

(b)   If the value of OWED is less than 30, the IF statement will cause a branch to the statement numbered _____ .

- - - - - - - - - - - - - - - - -

(a) Statement number 30, because (OWED - 40.) = (40. - 40.) = 0. and the second branch will be taken.

(b) Statement number 40 since (OWED - 40.) will always be negative, so execution will branch to the statement numbered with the first statement number.

9.   We will now try to confuse you on purpose! Be careful. Using this statement,

```
        IF (MYAGE - 21), 15, 18, 13
```

select the appropriate age ranges that will satisfy the branch indicated.

Branch to state- ment number		Value of MYAGE
_____ (a) 13	(1)	less than 17
_____ (b) 15	(2)	13
	(3)	21
_____ (c) 18	(4)	18
	(5)	greater than 21
	(6)	under 19 and older than 15

- - - - - - - - - - - - - - - - - -

(a) Branch to 13 if MYAGE is greater than 21, which would be answer 5.

(b) Branch to 15 if MYAGE is less than 21, thus answers 1, 2, 4, and 6 are correct.

(c) Branch to 18 if MYAGE is exactly equal to 21, thus 3 is correct.

Hope you didn't confuse the statement numbers with the values of MYAGE.

10. This statement

```
        IF (B*B - 4. *A*C), 100, 300, 200
```

tests the value of the expression B * B - 4. * A * C and branches to the statements numbered 100, 300, and 200 if the value of the expression is negative, zero, or positive, respectively.

Write an arithmetic IF statement which tests the value of the expression PREVSS + .058 * GROSS - SSLIMT and branches to the statement numbered 100 if the value of the expression is negative or zero. If the value of the expression is positive branch to the statement numbered 200.

- - - - - - - - - - - - - - - - - - -

```
        IF (PREVSS + .058*GROSS - SSLIMT), 100, 100, 200
```

11. Any program performing input must recognize when there are no more records left to input. If you design such a program you would eventually run

out of input records (after all, how many employees could you have?). To indicate that there are no more data records, it is a common practice to include, after the last input record, another record with a special code. As an example, a negative number may be typed in the field indicating an amount of hours worked. An hourly pay rate of 0 could also be used for such a special code. If no indication is given to the computer that there is no more data, the computer may stop. This is frowned upon in most large systems, since it may require manual intervention by the computer operator to get the next job onto the computer. When the computer stops normally, as with the STOP statement, this does not happen. Frame 8 of Chapter Eleven discusses another way to determine when no more input data records exist.

Here is a little program. <u>Program objective:</u> (1) This program reads in a card on which an employee number, pay rate, and number of hours is punched, as shown below.

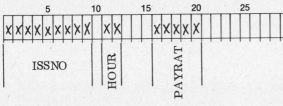

The last data card has a -1 punched in the HOUR field. (2) If HOUR is negative, the program will stop. (3) The program then computes the gross wage (GROSS) as GROSS = HOUR * PAYRAT. (4) Then it prints the ISSNO, HOUR, PAYRAT, and GROSS values. (5) And returns to read the next data card.

On the next page is the coded program.

---

*In case you don't remember these algebraic inequality symbols, look at the chart furnished here.

Symbol	Example	Relation
<	a < b	a is less than b
<=, ≤	a ≤ b	a less than or equal to b
>	a > b	a greater than b
>=, ≥	a ≥ b	a greater than or equal to b

These symbols are not FORTRAN notation, but they are used in COMMENT statements and in flowcharts.

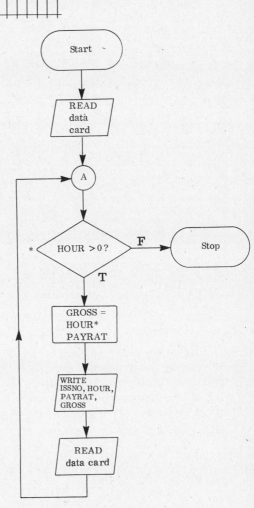

```
C
C  READ DATA CARD
C
100    READ (5, 121) ISSNØ, HØUR, PAYRAT
121    FØRMAT (I9, 1X, F2.0, 3X, F5.2)
C
C  TEST IF HØUR < 0 -- LAST DATA CARD
C  BRANCH TØ STØP
C
150    IF (HØUR) 400, 200, 200
200    GRØSS = HØUR * PAYRAT
C
C  PRINT ISSNØ, HØUR, PAYRAT, AND GRØSS
C
C
       WRITE (6, 351) ISSNØ, HØUR, PAYRAT, GRØSS
351    FØRMAT (1X, I9, 5X, F3.0, 5X, F6.2, 5X, F9.2)
C
C  READ DATA CARD
C
       READ (5, 121) ISSNØ, HØUR, PAYRAT
C
C  RETURN TØ TEST IF HØUR < 0
C
       GØ TØ 150
C
C  STØP
C
400    STØP
       END
```

Notice that the output fields of PAYRAT and HOUR are one position longer than on input to provide a position for the decimal point to be printed.

Modify statement numbered 150 so that the program will branch to the STOP statement if the value of PAYRAT is equal to zero. (Use your FORTRAN Coding Form.)

- - - - - - - - - - - - - - -

```
150    IF (PAYRAT) 400, 400, 200
```
or
```
150    IF (PAYRAT) 200, 400, 200
```

The only difference in these statements is what the program "should" do if PAYRAT is less than zero. In the first statement, control would be transferred to the STOP statement, and in the second statement, a negative value of GROSS would be computed. From our experience, you really should use the first statement since you would not want to continue processing with incorrect data.

12. This statement

```
      IF (HØUR -40.) 130, 140, 150
```

can be considered to contain a test to decide if the value of HOUR is less than, equal to, or greater than 40, and to take a specific action in each case. In the same manner, this statement

```
      IF ((40.*RATE + 1.5*RATE*(HØUR-40.))- 400.)
     - 100, 200, 300
```

can be considered to contain a test to decide if the value of (40. * RATE + 1.5 * RATE * (HOUR - 40.)) is less than, equal to, or greater than 400.

Write an arithmetic IF statement which will cause a branch to the statements numbered 50, 60, and 80 if the value of the integer expression I - I/J * J is less than, greater than, or equal to 10, respectively.

- - - - - - - - - - - - - - - - - -

```
      IF ((I-I/J*J) - 10) 50, 80, 60
   or IF (I-I/J*J - 10) 50, 80, 60
```

You can use either statement since the inner parentheses in the first statement simply serve to group the expression I - I/J * J.

13. Write an arithmetic IF statement which will cause a branch to the statements numbered 30, 253, and 670 if the value of the expression ALOAN - DISCNT is less than, equal to, or greater than 1000, respectively.

- - - - - - - - - - - - - - - - - -

```
      IF (ALØAN - DISCNT - 1000.) 30, 253, 670
   or IF ((ALØAN - DISCNT) - 1000.) 30, 253, 670
```

Note that these parentheses are not necessary since, by the hierarchy of expression evaluation, the expression is evaluated from left to right.

14. Now modify the program in frame 11 so that people who work more than 40 hours for the pay period will receive time and one-half for the excess hours. Modify the program in this way: (1) If HOUR is greater than 40, the gross wage is GROSS = PAYRAT * (40. + 1.5 * (HOUR - 40.)). (2) If HOUR

is less than or equal to 40, the gross wage is GROSS = PAYRAT * HOUR.
(Hint: You must be sure you only compute the gross value once.) The flowchart for the complete program is below.

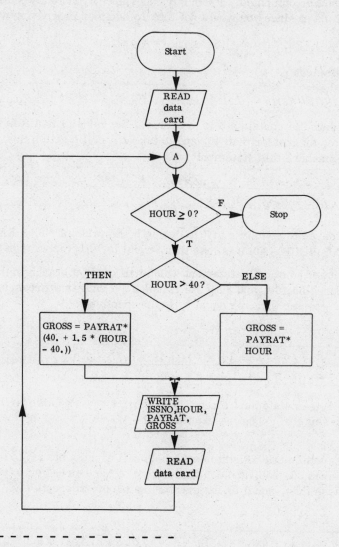

- - - - - - - - - - - - - - - - - - - -

Our program is shown on the next page. It is <u>very important</u> that you included
a statement such as GO TO 350, which we used to branch over the part of the
program which computed GROSS for HOUR greater than 40. If you did not do
this, then when HOUR is less than or equal to 40, GROSS will be computed <u>two</u>
times—the second time possibly incorrectly since (HOUR - 40.) may be
negative.

```
C
C  READ DATA CARD
C
100      READ (5, 121) ISSNØ, HØUR, PAYRAT
121      FØRMAT (I9, 1X, F2.0, 3X, F5.2)
C
C  TEST IF HØUR < 0 -- LAST DATA CARD
C  BRANCH TO STØP
C
150      IF (HØUR) 400, 200, 200
C
C  TEST IF HØUR > 40  BRANCH TØ 260
C  ELSE BRANCH TØ 240
C
200      IF (HØUR - 40.) 240, 240, 260
C
C  HØUR LESS THAN ØR EQUAL TØ 40.  CØMPUTE
C  GRØSS=HØUR*PAYRAT AND BRANCH TØ WRITE STATEMENT
C
240      GRØSS = HØUR * PAYRAT
         GØ TØ 350
C
C  HØUR GREATER THAN 40, CØMPUTE GRØSS BASED ON
C  OVERTIME FØRMULA
C
260      GRØSS = PAYRAT * (40. + 1.5*(HØUR-40.))
C
C  PRINT ISSNØ, HØUR, PAYRAT, AND GRØSS
C
350      WRITE (6, 351) ISSNØ, HØUR, PAYRAT, GRØSS
351      FØRMAT (1X, I9, 5X, F3.0, 5X, F6.2, 5X, F9.2)
C
C  READ NEXT DATA CARD
C
         READ (5, 121) ISSNØ, HØUR, PAYRAT
C
C  RETURN TØ TEST IF HØUR < 0
```

(continue on next page)

```
C
         GØ TØ 150
400      STØP
         END
```

15. Some programs you will write (soon!) will require the use of a variable which will function as a counter (adder) or accumulator. As an example, this statement

```
         I = I + 1
```

illustrates the variable I accumulating a value of one. In this statement the present value of I is increased by one and this new value is stored in I. Some people refer to this as "incrementing I by one." Here are other examples of accumulators.

```
         KØUNT = KØUNT + ISTEP
```

```
         SUM = SUM + TERM
```

The first example adds the value of ISTEP to the current value of KOUNT, and the second example adds the value of TERM to the current value of SUM.

A general rule for using such variables is <u>always</u> initialize (start at some known value) those variables which serve as counters or accumulators. Unless you initialize such a variable, you may not know what value is stored in the variable. For example, the following program segment reads a single data value from each of ten input records and adds the values indicated.

```
         :
C
C  CHECK FØR 10TH DATA RECØRD
C
40       IF (K - 10) 50, 200, 200
C
C  READ A VALUE (ANUMB) AND ADD 1 TØ
C  THE RECØRD COUNT (K)
C
50       READ (5, 101) ANUMB
101      FØRMAT (F6.1)
125      K = K + 1
C
C  ACCUMULATE ANUMB IN ACCUM
C
150      ACCUM = ACCUM + ANUMB
```

(continue on next page)

```
         GØ TØ 40
200      •.••••|•.
```

This program segment will be correctly compiled. However, execution will probably give unpredictable results. Since K (the record counter) was never initialized to zero, either less than ten, ten, or more than ten records would be read (after all, the variable K might have been assigned to a memory location which had the value 63572 or 0 or -324 stored). In this case, hopefully some sort of arithmetic or input/output error may occur to halt execution.

What statements should be added to the program segment before the IF statement to initialize the values of K and ACCUM to zero?

- - - - - - - - - - - - - - - - - -

```
         K = 0
         ACCUM = 0.
```

16. Let's examine the statements numbered 125 and 150 in this program segment.

```
         K = 0
         ACCUM = 0
40       IF (K - 10) 50, 200, 200
50       READ (5, 101) ANUMB
101      FØRMAT (F6.1)
125      K = K + 1
         :
150      ACCUM = ACCUM + ANUMB
         GØ TØ 40
200      •.••••|•.
```

Statement 125 adds one to the present value of K and stores this new value in K. Of course, this statement destroys the old value of K. In the same sense,

statement 150 can be considered as adding _____ to the present

value of _____ and storing this new value in _____.

- - - - - - - - - - - - - - - - - -

ANUMB, ACCUM, ACCUM

17. Write a FORTRAN statement which increments a variable INTVAR by five and stores this new value in INTVAR.

- - - - - - - - - - - - - - - - - -

```
         INTVAR = INTVAR + 5
```

18. We want you to write a simple program to count a number of data records. Assume each record has the format: positions 1-4, a positive integer; positions 5-9, a real number with format F5.2. After the last data record to be counted, a blank record is inserted (will be read by FORTRAN as zeros). The output of the program is the number of data records (not including the blank record). We will give you a flowchart.

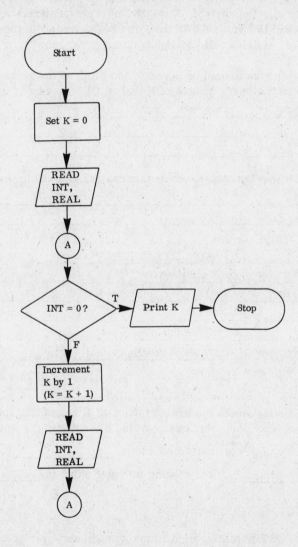

```
C   INITIALIZE COUNTER-K AND READ DATA RECORD
C
    K = 0
100 READ (5, 101) INT, REAL
101 FORMAT (I4, F5.2)
C
C CHECK IF INT = 0.  IF TRUE BRANCH TO PRINT K
    ELSE INCREMENT K BY 1
C
110 IF (INT) 150, 400, 150
150 K = K + 1
C
C READ NEXT DATA RECORD
C
    READ (5, 101) INT, REAL
C
C BRANCH TO DECISION
C
    GO TO 110
C
C PRINT K AND STOP
C
400 WRITE (6, 401) K
401 FORMAT (1X, I5)
    STOP
    END
```

For the purposes of this program, it was really not necessary to include the variable REAL in the READ statement list since it served no purpose.

19. You will now write another program. Don't be nervous; it looks a lot like the program in frame 33 of Chapter Three. (That is a hint!) Program objective: (1) This program reads an integer constant located in positions 1 to 3 of an input record (call it the constant N). (2) Then for each integer K from 1 to N, it computes its square (call it KSQUAR) and its cube (call it KCUBE). (3) The program then prints out the value of K, KSQUAR, and KCUBE for each value of K from 1 to N. The flowchart is on the next page. Assume the value of N is equal to or greater than 1.

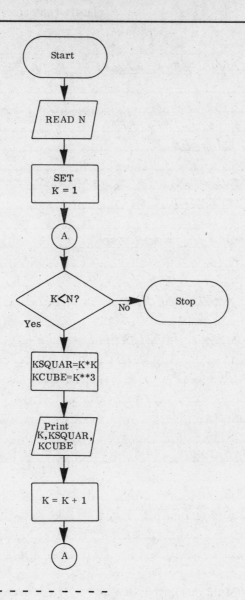

- - - - - - - - - - - - - - - - - -

Our program is below.

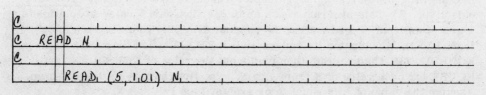

(continue on next page)

```
101    FORMAT (I3)
C
C   INITIALIZE COUNTER (K) TO ONE
C
       K = 1
C
C   TEST IF K = N  IF TRUE STOP, ELSE GO TO 120
C
110    IF (K - N) 120, 200, 200
C
C   COMPUTE KSQUAR = K*K
C   AND KCUBE = K**3
C
120    KSQUAR = K*K
       KCUBE = K**3
C
C   PRINT K, KSQUAR, AND KCUBE
C
       WRITE (6,151) K, KSQUARE, KCUBE
151    FORMAT (1X, I3, 5X, I7, 5X, I12)
C
C   INCREMENT K BY 1
C
       K = K + 1
       GO TO 110
200    STOP
       END
```

20. The following program reads in an integer constant (N) and adds all the integers from 1 to N (computes 1+2+3+...+N). <u>Program objective</u>: This program computes the sum of the first N integers by: (1) reading in an integer constant from columns 4 to 6 of a data card; (2) initializing an accumulator (NACCUM) to zero and a counter (KOUNT) to zero; (3) testing to see if the value of KOUNT is equal to N, at which time the value of the accumulator NACCUM is printed along with the value of N. If the value of KOUNT is less than N, execution continues at (4); (4) adding 1 to the value of KOUNT and adding KOUNT to the value of the accumulator NACCUM; (5) Execution then branches to (3) to test the value of KOUNT.

Assume N is greater than zero. The flowchart and program are on the next page.

```
C
C   READ DATA CARD TO OBTAIN N
C
        READ (5, 101) N
101     FORMAT (3X, I3)
C
C   INITIALIZE ACCUMULATOR (NACCUM)
C   AND COUNTER KOUNT TO VALUE
C   OF ZERO
C
        KOUNT = 0
        NACCUM = 0
C
C   TEST VALUE OF KOUNT, IF KOUNT
C       < N BRANCH TO 150, ELSE
C   BRANCH TO WRITE STATEMENT 200
C
125     IF (KOUNT - N) 150, 200, 200
C
C   INCREMENT KOUNT BY 1 AND
C   NACCUM BY KOUNT
C
150     KOUNT = KOUNT + 1
        NACCUM = NACCUM + KOUNT
C
C   BRANCH TO TEST VALUE OF KOUNT
C
        GO TO 125
C
C   PRINT N AND NACCUM
C
200     WRITE (6, 201) N, NACCUM
201     FORMAT (1X, I3, 5X, I6)
C
C   STOP
C
        STOP
        END
```

Start

READ N

Set
KOUNT = 0
NACCUM = 0

A

KOUNT = N?   F → B

T

Add 1 to KOUNT
Add KOUNT to
NACCUM

A

B

Print N,
NACCUM

Stop

<u>Input</u>(N)   <u>Output</u>(N, NACCUM)
3   3   6
5   5   15
20   20   210

One problem with this program is that the printed output consists of two numbers without any explanation of what they mean. You will learn how to write explanatory output messages for this program in Chapter Five.

Modify this program to multiply together the integers from 1 to N. Be careful how you initialize the value of the accumulator of the product of the integers. Use a format of I11 to output NACCUM.

```
C
C  READ DATA CARD TO OBTAIN N
C
      READ (5, 101) N
101   FORMAT (3X, I3)
C
C  INITIALIZE ACCUMULATOR (NACCUM) TO ONE AND
C  COUNTER KOUNT TO ZERO
C
      NACCUM = 1
      KOUNT = 0
C
C  TEST VALUE OF KOUNT, IF KOUNT < N BRANCH TO 150
C  ELSE BRANCH TO WRITE STATEMENT 200
C
125   IF (KOUNT - N) 150, 200, 200
C
C  INCREMENT KOUNT BY 1 AND MULTIPLY NACCUM BY KOUNT
C
150   KOUNT = KOUNT + 1
      NACCUM = NACCUM * KOUNT
C
C  BRANCH TO TEST VALUE OF COUNT
C
      GO TO 125
C
C  PRINT N AND NACCUM
C
```

(continue on next page)

```
200.    WRITE (6, 201) N, NACCUM
201.    FORMAT (1X, I3, 5X, I11)
C
C  STOP
C
        STOP
        END
```

If you plan to run this program on a computer you should limit the value
of N to less than 15 because the product of the first thirteen integers is
6,227,020,800. The value may approach the magnitude of the largest integer
your computer can store. Those of you who know a little mathematics may
have recognized this problem as the computation of the factorial function (n!).

21. Consider the following FORTRAN statements from a payroll application
program.

```
        FICA = YTDPAY * FICART
        EXCESS = FICA - TLIMIT
        IF (EXCESS) 30, 30, 20
```

In this sequence, we determine if we've reached the maximum amount of
FICA (Social Security) tax to be deducted from an employee's salary. The
first statement calculates a tentative year-to-date FICA deduction (FICA) by
multiplying the FICA tax rate (FICART) by the year-to-date salary (YTDPAY).
The second statement computes EXCESS as the difference between the tentative
FICA tax (FICA) and the tax limit set by the government (TLIMIT). Finally,
we test whether the tentative FICA tax has exceeded TLIMIT in the IF statement. The value of EXCESS will be negative, zero, or positive, depending
upon the relationship of FICA and TLIMIT:

   EXCESS is negative if FICA is less than TLIMIT;
   EXCESS is zero if FICA equals TLIMIT;
   EXCESS is positive if FICA is greater than TLIMIT.

   Now, if you don't need the value of FICA in the above sequence, we could
simplify our statement sequence to

```
        EXCESS = (YTDPAY * FICART) - TLIMIT
        IF (EXCESS) 30, 30, 20
```

Furthermore, if we don't require the value EXCESS for any subsequent calculation, we could just as well reduce our previous two statements to one statement.

```
        IF ((YTDPAY*FICART)-TLIMIT) 30, 30, 20
or      IF (YTDPAY*FICART-TLIMIT) 30, 30, 20
```

Note that the last example takes advantage of the fact that the hierarchy of
operations will properly calculate the expression contained within the IF statement's parentheses.

By now you should be able to reduce each of the following program segments to one IF statement.   Go ahead and try them.

(a)
```
DIFF = FENCED - AREA
IF (DIFF) 110, 120, 130
```

(b)
```
AREA = PI * RADIUS**2
DIFF = FENCED - AREA
IF (DIFF) 110, 120, 130
```

(c)
```
RADIUS = DIAM/2.
PI = 3.1416
AREA = PI * RADIUS**2
DIFF = FENCED - AREA
IF (DIFF) 110, 120, 130
```

(d)
```
ØLDHIT = RECØRD + PAYØLA
NEWHIT = NEWPAY - 3 * ØLDHIT
RATING = NEWHIT - MØNEY
CAUGHT = RATING - 100.
IF (CAUGHT) 20, 40, 60
```

- - - - - - - - - - - - - - - - - -

(a)
```
IF (FENCED - AREA) 110, 120, 130
```

(b)
```
IF (FENCED - (PI * RADIUS**2)) 110, 120, 130
```
or
```
IF (FENCED - PI * RADIUS**2) 110, 120, 130
```

(c)
```
IF (FENCED - (3.1416 * (DIAM/2.)**2))
-    110, 120, 130
```
or
```
IF (FENCED - 3.1416 * (DIAM/2.)**2)
-    110, 120, 130
```

or (if you are really slick)
```
IF (FENCED - 3.1416 * DIAM**2 / 4.)
-    110, 120, 130
```
since (DIAM/2.)**2 is equivalent (algebraically) to DIAM**2/4.

(d)
```
IF (NEWPAY - 3 * (RECØRD + PAYØLA) - MØNEY
-    - 100) 20, 40, 60
```

We did mix some modes in this last exercise. If your compiler does not accept mixed mode expressions, you should change the names of the variables.

22. What do you think is wrong with each of the following statement sequences?

(a)

```
        IF (BRANCH) 20, 20, 20
```

(b)

```
        AMOUNT = -50.
100     IF (AMOUNT) 100, 110, 120
```

(c)

```
30      AMOUNT = AMOUNT + 1
        IF (AMOUNT) 30, 40, 50
```

- - - - - - - - - - - - - - - - - -

(a) Nothing. But why not use a GO TO 20 statement since the program will branch there under any circumstance?

(b) These statements will cause the computer to execute the IF statement continually—until the computer operator causes the machine to halt. Never branch to the IF statement you are executing. In this case AMOUNT has been given the value -50. However, a different value could have been assigned to the variable AMOUNT in another part of the program and the program could then branch to the statement numbered 100. In such a case the IF statement would not be incorrect.

(c) Sorry, there is nothing wrong with this sequence of statements. If the value of AMOUNT happens to be negative the statement sequence will increment the value of AMOUNT by 1 until AMOUNT becomes equal to or greater than zero.

Summary of Arithmetic IF Statement

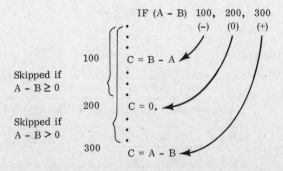

STOP Statement

23. Eventually, after your program has completed what it was supposed to do, you probably would like it to terminate execution. FORTRAN has a clever way to do this; you use this statement.

```
        STØP
```

A program may contain more than one STOP statement.

Consider the following program statement sequence.

```
        IF (VALUE) 101, 102, 103
101     STØP 1
102     STØP 2
103     STØP 3
```

This sequence illustrates a situation in which it would be useful for the computer operator to know which STOP statement caused the computer to halt (cease execution). The STOP statement may optionally contain an unsigned integer value, ranging from 1 through 32767. After a STOP statement has been executed the program can only be restarted by reloading the program into the computer memory.

What is wrong with the following statement?

```
        STP
```

- - - - - - - - - - - - - - - - - -

Perhaps nothing, if you are a race car driver, but a computer will flag (identify) this statement as an error. The statement should be

```
        STØP
```

Even though you may have guessed, the STOP statement is an executable statement. We thought we would just tell you anyway.

PAUSE Statement

24. The STOP statement, as you know, terminates execution of a program. Sometimes, however, you may want to temporarily pause in the program and then resume program execution at the next executable statement. For example, you may want the computer operator to mount and position a special form on the printer, such as payroll checks. After the computer operator has performed these chores, he/she resumes program execution.

For purposes such as these, and many others, you simply write the FOR-
TRAN statement

```
      PAUSE
```

The PAUSE statement writes the following message on the computer console
typewriter: PAUSE 00000.

How is the computer operator supposed to know what this means? Simple.
You submit a slip of paper with your program telling the operator what tasks
to perform when the computer produces the message PAUSE 00000.

How does the PAUSE statement differ from the STOP statement?

- - - - - - - - - - - - - - - - - -

The PAUSE statement differs from the STOP statement in that it causes the
program to continue execution with the statement following the PAUSE. After
a STOP statement, the program execution cannot be resumed without starting
the program from its beginning.

25. Sometimes the operator performs tasks which vary according to the
reason for the PAUSE statement. In this case you can use an alternate form
of the PAUSE statement,

```
      PAUSE n
```

where n is a string of 1 to 5 digits. For the exact installations implementation check your FORTRAN manual.

When the computer executes the PAUSE n statement, the computer prints
the following message on the console typewriter: PAUSE n. The operator
can then look up the meaning of the number to find what operations he is to
perform. Of course, you would have to supply the operator with a list of the
meanings for each of the various PAUSE statements. After a pause the operator must press a start key or something comparable on the computer to
start things going again.

If you wish to cause the message PAUSE 0341 to be printed on the console
typewriter, what statement should you write?

- - - - - - - - - - - - - - - - - -

```
      PAUSE 0341
```

END Statement

26. How can the FORTRAN compiler tell when it has read the last FORTRAN statement in a program? Certainly not because of "seeing" a STOP statement, since a program can contain more than one STOP statement. The answer is that FORTRAN compilers require an

	END

statement at the physical end of each FORTRAN program (source program). This statement tells the compiler that "there are no more FORTRAN statements in the program currently being compiled." All programs written in FORTRAN are incomplete until an END statement is placed after the last statement in each source program. The END statement is a nonexecutable statement.

Is the following program correct? _____

20	A = 4.
	C = A**2
	END
15	D = 1.
	STØP 7
	F = A + B * C**D
	GØ TØ 20

— — — — — — — — — — — — — — — — — — — —

No! The END statement must be the last written statement in the source program. Thus, the END statement belongs after the GO TO 20 statement. In fact, the compiler would compile the first sequence as a complete program, and then attempt to compile the second sequence as another program.

Self-Test

1. The following statements are written incorrectly. Identify all errors.

(a) GO TO -5 _____

(b) GO TO 10, 20 _____

(c) 20 GO TO 20 _____

(d) 10 FORMAT (I5)
       GO TO 10 _____

(e) I = 10
       GO TO I _____

2. What happens after a PAUSE statement is executed? _____

_____

3. Which of the following are incorrect and why?

(a) SPOT 10 _____

(b) STOP _____

(c) :
    END
    GO TO 100
    :   _____

4. Which of the following statements are written incorrectly and why?

(a) IFF (X-5) 5, 10, 20 _____

(b) IF ((X-A)**5 10, 20, 30 _____

(c) IF (A-B), 10, 20, 30, 40 _____

(d) IF (K-I) 3, 4, 4 _____

(e) IF (Z+Y) 10, 10, 10 _____

(f) 15 IF ((ALPHA*BETA)+ZETA) 5, 10, 15 _____

(g) IF (ALPHA = 5) 5, 10, 15 _____

5. Indicate the statement number to be executed after each of the following statements.

(a) GO TO 25 _____

(b) I = 5
    J = 3
    IF (J-I) 10, 10, 20 _____

(c) X = 5.0
    Y = 3.0
    I = 2
    IF ((X+Y)**I) 10, 15, 38 _____

6. Write an IF statement for the following two examples. (Use your coding form.)

(a) If the variable ALPHA is negative, control goes to statement 5; if positive, to 15; if zero, to 10.

(b) If the expression ((X*Y)**I)+D is negative or zero, control goes to 10; otherwise, to 20.

7. What value will be printed when the following program has been executed?

```
     I = 1
10   J = 2
     K = I + J
     I = I + 1
     IF (I - 3) 10, 10, 20
20   WRITE (6, 30) K
30   FORMAT (I2)
     STOP
     END
```

8. Write a FORTRAN program which adds all integers from 1 to 10. (Use your coding form.)

9. Write a program to convert all integer Fahrenheit temperatures from -40 F to 100 F to Celsius temperatures. The conversion formula is given by

$$C = \frac{5}{9}(F - 32)$$

All Celsius temperatures are to be rounded to two decimal places. You may use an F6.2 format code to obtain the necessary rounding (see frame 53 of Chapter Three). Print the Fahrenheit and Celsius temperatures, in this order. Leave at least ten print positions between the printed values.

10. Here's a bonus question. It's a little more difficult. See how you do. The quadratic equation $Ax^2 + Bx + C = 0$ has real solutions if $B^2 - 4AC \geq 0$. In this case the solutions are given by the equations $x = \dfrac{-B + (B^2 - 4AC)^{1/2}}{2A}$ and $x = \dfrac{-B - (B^2 - 4AC)^{1/2}}{2A}$. Write a program which reads a data card for values of A, B, and C (punched in columns 1-8, 9-16, and 17-24 of the card in F8.2 format), computes the solutions if $B^2 - 4AC \geq 0$, and prints the values of A, B, C, and the two roots. If $B^2 - 4AC < 0$, read the next data card. The last data card has a value of 0 punched in the field for A.

Answers to Self-Test

1. (a) Statement number must be an unsigned integer. (frame 1)
    (b) Only one statement number is allowed. (frame 2)
    (c) A GO TO statement cannot refer to itself. (frame 3)
    (d) A GO TO statement must refer to an executable statement. (frame 5)
    (e) A GO TO statement must contain a statement number. (frame 2)
2. The computer halts and a message PAUSE 00000 is displayed on the system printer. (frame 24)

3. (a) Wrong spelling; should be STOP. (frame 23)
(c) The key word END must appear at the physical end of the program. (frame 26)

4. (a) Wrong spelling and the expression has wrong mode; should be IF (X-5. 0) 5, 10, 20.
(b) Right parenthesis missing.
(c) Exactly three statement numbers are allowed; no comma after the third statement number. Should be IF (A-B) 10, 20, 30.
(e) At least two statement numbers must differ.
(f) An IF statement must not refer to itself.
(g) Only an expression is allowed; ALPHA = 5 is an assignment statement. (frame 6)

5. (a) 25 (frame 1)
(b) 10 (frame 7)
(c) 38 (frame 7)

6. (a) IF (ALPHA) 5, 10, 15 (frame 10)
(b) IF (((X*Y)**I)+D) 10, 10, 20 (frame 10)

7. 5 (frame 6)

8.

```
C
C   INITIALIZE COUNTER (K) AND ACCUMULATOR
C      ISUM TO ZERO
C
       ISUM = 0
       K = 0
C
C   TEST IF COUNTER = 10
C
5      IF (K - 10) 10, 20, 20
C
C   INCREMENT K BY 1 AND ISUM BY K
C
10     K = K + 1
       ISUM = ISUM + K
C
C   BRANCH TO TEST K
C
       GO TO 5
C
C   PRINT ISUM
C
C
```

(continue on next page)

```
20      WRITE (6, 101) ISUM
101     FØRMAT (1X, I4)
        STØP
        END
```

(frames 15-17)

9.

```
C  F REPRESENTS FAHRENHEIT TEMPERATURE
C  C REPRESENTS CELSIUS TEMPERATURE
C  INITIALIZE F TØ -40
C
        F = -40.
C
C  TEST IF F > 100
C
100     IF (F - 100.) 150, 150, 300
C
C  CØMPUTE CELSIUS TEMPERATURE
C
150     C = 5.19 * (F - 32.)
C
C  PRINT F AND C
C
        WRITE (6, 201) F, C
201     FØRMAT (1X, F6.2, 10X, F6.2)
C
C  INCREMENT F BY ØNE AND BRANCH TØ 100
C
250     F = F + 1.
        GØ TØ 100
C
C  STØP
C
300     STØP
        END
```

(frames 15-17)

10.

```
C
C   READ DATA CARD FØR A, B, AND C
C
100     READ (5, 101) A, B, C
101     FØRMAT (F8.2, F8.2, F8.2)
C
C   TEST IF LAST DATA CARD (A = 0)
C
110     IF (A) 120, 200, 120
C
C   CØMPUTE B**2 - 4.*A*C AND TEST TO SEE IF
C       GREATER THAN ØR EQUAL TØ ZERØ
C
120     D = B * B - 4.*A*C
        IF (D) 100, 150, 150
C
C   CØMPUTE SØLUTIØNS X1 AND X2
C
150     X1 = (-B + D**.5)/(2.*A)
        X2 = (-B - D**.5)/(2.*A)
C
C   PRINT A, B, C, X1, X2
C
        WRITE (6, 201) A, B, C, X1, X2
201     FØRMAT (1X, F9.2, 5X, F9.2, 5X, F9.2, 5X,
       -    F10.3, 5X, F10.3)
C
C   READ NEXT DATA CARD AND BRANCH TØ TEST LAST DATA CARD
C
        READ (5, 101) A, B, C
        GØ TØ 110
C
C
C   STØP
C
200     STØP
        END
```

(frame 11)

CHAPTER FIVE
Intermediate Input and Output

By using the material in Chapters Three and Four, you can write some complex programs which can give you alot of output data. However, someone else looking at your output pages might wonder what all the numbers mean and why your output lines are always single-spaced. After a few months, even you may wonder what your printed output represented.

Thus, it is necessary for you to learn some more format control techniques. The material you will study in this chapter will enable you to write program statements which can:

- vary output line spacing and even skip to the next page using carriage control techniques;

- input data appearing on more than one card with one READ statement;

- output data from the computer onto more than one printed line by a single WRITE statement;

- simplify FORMAT statements by using repetition factors and parentheses;

- print textual materials to write headings and to identify output data values, using the H or the single quote (') format codes;

- use an A (alphanumeric) format code for numeric and non-numeric data;

- take into account the record length of the input and output devices you are using;

- read or write more data than the FORMAT statement should allow.

Carriage Control Characters

1. Do you remember The Case of the Vanishing "9"? If you have forgotten, please refer to frames 26-28 of Chapter Three. We solved the problem of the vanishing "9" by always inserting a 1X format code at the beginning of the FORMAT statement, as in the statement on the next page.

```
101    FØRMAT (1X, I3, 10X, F3.1)
```

The 1X code inserts a blank into the first position (carriage control position) of the output record. However, other characters can be placed in the carriage control position for different purposes.

The output record sent to the printer is assembled from data stored in the computer. For example, these statements create an output record as shown.

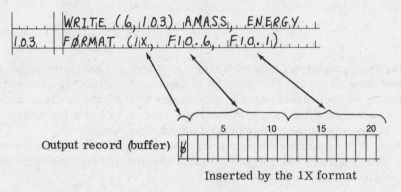

Inserted by the 1X format

The 1X format code only allows the printer to space one line before printing. What do we do if we don't want to space (advance) only one line before printing? Below is a table of the carriage control characters that allow us to control vertical line spacing and advancing to a new page before printing.

First character	Carriage advances before printing
blank (b)	one line
0	two lines
+	no advance (prints on previous line written)
1	to first line of the next page

Note: When we say "carriage control advances x lines before printing," we mean output will appear on the x'th line after the last line printed; that is, x-1 lines are skipped. For x = 2:

skipped line → ＿＿＿＿＿＿＿ ← printed lines
            ＿ ＿ ＿ ＿ ＿ ＿ ＿
            ＿＿＿＿＿＿＿

If either by intention or mistake you insert other characters in the carriage control position of the output record they will generally be ignored, depending on the printer. Check with your computer installation to determine what characters (in addition to +, blank, zero, and 1) are acceptable.

If we send the following characters to the printer, what character will be used for carriage control and which characters will actually be printed?

Character position

| | | | 5 | | | 10 | | | 15 | | | 20 |

Output record

| 0 | 3 | . | 2 | 4 | | 9 | 1 | 2 | 4 | | | | | | | | | | | |

- - - - - - - - - - - - - - - - - -

The character 0 will be used for carriage control. As a result the printer will advance two lines (skip one line). That is, the printer will be on the second available line. The remaining characters will be printed as follows.

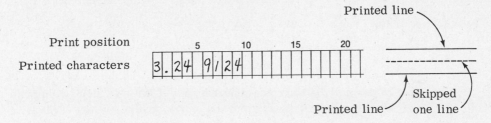

Print position

Printed characters

2. All right, we have got the carriage control characters. But how do we insert them in the output record? You might be wondering also. One method is to surround the carriage control character with single quotes ('). The character enclosed in these quotes is called <u>literal data</u> (which will be covered in detail in frames 26 to 28). As an example, the following FORTRAN statements will command the printer to advance the printing mechanism two lines (that is, one line will be skipped and the printing mechanism will be positioned on the next available line ready to print).

```
      WRITE (6,401) WATCH, THIS
401   FORMAT ('0', F7.2, 3X, F9.1)
```

The format entry '0' inserts the character zero in the first position of the output record. (The output record is sometimes called an <u>output buffer</u>.) Starting in position two, the output record contains the data stored in the variable WATCH. Then, the format code 3X skips print positions 9, 10, and 11 of the output record. Finally, the value of the variable THIS is inserted into the output record beginning at position 12. A schematic representation is shown on the next page.

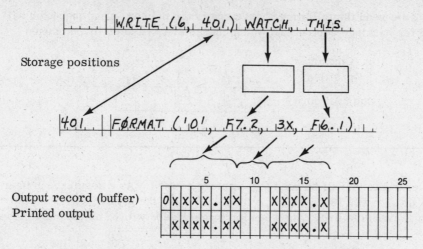

To insert a: blank   use ' ' (leave a space between the quotation marks)
             +   use '+'
             1   use '1'
             0   use '0'

Now some of you may be worrying what happens if we read all 80 columns of a card into storage and want to print out the entire contents of the card on one line. Won't we lose the 80th character since we have added a carriage control character at the beginning of the output record? No. The carriage control character is never printed! Also, most printers have more than 80 print positions, so you will have plenty of room. If you are still worrying about this, take a peek at frame 24.

(a) Rewrite the FORMAT statement (401) above so that the printer will print without advancing.

(b) Rewrite the same statement so that the printer will space one line before printing the data stored in the variables WATCH and THIS.

- - - - - - - - - - - - - - - - - - - -

(a)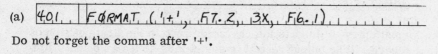

Do not forget the comma after '+'.

(b)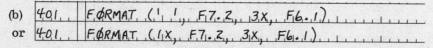

(if you remembered what we did in Chapter Three)

3.   The second technique which enables you to insert characters into a record uses the H format code, which we will cover in more detail later in this chapter. In a nutshell this technique works as follows: The letter H is preceded by the digit 1 and followed by the desired carriage control character.

Here is a table comparing both methods.

'literal format	H format
'b̷'	1Hb̷
'0'	1H0
'1'	1H1
'+'	1H+

Here is the example from frame 2 with the H format code.

```
       WRITE (6,401) WATCH, THIS
401    FORMAT (1H0, F7.2, 3X, F6.1)
```

The H format code is part of all standard FORTRAN systems. On the other hand, the 'literal' format code is a part of the FORTRAN 77 and is implemented by most 1966 FORTRAN compilers. The FORTRAN manual of your system will tell you which features are available. The 'literal' format code is more convenient to use and is preferred by many experienced programmers. Our book also reflects this preference.

The format code 1H+ will cause the printer to _____

while the format code _____ will cause the printer to space two lines before printing.

- - - - - - - - - - - - - - - - - - -

not space before printing; 1H0

4. Here is an example to remind you that you better not forget the carriage control character, and if you do forget it, you might expect some computer room disasters.

A business assigned each of its products a six-digit integer product number, each starting with a 1. When a product is sold, a transaction card is punched for the sale of the item in the following format.

Columns		Variable name
1–6	Product number (6-digit integer of which first digit is 1)	NUMBER
7	Store number (1-digit integer)	NSTORE
10–15	Number sold (5-digit integer)	NSOLD

Notice that we are using meaningful variable names. It is good programming practice to use meaningful variable names since they make a program easier for people to understand.

At the end of the week, all of the transaction cards are collected together and processed by the following program. Device 5 is the card reader and device 6 is the line printer.

```
           ⋮
      NTØTAL = 0
50    READ (5, 62), NUMBER, NSTØRE, NSØLD
62    FØRMAT (I6, I1, 2X, I6)
C  IF NSTØRE FIELD IS SET EQUAL TØ ZERØ
C  PRØGRAM WILL STØP
      IF (NSTØRE) 100, 100, 70
70    NTØTAL = NTØTAL + NSØLD
           ⋮
80    WRITE (6, 62) NUMBER, NSTØRE, NSØLD
           ⋮
      GØ TØ 50
100   WRITE (6, 401), NTØTAL
401   FØRMAT ('1', 30X, I8)
      STØP
      END
```

What do you think will occur each time the statement numbered 80 is executed? (Hint: Look at the specifications for the variable NUMBER.)

The printer will print the data at the top of a new page each time it executes the statement numbered 80 because 1 is put into the carriage control position by the variable NUMBER.

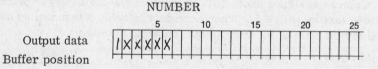

Imagine the computer operator looking dumbfounded at the printer which is shooting out pages at a fantastic rate. Watch the computer operator run to the printer. Run, computer operator, run. Watch him push the STOP button to stop the printer. Listen to him swear!

5.   If we want to start printing in print position 10, after advancing one line, the FORMAT statement looks like this.

```
301   FØRMAT (1X, 9X, ... )
```

Since the 1X inserts a blank into the carriage control position and the 9X inserts nine blanks into the printed line, this statement can be rewritten as

```
301   FØRMAT (10X, "..")
```

where the first blank is taken as the carriage control character.

Write a FORMAT statement which would start printing in print position 34 after advancing one line. Call this statement 103.

- - - - - - - - - - - - - - - - -

```
      103   FØRMAT (1X, 33X, "..")
or    103   FØRMAT (34X, "..")
```

    1X for the carriage control position
and 33X to skip the first 33 print positions
   34X

/ Format Code

6. Some computer applications require reading the values of variables from more than one record (or card). We can use one READ statement to read in the variables, but we need some method to indicate that the values will be found in separate records (cards). The FORTRAN language uses the slash symbol (/) within the FORMAT statement to indicate that the next record is to be processed. In this pair of statements,

```
          READ (5, 128) VALUE1, VALUE2
    128   FØRMAT (2X, F8.2/6X, F5.0)
```

VALUE1 is obtained from columns 3 through 10 in the first record, and VALUE2 is obtained from columns 7 through 11 in the second record.

Note that we do not place a comma either immediately before or after the slash. The reason? In FORTRAN, the comma and slash both serve as separators in a FORMAT statement, but here the similarity ends. The comma instructs the computer to look for another item in the same record; the slash, however, tells the computer that any additional input must come from the next record in sequence.

Write a set of FORTRAN statements to read the value of IN from columns 4 to 8 of a card and the value for KADINK from columns 1 to 5 of the next card. Device 5 is the card reader.

- - - - - - - - - - - - - - - - -

```
          READ (5, 131) IN, KADINK
    131   FØRMAT (3X, I5/I5)
```

7.   From the last frame, you may have deduced the general rule: each slash means ignore the remainder of the current record and obtain the next record. From which record would each of the following variables be read?

```
         READ (5, 131) VAL1, VAL2, VAL3, INTVAL
131.     FORMAT (F7.2/10X, F5.2, F5.2/I3)
```

VAL1 _____   VAL3 _____

VAL2 _____   INTVAL _____

- - - - - - - - - - - - - - - - - -

VAL1, record 1;   VAL2, record 2;   VAL3, record 2;   INTVAL, record 3

8.   Let's try another one which might be tricky. From which record would each of the following variables be read?

```
         READ (5, 131) LENGTH, IWITH, IHITE
131.     FORMAT (///, 15X, I6, I6//I10)
```

LENGTH _____   IHITE _____

IWITH _____

- - - - - - - - - - - - - - - - - -

LENGTH, record 3; IWITH, record 3; IHITE, record 5. When reading the records, the computer refers to the FORMAT statement. Since a slash is written, no data is to be stored for the first record. The computer then reads for the second record, but the second slash instructs it that no data is to be stored there. So the computer reads the third record, and success! Data is to be stored from columns 16 through 21 and 22 through 27. The next slash tells the computer to ignore the rest of the third record. The fourth record is skipped and data from the fifth record is stored, using the I10 format.

9.   Write a FORMAT statement corresponding to the READ statement below,

```
         READ (5, 161) AMASS1, SPEED1, AMASS2, SPEED2
```

so that: Variable is read from Record
          AMASS1   2
          SPEED1   4
          AMASS2   4
          SPEED2   5

All variables are to have a F7.3 format code. Call this statement 161.

- - - - - - - - - - - - - - - - - -

```
161.     FORMAT (//F7.3//F7.3, F7.3/ F7.3)
```

10. In a business operation, we may want to read and process certain data for each employee from an employee master file. Suppose the master file contains five cards (or records) for each employee, each record containing different information. Prepare the applicable READ and FORMAT statements to input the variables below.

Description	Variable	Columns
record 1		
employee number	NUMEMP (integer)	2-10
department number	NUMDEP (integer)	11-13
record 2—skip		
record 3		
job code	JOBCD (integer)	2-3
hourly pay rate		
(xx. xx)	RATE (real)	6-10
record 4—skip		
record 5—skip		

- - - - - - - - - - - - - - - - - - -

```
      READ (5,121) NUMEMP, NUMDEP, JOBCD, RATE
121   FORMAT (1X, I9, I3// 1X, I2, 2X, F5.2//)
```

The first slash after the I3 tells the computer to go to the next record. Since the computer was working with the first record, it then reads the second record. However, there is another slash that follows, which instructs the computer to read the next record, so the computer reads the third record to obtain the values for job code and hourly pay rate. Finally, to get the computer ready for the next set of employee's records, we must use two slashes to skip the rest of the third and fourth records. Now we are at the fifth record, but the parenthesis at the end of the FORMAT statement skips this record.

11. You will, eventually, want to write the data values of a WRITE list on more than one printed line (record). That is, you will want to create many output records (lines) for a single WRITE list. This is done by using the slash (/) format code. That's right, the same / you have used for READ statement formats. For printed output, the slash indicates the termination of a printed line, but it is the carriage control character that actually advances the paper in the printer—with one exception: two or more slashes in succession will cause skipping of lines in the same manner that slashes cause records to be skipped when reading. Consider these statements.

```
      WRITE (6,201) MORE, THAN, ONE, LINE
201   FORMAT ('1', 10X, I3, 2X, F8.2 / 8X,
         F10.7/1H, I6)
```

Notice the variety of carriage control methods that we have used. The printed output will be as shown on the next page.

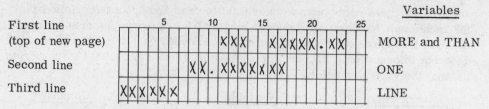

					5					10					15					20					25		Variables

First line (top of new page) — X X X X X X X . X X — MORE and THAN

Second line — X X . X X X X X X — ONE

Third line — X X X X X X — LINE

The following statements will illustrate the use of multiple slashes (two or more) to advance the paper in the printer.

```
       WRITE (6,301) STRE, AKERS, ARE, SWIFT,
      -   RUNN, ERS
301    FORMAT (1X, F10.4, F8.2, F7.2//1X,
      -   F9.3///1X, F8.4, F7.2)
```

The printer will print on Line the Variables with the Format

	Line		Variables		Format
	1		STRE		F10.4
	1		AKERS		F8.2
	1		ARE		F7.2
// skips 1 line	3		SWIFT		F9.3
/// skips 2 lines	6		RUNN		F8.4
	6		ERS		F7.2

Thus, three slashes (///) make the printer skip two lines (advance three lines).

On the print grid we have provided for you below, indicate where the various data values and their associated variables will be printed for the following statements.

```
       WRITE (6,101) HOPE, YOU, GET, TH, IS
101    FORMAT (' ', 2X, F10.3/'0', F6.2//  1H ,
      -   F8.2, F8.2, 2X, I5)
```

Assume ' ' starts the output on the first line below.

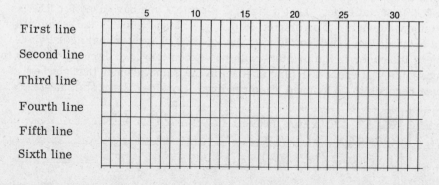

First line
Second line
Third line
Fourth line
Fifth line
Sixth line

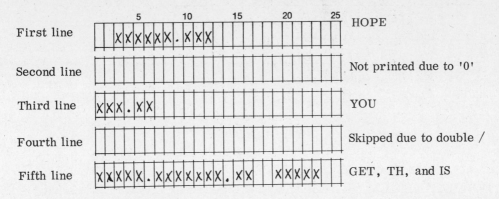

First line — HOPE

Second line — Not printed due to '0'

Third line — YOU

Fourth line — Skipped due to double /

Fifth line — GET, TH, and IS

There is no sixth line, sorry.

12. Write a FORMAT statement, numbered 104, corresponding to this WRITE statement,

```
      WRITE (6,104) A, B, I, D, I3, J, P
```

such that the data is printed as follows.

Variable	is written on Line	with the Format
A	1	F8.3
B	3	F4.1
I	3	I5
D	4	F8.1
I3	7	I7
J	7	I2
P	8	F8.3

- -

```
104    FORMAT (1X, F8.3,//1X, F4.1, I5/1X,
    -    F8.1///1X, I7, I2/1X, F8.3)
or 104 FORMAT (' ', F8.3 /'0', F4.1, I5 /' ',
    -    F8.1 // '0', I7, I2 /' ', F8.3)
```

if you feel fancy today.

13. The / format code allows you to eliminate multiple READ and WRITE statements. The set of WRITE statements and their associated FORMAT statements which follow will write four printer lines.

```
      WRITE (6,104) A
      WRITE (6,104) B
      WRITE (6,104) C
      WRITE (6,104) D
104   FORMAT (1X, F8.2)
```

It can also be written as

```
      WRITE (6,201) A, B, C, D
201   FORMAT (1X, F8.2/1X, F8.2/1X, F8.2/
             1X, F8.2)
```

Write a single READ and FORMAT statement to eliminate the multiple READ statements in this program segment. Number the FORMAT statement 301.

```
      READ (5,103) A, I
      READ (5,103) B, J
      READ (5,103) C, K
103   FORMAT (F8.2, I7)
```

- - - - - - - - - - - - - - - - - -

```
      READ (5,301) A, I, B, J, C, K
301   FORMAT (F8.2, I7/F8.2, I7/F8.2, I7)
```

Repetition Factors

14. In some applications, you might find that one or a series of format specifications repeat themselves. The example below reveals a consecutive repetition of the I7 specifications.

```
121   FORMAT (1X, 3X, I7, I7, 3X, I7, I7)
```

We can abbreviate I7, I7 by writing 2I7, where 2 is called a repetition factor and always precedes the item(s) repeated. In this instance the item repeated is I7; therefore, we have 2I7. The repetition factor indicates how many times the specification code is to be repeated.

See if you can rewrite the above FORMAT statement by using the repetition factor with the I7 specification.

- - - - - - - - - - - - - - - - - -

```
121    FORMAT (1X, 3X, 2I7, 3X, 2I7)
```

15. You may also have noticed another repetition in frame 14, that of the two items 3X and 2I7. In Chapter One we explained how the proper use of parentheses can make an arithmetic statement easier to understand and less ambiguous. Suppose we enclose the repeated items (or groups of format specifications) in parentheses. We obtain the following.

```
121    FORMAT (1X, (3X, 2I7), (3X, 2I7))
```

Since the two underlined items are repetitive, we can use the technique described in frame 14 to reduce this statement to

```
121    FORMAT (1X, 2(3X, 2I7))
```

Notice the placement of commas. The general rule is that a comma must follow each specification, except for the last within the FORMAT statement. The specification within the parentheses—(3X, 2I7)—is treated as a specification for itself. For this reason no comma follows the 2I7, but one does follow the close parenthesis: (3X, 2I7), (3X, 2I7).

Try to rewrite the following FORMAT statements using repetition factors wherever applicable.

```
(a)  123    FORMAT (F3.0, 4X, I2, I2, F3.1, 4X, I2, I2, F3.1)
(b)  124    FORMAT (7X, 3I2, F7.3, 2X, 3I2, F7.3, 2X, 3I2)
(c)  125    FORMAT (2(1X, I4), 3X, 2(1X, I4), 4X, F6.1)
```

Hint: 4X can be written as 3X, 1X.

- - - - - - - - - - - - - - - - - -

```
(a)  123    FORMAT (F3.0, 2(4X, 2I2, F3.1))
```

Underlining the specifications which are repetitive, we have
      123   FORMAT (F3.0, 4X, I2, I2, F3.1, 4X, I2, I2, F3.1)
We then rewrite the statement (mentally).
      123   FORMAT (F3.0, (4X, 2I2, F3.1), (4X, 2I2, F3.1))
And finally,
      123   FORMAT (F3.0, 2(4X, 2I2, F3.1))

```
(b)  124    FORMAT (7X, 2(3I2, F7.3, 2X), 3I2)
or   124    FORMAT (7X, 3I2, 2(F7.3, 2X, 3I2))
```

```
(c)  125    FORMAT (2(2(1X, I4), 3X), 1X, F6.1)
```

If you were correct for statement 125, go on to frame 16. Otherwise, here is an explanation. Let's underline the repetitive groups in the statement.

     125   FORMAT (2(1X, I4), 3X, 2(1X, I4), 3X, 1X, F6.1)

Note that 3X, 1X means the same thing as 4X. From this we have

     125   FORMAT ((2(1X, I4), 3X), (2(1X, I4), 3X), 1X, F6.1)

which we can condense to

     125   FORMAT (2(2(1X, I4), 3X), 1X, F6.1)

16. The use of repetition factors and parentheses can simplify FORMAT statement coding. However, such a use may also create errors for the unwary programmer. Consider this statement.

| 201 | FORMAT (1X, F8.2/1X, F8.2/1X, F8.2/1X, F8.2) |

Statement 201 under the demand of the statement

| | READ (5, 201) A, B, C, D |

will read four data cards. Using parentheses for grouping 1X, F8.2/ factors, we obtain

| 201 | FORMAT ((1X, F8.2/), (1X, F8.2/), (1X, F8.2/), 1X, F8.2) |

which, using repetition factors, becomes

| 201 | FORMAT (3(1X, F8.2/), (1X, F8.2) |

This is, of course, equivalent to the first FORMAT statement.

However, if your sense of beauty and symmetry is offended by such an awkward looking expression and you have the urge to reduce this even more to

| 201 | FORMAT (4(1X, F8.2/)) |

you will get into trouble. Can you tell us why? _____

_____

- - - - - - - - - - - - - - - -

Your answer should be something like: This FORMAT statement will use five cards. After the data value of D is read from the fourth data card, the / causes the next record to be read—but nothing from this card is stored in the computer's memory.

17. Let's test your understanding by going in reverse. Here are some examples using repetition factors. Expand each of the following FORMAT statements until you are left with no repetition factors or sets of parentheses.

| 126 | FORMAT (2(3X, F2.0, /X, 2I2), 3F7.2, (1X, 2I3) |
| 127 | FORMAT (F7.1, 2(2F7.1, I2), 2X, 3I9.) |

- - - - - - - - - - - - - - - -

126	FORMAT (3X, F2.0, 1X, I2, I2, 3X, F2.0, 1X,
-	I2, I2, F7.2, F7.2, F7.2, 1X, I3, I3)
127	FORMAT (F7.1, F7.1, F7.1, I2, F7.1, F7.1,
-	I2, 2X, I9, I9, I9)

18. Repeating groups may also contain slashes. Rewrite the following FORMAT statement using repetition factors.

| 133 | FORMAT (I3/F6.2, F6.2, I4/F6.2, F6.2, |
| - | I4/I5) |

- - - - - - - - - - - - - - - - - - - -

| | 133 | FORMAT (I3/2(2F6.2, I4/), I5) |
| or | 133 | FORMAT (I3, 2(/2F6.2, I4)/I5) |

19. This and the next three frames contain practice problems. If you wish, you may skip to frame 23.

Here is a compact FORMAT statement. Expand it so that there are no repetition factors.

| 134 | FORMAT (2(/ 2F8.3, 2I1).) |

- - - - - - - - - - - - - - - - -

| 134 | FORMAT (/F8.3, F8.3, I1, I1/F8.3, F8.3, |
| - | I1, I1) |

20. The FORMAT statement below can be rewritten using repetition factors; do it.

| 132 | FORMAT (F6.3, I3, F4.1, F6.3, I3, F4.1, I5) |

- - - - - - - - - - - - - - - - - -

| 132 | FORMAT (2(F6.3, I3, F4.1), I5) |

21. Now try expanding the FORMAT statement on the next page into one with no repetition factors.

```
1,35     FØRMAT (F3.0/3(I2, 1X/))
```

- - - - - - - - - - - - - - - - -

```
1,35     FØRMAT (F3.0/I2, 1X/I2, 1X/I2, 1X/)
```

22. Rewrite this FORMAT statement using repetition factors.

```
1,36     FØRMAT (I6, 1X/I6, 1X/I6, 1X)
```

- - - - - - - - - - - - - - - -

```
      1,36     FØRMAT (I6, 1X, 2(/I6, 1X))
or    1,36     FØRMAT (2(I6, 1X/), I6, 1X)
```

23. Frames 15 and 16 show how parentheses are used to group format codes. We will now use parentheses to group grouped format codes. This FORMAT statement

```
1,21     FØRMAT (3X, F6.2, I4, F6.2, I4, 3X, I2, F6.2, I4,
    -      F6.2, I4, 3X, I2, F12.7)
```

can be changed to

```
1,21     FØRMAT (3X, (F6.2, I4), (F6.2, I4), 3X, I2, (F6.2,
    -      I4), (F6.2, I4), 3X, I2, F12.7)
```

and further reduced to

```
1,21     FØRMAT (3X, (2(F6.2, I4), 3X, I2), (2(F6.2, I4),
    -      3X, I2), F12.7)
```

and finally

```
1,21     FØRMAT (3X, 2(2(F6.2, I4), 3X, I2), F12.7)
```

This is called a <u>nest</u> of group format specifications. A nest consists of groups contained within groups. This example is the deepest nest allowed in FORMAT statements. The rule is: <u>A group within another group cannot itself contain another group</u>. This rule only applies to FORMAT statements and not to arithmetic or logical statements (see Chapter Six for these). Thus

```
3,0,1    FØRMAT (2(3(F10.2, I7), 2X, 4(I3, I5)), I4)
```

is allowed since the (F10.2, I7) and (I3, I5) groups contain no other group. Note that the parenthesis count never can exceed three.

```
301.    FØRMAT.(2 (3 (F10.2,I7).,  2X,  4(I3, I5)).,  I4).
        +1 +2 +3              +2          +3      +2+1      0
```

In the statement below, however, the parenthesis count is too high.

```
401.    FØRMAT.(I4, 3(2X, 3(I4, 2(3X, F8.2), I3), F8.2), I3)
        +1      +2    +3    +4          +3    +2        +1      0
                            ↑
```

Statement 401 is not allowed since the group (I4, 2(3X, F8.2), I3) contains the inner group (3X, F8.2), while itself being contained in the group 3(2X, 3(I4, 2(3X, F8.2), I3), F8.2).

(a) Is this statement allowed? _____

```
302    FORMAT  (IX, 2(I5, 3X, 2(I4, F10.3, 2(F8.2)), 3X).,
       -     F10.3).
```

(b) Is this statement allowed? _____

```
104.    FØRMAT  (((2X, I5)., 3(I4, F8.2, 2X)., F4.1)),
```

(c) Use parentheses to group the format codes in this statement as much as possible.

```
101.    FØRMAT  (IX, F5.2, F10.4, 2X, I5, F10.4, 2X, I5, 4X,
        -    F5.2, F10.4, 2X, I5, F10.4, 2X, I5, 4X, I1).
```

- - - - - - - - - - - - - - - - - -

(a) Not allowed. Using the parenthesis count, this count becomes four at the left parenthesis of (F8.2).
(b) Allowed. The parenthesis count never exceeds three.
(c) The original FORMAT statement can be reduced to

```
101    FØRMAT  (IX, F5.2, 2(F10.4, 2X, I5), 4X, F5.2,
       -    2(F10.4, 2X, I5), 4X, I1)
```

which reduces to

```
101.    FØRMAT  (IX, 2(F5.2, 2(F10.4, 2X, I5), 4X), I1).
```

Record Length

24. The format specifications define the location, width, and data type of each field in an input or output record. Furthermore, to illustrate, if you specify

many variables to be read from one 80-column card, be careful that the sum of all the field widths does not exceed 80. To test for legality, add all field widths including the skips. For example, this statement is legal.

```
101   FØRMAT (5F10.5, 5X, 5I5)
```

But this statement is illegal.

```
201   FØRMAT (8F15.5)
```

Are the following statements legal for an 80-column card input?

(a)
```
301   FØRMAT (3I5, 15X, 7F10.3)
```

(b)
```
701   FØRMAT (I5, 7I3, 10X, F10.4, 5X, I3)
```

- - - - - - - - - - - - - - - - - -

(a) FORMAT statement 301 is illegal since 3I5 requires 15 columns

                                15X requires 15 columns

                            7F10.3 requires <u>70</u> columns

                                     Total   100 columns

(b) FORMAT statement 701 is legal since I5 requires 5 columns

                                7I3 requires 21 columns

                            10X requires 10 columns

                      F10.4 requires 10 columns

                              5X requires 5 columns

                              I3 requires <u>3</u> columns

                                     Total   54 columns

25. Before we continue, we should discuss record length for printers. The record length for a printer is equal to the number of print positions on the printer plus one (for the carriage control character). You should find out the number of print positions on your printer since if you exceed the record length with a FORMAT statement your compiler may refuse to accept the statement. A word to the wise should be sufficient; however, we know better.

Let's assume we have a printer with 132 print positions. Thus, the maximum record length is 133 (132 + 1 carriage control position). These statements will work fine with our printer.

```
        WRITE (6, 302) A, GØØD, GUY
302   FØRMAT ('1', 25X, F10.4, 50X, F10.2, 20X, F5.1)
```

However, the output from the following will not fit on one line.

```
        WRITE (6, 501) A, BAD, EGG
501   FØRMAT ('1', 50X, F10.4, 80X, F12.7)
```

Will these statements work with our printer?

	WRITE (6,801) IM, NØT, SURE
801	FØRMAT ('0', 60X, I5, 30X, I10, 5X, F12.7)

- - - - - - - - - - - - - - - - - -

Yes, because the record length is 123. Remember to count the carriage control character.

T Format Code

26. The X format code allows you to space between fields for output and input. If there are many fields you must count the spaces between adjacent fields. This is a lot of work especially when you can use the T format code. The T code allows you to specify where a field starts for output and input. As an example

	WRITE (12, 150) A, IN3, D
150	FØRMAT (1X, T31, F12.2, T51, I6, T66, F8.4)

would cause the printing of the values of A, IN3, and D to start at print positions 30, 50, and 65 on a page.

|← A →| | IN3 | |← D →|

3	4	5	5	6	7
0	2	0	5	5	2

Why does T31 imply to start printing at position 30? When a print buffer is filled by the CPU, the first character in the buffer is used for carriage control. You must specify a number one more than the position you wish to start printed output: hence T51 will start the value for IN3 at print position 50. This will vary between FORTRAN compilers. Check your installation's FORTRAN manual. This makes formatting a lot easier since it is not necessary to count the spaces between the fields. You are specifying the absolute location of the start of the field by using the T code. When you use the X code you specify a relative position between fields. The T and X codes can be mixed in a format statement. You are even allowed to write information backwards on a line by specifying T positions with decreasing values. The statements above can be written as:

	WRITE (12, 180) D, IN3, A
180	FØRMAT (1X, T66, F8.4, T51, I6, T31, F12.2)

There is one problem though. If you use the T codes only to position all of the output, you may be in for some extra work if someone says "That looks very neat but could you move the whole thing to the left by two spaces?"

Create some WRITE and FORMAT statements to produce the following report format. Device 6 is the printer.

```
2            3           5
7            8           2
SALSMN #     ANN. SALES  ANN. COMMIS.

   XXXX        XXXXXXXX    XXXXX.XX

2            3           5
9            9           3
```

```
        WRITE (6, 140)
140.    FØRMAT (/IX, T28, 'SALSMN #', T39, 'ANN.',
      -    'SALES', T53, 'ANN. COMMIS.'/)
        WRITE (6, 150) ISALES, IANSLS, CØMIS
150.    FØRMAT (/IX, T30, I4, T40, I8, T54, F8.2)
```

27. The T format code can also be used to reread either a part of, or a complete input record. Suppose a record contains, in position 10, a record-type code (either 1 or 2). If the code is 1 then positions 21 through 32 contain two integers of format I6. If the code is 2 then positions 21 to 32 contain two real numbers of format F5.1 and F7.3, respectively. The problem with reading such a record is that it may be impossible to predict the value of the record-type code before the record is read. To eliminate having to guess the value of the code, we will read the record twice: the first time assuming the values are integers and the second time assuming the values are real. Notice that we will only use one READ statement. Here is our solution

```
        READ (11, 300) ITYPE, I1, I2, R1, R2
300.    FØRMAT (T10, I1, T21, I6, I6, T21, F5.1, F7.3
```

We do not reread the record-type code in position 10 since it is not necessary to do so.

There are many other applications which use FORTRAN's ability to reread a field or fields. Here is one you can do now.

Positions 11 through 14 of a record contain an employee number. Position 21 of the same record contains a 'check digit'. The check digit is supposed to be equal to the remainder after the sum of the digits of the employee number is divided by 9. This type of check digit is used to try to identify mispunched numbers. As an example, employee number 5262 would have a check digit of 6 since (5+2+6+2)=15 and 15/9 leaves a remainder of 6.

Write a READ and FORMAT statement which stores the whole employee number in NEMPLY and the digits of the employee number in N1, N2, N3, and N4. The check digit will be stored in NCHECK.

```
       READ (5, 100). NEMPLY, M1, N2, N3, N4, MCHECK
100.   FØRMAT (T11, I4, T11, 4I1, T21, I1)
```

The T format code can be very useful, indeed!

Literal Data—H Format Code

28. A FORTRAN program can write fixed textual materials such as messages or report headings. These messages will be the same each time the program is run. These textual materials are commonly called <u>literal data</u>. All such literal data must appear in a FORMAT statement. No item in a WRITE statement list corresponds to the literal data in a FORMAT statement. Literal data is printed when a WRITE statement refers to a FORMAT statement which contains literal data. The standard form for literal data is

```
301.   FØRMAT(IX, 20HTHIS IS LITERAL DATA),
```

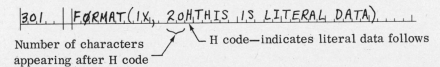

Number of characters
appearing after H code

H code—indicates literal data follows

This statement shows there are three parts necessary to write literal data:

1. an integer (in this case, 20) indicating the number of characters (including special characters and blanks) that appear after the format code H;
2. the format code H, indicating that literal data follows;
3. the literal data.

This data is printed by using these statements.

```
       WRITE (6, 301).
301.   FØRMAT (IX, 20HTHIS IS LITERAL DATA)
```

Complete the following FORMAT statement.

```
251.   FØRMAT (IX,    THIS DØES NØT LØØK SØ EASY)
```

- - - - - - - - - - - - - - - - - - - -

```
251.   FØRMAT (IX, 26HTHIS DØES NØT LØØK SØ EASY)
                   1234567891111111112222222
                         0123456789 0123456
```

Counting the amount of characters and blanks can be a source of error. We must count accurately or the FORMAT statement will not compile.

Literal Data—Another Way

29. Counting characters and blanks is a common source of error. Most 1966 FORTRAN compilers offered an alternative form for writing literal data. Furthermore, this alternative form became part of the FORTRAN 77 standard. This statement

```
251     FORMAT ( 1X, 20HTHIS IS A BETTER WAY)
```

can be written as

```
251     FORMAT ( 1X, 'THIS IS A BETTER WAY')
```

The literal data is enclosed in apostrophes or with asterisks (*). Check your computer's FORTRAN manual to see what you can use. By using apostrophes (or asterisks) you do not have to count the characters and blanks of the literal data. So, to print out FEE, FI, FO, FUM! I SMELL THE GLORY OF APOSTROPHES, you simply use the following statements.

```
        WRITE (6, 301)
301     FORMAT (' FEE, FI, FO, FUM! I SMELL THE GLORY'
       -    ' OF APOSTROPHES')
```

We placed the carriage control character (a blank here) before FEE in the FORMAT statement inside the apostrophes. Normally our WRITE statement would also include data values from storage areas. However, in our example the WRITE statement had no list (since no data values were being written from storage areas). In this Guide, we will use apostrophes to indicate literal data.

Write program statements to print I LIKE THIS BETTER on a printer (device 6). Use a blank for carriage control. Number the FORMAT statement 21.

- - - - - - - - - - - - - - - - - - - -

```
        WRITE (6, 21)
21      FORMAT (' I LIKE THIS BETTER')
```

30. If you are going to use apostrophes to indicate literal data in FORMAT statements, you should be aware of the following trap.

```
        WRITE (6, 101)
101     FORMAT (' MRS. O'REILLY'S COW')
```

No FORTRAN compiler will pass that FORMAT statement since it is incorrect! "Incorrect?" you say. "What's wrong with it?" The two (yes, two) errors in the statement are the apostrophes between the O and R and the Y and S. This is not an anti-Irish computer; but, you see, a compiler cannot understand English and thus the apostrophe after the O would indicate the end of literal data. The next character, R, is not a comma or other format code, thus the computer would flag the R as an error. To indicate a literal apostrophe, use two apostrophes. As an example, DON'T becomes DON''T.

With this last example in mind, correctly complete the following.

```
        WRITE (6,101)
101     FORMAT (' MRS. O_REILLY_S COW')
```

```
        WRITE (6,101)
101     FORMAT (' MRS. O''REILLY''S COW')
```

With the H format code, however, each apostrophe is a character; do not replace each literal apostrophe with two apostrophes. Here is our example.

```
101     FORMAT (20H MRS. O'REILLY'S COW)
```

31. Now you will learn how to write those marvelous headings you see printed from other people's programs. We will assume a printed line has 132 print positions. Suppose you want to print the following heading.

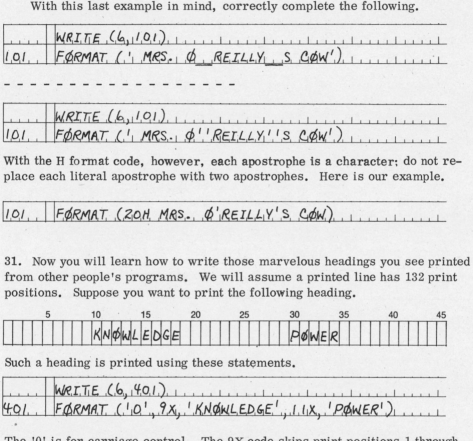

Such a heading is printed using these statements.

```
        WRITE (6,401)
401     FORMAT ('0',9X,'KNOWLEDGE',11X,'POWER')
```

The '0' is for carriage control. The 9X code skips print positions 1 through 9. The 11X code skips positions 19 through 29.

Write statements to cause the computer printer to print at the top of the page the following heading.

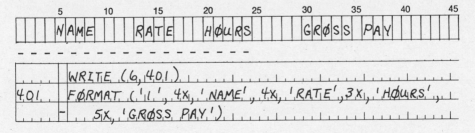

```
        WRITE (6,401)
401     FORMAT ('1', 4X, 'NAME', 4X, 'RATE',3X, 'HOURS',
        -  5X, 'GROSS PAY')
```

In our example we have only shown a small part of a printed line. Generally you use a whole printed line. In such a case you will want to use a print chart (as shown in reduced form on page 178) to organize positions for data values and headings.

32. How do you decide where you should place headings on a page? Most general information headings such as report names, dates, and so on are centered at the top of a page. Several lines should be skipped before printing other lines. Column headings are usually centered above the data they specify. You should try to arrange the output data so that adjacent columns are separated. A rule of thumb is to use at least four print positions between adjacent columns (if you can spare the room). This increases readability.

You should use the print chart to map out positions for data and headings. If your printed output doesn't look just right to you, change your FORMAT statements a little. See frame 16 of Chapter One for examples of headings and spacing of columnar output data.

33. Now let's use some WRITE statements that include data values as well as literal data.

```
      |RATE = 3.5
      |TIME = 2.4
      |DISTAN = RATE * TIME
      |WRITE (6,701) RATE, TIME, DISTAN
701   |FORMAT (' RATE=',F10.3,' TIME=',F8.2,
   -  |       ' DISTANCE=',F12.7)
```

Or, if you prefer the H format specification, here is a FORMAT statement to suit you.

```
701   |FORMAT (6H RATE=,F10.3,6H TIME=,F8.2,
   -  |       10H DISTANCE=,F12.7)
```

Either of these FORMAT statements would cause an output as follows:

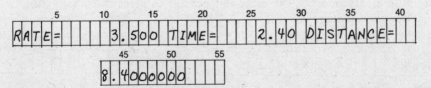

Isn't this a nice method of displaying the values of RATE, TIME, and DISTAN? As the arrows show, all items in the WRITE list correspond to format codes and not to the literal data.

You should also notice the blank just before the literals TIME and DIS-TANCE. These blanks cause a space between: the third fractional digit of

132/10/6 PRINT CHART   PROG. ID. _FRBNY780_   PAGE _1_

(SPACING **132** POSITION SPAN, AT 10 CHARACTERS PER INCH, 6 LINES PER VERTICAL INCH)   DATE _8/23/76_

PROGRAM TITLE _FRBNY QUARTERLY ADJUSTED FIGURES_

PROGRAMMER OR DOCUMENTALIST: _I. M. GOLDFINGER_

CHART TITLE _QUARTERLY ADJUSTED FIGURES_

NOTE: Dimensions on this sheet vary with humidity. Exact measurements should be calculated or scaled with a ruler rather than with the lines on this chart.

FRBNY780-1-3

FEDERAL RESERVE BANK OF NEW YORK

QUARTERLY ADJUSTED FIGURES

197X - 197X

(MILLIONS OF DOLLARS)

1 9 7 X

I   II   III   IV

1 9 7 X

I   II   III   IV

TOTAL RESERVES

GOLD STOCK

FOREIGN EXCHANGE

NET IMF POSITION

U. S. ASSETS

INTERBANK CLAIMS

TOTAL CLAIMS

LOANS TO MEMBER BANKS

F. R. FLOAT

VAULT CASH

TIME DEPOSITS

DEMAND DEPOSITS

XXXXXX   XXXXXX   XXXXXX   XXXXXX   XXXXXX   XXXXXX   XXXXXX   XXXXXX

XXXXXX

XXXXX X

XXXXXX

XXXXXX   XXXXXX   XXXXXX   XXXXXX   XXXXXX   XXXXXX   XXXXXX   XXXXXX

XXXXXX   XXXXXX   XXXXXX   XXXXXX   XXXXXX   XXXXXX   XXXXXX   XXXXXX

XXXXXX

XXXXXX

XXXXXX

XXXXXX

XXXXXX

CARRIAGE CONTROL

RATE (the 0) and the literal TIME; and the second fractional digit of TIME (the 0) and the literal DISTANCE. The equal signs appearing in the literals RATE=, TIME=, and DISTANCE= also separate the literal words from the printed data values.

What would be printed by the following program segment?

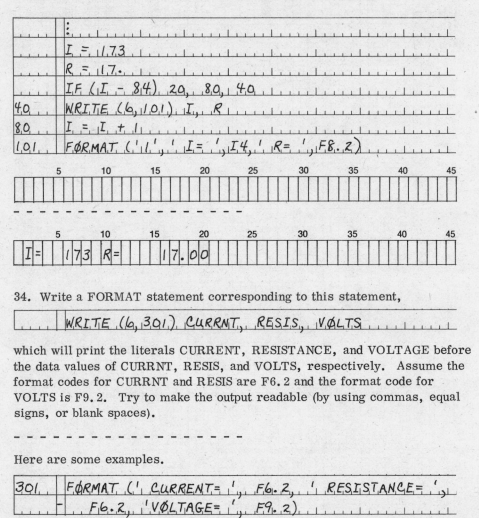

34. Write a FORMAT statement corresponding to this statement,

```
        WRITE (6,301) CURRNT, RESIS, VØLTS
```

which will print the literals CURRENT, RESISTANCE, and VOLTAGE before the data values of CURRNT, RESIS, and VOLTS, respectively. Assume the format codes for CURRNT and RESIS are F6.2 and the format code for VOLTS is F9.2. Try to make the output readable (by using commas, equal signs, or blank spaces).

- - - - - - - - - - - - - - - -

Here are some examples.

```
301    FØRMAT (' CURRENT= ', F6.2, ' RESISTANCE= ',
   -      F6.2, 'VØLTAGE= ', F9.2)
```

or, spreading things out a bit more:

```
301    FØRMAT (' CURRENT= ', F6.2, 10X,
   -      ' RESISTANCE=', F6.2, 10X, 'VØLTAGE=',
   -      F9.2)
```

In this last statement it wasn't necessary to leave a blank before the literals RESISTANCE and VOLTAGE since the 10X format codes ensure blanks between the data values and literals.

A Format Code

35. Your own life experiences have suggested to you that computers can process alphanumeric data—data consisting of numeric and non-numeric characters (i.e., names, addresses, and so on). The A format code will enable you to write programs which transmit characters to and from variables and assign characters from one variable to another variable. A variable which contains alphanumeric characters should not be used in arithmetic operations (after all, when did you last square an address?). Let us consider the following:

```
        READ (5, 100) B
100     FORMAT (F4.0)
```

These statements identify the storage location labeled B which is to be loaded with a real value transmitted from the first four columns of a punched card.

Now, consider this pair of statements.

```
        READ (5, 100) B
100     FORMAT (A4)
```

The READ statement will store in location B alphanumeric data (such as alphabetic characters, numerical digits, or special characters) from the first four characters of the input record. The variable which stores alphanumeric data may be either INTEGER or REAL (or CHARACTER, which we discuss in Frame 37, of this chapter). The number of characters stored by such a variable, however, is dependent upon your installation's implementation of the INTEGER and REAL variables. Unless otherwise stated, we will assume that both INTEGER and REAL variables can store four alphanumeric characters.

Try an exercise.

(a) Write a pair of statements to read a punched card as shown below, and store the data ROME in the variable HAPPY.

```
            1 1 1 1
    123456789 0 1 2 3      Card columns
    ƀƀƀƀƀƀƀƀƀƀROME          Card values
```

(b) Write a pair of statements to write the data contained in the variable HOOKER commencing in print position 11 on the printer. (Note: The variable HOOKER contains the data RAIN.)

- - - - - - - - - - - - - - - - - -

(a)   READ (5, 100) HAPPY
    100 FORMAT (9X, A4)
(b)   WRITE (6, 100) HOOKER
    100 FORMAT (11X, A4)

36. The general form of the A format code is:

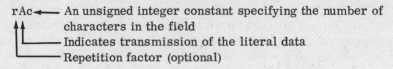

rAc◄── An unsigned integer constant specifying the number of
characters in the field
── Indicates transmission of the literal data
── Repetition factor (optional)

It is wise to discuss several points before we proceed.

Alphanumeric (sometimes called alphameric) data can be stored in integer, real, logical, double precision or character type variables (see Chapter Eight for these)—but don't try arithmetic with variables storing alphanumeric data.

The computer you use determines how many alphanumeric symbols can be stored in a variable. Double precision variables would store eight or more characters. Check your computer FORTRAN manual to find the maximum number of characters which can be stored for each variable type.

In many applications a character string is too long to be represented by any one variable. For example, the Police Department wants to store data in connection with an individual's driver's license. A typical number might be F18883Ƀ88848Ƀ283531-46. This number contains twenty-two characters, and in FORTRAN, cannot be stored in one real or integer variable. In fact we need six such variables (6 x 4 = 24). Here is a program segment which reads and writes such a character string.

	READ (5, 101), L1, L2, L3, L4, L5, L6
101	FORMAT (5A4, A2)
	WRITE (6, 151), L1, L2, L3, L4, L5, L6
151	FORMAT (11X, 5A4, A2)

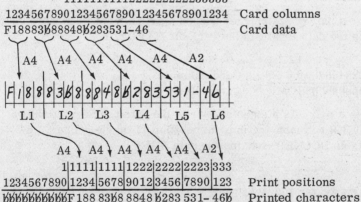

```
                 1111111111222222222233333
                 12345678901234567890123456789001234   Card columns
                 F18883Ƀ88848Ƀ283531-46               Card data
```

```
         A4    A4   A4   A4    A4    A2

       |F|1|8|8|8|3|Ƀ|8|8|8|4|8|Ƀ|2|8|3|5|3|1|-|4|6|
         L1  |  L2  |  L3  |  L4  |  L5  |  L6

         A4   A4   A4   A4   A4  A2
```

```
              1|1111|1111|1222|2222|2223|333
       1234567890|1234|5678|9012|3456|7890|123     Print positions
       ƁƁƁƁƁƁƁƁƁƁƁF188 83Ƀ8 8848 Ƀ283 531- 46Ƀ     Printed characters
```

A punched card has the data:

```
              1111111111122222222223333
       12345678 90 123 456 789 01 234 56 78 90 12    Punched card columns
       THISƁISƁAƁLONGƁSENTENCEƁTOƁPUNCH             Punched characters
```

Code FORTRAN statements to read and write this character data, starting in print position 10 of a new page on a **printer,** (device 6).

- - - - - - - - - - - - - - - - - -

Here's a good way to do it.

. . . .	READ (5, 101), L1, L2, L3, L4, L5, L6, L7, L8
101	FØRMAT (8A4)
. . . .	WRITE (6, 151), L1, L2, L3, L4, L5, L6, L7, L8
151	FØRMAT ('1', 9X, 8A4)

The use of array variables (Chapter Seven) and implied DO loops (Chapter Nine) can considerably shorten the lists in both the READ and WRITE lists.

Character Variables

37. If you don't have a FORTRAN 77 compiler you should probably skip this frame. We mentioned before (frame 35) that FORTRAN allows four alphanumeric characters to be stored in a variable. But what if you want to store a social security number (9 characters long) or a name (up to 12 characters long)? What do you do?

Well, you can use many variables and store four characters in each variable or you can use a character variable. Let's say we want to store a ten character **alphanumeric stock code.** By placing the statement at the beginning of a program

CHARACTER * 10 STOCK

we can then read in a stock code from a record by using the statements

. . . .	READ (11, 200) STOCK
200	FØRMAT (A10)

This is definitely more natural than dividing the stock code into four character (or less) chunks. Notice how the format code A10 is used to read in ten alphanumeric characters. We have postponed a larger discussion of CHARACTER variables to Chapter 8.

Character variables can be used for both input and output. If your program contains two character variables FNAME (8 characters) and LNAME (12 characters), create a WRITE and FORMAT statement to print out the value of LNAME followed by a comma and then the value of FNAME.

- - - - - - - - - - - - - - - - - -

. . . .	WRITE (6, 100) LNAME, FNAME
100	FORMAT (/1X, A12, ',', A8)

FORMAT Statement Repetitions

38. Look carefully at this pair of statements.

> READ (5, 600) A, B, C, D, E
> 600   FORMAT (F10.3, F6.2)

The variable list in the READ statement has five items. However, the FOR-
MAT statement has only two specifications in the list and thus will only anticipate two values on a record. When the READ statement is executed the computer refers to the FORMAT statement and, as a result, stores data from the
first ten positions as the value of A and the next six positions as the value of
B. Because the FORMAT statement indicates only two variables are to be read
from a record, the third variable in the READ list, C, will have to come
from the next record. So the computer reads the next record and stores data
from the first ten positions as the value of C and the next six positions as the
value of D.

   The general rule is: When the list of variables in the READ statement is
greater than the number of format specifications in the FORMAT statement,
a single READ statement causes additional records to be read until all the required data is obtained.

   Will the value for the variable E be read from the second, third, or
fourth record?_____

- - - - - - - - - - - - - - - - - - - -

Variable E will be obtained from the third record.

39. Upon storing all of the values requested by the READ list, the computer
will ignore any remaining specifications in the FORMAT statement. In the

statements below, how many records are read?_____

	READ (5, 101) A, B, C, D, E, F, G
101	FORMAT (2F5.2, F4.1)

- - - - - - - - - - - - - - - - - - -

Three records (Positions 6 to 80 of the third record will be ignored because
values have been stored for all variables in the READ list.)

40. Let's reduce the FORMAT statement in frame 13 (numbered 301) to a
simpler form. Since the purpose of the FORMAT statement was to read
three records, it was necessary to use these statements.

	READ (5, 301) A, I, B, J, C, K
301	FORMAT (F8.2, I7/F8.2, I7/F8.2, I7)

However, since a FORMAT statement will be used repeatedly until the READ statement list is satisfied, these statements can be rewritten as:

```
       READ (5, 301) A, I, B, J, C, K
30 1   FØRMAT (F8.2, I7)
```

Write a set of FORTRAN statements to read the:

Value	from Record	with Format
A1	1	F8.3
A2	1	F7.0
B1	2	F8.3
B2	2	F7.0
X	3	F8.3

Assume the values of A1, B1 and X are found in positions 10-17 of each record, and the values of A2 and B2 are found in positions 20-27 of each record.

- - - - - - - - - - - - - - - - - - - -

```
       READ (5, 301) A1, A2, B1, B2, X
30 1   FØRMAT (9X, F8.3, 2X, F7.0)
```

41. Rewrite the FORMAT statement below without using slash marks.

```
       WRITE (6, 201) A, B, C, D
20 1   FØRMAT (1X, F8.2/1X, F8.2/1X, F8.2/1X, F8.2)
```

- - - - - - - - - - - - - - - - - -

```
       WRITE (6, 201) A, B, C, D
20 1   FØRMAT (1X, F8.2)
```

This example also came from frame 13. Isn't life nice now?

42. These statements will obviously read values for A, I, and C from one card.

```
       READ (5, 201) A, I, C, J, E, K
20 1   FØRMAT (F4.1, (I2, F8.3))
```

What happens next? Well, the values for J and E will be read from the next card (record) using the format codes I2 and F8.3, respectively. Why didn't format control return to the first format specification F4.1? The answer is that the set of parentheses forming the group (I2, F8.3) of format codes caused the format control to return to this specification. When a READ or

WRITE statement demands more format codes than the FORMAT statement "appears" to have, format control always returns to the last left parenthesis in the FORMAT statement and thus to a new record. Thus, the value of K is read from the next card (the third card) with the format code I2.

These statements cause the printer to write the data values of each variable as follows.

. . . . .	WRITE (6, 201), R1, I2, R3, I4, R5, I6, R7, I8, R9 . . . .
201 . .	FØRMAT (1X, F8.2, 2(1X, I3, F6.1)) . . . . . .

Variable	Format code	Line record	
R1	F8.2	1	
I2	I3	1	
R3	F6.1	1	
I4	I3	1 ⎞ These come from the
R5	F6.1	1 ⎠ repetition factor 2.
I6	I3	2 ⎫ These come from the group
R7	F6.1	2 ⎪ repetition since format
I8	I3	2 ⎪ control returns to the last
R9	F6.1	2 ⎭ group repetition.

A new record is read whenever format control returns to the group repetition. The format code 1X simply advances the printer one line before printing the values of I6, R7, I8, and R9.

Does it blow your mind? Read this frame again before answering the question. Given these statements, please complete the following table.

. . . . .	WRITE (6, 301), SEE, IF, YØU, KAN, GET, THIS, ØNE . . .
301 . .	FØRMAT (1X, 2(F3.1, I4)/(1X, F6.1)) . . . . . .

Variable	Format	Prints on line (record)
SEE	F3.1	1
IF	I4	1
YOU	_____	_____
KAN	_____	_____
GET	_____	_____
THIS	_____	_____
ONE	_____	_____

- - - - - - - - - - - - - - - -

YOU	F3.1	1
KAN	I4	1
GET	F6.1	2
THIS	F6.1	3 (new record)
ONE	F6.1	4 (new record)

If there were no parentheses around the format codes 1X and F6.1, format control would have been returned to the F3.1, I4 group (which would have the last left parenthesis). Thus, a WRITE error would have occurred when the printer tried to write the value of THIS using an I4 code since THIS is a real variable.

43. Let's apply what we have learned about input statements to a practical problem. Suppose we have a file (deck of punched cards) containing data concerning our employees. Each employee has three records (or cards), and the records are in the same sequence throughout the file. Our objective is to determine the number of employees that work in department 15 whose pay rate is $5.00 or more. To indicate the last record in the file, the value 999 has been placed in the position of the department number. Have the computer pause after the last record has been read. Here are the record layouts for each employee.

Card 1

1	Emp#	Dept	Employee name			Hired			Term't			Remarks
cd			First	M	Last	M	D	Y	M	D	Y	

Columns: 9999999999... 1 2 3 4 5 6 7 8 9 10 11 12 13 14 15 16 17 18 19 20 21 22 23 24 25 26 27 28 29 30 31 32 33 34 35 36 37 38 39 40 41 42 43 44 45 46 47 48 49 50 51 52 53 54 55 56 57 58 59 60 61 62 63 64 65 66 67 68 69 70 71 72 73 74 75 76 77 78 79 80

Card 2

2	Emp#	Street	City	St	Zip	Telephone A/C
cd						

Columns: 1 ... 80

Card 3

3	Emp#	Begin			Job code	Pay rate	
		M	D	Y			

Columns: 1 2 3 4 5 6 7 8 9 10 11 12 13 14 15 16 17 18 19 20 21 ... 80

Here are some hints: Draw a simple flowchart to illustrate the sequence of operations and tests that you want to take place. Then write your program statements. To skip two cards, use these statements,

```
          READ (5, 20002)
20002     FORMAT (/)
```

which skip the first card due to the / and the second card due to the) in the FORMAT statement.

- - - - - - - - - - - - - - - - - - - -

Here's one possible solution. First we drew a structured flowchart to enable us to easily prepare the program coding.

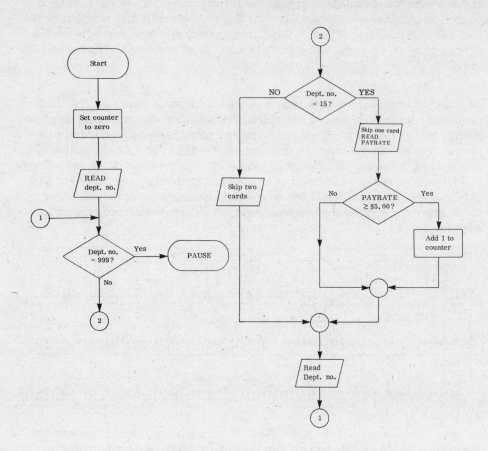

The actual program follows. We have placed numerous comments throughout the program to help you understand the logic flow. The program would work without the comments, but it would be more difficult to understand, especially if someone other than the original programmer were using it.

```
C   SET THE COUNTER TO ZERO
        ICOUNT = 0
C
C   READ THE DEPARTMENT NUMBER
1       READ (5, 10001) IDEPT
10001   FORMAT (5X, I3)
C
C   TEST DEPARTMENT NUMBER; BRANCH TO PAUSE IF 999
        IF (IDEPT - 999) 20000, 60000, 60000
C   TEST DEPARTMENT NUMBER; BRANCH IF 15
20000   IF (IDEPT - 15) 30000, 40000, 30000
C
C   SKIP TWO CARDS
30000   READ (5, 30001)
30001   FORMAT (/)
C
C   BRANCH TO READ NEXT CARD
        GO TO 55000
C
C   READ THE PAYRATE AFTER SKIPPING A CARD
40000   READ (5, 40001) PYRATE
40001   FORMAT (/ 15X, F5.2)
C
C   TEST IF PAYRATE LESS THAN $5.00; BRANCH TO 1
C   IF LESS
        IF (PYRATE - 5.00) 1, 50000, 50000
C
C   INCREMENT COUNTER BY 1
50000   ICOUNT = ICOUNT + 1
C
C       READ NEXT CARD
C
55000   READ (5, 10001) IDEPT
C
C       BRANCH TO TEST FOR IDEPT = 999
C
        GO TO 20000
```

(continue on next page).

```
|C   |    ||
|C  PAUSE
|60000| PAUSE
|    |   :
|    |  END
```

44. There is a variation on the I format code for those of you who have a
FORTRAN 77 compiler. Let's assume I = 735, then the statements

```
|      |  WRITE(11, 90) I
|90    |  FORMAT(1X, I6.4)
```

will print

0735

What has happened? A format code of I6 would have simply printed 735.
The .4 in the I6.4 code mandated that at least four digits be printed even
though 735 only requires three digits. That is why a zero (0) was printed.
So what, you say, who would ever use something like this? There are times
when you want to have no blanks in front of a number (like on a check amount).
Here's another example, this time using the format code I6.0.

```
|      |  I = 0
|      |  WRITE (12, 120) I
|120   |  FORMAT (1X, I6.0)
```

will print

No, the printer didn't leave out the line! Since I = 0, and the format code
I6.0 specifies at least 0 digits printed, nothing is printed.

If this form of the I code is used for input, the .d part of the code is ignored.
Thus, I8.3, when used as an input format code, is the same as I8.

What will be printed by the program segment

```
|      |  I = 75
|      |  J=5356
|      |  K = 0
|      |  L = 414
|      |  WRITE (10, 200) I, J, K, L
|200   |  FORMAT (1X, I4.3, I6.0, I4.0, I5)
```

- - - - - - - - - - - - - - - -

```
b075 | bb5356 | bbbb | bb414
 1    4 5      1 1    1 1    1
              0 1    4 5    9
```

Self-Test

(Use device 5 as an 80-column card reader, device 6 as a 132 print position printer.)

1. What is wrong with the following statements used for a print file?

(a) `30    FORMAT (6HTHIS IS)`

(b) `40    FORMAT ('1',20X,'HIY ADERE',70X,'HOPE YOU', 'LIKE $1,000,000',50X,'HI')`

(c) `30    FORMAT (2X,(F8.2,3(I10,F3.0,2(I5,6X))),I3)`

(d) `30    FORMAT ('THIS IS)`

2. What will the following statements cause the computer to do? _____

```
30    WRITE (6,300)
300   FORMAT ('1'/)
      GO TO 30
```

3. (a) Rewrite this FORMAT statement as simply as possible by using repetition factors.

`10    FORMAT (F6.2,F6.2,F6.2,2X,I4,I4)`

   (b) Rewrite this FORMAT statement as simply as possible by using repetition factors.

`20    FORMAT (F7.4,I5,F7.14,I5,2X,I3,I3,I3)`

4. How many lines would be used on a printer page by these program statements? _____

```
      WRITE (6,30) REALLY, KRAZY, THESE, SILLY, EXAM,
      PLES
30    FORMAT ('0',F8.3/'+',10X,I5/' ',F6.2,(1X,F8.2))
```

5.   By using the T format code, write a READ and FORMAT statement to read a record from device # 11 and to store the data from position 11 through 16 in an integer variable (LINKNO) and from positions 91 through 110 in a character variable DSCRPT. Assume DSCRPT has been described by a CHARACTER * 20 DESCRPT statement at the beginning of the program.

6.   These statements will use how many cards during a READ? _____

```
      READ (5,25), I, J, FØX
25    FØRMAT (I3//I2//F5.2)
```

7.   How many data cards do the following statements require? _____

```
      READ (5,24), HØW, MANY, CARDS, DØ, I, USE,
   -     HERE
24    FØRMAT (F8.3, 3X, I5, 2X, F6.2)
```

8.   What is wrong with the FORMAT statement for the following program statements?

```
      WRITE (6,250), A, B, C, D, E, F, G
250   FØRMAT (' ', 7F20.7)
```

9.   Do the following sets of program statements produce the same output?
_____

```
Set 1       WRITE (6, 50)
       50   FØRMAT (3X, 'PHIL''S BEARD')

Set 2       WRITE (6,100)
      100   FØRMAT (1H, 14H   PHIL'S BEARD)
```

10. What will the program below print? _____

```
      KØUNT = 3
20    I = 15
      J = 13
```

(continue on next page).

```
         L = I * J
         WRITE (6, 100) I, J, L
100      FØRMAT ('1', 'I= ', I3, ',J= ', I3, ', L= ',
        -     I5)
         IF (KØUNT - 3) 20, 40, 20
40       STØP
         END
```

Write the output here.

```
   5      10      15      20      25      30      35      40      45
| | | | | | | | | | | | | | | | | | | | | | | | | | | | | | | | | | | | | | | | | |
```

11. What will be the output from the statements

```
         WRITE (8, 100)
100      FØRMAT (1X, T31, 'MY JØB', T28, 'KEEPS',
        -     T116, 'MUMBØ', T42, 'FØREVER',
        -     T22, 'JUMBØ', T11, 'THIS')
```

12. Write a program segment which will print literals on three lines as follows:

GHF CORPORATION (centered on the top of a new page)
MAKERS OF EVERYTHING FOR EVERYONE (centered, two lines below line 1)
MAKE CHECKS PAYABLE TO CASH (centered, one line below line 2)

13. Write a program which will print out a table with three columns consisting of an integer (N), its square (NSQUAR), and its cube (NCUBE). Let the integer vary from 1 to 100 in increments of one. Each column should have a heading. (Hint: Look at the answer to frame 33 of Chapter Three. Leave at least ten spaces between columns.)

14. Write a pair of WRITE and FORMAT statements which will print the values stored in the variables ONLY, BY, USING, PAREN, and THESES. Each variable should be printed using an F12.7 format code. One is to be printed on a line. Do not use any / format codes in your answer. Only use one WRITE statement.

15. Write FORTRAN statements to read the data punched in columns 4-15 of the punched card below. Use the three variables D1, D2, and D3.

```
   5      10      15      20      25      30      35      40      45
| | |D|E|S|E|R|T| |I|N|N| | | | | | | | | | | | | | | | | | | | | | | | | | | | | |
```

16. Write FORTRAN statements to write the variables in problem 13 in the order D3, D2, D1. What will be printed? _____

Answers to Self-Test

1. (a) The literal THIS␢IS requires seven print positions—only six have been specified in the 6H format code. (frame 28)

(b) Assuming a printer with 132 print positions, this FORMAT statement demands 173 print positions. It is too long. Also note that there was no indicator for the continuation line.

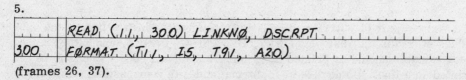

(frame 25)

(c) There are too many sets of nested parentheses. The (I5, 6X) group is causing the problem. (frame 23)

(d) There are not enough apostrophes. The correct statement is

30 FORMAT (' THIS IS ')

2. The computer will command the printer to constantly skip to the next page, which means blank paper will shoot out of the printer. (frame 2)

3. (a) 10 FORMAT (3F6.2, 2X, 2I4) (frame 14)

(b) 20 FORMAT (2(F7.4, I5), 2X, 3I3) (frame 15)

4. Five lines:

'0' causes a double space (two lines)—value of REALLY;

'+' prints on the second line (did we get you here?)—value of KRAZY;

' ' prints on the third line—values of THESE and SILLY;

group repetition prints on the fourth line—value of EXAM; and

group repetition prints on the fifth line—value of PLES.

(frames 2, 6, 15)

5.

```
      READ (1,300) LINKNØ, DSCRPT
300   FØRMAT (T11, I5, T91, A20)
```

(frames 26, 37).

6. Five cards (frame 7)

7. Three cards (frame 38)

8. The FORMAT statement demands a printer with 140 (7 x 20) print positions. This number exceeds the 132 positions assumed for device number 6. (frame 25)

9. Yes. Set 1 statements start printing in print position three. The first character in the output record (the carriage control character) was a blank

donated by the first X of the 3X format code. The double apostrophes (") are necessary to insert a single apostrophe in the printed output. Of course, in Set 2 only a single apostrophe is necessary when using the H code. (frames 28, 29)

10.

	5	10	15	20	25	30	35	40	45

```
I=  IS, J= -13, L=  -195
```

(frame 33)

11.

THIS MUMBO JUMBO KEEPS MY JOB FOREVER

(frame 26)

12.

```
        WRITE (6,101)
101     FØRMAT ('1', 58X, 'GHF CØRPØRATIØN'/ '0',
        -49X, 'MAKERS ØF EVERYTHING FØR EVERYØNE'/
        -1X, 52X, 'MAKE CHECKS PAYABLE TØ CASH')
```

You could have used the H code instead of using apostrophes. The /'0' codes could have been replaced by //1X. (frames 1, 28-31)

13.

```
C
C  INITIALIZE N TØ
C
        N = 1
C
C  WRITE CØLUMN HEADINGS WITH 10 SPACES
C
        WRITE (6,101)
101     FØRMAT ('1', 21X, 'N', 12X, 'SQUARE', 11X, 'CUBE')
C
C  TEST IF N IS LESS THAN 101;
C      AND BRANCH TO 150. IF N >=101 BRANCH TØ STØP
C
140     IF (N- 101) 150, 300, 300
C
```

(continue on next page).

```
C    COMPUTE NSQUAR=N*N AND NCUBE=N**3
C
150   NSQUAR = N * M
      NCUBE = N**3
C
C  PRINT N, NSQUAR, AND NCUBE
C
      WRITE (6, 201) N, NSQUAR, NCUBE
201   FORMAT (1X, 20X, I3, 10X, I5, 10X, I7)
      N = N + 1
      GO TO 140
300   STOP
      END
```

(frames 28–32)

14.

```
      WRITE (6, 101) ONLY, BY, USING, PAREN, THESES
101   FORMAT (1X, F12.7)
```

(frame 40)

15.

```
      READ (5, 101) D1, D2, D3
101   FORMAT (3X, 3A4)
```

(frames 35–36)

16. The statements are

```
      WRITE (6, 201) D3, D2, D1
201   FORMAT (5X, 3A4)
```

The output corresponding to these statements will be

(frames 35, 36)

CHAPTER SIX
Additional Control Statements

By now you've covered enough ground so that you can write practical elementary FORTRAN programs. With the many commands you've learned up to this point, you could also write more complex FORTRAN programs . . . but with great difficulty. So, in these next chapters we aim to provide you with additional FORTRAN features to make your programming life easier and your efforts more effective.

This chapter is an important foundation for the subsequent chapters. In it you will learn to use:

- the DO and CONTINUE statements to repeat the execution of a FORTRAN statement sequence;
- the logical IF statement that will execute a statement if an expression is true, but will not if the expression is false;
- the logical block IF statement that will execute one block of FORTRAN statements (group of zero or more statements) if an expression is true, but will execute a different block if that expression is false;
- the computed GO TO statement for selective unconditional branching.

You will also learn how the FORTRAN 77 implementation of the DO statement differs from the 1966 FORTRAN standard.

In this and subsequent chapters, we will usually omit the FORMAT statement from examples for the sake of simplicity.

DO Loops

1. In Chapter Three you learned about the IF statement. You may have noticed that this statement could be used to repeat a group of FORTRAN statements. On the next page is a program sequence which we used to calculate a student's grade average. We've added some arrows and notations to help you understand the program flow.*

---

*We've numbered the statements in columns 1 through 5 for many of our illustrative program segments. In practice, you would generally number only those statements that are referenced in a branching statement or an input/output statement. Otherwise statement numbering serves only to document the program, and has no effect upon its execution.

The objective of this loop is to cause the READ statement and summation to occur three times.

```
              TØTAL = 0
5             INDEX = 1
10            READ (5,100) GRADE
20            TØTAL = TØTAL + GRADE
30            INDEX = INDEX + 1
35            IF (INDEX - 3) 10, 10, 40
40            AVG = TØTAL/3.
              WRITE (6,200) AVG
```

INDEX < 4   Range of loop

INDEX = 4

The repetition of statements 10 and 20 was controlled by three statements: 5, 30, and 35. Statement 5 initialized a counting variable (control variable), called INDEX in this example, to the value 1.

Following each execution of the READ statement 10 and the assignment statement 20, the computer incremented the counter by a fixed or constant value of 1.

The IF statement, number 35, determined whether it was necessary to take another trip through the loop or to continue execution at the next sequential statement, 40. Thus, only a counter value (variable INDEX) in excess of 3 (which is the limit in our program segment) would cause execution to continue in a sequential manner.

    a) Which statements in the program segment below control the loop?

    b) How many trips will be taken through the statement sequence 100 through 175?

```
50     SUM = 0.
75     INDEX = 3
100    SUM = SUM + 1.
125    WRITE (6,1000) SUM
150    INDEX = INDEX + 1
175    IF (INDEX - 50) 100, 100, 200
200    AVG = SUM/48.
```

- - - - - - - - - - - - - - - -

    a) 75, 150, and 175.

    b) 48 trips. (You may have to use your fingers for this, but here's how it goes: the first trip gives an index value of 4 for statement 175; the second trip through gives us a value of 5; for the 48th trip, it would have a value of 51—causing execution to continue with statement 200 rather than statement 100.)

2. Look at our example again, on the next page. Notice in particular statements 5, 30, and 35.

— Initial value

	TØTAL = 0	
5	INDEX = 1	
10	READ (5,100) GRADE	
20	TØTAL = TØTAL + GRADE	incremental
30	INDEX = INDEX + 1	parameter
35	IF (INDEX - 3) 10, 10, 40	terminal
40	AVG = TØTAL/3.	parameter
	WRITE (6, 200) AVG	

Range of loop { (statements 10 through 35)

Let's play computer. The statements above are executed in the order in which they appear, unless otherwise directed. We've completed sentence (a) below. You complete the others.

(a) We start by initializing both variables, setting TOTAL equal to 0 and IN-DEX equal to 1 . These are called initial values .

(b) After executing statement 30, INDEX has the value of _____ . The digit 1 in the expression INDEX + 1 is called an incremental parameter.

(c) The digit 3 in the expression (INDEX - 3) is called the terminal para-meter. In statement 35, the expression (INDEX - 3) is evaluated and results in a value of _____ .

(d) Therefore, the IF statement tells the computer to execute which state-ment next? _____

(e) Again, statement 30 increments the variable INDEX by _____ . The value of INDEX is now _____ . The digit 1 is called the _____ .

(f) However, statement 35 transfers control to statement _____ .

(g) After statement 30 is executed again, INDEX contains the value _____ .

(h) Finally, the IF statement (statement 35) transfers control out of the loop, to statement _____ .

(i) Hmmm... how many trips would be taken through the statement sequence 10 through 35 (how many times will statements 10, 20, 30, and 35 be executed)?

(j) Looping is the process of repeating a sequence of computer instructions more than one time. The statements within that sequence are within the range of the loop. Peek back at the example above to answer this question:

The range of the loop is from statement 10 through statement _____ .

(b) INDEX has the value of 2; (c) –1, a negative value; (d) 10; (e) 1, 3, incremental parameter. (f) 10; (g) 4; (h) 40; (i) three; (j) 35

3.   By now we have sufficiently hinted that there must be a simpler way to create loops in a program, and there is: DO loops. We've illustrated a program segment below which has been written two ways: first, the old way, and then the new way—using a DO loop.

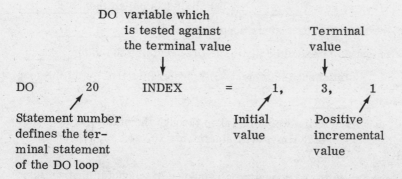

```
                  ┌        │ TØTAL = 0
                  │   5    │ INDEX = 1
Range             │   10   │ READ (5, 100), GRADE
of loop      ┤   20   │ TØTAL = TØTAL + GRADE
                  │   30   │ INDEX = INDEX + 1
                  └   35   │ IF (INDEX - 3) 10, 10, 40
                      40   │ AVG = TØTAL / 3.
                          │ WRITE (6, 200), AVG
                          │
                          │ TØTAL = 0
DO statement →        │ DØ 20 INDEX = 1, 3, 1
Range             ┤ 10   │ READ (5, 100), GRADE
of loop      └ 20   │ TØTAL = TØTAL + GRADE
                      40   │ AVG = TØTAL / 3.
                          │ WRITE (6, 200), AVG
```

Let's take a closer look at this DO statement.

$$
\begin{array}{ccccccc}
 & & \text{DO variable which} & & & & \\
 & & \text{is tested against} & & & \text{Terminal} & \\
 & & \text{the terminal value} & & & \text{value} & \\
 & & \downarrow & & & \downarrow & \\
\text{DO} & 20 & \text{INDEX} & = & 1, & 3, & 1 \\
 & \nearrow & & & \nearrow & \nearrow & \\
\text{Statement number} & & & \text{Initial} & & \text{Positive} & \\
\text{defines the ter-} & & & \text{value} & & \text{incremental} & \\
\text{minal statement} & & & & & \text{value} & \\
\text{of the DO loop} & & & & & &
\end{array}
$$

"Landsakes," you say. "The DO statement has apparently taken the place of statements 5, 30, and 35. Oh, true joy." Yes, the DO statement:
   1. initializes the DO variable (here, INDEX);
   2. increments the DO variable after statement 20 has been executed;
   3. tests the DO variable to determine if it is greater than the terminal value (in our example that was 3). The result of the test

causes control to return either to the beginning of the range of the DO loop or to the next executable statement after the ranges of the DO loop (here, statement 40).

What do the numbers 100, 20, and 50 in this DO statement mean?

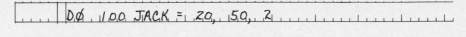

- - - - - - - - - - - - - - - - - - -

100 indicates the last statement numbered within the range of the DO loop. The DO variable JACK will have an initial value of 20. The statements immediately following the DO statement through and including statement 100 (as specified by the DO) will be executed until the DO variable value exceeds 50, which is the terminal value for the DO variable. When the variable exceeds this limit, execution then continues with the next executable statement following the DO loop range.

4. This is the general form of the DO statement.

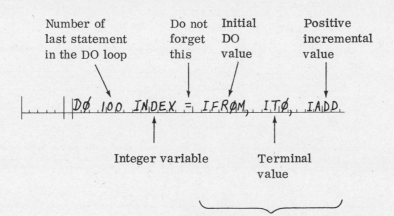

The DO statement is a FORTRAN command to commence an automatic process, controlled exclusively by the DO statement, to repeat the execution of all statements following the DO up to and including the statement (in our example) 100. The controlling factors of the loop are the three integer variables (or constants):

INDEX = IFROM, ITO, IADD

control parameters

When first entering the loop, the computer sets the DO (or counter) variable INDEX to the value specified by the variable IFROM (or constant if specified), so that INDEX = IFROM acts as an assignment statement. Upon reaching the last statement within the DO loop range, the computer increments the DO variable INDEX by the (positive) value of the variable IADD (or constant), just as if we had the assignment statement INDEX = INDEX + IADD. The computer then compares the value of INDEX to the value of the variable ITO (or constant), and if the value of INDEX <u>does not</u> exceed it, the computer makes another "trip" through the loop, beginning with the executable statement following the DO statement. However, if the value of INDEX <u>does</u> exceed ITO, the computer makes a <u>normal</u> exit from the DO loop by executing the next executable statement that follows the DO loop range. This process is diagrammed below.

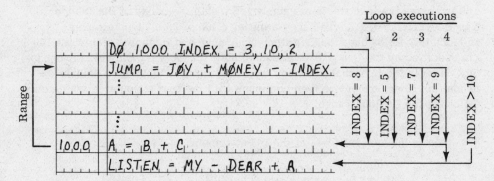

In the statements below, how many times will the computer execute the loop? _____

```
          J = 2
          K = 17
          L = 3
          DØ 5 I = J, K, L
          :
5         INDEX = 1
```

- - - - - - - - - - - - - - - -

6 times:

Trip count	Value of DO variable I
1	2
2	5
3	8
4	11
5	14
6	17

Remember, the loop is repeated until the value of the DO variable exceeds the terminal parameter value (whether the terminal parameter is a constant or the value of an integer variable).

5.   In our slick DO loop program segment of frame 3, the computer increments the DO variable INDEX by 1 after each trip through the DO loop range.

		TØTAL = 0
		DØ 20 INDEX = 1, 3, 1
10		READ (5, 100) GRADE
20		TØTAL = TØTAL + GRADE
40		AVG = TØTAL/3.
		WRITE (6, 200) AVG

If we wanted to increment by 2 instead of 1, we would rewrite the DO statement.

		DØ 20 INDEX = 1, 3, 2

This will cause the loop to be executed twice rather than three times.   You
may use any positive integer other than 1 as an increment, if your program
requires it.   We'll cover this in greater detail in frame 11.

   If you wanted to increment the DO variable IMWISE by 7 on each pass
through the DO loop range, how would you change this DO statement?

		DØ 50 IMWISE = 1, 30, 4

- - - - - - - - - - - - - - - - - - -

		DØ 50 IMWISE = 1, 30, 7

6.   The increment does not have to be specifically specified in the DO statement; but if you do omit specifying it, the FORTRAN compiler assumes that
it has a value of 1.

   What is the difference between these two DO statements?

		DØ 125 INDEX = 3, 50
		DØ 125 INDEX = 3, 50, 1

- - - - - - - - - - - - - - - - - - -

Both DO statements are equivalent, except that in the first the increment is
implied to have a value of 1, whereas in the second it is specified as 1.

7.   The DO statement is an effective command for repeating a program sequence two or more times.   The compiler usually generates more efficient

computer instructions from a DO statement than it does from a series of assignment and IF statements (like we illustrated in frame 1).

Let's practice writing a DO statement. Write a DO statement which has:

range through statement 50070
Do variable named NUMBER
initial value of 16
terminal value of 40 } DO loop parameters
increment of 1

- - - - - - - - - - - - - - - - - - - -

Either answer is correct.

| | DØ 50070 NUMBER = 16, 40, 1 |
| | DØ 50070 NUMBER = 16, 40 |

Remember that the increment is assumed to be the value 1 if its value is not specified.

8. Now write a DO statement which has these characteristics:

range—statement 187
increment—value stored in variable INC
DO variable—LIGHT
terminal value—188000
initial value—stored in variable IBEGIN

- - - - - - - - - - - - - - - - - - - -

| | DØ 187 LIGHT = IBEGIN, 188000, INC |

9. Using this FORMAT statement,

| 100 | FØRMAT (' MY NAME IS CHARLES ATLAS.') |

write a program (don't panic) segment to print out the literal MY NAME IS CHARLES ATLAS. (remember the period!) fifty times.

- - - - - - - - - - - - - - - - - - - -

This is one possible answer.

	DØ 10 INDEX = 1, 50
10	WRITE (6,100)
100	FØRMAT (' MY NAME IS CHARLES ATLAS.')
	STØP
	END

10. Indicate whether each of these DO statements are incorrect, and if so, why.

Invalid and reason

(a) `DØ 56 X = 1, 3, 1`

(b) `DØ   100 K = 16, 20`

(c) `DØ 10,004 J1,234 = M1, M2, 3`

(d) `DØ 87 M = 25, JACK, JILL`

(e) `DØ 690 LUMPS = 3.4, 6.6, .2`

- - - - - - - - - - - - - - - - - -

(a) and (e) are invalid. 1966 FORTRAN specifies that the DO variable and the three control parameters (which may be variables or constants) must be integer. (However, FORTRAN 77 permits real variables and constants! We'll discuss FORTRAN 77 beginning with **frame 23.**)
(b) is invalid because the DO statement must begin after column 6.
(c) and (d) are both valid DO statements.

Comparison of Loop Control

Now that you've had some experience writing DO statements, let's review the two methods of loop control.

| | Loop control method | |
Characteristic	DO statement	IF statement
execution speed	efficient computer instructions cause greater speed	executes slower than DO statement
number of statements required to control the loop	one statement: DO statement	three statements: initialize counter increment counter test counter, branch
program documentation and ease of understanding loop	loop control is self-documented	loop is not easily identified because three statements are required to define loop

DO Loop Increment

11. This and the following frames will discuss the finer aspects of the 1966 FORTRAN implementation of the DO statement for loop control. The increment of the DO statement must be a positive or unsigned value (or constant). So the DO statement can only cause the control variable to be incremented in a positive direction.

If, for some reason, the terminal value were less than the initial value, the DO loop would execute just once. For instance, in the example below, if the value of L were 7, the loop would be executed two times.

```
READ (5, 301), L
DØ 207 J = 5, L, 2
```

How many times would the loop be executed if L had the value of 4?

_____

– – – – – – – – – – – – – – – – – –

The loop would be executed just once because the terminal value of 4 is less than the initial value of 5.

12. How many times would the loop in frame 11 be executed if L had the value of 5? _____

– – – – – – – – – – – – – – – – – –

Once; the loop is <u>repeated</u> only when the DO variable has a value <u>not</u> greater than the terminal variable or constant.

DO Loop Control Variable

13. Once inside the range of the DO loop, your program may use the values contained in any of the DO and parameter variables of the DO statement, provided there is no attempt to change their values. The program below simply illustrates how a program can use the value of the DO variable.

Problem: What is the sum of the numbers 1 through 6, or $1 + 2 + 3 + 4 + 5 + 6 = ?$

Solution: Use an expensive computer and this program.

```
          ISUM = 0
          DØ 10 INDEX = 1, 6
10        ISUM = ISUM + INDEX
          WRITE (6, 100) ISUM
100       FØRMAT (' SUM ØF FIRST SIX PØSITIVE'
        - ' INTEGERS IS ', I4)
          STØP
          END
```

DO loop range { applies to lines statement 10 through statement 100 }

Note that the program on the preceding page uses the variable ISUM as both a work variable and a final result.

Try your hand at writing a program to calculate the sum of the squares of the integers 1 through 6, or $1^2 + 2^2 + 3^2 + 4^2 + 5^2 + 6^2 = ?$ If you're clever, you can use most of our program example.

- - - - - - - - - - - - - - - - - - - -

```
          ISUM = 0
          DO 10 IVALUE = 1, 6
10        ISUM = ISUM + IVALUE * IVALUE
          WRITE (6, 100) ISUM
100       FORMAT (' SUM OF SQUARES OF FIRST SIX'
        - ' POSITIVE INTEGERS IS', I4)
          STOP
          END
```

The use of NUMBER * NUMBER is preferable over NUMBER ** 2 because the computer calculates it more efficiently.

14. What's wrong with this DO loop segment?

```
          DO 80000 J = 6, 34, 7
          :
          J = J + 1
          :
80000     WRITE (6, 80001) J
```

- - - - - - - - - - - - - - - - - - - -

The assignment statement J = J + 1 violated the rule that it is not permissible to alter the value of the DO variable while inside the range of the DO loop.

15. Although 1966 FORTRAN currently limits DO statements to using positive integer values, you may use the DO statement to control loops that require decreasing values or real values.

Decreasing value. This segment illustrates how you can use a DO statement to cause a variable to assume values in a declining sequence.

```
          DO 100 J = 2, 102, 2
          K = 52 - J
          :
```

The variable K will be assigned the values in a sequence 50 through -50 in decrements of 2 (that is, 50, 48, 46,..., -48, -50).

FORTRAN 77 allows decreasing values. If you either have access to a FORTRAN 77 compiler or are interested in this new feature, see frame 23.

Real value. By using an assignment statement, the segment below illustrates how the integer value of the control variable can be converted to real and used within the range of the loop.

```
       DØ 00650 M = 6, 600, 3
       EM = M
       EM = EM/2.
       :
```

The variable EM will be assigned the sequence of values from 3.0 through 300.0 in increments of 1.5 (that is, 3.0, 4.5, 6.0,..., 298.5, 300.0). FORTRAN 77 strikes again—because it allows real variables as well as integer variables. For a more complete discussion, see frame 23.

(a) Write a program segment that is to print a series of numbers 100.0 through 0.0 in decrements of .4; use the IF statement method of controlling the loop. (Refer to frame 1 if you forgot the IF statement method.)

(b) Now write a program segment that is to accomplish the same result as (a) above, but use a DO statement to control the loop.

- - - - - - - - - - - - - - - - - - - -

(a) This is one correct solution.

```
             AMØUNT = 100.0
       1     WRITE (6,351) AMØUNT
       351   FØRMAT (' ', F5.1)
             AMØUNT = AMØUNT - .4
             IF (AMØUNT) 2, 1, 1
       2     :
```

(b)
```
             DØ 1 K = 4, 1004, 4
             AMØUNT = 1004 - K
             AMØUNT = AMØUNT/10.
       1     WRITE (6,351) AMØUNT
       351   FØRMAT (' ', F5.1)
```

The computer performs addition and subtraction more rapidly than it performs multiplication and division. To this extent, (a) may be a more efficient solution to our problem than (b), even though the DO method is otherwise more efficient for controlling a loop than the IF statement method.

Answer (b) illustrates the general principle of using a DO loop when the value of a variable is to be decremented rather than incremented under 1966 FORTRAN. When you write a program under 1966 FORTRAN which requires decrementing, you will have to judge which of the methods illustrated, (a) or (b), is most applicable.

Ending the DO Loop

16. The last statement in the range of the DO must be <u>executable</u>. Therefore, you would not want to use a FORMAT, DIMENSION, END, or other nonexecutable statement as the last statement in the DO loop range.

FORTRAN will not accept certain executable statements as the last statement in the DO loop range; these include another DO, GO TO, arithmetic IF (in contrast to the logical IF which you will cover starting in **frame 28**), STOP, RETURN (Chapter Ten), and PAUSE.

If, for some reason, a "forbidden" statement happens to be the last statement in a DO loop, follow the forbidden statement by a do-nothing statement called CONTINUE and specify this to be the end of the DO loop instead. The CONTINUE statement is executable, but really has no effect other than instructing the computer to execute the next instruction in sequence. In the above situation, though, it assists the compiler in delineating the end of the DO loop.

Use a CONTINUE statement to correct this DO segment.

```
         Z = 0.0
         DO 50 I = 1, 200
         Z = Z + 3.
50       IF (75. - Z) 100, 100, 50
```

- - - - - - - - - - - - - - - - - - -

An arithmetic IF statement is the last statement in the DO loop. We can correct this situation by adding a CONTINUE statement.

```
         Z = 0.0
         DO 50 I = 1, 200
         Z = Z + 3.
         IF (75. - Z) 100, 100, 50
50       CONTINUE
```

DO Loop Indentation

17. Good programmers both indent the statements within the range of a loop and use a CONTINUE statement as the last statement within the range of a loop, even though another type of statement would be satisfactory for program execution. The end result of following these two practices is a more readable program.

On the next page, notice how documentation method 1 more clearly identifies the statements within the range of the loop than does method 2.

Documentation method 1

```
          READ (5, 1471) INPUT
          DØ 96 K = 15, 19, 2
              J = K * INPUT
              WRITE (6, 1482) J
96        CØNTINUE
          L = J ** INPUT
          WRITE (6, 1482) L
```

Documentation method 2

```
          READ (5, 1471) INPUT
          DØ 96 K = 15, 19, 2
          J = K * INPUT
96        WRITE (6, 1482) J
          L = J ** INPUT
          WRITE (6, 1482) L
```

Rewrite the solution to frame 16, indenting the statements within the range of the loop.

- - - - - - - - - - - - - - - - - -

```
          Z = 0.0
          DØ 50 I = 1, 200
              Z = Z + 3.
              IF (75. - Z) 100, 100, 50
50        CØNTINUE
```

DO Loop Flowcharting

18. The computer industry has not yet adopted a standard flowcharting symbol for the DO loop, although a number of methods are used. Two methods are shown on the next page.

Method 1.

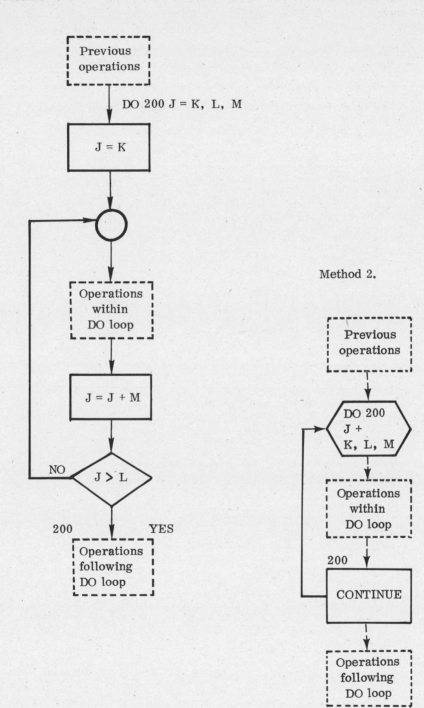

Method 2.

We prefer the second method on page 219, since it represent the DO statement under both 1966 FORTRAN and FORTRAN 77. Although it does not show the individual operations of the DO statement, it clearly identifies the range of the DO loop and is easy to draw. We use the ⟨　　⟩ to indicate the beginning of the DO loop by writing the DO statement inside the symbol. To indicate the end of the DO loop range, we use the symbol ▭ with the statement number written above the top left corner.

The flowchart at the right depicts the program segment at the left.

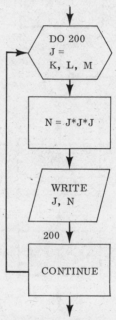

```
      DO 200 J = K, 4, M
         N = J*J*J
         WRITE (6, 191) J, N
191   FORMAT (' ', I3, 1X, I6)
200   CONTINUE
```

Now you flowchart this program segment. Draw your flowchart in the space provided, or on a separate sheet of paper if you need more room.

```
      DO 405 K = 4, 4000, 4
         AMOUNT = 4000 - K
         AMOUNT = AMOUNT/10.
         WRITE (6, 351) AMOUNT
351   FORMAT (' ', F5.1)
405   CONTINUE
```

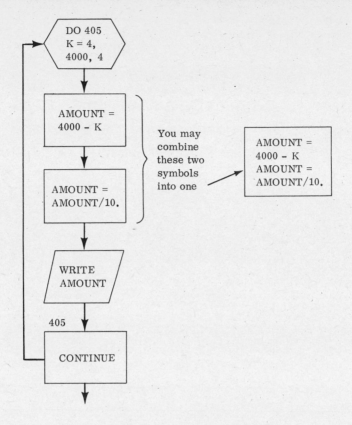

DO Loop Termination

19. A branch from a statement <u>within</u> the range of a DO loop to a statement <u>outside</u> the DO loop will terminate the DO loop. This is called an <u>abnormal termination</u> because a branch caused the termination of the DO loop rather than the loop running its course.

Here's the solution to frame 17 again. We've also flowcharted the segment (on the next page) so that you can visually note how the branch causes execution to leave the range of the loop.

```
         Z = 0.0
         DØ 50 I = 1, 200
            Z = Z + 3.
            IF (7.5.-Z) 100, 100, 50
50       CØNTINUE
```

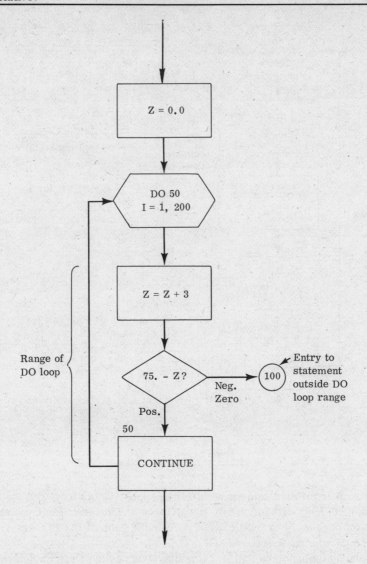

For the program segment and flowchart on the next page, answer the questions which follow. We've indicated the general flow of the program by using just the flowchart symbols without writing anything inside them.

		DØ 96 NUMBER = 1, 100, 1
		READ (5, 301) INPUT
		IF (INPUT) 97, 97, 95
95		⋮
		⋮
96		CØNTINUE
97		⋮

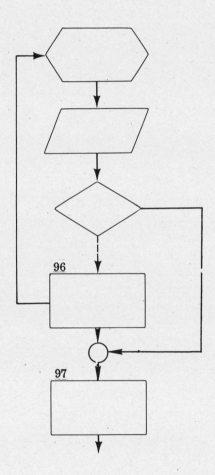

Using the above program segment, how many cards will be read if:

(a) all values of INPUT are positive? _____

(b) the 27th card has a negative value? (Assume the first 26 are positive.)

_____

(c) the first card has a zero value? _____

- - - - - - - - - - - - - - - - - - -

(a) 100 cards will be read; that is, one card on each trip of the loop. (b) 27 cards; the 27th card will cause a branch out of the range of the loop (because of the action of the IF statement). (c) 1 card.

20. In frame 13 you learned that your program may use the value of the DO variable while <u>within</u> the range of the DO, provided there was no attempt to change its value. Whether your program may use the value of the DO varia-ble <u>outside</u> the range of the loop depends upon both the method of termination (normal or abnormal) and the FORTRAN compiler (1966 FORTRAN or FORTRAN 77). Here's a table to peruse:

Value of the DO Variable

Termination	FORTRAN Standard	
	1966	1977
Normal	Undefined	Defined*
Abnormal	Defined and contains the value when termin-ation occurred	

* The DO variable also contains the value it had at the time the loop ter-minated—remember that the DO variable was incremented (or decremented) before normal termination of the DO loop occurred; for example, in the statement DO 80 M = 10, 7, -1, the value of M after normal termination will be 6.

Refer back to the program segment in frame 19 to answer these questions. What is the value of NUMBER:

(a)   after 100 cards have been read and execution leaves the range of the DO loop? _____

(b)   after the 27th card has been read and execution branches out of the DO loop range? _____

(c)   after reading the first card and branching to statement 97? _____

- -

(a) NUMBER, under 1966 FORTRAN, is not defined because the loop was normally terminated; with respect to FORTRAN 77, NUMBER will have a value of 101; (b) 27 because the loop was abnormally terminated; (c) 1. At this point you should realize that the value of the DO variable will contain the number of cards read if there is an abnormal termination of the loop. You may apply this concept to any program using a DO loop.

Nested DO Loops

21. In some programming applications, you may want to have one or more DO loops contained in another DO loop. A DO loop contained inside another is called a nested DO loop. Your FORTRAN manual will indicate how many DO loops may be contained in each other, which is called the depth of the nesting. For example, these DO loops are nested two deep.

```
1        5 6 7    10      15      20      25      30      35
         ITRIP = 0
         DO 27 J1 = 10,14,1
            DO 26 J2 = 1,2,1
               ITRIP = ITRIP + 1
               WRITE (6,141) ITRIP, J1, J2
26          CONTINUE
27       CONTINUE
```

Look at the flowchart of these nested DO loops on the next page.

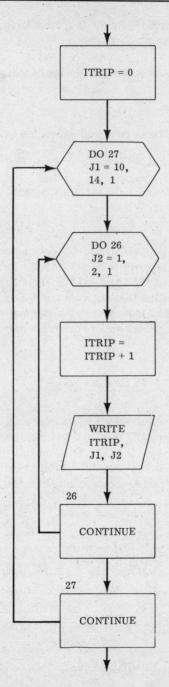

Note that the innermost loop (2) will "trip" most frequently whereas the outermost loop (1) "trips" the least. To further illustrate the action of the nested loops, we've presented part of the output from the above program segment, on the next page.

| | Values of control variables | |
Trip	J1	J2
1	10	1
2	10	2
3	11	1

Complete the entries in the table beginning with trip 4 and continue until all of the loops have been normally terminated.

Trip	J1	J2
4		

- - - - - - - - - - - - - - - - -

Trip	J1	J2
4	11	2
5	12	1
6	12	2
7	13	1
8	13	2
9	14	1
10	14	2

22. The rules of using the value of the control variables as discussed in frames 4 and 13 also apply to nested loops. Later you will find additional discussion of DO loops as you learn about other features of the FORTRAN language. Your FORTRAN manual will show many other ways of nesting DO loops.

Now, draw a flowchart of a program using nested DO loops which will print two numbers and the result of their multiplication. Each number in the pair will range from 1.3 to 1.9 in increments of .1. Then code your program in FORTRAN, using a separate sheet of paper for your flowchart. (Hint: Each control variable should range in value from 13 through 19; if you then convert its value to REAL and divide by 10, you will have the proper value for multiplication.) The results printed by your program might look like this:

```
1.3 times 1.3 equals 1.69
1.4 times 1.3 equals 1.82
1.5 times 1.3 equals 1.95
    :
    :
1.8 times 1.9 equals 3.42
1.9 times 1.9 equals 3.61
```

- - - - - - - - - - - - - - - -

Here's one possible answer:

```
      DO 26 N1 = 13,19
        DO 25 N2 = 13,19
          P1 = N1
          P1 = P1/10.
          P2 = N2
          P2 = P2/10.
          ANSWER = P1*P2
          WRITE (6,481) P2, P1,
     -    ANSWER
25      CONTINUE
26    CONTINUE
```

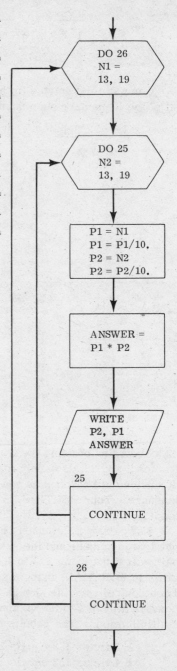

FORTRAN 77 DO STATEMENT

23. If you don't have access to or aren't interested in the FORTRAN 77 implementation of the DO statement, go to the DO statement summary on page 233.

As we first mentioned in frame 11, 1966 FORTRAN allowed at least one execution of the DO range. But this could cause a problem, as in the following example.

$$
\left.
\begin{array}{l}
\text{MIN } = 5 \\
\text{MAX } = 2 \\
\text{DO 30 J = MIN, MAX, 2} \\
\quad \cdot \\
\quad \cdot \\
\quad \cdot
\end{array}
\right\}
\begin{array}{l}
\text{range of} \\
\text{the DO} \\
\text{statement}
\end{array}
$$

```
    30  CONTINUE
        KARDS = JACK + NINE
```

The statements within the DO range were executed once, even though the value of MIN exeeded MAX. Why? Because 1966 FORTRAN tests the value of the DO variable <u>following the execution of the DO range</u> (remember frame 17). So our program compiled properly but did not execute correctly.

The program would compile if we used a variable for the initial and/or terminal parameters (as we did), because the compiler won't be able to determine the correctness of the DO statement— unless the compiler is very sophisticated.

On the other hand, if you used constants for both the initial and terminal parameters, the compiler would flag the DO statement as erroneous because the terminal value was less than the initial value.

FORTRAN 77 surmounted these problems by providing for the <u>computation of the number of trips</u> to be taken through the DO range <u>before executing the DO range</u>, and allowing positive <u>or</u> negative increments. So our program, when compiled under FORTRAN 77, would not execute the DO range, but would branch to and execute the statement <u>immediately following the end of the DO range.</u>

```
        KARDS = JACK + NINE
        DO 20 J = 8, 3, -1
            ·

            ·

            ·
    20  CONTINUE
        CANDY = NUTS + CARMEL
```

(a) Would the above DO statement successfully compile under 1966 FORTRAN? FORTRAN 77?

(b) Which FORTRAN standard allows a negative incremental parameter?

(c) Which FORTRAN standard provides for testing the value of the DO variable after executing the DO range?

(d)   Which FORTRAN standard computes the number of trips to be taken
through the DO loop before executing the statements within the DO range?

(a)   While FORTRAN 77 would successfully compile this statement, 1966
FORTRAN would flag it as erroneous because the terminal parameter is less
than the initial value and the incremental parameter is negative;   (b) FOR-
TRAN 77 permits negative incremental parameters;   (c) 1966 FORTRAN;
(d) FORTRAN 77.

24. In summary, the major difference between FORTRAN 77 and the 1966
FORTRAN implementation of the DO statement is FORTRAN 77 provides for
computing the number of trips to be taken through the loop, if any, before
executing the statements of the DO range.   In our previous frame, we used

$$DO \quad 20 \ J = 8, \ 3, \ -1$$

which will have a trip count of 6.   Let's verify this.   On the first trip, J
has a value of 8; on the second trip, J equals 7.   And counting on your
fingers, ... J has a value of 3 on the sixth trip.
    You don't really have to take off your shoes in order to count trips on
both hands and toes in order to properly implement FORTRAN 77.   The
little formula below (which you can copy on to your shirt sleeve or handkerchief) will give you the exact number of trips or iterations that FORTRAN 77
will cause through the range of the DO loop.

Maximum of either zero or K, where K is the integer value
    of the expression $\dfrac{(M2 - M1 + M3)}{M3}$

where   M1 is the initializing parameter,
            M2 is the terminal parameter, and
            M3 is the incremental parameter.

In summary form, the number of trips are equal to
            MAX (INT ((M2 - M1 + M3)/M3), 0)

Let's use the formula to compute the trip count (instead of our fingers).
First, we substitute 8, 3, and -1 for M1, M2, and M3 respectively.
            MAX (INT ((3 - 8 + (-1))/(-1)), 0)
Then we combine terms.
            MAX (INT ((-6)/(-1)), 0)
Finally, we divide.
            MAX (INT (+6), 0)
And the maximum value of (zero or 6) is 6.
    Let's practice using our convenient formula.   In the following table we've
given you the values of the initial, terminal, and incremental parameters.   It's
your job to compute and fill in the number of trips to be taken through the
DO loop under FORTRAN 77.

DO   12345 NUMBER = M1, M2, M3

	M1	M2	M3	number of trips
(a)	6	12	2	
(b)	12	6	-2	
(c)	12	6	2	
(d)	7	2	-3	

(a) 4 trips; (b) 4 trips; (c) 0 trips; (d) 2 trips... the integer value of $\frac{-8}{-3}$ is 2.

25. FORTRAN 77 ended many of the restrictions placed upon the DO statement by 1966 FORTRAN. If you're lucky enough to have access to a FORTRAN 77 compiler, you have another benefit. Under 1966 FORTRAN you were limited to using positive integer constants and/or variables as parameters in the DO statement; likewise, the DO variable had to be integer.

In contrast, FORTRAN 77 permits the use of real and/or integer variables in the DO statement, as well as arithmetic expressions for the initializing, terminal, and/or incremental parameters. This means, under FORTRAN 77, a parameter can be any of the following: real, integer, positive, negative, a simple variable, a constant, or an arithmetic expression. What a mouthfull!

Now it's your turn to solve the problem in frame 15 of this Chapter using the DO statement implemented under FORTRAN 77. Write a program segment that is to print a series of numbers 100.0 through 0.0, in decrements of .4.

- -

This is one correct solution:
```
        DO 10 AMOUNT = 100.0, 0.0, -.4
    10  WRITE (6,11) AMOUNT
    11  FORMAT (' ', F5.1)
```

Slick, isn't it?

26. In frame 25, we stated that FORTRAN 77 supported the parameters of the DO statement, whether they be arithmetic expressions, simple variables, and/or constants. We are now going to use all three in the DO statement.

In the table below, we've computed the number of trips for the first two illustrations. It's your job to fill in the missing values from the table. To assist you, we have included some notations as to how we computed our two answers. Now, if you don't remember the formula for computing the trip count, refer either to your shirt sleeve, handkerchief, or frame 24.

DO 80 C = ((F - 32.)*(5./9.)), BOIL,.1

.

.

value of BOIL	value of F	initial value of C	number of trips through
100.0	212.0	100.0	1
100.0	210.2	99.0	11
(a) 100.0	77.0	25.0	
(b) 30.0	152.0		

$$\frac{(100 - 100 + .1)}{.1} = 1$$

$$\frac{(100 - 99 + .1)}{.1} = \frac{1.1}{.1} = 11$$

- -

(a) 521 trips; the initializing parameter has a value of 25.0;

$$\frac{77. - 25. + .1}{1.} = 521$$

(b) C has an initial value of 66.7 (which is 66.6666... rounded) and no trips will occur through the loop, since zero is greater than -367

$$\frac{30 - 66.7 + .1}{.1} = -367$$

27. Two very general representations of the DO statement DO 70 I = 1, 200 follow.

Loop A   Loop B

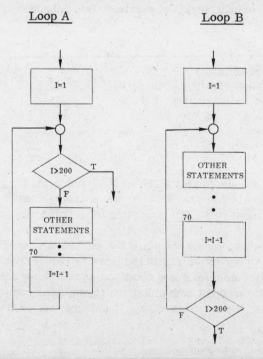

Which more closely illustrates implementation of the DO statement (a) under 1966 FORTRAN? (b) FORTRAN 77?

‒ ‒ ‒ ‒ ‒ ‒ ‒ ‒ ‒ ‒ ‒ ‒ ‒ ‒ ‒ ‒ ‒

(a) loop B, because the loop is executed at least once before the DO variable is tested; (b) loop A because I is tested at the beginning of the DO range.

Summary of DO Statement

The DO statement is a control statement which can cause repetitive execution of one or more subsequent statements. Its general form is:

DO sn index = ifrom, ito, inc

where	FORTRAN 77	1966 FORTRAN
sn	is the number of the terminal statement which defines the end of the DO loop range.	
index	is an integer or real variable called a DO variable.	is an integer variable called a DO variable.
	The DO variable does not control execution of the loop.	The DO variable is used to control execution of the DO loop.
	While the DO variable is defined, other FORTRAN statements may access and use its value. The DO variable is first defined when the DO statement is executed.	
	Once defined, the DO variable retains its last value.	The DO variable becomes undefined following normal termination of the DO loop.
ifrom	is an integer or real arithmetic expression.	is an integer variable or constant, having a positive value.
	The DO variable is initialized to this value before the first execution of the DO loop statements.	

ito	is an integer or real arithmetic expression.	is an integer variable or constant, having a positive value.
	The DO variable is never tested against this value, although the DO variable value will approach this value as the DO variable is incremented with each DO loop execution.	After executing the statements in the DO loop range, the DO variable is tested against this value. Execution continues with the next statement if the DO variable exceeds this value. Otherwise, the DO loop is again executed.
inc	is an integer or real arithmetic expression, having a nonzero value.	is an integer variable or constant, having a positive value.
	This parameter is optional. When it is not specified, it has an assumed value of 1. The DO variable is incremented by this value after each execution of the DO range, prior to testing.	
Testing	of the trip count occurs before executing the DO loop.	of the DO variable occurs after executing the DO loop.

The last statement within the range of a DO loop must be an executable one. However, the following executable statements are prohibited: STOP, PAUSE, another DO, GO TO, arithmetic IF, or RETURN. A CONTINUE statement is always acceptable as the last statement of a DO loop range.

A DO loop may be entirely contained within another loop. This is called nesting. The number of nesting levels permitted is determined by your FORTRAN compiler.

While not illustrated in this chapter, the control variable of an outer DO loop may be used as the parameter of any inner DO statement. This is a sophisticated application of the simple rules set forth in frame 4.

Chapter Seven will illustrate more practical applications of the DO statement after you have been introduced to array variables.

By using the ⬡ symbol and the ▭ symbol, you can flowchart the range of a DO loop, such as in the nested loop (two deep) shown on the next page.

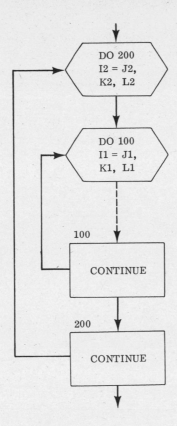

Logical IF Statement

28. In Chapter Three, we discussed the arithmetic IF statement. FORTRAN provides us with another kind of IF statement—the <u>logical</u> IF statement. Look carefully at these examples of logical IF statements.

```
       IF (AXLE .GT. 8.) WEIGHT = AXLE * TØN
       IF (SKY .EQ. BLUE) GØ TØ 10
       IF ((SKY .EQ. BLUE) .AND. NØRAIN) WRITE
     -   (6, 100) TEMP
       IF (CHEAT .ØR. .NØT. THIEF) TERMS = YEARS*2.
```

Like the arithmetic IF, the logical IF statement contains the word IF and one or more expressions within a set of parentheses. The logical IF has three parts:

$$\underbrace{\text{IF}}_{1} \quad \underbrace{\text{(logical expression)}}_{2} \quad \underbrace{\text{executable statement}}_{3}$$

1. The word IF.
2. A logical expression enclosed within a single pair of parentheses (the logical expression must be capable of being evaluated as either true or false).
3. An executable FORTRAN statement that will be performed only if the expression in part 2 is evaluated as true. Execution then normally proceeds to the next executable statement in either case.

Here's a flowchart which illustrates the concept of the logical IF statement.

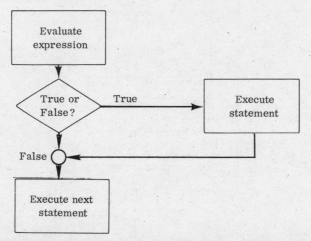

As we saw in Chapter Two, an arithmetic expression results in or represents the computation of a numerical value. For example, if A equals 5.0 and B equals 3.0, then the expression A + B**2 can be evaluated as 5.0 + 3.0**2, or 14.0.

Logical expressions result in the computation of a logical value which can be either <u>true</u> or <u>false</u>.

While an arithmetic expression is a collection of constants and/or variables connected by <u>arithmetic</u> operators, such as +, -, *, /, and **, a logical expression consists of a combination of constants, variables, or arithmetic expressions connected by <u>logical</u> operators. *

You can easily identify logical expressions because they all involve <u>logical</u> or <u>relational</u> operators which are preceded and followed by periods. For example, here are three logical expressions.

HOURS .GT. 40.
X .EQ. Y
(X .LE. Y) .OR. (A .GE. B)

---

*To minimize any confusion, we will discuss in this chapter only simple logical expressions which consist of comparisons between the values of arithmetic expressions. In Chapter Nine we will discuss logical expressions which also include <u>logical</u> constants and variables.

On the basis of what you know so far, which of the following are logical expressions?

_____ (a) X + Y - 2

_____ (b) A/B .GT. C**2

_____ (c) (IZIP .LE. 10025) .AND. (ADRES .EQ. 292.)

_____ (d) (THIS - IS**2) * SNEAKY

- - - - - - - - - - - - - - - - - -

Choice (b) is a logical expression because it contains the relational operator .GT. Choice (c) is a logical expression because it contains the relational operators .LE. and .EQ. and the logical operator .AND.

Relational Operators

29. The logical expression uses relational operators to form logical expressions which <u>compare</u> values. These are the relational operators.

Operator	Meaning
.GT.	greater than (>)
.GE.	greater than or equal to (≥)
.EQ.	equal to (=)
.LT.	less than (<)
.LE.	less than or equal to (≤)
.NE.	not equal to (≠)

For example, to say in FORTRAN that the number 15 is greater than 5, we would write 15 .GT. 5; because 15 is greater than 5, the expression would have the value of <u>true</u>.

For each of the following, write a logical expression and then indicate whether its value is true or false (T or F).

		Expression	Value
13 greater than 12	(a)	_____	____
13 greater than or equal to 13	(b)	_____	____
12 equals 13	(c)	_____	____
12 less than 13	(d)	_____	____
14 less than or equal to 13	(e)	_____	____
31 not equal to 13	(f)	_____	____

- - - - - - - - - - - - - - - - - -

(a) 13 .GT. 12—T; (b) 13 .GE. 13—T; (c) 12 .EQ. 13—F; (d) 12 .LT. 13—T; (e) 14 .LE. 13—F; (f) 31 .NE. 13—T

30. Remember, in a logical IF statement, the statement to the right of the logical expression will be executed only if the evaluated logical expression has the value of true. If it is false, execution simply proceeds with the next executable statement.

Compare the program segment below with the flowchart.

```
      NEED = 0
      IF (INSTK .LT. 10) NEED = 10
      INSTK = INSTK + NEED
```

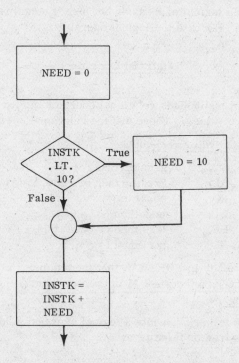

The logical IF statement compares the values of INSTK and the constant 10.

If the value of INSTK is less than 10, the expression is _____ (true/false). The executable statement to the right of the evaluated expression will be executed if the expression is true; otherwise execution will commence with the next executable statement following the logical IF statement in the program.

To illustrate, if INSTK has the initial value of 25, the evaluated expression will be false (because 25 is not less than 10). In that case, the statement NEED = 10 will not be executed and INSTK will have a final value of 25 (because 25 equals 25 plus 0).

What will be the final value of INSTK if the initial value is 9? _____

- - - - - - - - - - - - - - - - - - - -

true; 19 (19 equals 10 plus 9)

31. It is permissible to have arithmetic operators in the logical expression. The relational operators are performed after the arithmetic. In the next example, first evaluate the arithmetic expression (INSTK - IUSED) and then use the results to evaluate the logical expression. Notice the parentheses in the IF statement. The innermost parentheses are not actually needed because the arithmetic expression is evaluated first according to the hierarchy we discussed in Chapter Two.

(a) Flowchart this program segment in the space below. (Some of the variables have received their values elsewhere in the program.)

```
MIN = 10
NEED = 0
IF ((INSTK - IUSED) .LT. MIN)
-  NEED = MIN + IUSED - INSTK
```

(b) How does the program segment below differ from the one above?

```
NEED = 0
IDIFF = INSTK - IUSED
IF (IDIFF .LT. 10) NEED = 10 + IUSED - INSTK
```

- - - - - - - - - - - - - - - - -

(a) On the next page is one method of flowcharting the program segment. Note that MIN is initialized to the value 10. If MIN is used only in the IF statement, we could eliminate the assignment statement and substitute the value 10 directly in the logical IF statement.

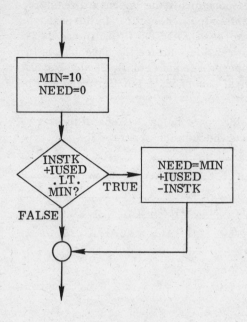

(b) For ease of comparison, we've flow-
charted the second program segment.
Look familiar? Both program segments
accomplish the same end objective: to
calculate the value of NEED. Both segments will produce identical answers.
Note that we substituted the constant 10
in the logical expression for the variable
MIN. We were also able to eliminate the
assignment statement MIN = 10. We did
add an assignment statement to calculate
IDIFF which we used in the logical expression—to clearly indicate how the
arithmetic expression is first evaluated.
When actually programming, you should
not calculate IDIFF unless it is used elsewhere in the program.

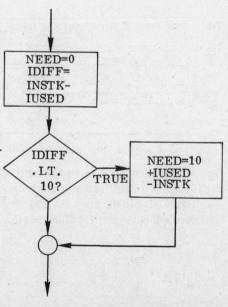

32. Draw a flowchart and write a program segment that will print the value of ITOTAL using a logical IF statement.

ITOTAL is the sum of NEED and INSTK.

Read the value of INSTK from the card reader (unit 5).

NEED has a value of 0 unless INSTK is less than 15, in which case NEED has a value of 20.

Write the value of ITOTAL on the printer (unit 8).

(Note: Don't bother with the FORMAT statements.)

- - - - - - - - - - - - - - - - - -

This is one possible answer. Note how we arrange the logical IF statement on two (or more) lines. For documentation purposes, you can place the logical expression on one line and the executable statement on the next, indented three spaces. This practice makes for easy reading of the program. Our flowchart is on the next page.

```
NEED = 0
READ (5,401) INSTK
IF (INSTK .LT. 15)
   NEED = 20
ITOTAL = INSTK + NEED
WRITE (8,501) ITOTAL
```

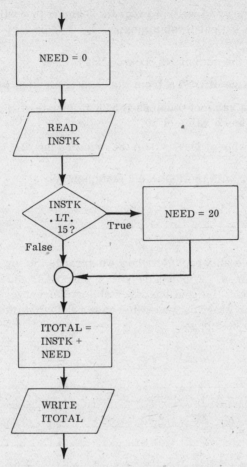

33. Using the program segment in frame 32, what value will be printed for ITOTAL given each of the following values for INSTK? To help you solve the problem, we filled in the first values.

Value of INSTK		Value of logical expression	Value of NEED	Value of ITOTAL to be printed
17	(a)	false	0	17
9	(b)			
15	(c)			
39	(d)			

- - - - - - - - - - - - - - - -

(b)	true	20	29
(c)	false	0	15
(d)	false	0	39

34. Now let's practice writing more complex logical expressions using arithmetic expressions. Rewrite the following as FORTRAN logical expressions.

Example: $a^2 < c - 1$ A * A .LT. C - 1.

(a) $4ac = e$ _____

(b) $j \neq 69$ _____

(c) $k - 5 \leq 19$ _____

   or, $k \leq 24$ _____

(d) $x + y > a^2 + b - c$ _____

- - - - - - - - - - - - - - - - -

(a) 4. * A * C .EQ. E; (b) J .NE. 69; (c) K - 5 .LE. 19, or K .LE. 24;
(d) X + Y .GT. A * A + B - C

35. In frame 30 you learned that the computer executes the executable statement to the right of the logical expression if the logical expression is true. All executable statements are permitted except another logical IF statement or a DO statement.

Write logical IF statements to perform the following.

(a) Print the value of TIRES if WHEELS + 1 is greater than 5.

(b) Add the value 1 to KOUNT if 2 times BABY equals FATHER plus AMOTHR.

- - - - - - - - - - - - - - - - -

(a)
```
      IF (WHEELS + 1. .GT. 5.)
     -   WRITE (8,371) TIRES
```

Your answer is also correct if you wrote the complete statement on one line. To save computation, you could have subtracted 1 from each side of the logical expression, as we have done below.

```
      IF (WHEELS .GT. 4.)
     -   WRITE (8,371) TIRES
```

This is more efficient because it saves the computer from having to add 1 to WHEELS each time the IF statement is executed.

(b)
```
      IF (2. * BABY .EQ. FATHER + AMOTHR)
     -   KOUNT = KOUNT + 1
```

36. In Chapter Two you learned the difference between integer and real variables. You should remember that a real variable will contain a value that is less precise than an integer variable because of the method in which the computer internally handles real (or floating point) values. Consequently you may

get unexpected results when using real variables in a logical expression. For
example:

```
      G = 4.
      IF (G/2. .EQ. 2.) GO TO 10045
```

Since the result of dividing G (which has an initial value of 4.0) by 2. could
be 1.999999 in FORTRAN, the logical expression could be false. Where possible, use integer variables or take into consideration that the arithmetic expression may have a "slight" error.

A programmer wrote the following program segment, but it didn't seem
to work properly.

```
      READ (5, 6841) B
      IF (B/2. .EQ. 18.)
     -   WRITE (8, 6851) HIT
```

If he read in a value of 36. for B, the computer failed to write the value of
HIT on the printer. We rewrote the logical IF statement (and added other
statements) so that the segment would properly operate.

```
      READ (5, 6841) B
      C = B/2. - 18.
      IF (C .LT. 0)                    } 1
     -   C = -C
      IF (C .LT. .001)                 } 2
     -   WRITE (8, 6851) HIT
```

1.   This sequence calculates
the difference, which should
be close to the value 0 if B has
the value of 36. If the difference is negative, it is converted to a positive one.

2.   This statement tests
whether the difference is
smaller than some accept-
able value, here .001.

Rewrite the program segment below so that it will accept an "error" of
.0001 as tolerable; the value of the variable Z is not used anywhere else in
the program.

```
      READ (5, 6861) X, Y, A
      Z = (X/Y)**3.4
      IF (Z .EQ. A) WRITE (8, 6871) X, Y, A
```

- - - - - - - - - - - - - - - - - -

```
      READ (5, 6861) X, Y, A
      Z = (X/Y)**3.4 - A
      IF (Z .LT. 0.) Z = -Z
      IF (Z .LT. .0001) WRITE (8, 6871) X, Y, A
```

Note that we subtracted the variable A on the second line; this is permissible because the value of Z is not used elsewhere in the program.

Logical Operators

37. You may also perform multiple comparisons in a logical expression by using the following additional FORTRAN logical operators.

.AND.

.OR.

.NOT.

The table below best explains the action of the above operators. In each example LE1 and LE2 represent two different logical expressions that are related by each of the above three operators.

Expression	Resulting true/false value
LE1 .AND. LE2	True only if both LE1 and LE2 are true. False if either LE1 or LE2 is false.
LE1 .OR. LE2	True if either LE1 or LE2 or both LE1 and LE2 are true. False if both LE1 and LE2 are false.
.NOT. LE1	True if LE1 is false, but false if LE1 is true.

This could get confusing, unless you've had Boolean algebra. We'll keep our examples simple. For each example below, we've indicated whether the expression is true or false.

Expression	Resulting value
(10 .EQ. 5) .OR. (16 .GT. 14)	True because 16 is greater than 14.

simple logical expression — simple logical expression

compound logical expression

(10 .EQ. 5) .AND. (16 .GT. 14)	False because one expression statement is false; both expressions must be true for the total to be true.
.NOT. (10 .EQ. 5)	True because the expression (10 .EQ. 5) is false.

It's not as bad as it looks—in fact, logical expressions are fun to write, once you get the hang of it. So let's practice a few.

Evaluate each of the expressions below, determining whether the resulting value is either true or false. For your convenience, we've provided a table that you can use as a worksheet, and we've even worked out the answer to the first problem. Assume I = 20 and J = 30.

(a) (I .GT. 10) .AND. (J .EQ. 30)   (e) (I .NE. 20) .OR. (J .GE. 30)
(b) (I .LT. 10) .AND. (J .LE. 30)   (f) (I .LT. 5) .OR. (J .EQ. 30)
(c) (I .EQ. 30) .AND. (J .LT. 40)   (g) (I .GE. 15) .OR. (J .GT. 50)
(d) .NOT. (I .LT. 50)   (h) (I .GT. 70) .OR. (J .LT. 5)

	Value of expressions first	second	Logical operator	Value of compound expression
(a)	T	T	.AND.	T
(b)				
(c)				
(d)				
(e)				
(f)				
(g)				
(h)				

- - - - - - - - - - - - - - - - - -

(b)	F	T	.AND.	F
(c)	F	T	.AND.	F
(d)	T		.NOT.	F
(e)	F	T	.OR.	T
(f)	F	T	.OR.	T
(g)	T	F	.OR.	T
(h)	F	F	.OR.	F

Now if you're interested in knowing the technical reason for the periods surrounding the logical operators, proceed to frame **38**; otherwise GO TO frame **39.**

38. Why is it necessary to write the relational and logical operators with periods? The answer is simple. Up to now the FORTRAN compiler would treat LE as an integer variable name—but if we tried to compare the variable XYZ with the value 13., XYZ LE 13. would confuse the compiler.

Some compilers ignore blanks and generally would consider XYZ LE as XYZLE, which is a legitimate real variable name. Similarly, comparing values 5 and 15 in the expression 5 LE 15 would cause the compiler to assume you were naming a variable 5LE15. But since variable names must begin with an alphabetic character, 5LE15 would be interpreted as a syntax error during compilation.

The periods enclosing the logical and relational operators let the compiler determine that the operators are logical (rather than illogical!).

Repair these logical expressions.

(a)   (A + B) . LE (C + D) _____

(b)   ((BE + CARE) . EQ. FULL) AND (HERE EQ 0.)

_____

- - - - - - - - - - - - - - - - - - -

(a) (A + B) . LE. (C + D)
              ↑

(b) ((BE + CARE) . EQ. FULL) .AND. (HERE . EQ. 0.)
                    ↑   ↑   ↑   ↑

39. Like arithmetic operations, logical and relational operations are also subject to a hierarchy.

Hierarchy	Operation	
1	( ) parentheses	
2	** exponentiation	
3	* multiplication	arithmetic
3	/ division	operators
4	+ addition	
4	– subtraction	
5	.GT. greater than	
5	.GE. greater than or equal to	
5	.EQ. equal to	relational
5	.NE. not equal to	operators
5	.LE. less than or equal to	
5	.LT. less than	
6	.NOT. not	logical
7	.AND. and	operators
8	.OR. or	

The arithmetic operations are performed first, then the relational operations, and finally logical operations. Here is an example.

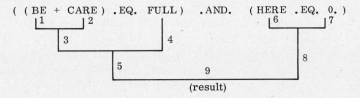

(result)

The computer will encounter BE + CARE as the first complete expression contained within a set of parentheses; the computer performs the addition of elements 1 and 2 which it then stores as an intermediate result, indicated by 3 in our diagram. Scanning to the right, FULL is the last "mini" expression that completes the larger expression ((BE + CARE) . EQ. FULL). The intermediate result 3 and FULL (4) are related, with the true or false value stored as an intermediate result, marked 5.

Continuing to scan to the right, the computer determines that HERE . EQ. 0. is another complete expression, which it then evaluates and stores a true or false value as the intermediate result 8. Finally, the intermediate results 5 and 8 are ANDed together, giving us the final result.

Remember, the evaluation takes place from left to right, and from innermost parentheses to outermost. Within parentheses, the rules for evaluating arithmetic expressions (from left to right) apply just as we described in Chapter Two.

Diagram the following expression in the same manner as we did the example. (Hint: Consider each side of the .AND. as separate expressions.)

WIDTH * DEPTH * HEIGHT .GT. 100. .AND. WEIGHT .LT. 250.

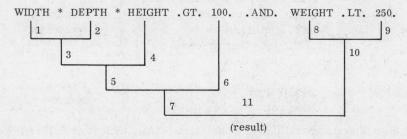

(result)

Remember that the computer scans and evaluates the expressions from left to right. The expression WIDTH * DEPTH * HEIGHT .GT. 100. is evaluated, followed by the evaluation of WEIGHT . LT. 250., and then the two results are ANDed which results in either a true or false value. So let's consider each side of the .AND. separately.

In the expression WIDTH * DEPTH * HEIGHT .GT. 100., the * operator has a higher priority over the .GT. operator, so it will be performed first. Because only two values can be multiplied at one time, the first two are multiplied and then the result (3) is multiplied by the variable HEIGHT (4). The result of the arithmetic operations (5) (in this instance, multiplication) is related to the constant 100.; if equal or less, a false value is stored; otherwise a true value is temporarily stored (7).

The .AND. has the lowest priority in our problem expression, so it will be performed last. Continuing our scan to the right, we then perform the

relation of WEIGHT .LT. 250., and store the true or false value as an intermediate result (10). Finally, the two intermediate results (7 and 10) are
ANDed which gives us our final true or false value (11).

40. We've supplied the values of L and M below. In each case, substitute
the numerical values and then evaluate the expression, determining whether
it is true or false. To assist you, we've worked out the answer to the first
as a guide. Here is the expression.

((L .LT. 35) .OR. (M .EQ. 15)) .AND. .NOT. L .GT. M

L	M		True/false
15	15	(a)	true

First, substitute the values for the variables in the expression: ((15 .LT. 35) .OR.
(15 .EQ. 15)) .AND. .NOT. 15 .GT. 15.
Expressions within parentheses will be
evaluated before those outside; thus, .OR.
will be performed before .AND..

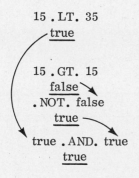

15 .LT. 35
true

15 .GT. 15
false
.NOT. false
true

true .AND. true
true

Second, evaluating the expression 15 .LT.
35 results in a true value; it is not necessary to evaluate the remainder of the .OR.
because it will be true if either is true.

Next, 15 .GT. 15 results in a false value
which is converted to true by the logic operation of .NOT..

Finally, both intermediate values of true
are ANDed, resulting in a final value of
true.

15	14	(b)	
36	15	(c)	
34	36	(d)	

- - - - - - - - - - - - - - - -

(b) false

15 .LT. 35
true

15 .GT. 14
true

.NOT. true
false

true .AND. false
false

L .LT. 35

L .GT. M

.NOT. L .GT. M

(c) false
(d) true

41. The earlier FORTRAN compilers did not permit logical IF statements. Likewise, if your FORTRAN compiler does not contain all of the ANS FORTRAN commands, it most likely does not permit the logical IF statement. In this frame we will show you how comparable results can be obtained by using either a logical or an arithmetic IF statement sequence.

Problem: Add 1 to KOUNT if PRICE is greater than .99

Logical IF Solution

```
          IF (PRICE .GT. .99) KOUNT = KOUNT + 1
```

Arithmetic IF Solution

```
          IF (PRICE - .99) 2, 2, 1
1         KOUNT = KOUNT + 1
2         CONTINUE
```

Both program segments will produce identical results, but the logical IF is easier to read and understand.

Write a program segment using logical IF statements that assign the sum of L and M to K if:

> L is less than or equal to M and L is less than 35, or
> L is less than or equal to M and M equals 15.

Otherwise K has the value of 100.

- - - - - - - - - - - - - - - - - - - -

```
          K = 100
          IF ((L .LE. M .AND. L .LT. 35) .OR. (L .LE.
    -     M .AND. M .EQ. 15) K = L + M
```

42. If you'd like some practice in analyzing a logical IF program, try drawing a flowchart of the program segment in frame 41. Otherwise, look at the answer to this frame on the next page and use it to answer frame 43.

- - - - - - - - - - - - - - - - - - -

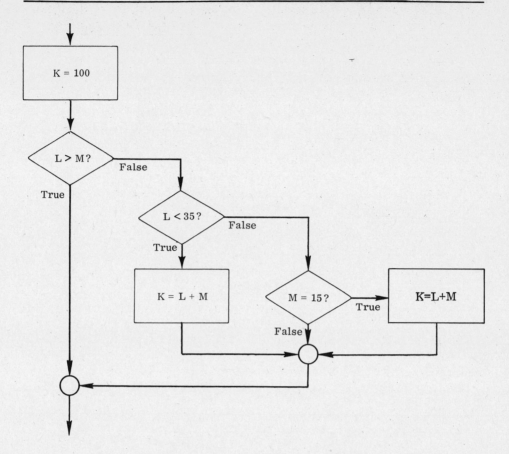

43. Here's your chance to rewrite the program segment for frame 41 using arithmetic IF statements instead. Use the flowchart in frame 42 to guide yourself.

- - - - - - - - - - - - - - - - - - -

		K = 100
		IF (L - M) 1, 1, 4
1		IF (L - 35) 3, 2, 2
2		IF (M - 15) 4, 3, 4
3		K = L + M
4		CONTINUE

44. The executable statement of the IF statement may be any except another logical IF or a DO statement. Look carefully at the following IF statements and determine which are incorrect and why.

Invalid and reason

(a)
```
IF (TIME .LT. HOUR)
-   DO 1000 J = 1, 25, 4
```

(b)
```
IF (J .EQ. 75 .OR. BIG
-   .GT. SMALL)
-   READ (5, 8041) VALUE
```

(c)
```
IF (BUNNY .LE. RABBIT)
-   IF (4 .GT. LITTLE)
-   GO TO 75000
```

(d)
```
IF (A .LT. 37.) GO TO 1004
```

- - - - - - - - - - - - - - - - - - -

(a) Invalid because the object of a logical IF statement cannot be a DO statement.

(b) Valid.

(c) Invalid because another logical IF statement cannot be the object of a logical IF statement.

(d) Invalid because only statement numbers are permitted in columns 1-5; the IF statement itself must begin after column 6.

45. In Chapter Eight we'll cover logical type variables which are variables that contain a value that the program treats as either .TRUE. or .FALSE.. Note that we wrote .TRUE. and .FALSE. in capital letters and with periods, because this is how we will write logical values for testing or initializing. You'll have to wait until Chapter Eight for more information. However, we think you're pretty smart, so here is a teaser: If the variable TEST has the value of .TRUE., what do you think will be the value of PIES?

```
        DOZENS = 37.
        PIES = 0
        IF (TEST) PIES = 12. * DOZENS
        WRITE (6,100) PIES
100     FORMAT ('  I LOVE PIES. '/' I WANT ', F7.0)
```

- - - - - - - - - - - - - - - -

One big tummy ache: 444 pies (12 times 37 equals 444).   The statement
PIES = 12. * DOZENS is executed because TEST has the value of .TRUE..

46. Let's practice using some simple logical IF statements in each of the
following problems.

(a)   Calculate SUM = PART1 + PART2 if the value of MICE is greater than 7
or AREA is greater than 36.4.

(b)   Write the message ERROR COUNT OF xx HAS EXCEEDED 7 to device 6
whenever KOUNT has a value exceeding 7.

(c)   Branch to statement 10040 if the sum of A and B is less than 95.3 and
I times J is less than 26.

- - - - - - - - - - - - - - - - - - - -

Here are some possible answers.
(a)   IF (MICE .GT. 7 .OR. AREA .GT. 36.4) SUM = PART1 + PART2, or
       IF ((MICE .GT. 7) .OR. (AREA .GT. 36.4)) SUM = PART1 + PART2
(b)   IF (KOUNT .GT. 7) WRITE (6,13011) KOUNT
       13011   FORMAT (' ERROR COUNT OF ', I2, ' HAS EXCEEDED 7')
(c)   IF (A + B .LT. 95.3 .AND. I * J .LT. 26) GO TO 10040, or
       IF ((A + B .LT. 95.3) .AND. (I * J .LT. 26)) GO TO 10040, or
       IF (((A + B) .LT. 95.3) .AND. ((I * J) .LT. 26)) GO TO 10040
Note how the first answer for each (a) and (c) takes advantage of the hierarchy
of operations.

Summary of Logical IF

The general form for the logical IF statement is

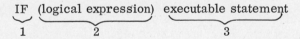

$$\underbrace{IF}_{1}\ \underbrace{(\text{logical expression})}_{2}\ \underbrace{\text{executable statement}}_{3}$$

1.   The word IF.
2.   A logical expression relating two or more variables (or, as you
will cover in Chapter Eight, a single logical variable) contained
within a pair of parentheses such that when evaluated, it will have
either a value of true or false.
3.   An executable statement other than another logical IF statement
or a DO statement.

The executable statement following the logical expression is executed
only if the expression is evaluated as true; otherwise execution continues
with the next executable statement following the logical IF statement. We
can flowchart this concept as shown on the next page.

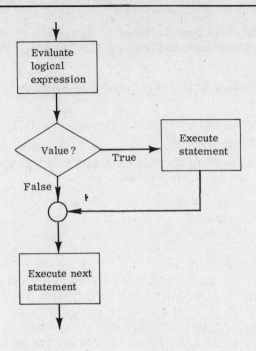

Frames 47 through 52 only apply to FORTRAN 77. If you don't have access to a FORTRAN 77 compiler or are not interested in the block IF statement, skip to frame 53.

BLOCK IF CONSTRUCT

47. The FORTRAN block IF construct (or structure) was implemented as part of the FORTRAN 77 standard. As you probably remember from a few frames ago, the logical IF statement causes execution of a single statement in the event the logical expression is true.

The (logical) block IF construct, however, gives you the expanded capability of executing a block (or group) of statements, and such block can be executed if the expression is either true or false. In the following frames, we'll show you how the block IF construct executes a block of statements. The important thing right now, though, is to remember that a block can contain from zero (none) to an unlimited number of statements. A block which contains no statements is called an "empty" block. Makes sense, doesn't it?

(a) What is the minimum number of statements a block may contain?

(b) Is it permissible for a block to contain more than 25 statements?

(c) In your own words, what is the primary difference between the logical

IF statement and the block IF construct? (Maybe you can think of two.)

- -

(a) A block may be empty, that is, contain no statements;
(b) yes;
(c) the logical IF statement causes execution of a single statement if the evaluated expression is true, but the block IF executes a <u>block of statements</u> if the expression is either <u>true or false.</u>

48. Here's an illustration of the block IF construct.

<pre>
1   7
     IF (SPEED .GT. LIMIT) THEN
         TICKET = .TRUE.
         FINE = 15.00 + 10.00 * (SPEED - LIMIT)
     ELSE
         TICKET = .FALSE.
     END IF
</pre>

Note the similarity between the block IF above and the logical IF statement. You also noticed, we hope, the new words THEN, ELSE and END IF. The block IF construct consists of seven parts, some of which are optional.

<pre>
     IF (logical expression) THEN
     1   2   3

         (zero to many)
         statements)   } 4

     ELSE
     5

         (zero to many)
         statements)   } 6

     END IF
        7
</pre>

1. The word IF.
2. A logical expression enclosed within a single pair of parentheses (the logical expression must be capable of being evaluated as either true or false).
3. The word THEN.
4. An IF-block, which may consist of any number of FORTRAN statements (including none). This block of statements will be executed if the expression is evaluated as <u>true</u>.

5.   The word ELSE.

6.   An IF-block, which may consist of any number of FORTRAN statements (including none). This block of statements will be executed if the expression is evaluated as <u>false.</u>

7.   The words END IF, which have the same nesting level as the IF statement (item 1 above).

While indention is optional, it certainly helps to make your programs more readable. If you only want to execute the IF-block when the expression is true, you may omit both items 5 and 6 above. Here's a flowchart which illustrates the concept of the block IF construct.

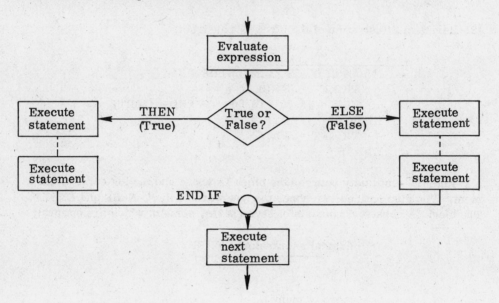

Flowchart the FORTRAN code which appears at the beginning of this frame.

- -

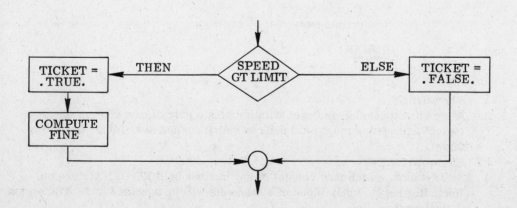

49. The block IF construct becomes easier to use...when you use it frequently. So, for some practice, we've rewritten the flowchart from frame
42 so that it is in the form of the block IF.

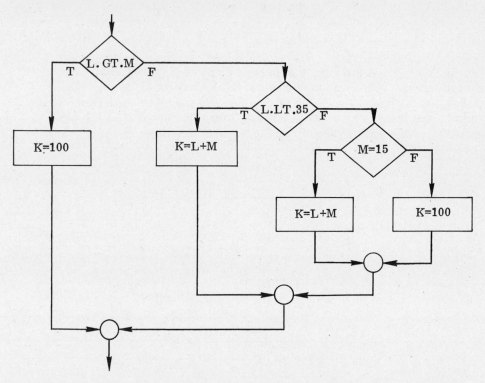

Okay, now it's your turn. Write the FORTRAN code, using the concept
of the block IF to correspond with the above flowchart. Don't forget to use
the END IF to terminate each level of IF. (Hint: an IF-block can contain
another block IF construct).

- -

You probably came up with something close to this solution.

```
1    7
    IF (L .GT. M) THEN
        K = 100
    ELSE
        IF (L .LT. 35) THEN
            K = L + M
        ELSE
            IF (M .EQ. 15) THEN
                K = L + M
            ELSE
                K = 100
```

<u>1   7</u>
        END IF
      END IF
    END IF

50. In frame 48, we told you that parts 5 and 6 are optional under certain circumstances: when no statements are to be executed in the event the logical expression evaluates as false. Rewrite your answer to frame 49 so that the statement   K = 100   is first, followed by your block-IF construct(s). Your answer should have only one ELSE statement.

- -

<u>1   7</u>
      K = 100

      IF (L .LE. M) THEN
        IF (L .LT. 35) THEN
          K = L + M
        ELSE
          IF (M .EQ. 15) THEN
            K = L + M
          END IF
        END IF
      END IF

51. Look at all those END IFs! Wow! FORTRAN 77 makes available the ELSE IF statement to make our work easier. For example,

<u>1   7</u>
    ELSE
      IF (M .EQ. 15) THEN

This statement defines the beginning of another IF level. Each If level needs an END IF statement to terminat it.

becomes
<u>1   7</u>
    ELSE IF (M .EQ. 15) THEN

In contrast, this defines an IF block. No END IF statement is required, except after the last IF block.

The answers to frames 49 and 50 take on a whole new look when we use the ELSE IF statement. We've coded the first few lines. You finish the coding.

```
1       7
        IF  (L .GT.  M) THEN
            K = 100
        ELSE IF (L. LT.  35) THEN
            K = L + M
        ELSE IF (M .EQ.  15) THEN

        _____

        _____

        _____

        END IF
```

Here are the missing three lines.

```
1       7
            K = L + M
        ELSE
            K = 100
```

52. As with the DO loop, you are not permitted to branch into the range (of a block-IF construct). We really have no idea how your program will "blow up" if you try it. And finally, you can even use DO loops within an IF-block. Just be sure the range of the DO loop is within the range of the IF-block.

Here's a flowchart which contains two DO loops. Write the FORTRAN code using the concept of the block IF statement as well as the ELSE IF.

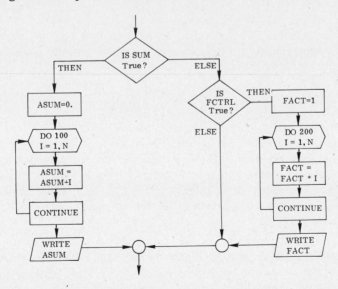

```
1       7
        IF (SUM) THEN
            ASUM = 0
            DO 100 I = 1, N
100         ASUM=ASUM + I          or            ASUM = ASUM + I
            WRITE (6,901) ASUM          100      CONTINUE
        ELSE IF (FCTRL) THEN
            FACT = 1
            DO 200 I = 1, N
200         FACT = FACT * I        or            FACT = FACT * I
            WRITE (6,902) FACT          200      CONTINUE
        END IF
```

Summary of Block IF

The general form for the block IF construct is

$$
\underbrace{\text{IF}}_{1} \quad \underbrace{\text{(logical expression)}}_{2} \quad \underbrace{\text{THEN}}_{3}
$$

$$
\left.\begin{array}{c}\text{(zero to}\\ \text{many statements)}\end{array}\right\} 4
$$

$$
\underbrace{\text{ELSE}}_{5}
$$

$$
\left.\begin{array}{c}\text{(zero to}\\ \text{many statements)}\end{array}\right\} 6
$$

$$
\underbrace{\text{END IF}}_{7}
$$

1. The word IF.
2. A logical expression relating two or more variables (or, as you will cover in Chapter Eight, a single logical variable) contained within a pair of parentheses such that when evaluated, it will have either a value of true or false.
3. The word THEN.
4. An IF-block, consisting of any number of FORTRAN statements, which will be executed if the expression evaluates as true.
5. The word ELSE. The word ELSE and the IF-block which follows aren't required when there aren't any to be executed if the expression evaluates as false.
6. An IF-block, consisting of any number of FORTRAN statements, which will be executed if the expression evaluates as false.
7. The words END IF.

The IF-block following the word THEN is executed only if the expression is evaluated as true; otherwise execution continues with the IF-block following the word ELSE, if it is present. We flowchart this concept as shown on the next page.

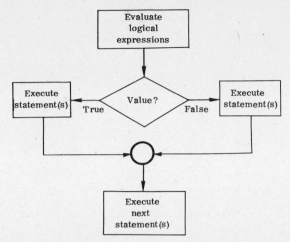

The words ELSE IF may be used to add additional IF-blocks which will be executed when the expression evaluated is true. The ELSE IF takes the general form

$$\text{ELSE IF} \quad \underbrace{\text{(logical expression)}}_{2} \quad \underbrace{\text{THEN}}_{3}$$

with the same rules applicable to the block-IF as described above.

Computed GO TO Statement

53. Back in Chapter Three you learned how to use the GO TO statement which causes an unconditional branch to another statement within your program. FORTRAN provides another kind of GO TO statement called the computed GO TO statement. Here's what such a statement looks like.

$$\underbrace{\text{GO TO}}_{1} \underbrace{(183, \ 37, \ 104)}_{2}, \underbrace{J}_{3}$$

1. GO TO or GOTO tells the FORTRAN compiler that what follows is a GO TO statement.
2. Upon detecting a left parenthesis, the FORTRAN compiler knows that this must be a computed GO TO statement, and it expects to find one or more statement numbers, each separated from the other by a comma, within the parentheses. Don't confuse the compiler by referencing a FORMAT statement, because the compiler will catch your error.
3. After sensing the rightmost parenthesis, the compiler looks for a comma which must be followed by an unsigned integer variable. This variable acts as a pointer when the computer is executing the program. If the pointer variable has the value 3 the computer will branch to the statement indicated by the third statement number from the left, here 104. If the pointer variable equals 2, the computer will branch to the statement referenced by the second statement number from the left, here 37.

Using the following computed GO TO statement, to what statement number will execution branch for each of the values of the pointer variable listed?

```
GØ TØ (10001, 29, 57630, 19, 10), INDEX
```

INDEX		Statement number
1	(a)	_____
2	(b)	_____
3	(c)	_____
4	(d)	_____
5	(e)	_____

- - - - - - - - - - - - - - - - - - -

(a) 10001; (b) 29; (c) 57630; (d) 19; (e) 10

54. Let's practice. Write a computed GO TO statement which will branch to:

statement 3400 if the pointer variable has a value of 5 or 6;
statement 3200 if the pointer has a value of 1 or 3;
statement 3300 if the pointer has a value of 2 or 4.

Assume the compiler will cause the branch to be to the next statement if the pointer value is anything else. Use NAME as the pointer variable.

- - - - - - - - - - - - - - - - - -

```
GØ TØ (3200, 3300, 3200, 3300, 3400, 3400),
NAME
```

55. Now write a computed GO TO statement which branches to statements 1001, 1002, 1005, or 1009, depending upon whether the value of the pointer variable J is any of the values 1 through 4 respectively.

- - - - - - - - - - - - - - - - - -

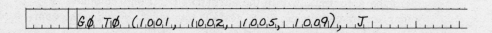

```
GØ TØ (1001, 1002, 1005, 1009), J
```

56. During program execution the pointer variable may have a negative or zero value, or even a value greater than the number of statement numbers within the parentheses. Depending upon your computer installation's FORTRAN compiler, the results will be either unpredictable or corrective action will be taken. Some compilers will merely ignore the computed GO TO statement in this instance and continue execution with the next executable statement in sequence.

What would happen if the variable ICODE had a value of 5 or 0?

```
       GØ TØ (20, 21, 22, 23), ICØDE
C  CØDE 1 - CLERICAL AND SECRETARIAL
20     BØNUS = SALARY / 52.
```

- - - - - - - - - - - - - - - - - -

Most compilers would cause execution to continue with statement 20, which happens to be the next executable statement. With other compilers, who knows . . .

57. If your compiler ignores the computed GO TO statement when the pointer variable is out of range, negative, or zero, you could take advantage of this feature to check for valid employee status codes. Note what happens if the value of the code (variable ICODE) is greater than 4 or less than 1.

```
       READ (1, 100) NAME, ID, ICØDE, SALARY, IDEPT
       GØ TØ (20, 21, 22, 23), ICØDE
C  INVALID CØDE - WRITE EXCEPTIØN REPØRT
       WRITE (6, 101) NAME, ID, ICØDE, SALARY, IDEPT
```

If ICODE has a value less than 1 or greater than 4, our program segment will print a message notifying us that something is wrong.

Write a program segment that will cause a branch to the statements indicated. If the pointer variable has an invalid value, have the segment write the message n IS NOT VALID. (where n is the value of the pointer) on the computer console (unit 6).

Value of pointer ICODE	Branch to statement number
1	201
2	923
3	925
4	9000

- - - - - - - - - - - - - - - - -

```
      GØ TØ (201, 923, 925, 9000), ICØDE
      WRITE (6,4001) ICØDE
4001  FØRMAT ('b', I2, 'bISbNØTbVALID.')
```

We used 4001 as the number of the FORMAT statement; you could have used another number, as long as it was not one of those indicated in the computed GO TO statement.

58. Again, assuming your compiler will ignore the computed GO TO if the pointer variable has a zero or out of range value, write a program sequence to branch to 30, 40, or 50, if I = 3, 4, or 5, respectively; otherwise execution is to continue with statement 20.

- - - - - - - - - - - - - - - - - - -

Here are two possible answers.
(1)   GO TO (20, 20, 30, 40, 50), I
      20 next statement

(2)   I = I - 2
      GO TO (30, 40, 50), I
      20 next statement

59. By now you should be an expert with computed GO TO statements. Which of the following statements are incorrect and why?

Incorrect and why

(a)
```
      GØ TØ (ITEAM, IRAH, ITEAM), INDEX
```

(b)
```
      GØ TØ (25, 20, 25), HIKE
```

(c)
```
      GØ TØ (19999), MØMMY
```

(d)
```
      GØ TØ (200, 250, 300) JAIL
```

(e)
```
55    GØ TØ (44, 55, 66), JUMP
```

- - - - - - - - - - - - - - - - - -

(a) Only statement numbers are permitted within the parentheses; variables are not allowed.

(b) The pointer variable must be an integer variable, not real as we have here. Change HIKE to MIKE and we'll be okay.

(c) This one is valid, even though we used only one statement number.

(d) We forgot the comma that belongs between the right parenthesis and the pointer variable JAIL.

(e) This one will work forever if JUMP has a value of 2 because the GO TO statement will loop back to itself repeatedly; never code a branch statement to branch back to itself.

Summary of Computed GO TO Statement

The computed GO TO statement has the following general form.

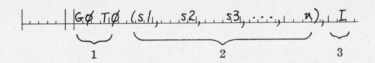

1. GO TO or GOTO (depending upon your compiler).
2. A list of statement numbers within parentheses, each statement number separated from another by a comma.
3. A comma followed by an integer variable which serves as a pointer to one of the statement numbers, depending upon its value. With many compilers, if the value of the pointer variable is either less than or greater than the number of statements referenced in the list, execution will continue with the next executable statement in sequence.

Self-Test

1. The statements below are logical IF statements. Rewrite the segment using an arithmetic IF statement.

```
      IF (AMOUNT .LT. 0.0) TALLY = 1
      IF (AMOUNT .EQ. 0.0) TALLY = 3
      IF (AMOUNT .GT. 0.0) TALLY = 2
```

2.   These three statements can be rewritten as one statement.   Are you a super-programmer?   Try!

```
        IF (AMØUNT) 20, 25, 25
20      AMØUNT = -AMØUNT
25      CØNTINUE
```

3.   Using DO loops, write a series of statements to write the values of "d" for each combination of "g" and "t" where

$$d = 1/2 \ gt^2;$$

g is from 29. to 35., in increments of . 25;

t is from . 1 to 10., in increments of . 1.

4.   Which of the following logical IF statements are incorrect, and why?

(a)
```
        IF (10. - TEN) XRAY = 7ØØ + MANY
```

(b)
```
        IF (TEST) ANSWER .EQ. TRUE
```

(c)
```
        IF ((V1 .LT. V2) .ØR. A = B) QUEEN =
       -    BREAD + HØNEY
```

(d)
```
        IF (A .GT. B) IF ((13 + I) .GT. 37) YØU =
       -    ARE - RIGHT
```

(e)
```
        IF (A .LT. B) B .GT. A
```

(f)
```
        IF (I .EQ. I1) DØ 97 JANET = 1, 3, 1
```

5. To which statement will execution branch for each value of JUMP?

```
      GØ TØ (15, 20, 10, 1, 9, 67), JUMP
5     LØØK = MYEYES * 2
```

Value of JUMP		Statement number	Value of JUMP		Statement number
0	(a)	_____	4	(e)	_____
1	(b)	_____	5	(f)	_____
2	(c)	_____	6	(g)	_____
3	(d)	_____	7	(h)	_____

6. What's wrong with the following GO TO statements?

(a)
```
      GØ TØ (100, 200, 300), JAIL + 37
```

(b)
```
      GØ TØ (100, 200, 300), HØME
```

(c)
```
      JUMPY = 3
300   GØ TØ (100, 200, 300), JUMPY
```

7. Rewrite this program segment of logical IF statements using the concept of the block IF. Use the ELSE IF statement in your answer.

```
1       7
        IF (AMØUNT .EQ. 1) TALLY = 9
        IF (AMØUNT .EQ. 2) TALLY = 4
        IF (AMØUNT .EQ. 3) TALLY = 7
        IF (AMØUNT .LT. 1) TALLY = 1
        IF (AMØUNT .GT. 3) TALLY = 5
```

8.   For the block IF construct below, give the value of K for the different values of L and M.

```
1       7
        IF (L .GT. M .OR. L .GE. 35 .AND. M .NE. 15) THEN
            K = 100
        ELSE
            K = L + M
        END IF
```

Value of L	Value of M	Value of K	Value of L	Value of M	Value of K
10	5	(a)_____	35	10	(e)_____
10	10	(b)_____	35	15	(f)_____
10	15	(c)_____	40	15	(g)_____
10	20	(d)_____	40	20	(h)_____

Answers to Self-Test

1.
```
        IF (AMØUNT) 10, 11, 12
10      TALLY = 1.
        GØ TØ 13
11      TALLY = 3.
        GØ TØ 13
12      TALLY = 2.
13      CØNTINUE
```

(frames 42-43)

2.
```
        IF (AMØUNT .LT. 0.0) AMØUNT = -AMØUNT
```

(frame 41)

3.

```
C    INITIALIZE VARIABLES
        G = 28.75
C    INCREMENT VARIABLE G
        DØ 1020 J = 1, 25
        G = G + .25
C        INCREMENT VARIABLE T
            DØ 1010 I = 1, 100
            T = I/10.
C        CALCULATE D AND WRITE VALUES
            D = (G * T * T) / 2.
            WRITE (6, 9010) D, G, T
9010        FORMAT (' ', 3F8.2)
1010        CONTINUE
1020 CONTINUE
```

(frames 21 and 22)

4.   All of the examples are wrong, and here's why.

(a) Because an assignment statement follows the expression tested by the IF statement, the compiler considers the IF statement to be a logical type; consequently, it expects the expression being tested to result in either a <u>true</u> or <u>false</u> value—but it doesn't. Instead, it results in an arithmetic value, and that's why it doesn't work. (frame 29)

(b) The expression ANSWER .EQ. TRUE contains the logical operator .EQ., but such an expression cannot be the object of any IF statement because it is not executable. If the programmer were attempting an assignment, he should have written IF (TEST) ANSWER = TRUE instead. (frame 29)

(c) The equal sign (=) in the tested expression is an arithmetic operator and cannot be used as a relational one. The statement should be rewritten as

```
      IF ((V1 .LT. V2) .ØR. A .EQ. B) QUEEN =
    -    BREAD + HØNEY
```

(frame 30)

(d) FORTRAN does not allow a logical IF statement to be the object of an IF statement, though you may find a compiler that has been extended to include this feature. (frame 35)

(e) The object of the logical IF statement must be an executable statement; B .GT. A is an expression—not a statement. (frame 29)

(f) A DO statement is not permitted as the object of any IF statement. (frame 35).

5.   (a) 5; (b) 15; (c) 20; (d) 10; (e) 1; (f) 9; (g) 67; (h) 5 (frames 42 and 45)

6. Each of the statements is incorrect.

(a) The pointer variable must be an unsigned integer variable—not an expression of two or more variables and/or constants. (frame 53)

(b) The pointer variable must be integer type, not real. (frame 53)

(c) Please don't do this program. It will compile okay, but the program will loop forever. Never have a statement branch back to itself. (frame 59)

7.
```
1       7
        IF (AMØUNT .EQ. 1) THEN
            TALLY = 9
        ELSE IF (AMØUNT .EQ. 2) THEN
            TALLY = 4
        ELSE IF (AMØUNT .EQ. 3) THEN
            TALLY = 7
        ELSE IF (AMØUNT .LT. 1) THEN
            TALLY = 1
        ELSE
            TALLY = 5
        END IF
```

(frame 51)

8. (a) 100; (b) 20; (c) 25; (d) 30; (e) 100; (f) 50; (g) 55; (h) 100
(frames 40 and 51)

CHAPTER SEVEN
Hurrah for Arrays

Often we want to write a program to run identical operations on a list of variables. For example, we might want to calculate the weekly average price of a security. To calculate the average price for each of 100 stocks over five days, up to now we would have required 500 variables as well as 100 repetitions of the program segment. How time consuming! But using arrays (subscripted variables, which we introduce in this chapter) along with the DO statement you've already learned, you can easily write a powerful and efficient FORTRAN program for this problem.

Similarly, you might want a program to edit incoming data by checking certain items against acceptable values stored in a table. If you wanted to test an item against each of the 100 possible acceptable values in the table, you certainly would not want to write 100 test statements! Using arrays and DO loops, you could code such a table search in just three lines.

Or imagine writing a program that assigns seats for specific plane flights. You could assign one variable to each seat—but how would you handle each separate flight? The coding could be foreboding! But using subscripted variables (arrays) along with direct access (disk, which will be presented in Chapter Eleven), programming such a seat reservation problem becomes a relatively easy task. In fact, the more you learn about FORTRAN, the more you'll appreciate the value of arrays.

When you complete this chapter you will be able to:

- correctly refer to a specific element in an array;

- write a DIMENSION statement in its proper place;

- specify and use two- and three-dimensional arrays.

One-Dimensional Array

1. The variables we have been using must start with an alphabetic character and have up to five additional digits and/or alphabetic characters. Now we will add some new wrinkles to make a new type of variable—called a subscripted variable.

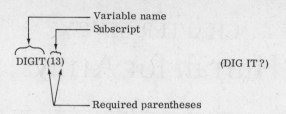

A subscripted variable consists of a variable name followed by a subscript enclosed in a single pair of parentheses.

DEEP(6) is a subscripted variable. DEEP6 is not a subscripted variable, but rather an "ordinary" variable (or a single variable name).

Which of the following are subscripted variables?

_____ (a) APPLE(6)   _____ (c) WAR73

_____ (b) AISLE5   _____ (d) JOYIS(21)

- - - - - - - - - - - - - - - - - - -

Choices (a) and (d) are subscripted variables.

2.   A subscripted variable name represents a set of consecutive locations as opposed to an unsubscripted variable (the type we've been using) which occupies one storage location inside the computer's memory. Here is a set (array) of five subscripted variables, each of which is called an array element.

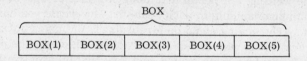

We call this set of subscripted variables either a one-dimensional array, a list, or a vector. The variable name BOX refers to the whole array. A reference to a specific array element is accomplished by subscripting the variable name with an integer subscript. Here are several examples: To refer to the fifth element in the array BOX we write BOX(5). To put the value 5.2 in the fifth element of the array BOX we write BOX(5) = 5.2. The statement WRITE (6,100) BOX(5) writes the value 5.2 on a printing device.

(a) Write a statement to read the value 8.2 from device 5 (a card reader) into the second element of the array GENE.

(b) A student programmer wrote the following:

    BOX(3) = 57.0
    BOX(5) = 389.0

What data values do you think the variables BOX(3) and BOX(5) now contain? _____

- - - - - - - - - - - - - - - - - - -

(a) READ (5, 100) GENE(2)

(b) The value 57.0 is stored in the third element of the array BOX, that is, BOX(3). 389.0 is the value of the fifth array element, BOX(5).

3. Suppose we want to read six scores into storage. We certainly would avoid writing the following FORTRAN statements with six different variables.

```
        READ (5, 100) THESE
        READ (5, 100) STAT
        READ (5, 100) EMENTS
        READ (5, 100) ARE
        READ (5, 100) RIDIC
        READ (5, 100) ULOUS
100     FORMAT (F3.2)
```

If the variables are to be stored consecutively within memory,

| THESE | STAT | EMENTS | ARE | RIDIC | ULOUS |

we could just as well use a six-element array (list) to represent the six variables. Let's call this list SCORES. Then each variable can be considered in a one-to-one relationship to each element in the array SCORES.

SCORES

THESE	STAT	EMENTS	ARE	RIDIC	ULOUS
SCORES(1)	SCORES(2)	SCORES(3)	SCORES(4)	SCORES(5)	SCORES(6)

We can now use the following program to transfer these data values into storage.

```
        DO 20 I = 1, 6
        READ (5, 100) SCORES(I)
20      CONTINUE
100     FORMAT (F3.2)
        :
        :
```

Thus, an array name enables us to represent a list of related variables compactly, by use of a single variable name. If the value of a specific array element is needed, it is referred to by its subscript. For example, when $I = 3$, the third score would be read in the above program. That is, this statement would be executed: READ (5, 100) SCORES(3).

If you want to represent a set of nine integer variables, how many elements should the integer array contain? _____

– – – – – – – – – – – – – – – – – – – –

The array should contain at least nine elements.

Note for mathematical buffs: The subscripting technique is well known in matrix algebra. A specific item within a matrix is referred to by a subscript. For example, the third value of the vector ALAN is written $ALAN_3$. The 3 printed to the lower right of the name ALAN is called a subscript. FORTRAN denotes a subscript by enclosing the subscript within a set of parentheses, such as ALAN(3).

4. The <u>variable name</u> in a subscripted variable follows the same rules as in an ordinary variable. The subscripted variable NUMBER(10) may contain an integer value. Whereas, the element GAMES(10) may store a real value. The subscripted variable NUMBERGAMES(10) is illegal since the variable name NUMBERGAMES exceeds six characters.

(a) Write a READ statement to transmit the value 53.5 from device 5 (a card reader) into a legal variable with the subscript 111.

(b) What value is contained in the element MAN(333) after the statement MAN(333) = 22.44 is executed?

– – – – – – – – – – – – – – – – – – – –

(a) READ (5, 100) GOOD(111)—or any other similar answer, as long as the variable name starts with a letter other than IJKLMN
(b) the value 22 (MAN is an integer variable name and so the element MAN(333) will store an integer value.)

5. Please keep firmly in mind that the purpose of a subscript is to indicate exactly which item in a list is being referenced. Fortran 77 allows you to start indexing an array element at either a positive, negative, or zero constant value. However, we will assume that the start for indexing the array variable is 1. That is, the first element is indexed as a name (1). Thus, the subscripted variable PSALM (73) refers to the 73rd element in a list called PSALM. However, to write PSALM (73.2) would be as meaningless as writing the address 73.2 Madison Avenue instead of 73 Madison Avenue. So the first rule is: <u>A subscript value must always be an integer</u> (whether it be positive, negative, or zero). For example, the following are correct: LEARN(66), LEARN(0), and LEARN(-66). But LEARN(66.0) and LEARN(66.9) have illegal subscripts.

Write a statement to subtract the fifth element of the variable name CLOTH from the eighth element of the variable name MAN. Store the result in the second element of the variable name STREAK.

– – – – – – – – – – – – – – – – – – – –

STREAK(2) = MAN(8) - CLOTH(5)

6. The second rule of subscripting is: <u>An integer variable may be used as a subscript</u>. 1966 FORTRAN requires the subscript to have a <u>positive</u> integer value. PSALM(I) is correct only if the integer variable I already contains a positive integer value under 1966 FORTRAN. Examine these examples.

(a)
```
1       I = 4
2       XEROX(I) = 27.5
```

When statement 1 is executed, the variable I has the value _____ .

So when statement 2 is executed the _____ th element in the array XEROX is referenced.

(b)
```
3       READ (5, 100), INDEX, V
4       VALUE(INDEX) = V + .37
```

In this example, suppose a punched card contains the values 5 and 360.7. When statement 3 is executed the variables INDEX and V contain the values _____ and 360.7, respectively. When statement 4 is executed the _____ th element in the array VALUE is referenced.

- - - - - - - - - - - - - - - - - -

(a) 4, fourth; (b) 5, fifth

7. The third rule states that <u>subscripted variables may have integer variable expressions as subscripts</u>.

```
        DO 25 MYAGE = 31, 65
        KOUNT(MYAGE - 21) = MYAGE * MYAGE
25      CONTINUE
```

In this example, because of the initial and terminal values of the DO variable the subscript expression MYAGE - 21 always results in a positive integer value. Therefore, it is a legal subscript. When the DO loop is entered the first time, the integer variable MYAGE has the value 31. So the expression MYAGE - 21 has the value 10. In all subsequent executions of the DO loop the subscript MYAGE - 21 when properly evaluated yields a positive integer value.

Under what circumstances may the following program segments be incorrect?

(a)
```
        I = -4
        ARRAY(I) = 27
```

(b)

```
READ (5,100) SCRIPT, V
VALUE (SCRIPT) = V + .37
```

(c)

```
     DO 25 MYAGE = 31, 65
     KOUNT(MYAGE - 31) = MYAGE * AGE
25   CONTINUE
```

- - - - - - - - - - - - - - - - - - -

(a) 1966 Fortran will not allow a subscript value of −4, although it is correct under Fortran 77.

(b) The subscript SCRIPT contains a real value which is not legal.

(c) On the first execution of the DO loop, the value of the expression MYAGE −31 is zero, which is not permitted in 1966 FORTRAN.

8.   Assume you have an array of ten elements called NUMBER with a lower bound of 1 and an upper bound of 10. Thus NUMBER (5) refers to the fifth element in the array NUMBER. NUMBER(4) refers to the preceding one, element 4. NUMBER(K - 1) refers to the element in the array preceding element NUMBER(K).

(a) Now, write an IF statement which would compare NUMBER(K) and NUMBER(K - 1). If NUMBER(K - 1) is greater than NUMBER(K), statement 60 would be executed; otherwise, control branches to statement 40.

(b) Write a statement to exchange the value stored in the elements NUMBER (K) and NUMBER (K - 1). You will need another storage location (called ITEMP) to do this.

- - - - - - - - - - - - - - - - - -

(a)

```
IF(NUMBER (K-1)-NUMBER(K)) 40,40,60
```

(b)

```
ITEMP = NUMBER(K)
NUMBER(K) = NUMBER(K-1)
NUMBER(K-1) = ITEMP
```

Interchange Sort

9.   Many computer applications use sorting programs to arrange data in a particular sequence. Numerous sorting techniques have been developed and in this and frame 10 we explain the interchange sort.

First, let us examine the strategy (algorithm) underlying our sort program. For simplicity, we will sort the sequence 7, 95, 33, 75, and 2 into ascending order (from low to high).

Algorithm:
(1) Compare the <u>first</u> number with the <u>second</u>.
(2) If the second number is smaller, exchange the two numbers.
(3) Repeat steps (1) and (2) using the first and third, first and fourth, and first and fifth. Now the smallest number occupies the first position.
(4) Repeat steps (1) through (3) using the second and third, third and fourth, and fourth and fifth numbers, respectively, for the first comparison in step (1).

And now, let's use this algorithm to sort the sequence 7 95 33 75 2 into ascending order. The table below applies the algorithm to this sequence. Each "pass" represents steps (1) through (4) of the algorithm.

Comparison	NUMBER(1)	NUMBER(2)	NUMBER(3)	NUMBER(4)	NUMBER(5)
Pass 1					
1	7	95	33	75	2
2	7	95	33	75	2
3	7	95	33	75	2
4	7	95	33	75	2
5	2	95	33	75	7
Pass 2					
1	2	95	33	75	7
2	2	33	95	75	7
3	2	33	95	75	7
4	2	7	95	75	33
Pass 3					
1	2	7	95	75	33
2	2	7	75	95	33
3	2	7	33	95	75
Pass 4					
1	2	7	33	95	75
2	2	7	33	75	95

The random sequence 7 95 33 75 2 was rearranged in ascending order 2 7 33 75 95. You may note that at each pass the smallest integer was transferred to the top of the sequence.

For five numbers we required a maximum of four passes (that is, one less than the number of items to be sorted). How many passes would be required for sorting 100 integers? _____

- - - - - - - - - - - - - - - - - - -

10. The following program finds the smallest integer in a set of 100 integers using the steps outlined below. The flowchart and program follow.

(1) Read 100 random integers from a card reader, each number punched on a separate card. An integer may have up to 4 digits including a sign.
(2) Find the smallest integer in the set.
(3) Print the message THE SMALLEST INTEGER IS XXXX.

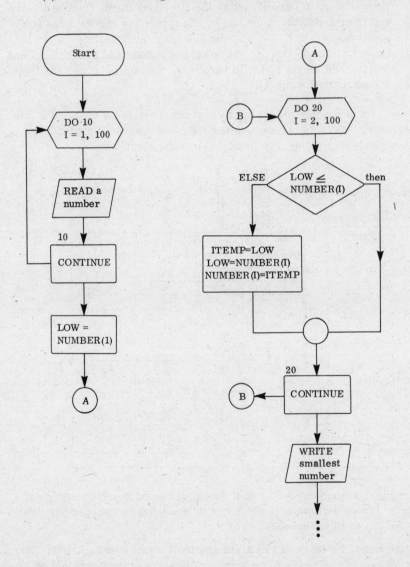

```
C  THIS PROGRAM FINDS THE SMALLEST INTEGER IN A
C       SEQUENCE OF 100 RANDOM NUMBERS
C       DIMENSION NUMBER(100)
C  READ 100 VALUES INTO THE ARRAY NUMBER
        DO 10 I = 1, 100
          READ (5, 101) NUMBER(I)
101     FORMAT (I4)
10      CONTINUE
C  FIND THE SMALLEST NUMBER
        LOW = NUMBER(1)
        DO 20 I = 2, 100
          IF (LOW .LE. NUMBER(I)) GO TO 20
15        ITEMP = LOW
          LOW = NUMBER(I)
          NUMBER(I) = ITEMP
20      CONTINUE
        WRITE (6, 201) LOW
201     FORMAT (' ', 'THE SMALLEST INTEGER IS ', I4)
        STOP
        END
```

(a) What is the purpose of this program segment?

```
        DO 20 I = 2, 100
          IF (LOW .LE. NUMBER(I) GO TO 20
15        ITEMP = LOW
          LOW = NUMBER(I)
          NUMBER(I) = ITEMP
20      CONTINUE
```

(b) If we had written this statement, what do you think would happen?

```
          IF (LOW .GE. NUMBER(I)), GO TO 20
```

- - - - - - - - - - - - - - - - - - - -

(a) The segment compares LOW to the number in the second position. If it is smaller or equal nothing is done. If it is larger, the two are exchanged. After this is done, it compares LOW to the third number and the process described is repeated until LOW is compared to all of the numbers in the array NUMBER. After the comparisons and interchanges, the number in LOW is the smallest integer.

(b) The segment would find the largest integer in the set.

11. Let us examine a program to perform these steps.

   (1) Read 100 integers, each punched on one card, into the array NUMBER. Each integer is up to four digits including a sign.

   (2) Sort the sequence into an ascending order.

   (3) Write the sorted sequence on a printer (device #6), one number per line.

The flowchart for the program follows:

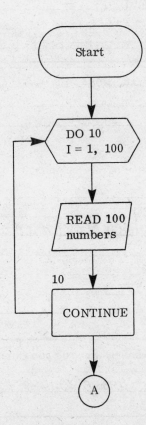

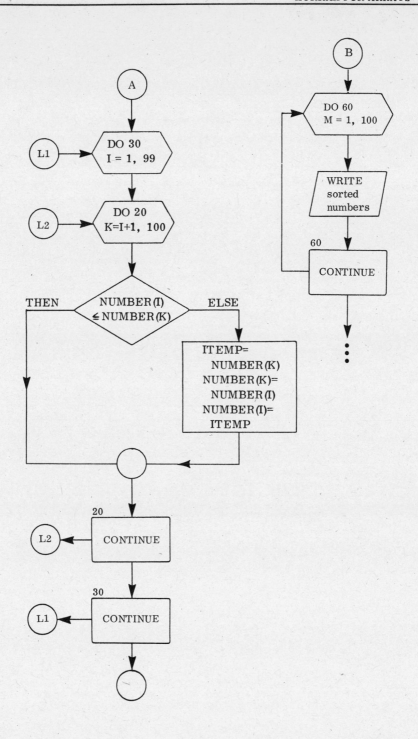

Here is the program.

```
C   THIS PROGRAM SORTS 100 RANDOM INTEGERS INTO AN
C       ASCENDING SEQUENCE. UP TO 4-DIGIT INTEGERS
C       MAY BE USED
C   THIS STATEMENT RESERVES 100 CONSECUTIVE VARIABLES
        DIMENSION NUMBER (100)
C   THIS DO LOOP READS 100 VALUES INTO 100 ELEMENTS
C       OF THE ARRAY NUMBER
        DO 10 I = 1, 100
            READ (5, 101) NUMBER(I)
101         FORMAT (I4)
10      CONTINUE
C   THIS DO CONTROLS THE NUMBER OF PASSES FROM 1 TO
C       99 - 99 PASSES IN TOTAL
        DO 30 I = 1, 99
C   THIS DO LOOP CONTROLS THE NUMBER OF COMPARISONS
C       WITHIN ONE PASS OF THE LIST
        DO 20 K = I+1, 100
C   THE IF AND SUBSEQUENT STATEMENTS PERFORM
C       STEPS 1-4 OF FRAME 9
            IF (NUMBER(I) .LE. NUMBER(K)) GO TO 20
            ITEMP = NUMBER(K)
            NUMBER(K) = NUMBER(I)
            NUMBER(I) = ITEMP
20      CONTINUE
30      CONTINUE
        DO 60 M = 1, 100
            WRITE (6, 201) NUMBER(M)
201         FORMAT (I4)
60      CONTINUE
            :
            :
```

WARNING. Some 1966 FORTRAN compilers may <u>not</u> accept the DO statement DO 20 K = I + 1, 100. If yours does not, use two statements

$$J = I + 1$$
$$DO \ 20 \ K = J, \ 100$$

in its place.

Now it's your turn. Write a program to:

(1) Read 100 integers, each punched on a separate punched card. (4 digits including a sign).

(2) Write the original sequnce on a printing device (number 6), one number to a line.

(3) Sort the sequence into a <u>descending</u> order.

(4) Write the sorted sequence on the printer.

(Hint: Change the relational operator in the IF statement of the last program.)

- - - - - - - - - - - - - - - - - - - -

```
C   THIS PROGRAM SORTS 100 RANDOM INTEGERS INTO A
C      DESCENDING SEQUENCE. UP TO 4-DIGIT INTEGERS
C      MAY BE USED
       DIMENSION NUMBER(100)
       DO 10 I = 1, 100
          READ (5, 101), NUMBER(I)
          WRITE (6, 202), NUMBER(I)
101    FORMAT (I4)
10     CONTINUE
       DO 30 I = 1, 99
       DO 20 K = I+1, 100
          IF (NUMBER(I) .GE. NUMBER(K)) GO TO 20
          ITEMP = NUMBER(K)
          NUMBER(K) = NUMBER(I)
          NUMBER(I) = ITEMP
20     CONTINUE
30     CONTINUE
       DO 60 L = 1, 100
60        WRITE (6, 202), NUMBER(L)
202    FORMAT (' ', I4)
       STOP
       END
```

Summary of the Rules for a Subscript

12. Fortran allows the use of arithmetic expressions for subscripts. A subscript can be of the form: an integer, an integer variable, an integer expression or an array element or a function reference. A subscript expression can also be a combination of each of these. However, there is one warning: it is

important that the evaluation of an expression not change any of the other parts of the expression that is being evaluated.

For example, an expression of the form N(I) + I, where N is a function, may cause the value of I to change during evaluation of the function N. Since evaluation of an expression is from left to right, the value of I (before the evaluation of the function N) would be different (after the evaluation of the function). Such games are specifically outlawed by FORTRAN 77.

The value of each subscript expression must be greater than or equal to the corresponding lower dimension bound in the array declarator (that's the dimension statement we talk about in the next frame) for the array. Likewise, the value of the subscript expression must not exceed the corresponding upper dimension bound declared in the declaration (dimension statement) of the array.

Identify the invalid subscripts in the following list.

_____	(a) EXER(17)		_____	(f) A(LEE + ABE)
_____	(b) CISE(Z + 3)		_____	(g) EXAM(N + 3.)
_____	(c) IS(-15)		_____	(h) PLE(-8 * L)
_____	(d) FUNNY(9 + LUNG)		_____	(i) HELP(N(7))
_____	(e) THIS(2 * MORE)		_____	(j) ME(0 * K)

- -

(b) Z is not an integer variable.
(f) ABE is not an integer variable.
(g) The number 3. is not an integer constant.

DIMENSION Statement

13. The compiler allocates memory for each variable. Since an array is stored in a number of consecutive memory locations, we must communicate to the compiler how many elements it must provide for. The DIMENSION statement gives this information to the compiler. Here is an example of a DIMENSION statement.

```
DIMENSION SAMPLE(200)
```

This statement informs the compiler that a variable SAMPLE is an array, contains 200 elements numbered from 1 to 200.

Another example of a DIMENSION statement
DIMENSION ANEW (-30:40)

informs the compiler that variable ANEW is an array which contains 71 elements. It is indexed by a subscript which has an integer values from -30 to +40. There are 71 values since index value 0 is also counted.

The DIMENSION statement must <u>precede</u> the first reference to the array name. Some compilers allow DIMENSION statements in the middle of a program as long as it appears before the use of the array name declared in the dimension statement. However, this is poor programming practice since it makes the programmer look throughout a whole program to find array declarations. Good programming practice is to declare all array elements used at the beginning of a program where they can be found.

Correct

	DIMENSION WEEP(1000)
	IF (WEEP(5)) 10, 10, 30
10	WEEP(5) = WEEP(5) + 1.
20	GO TO 40
30	WEEP(5) = 0.0
40	:
	:

Incorrect

	IF (WEEP(5)) 10, 10, 30
10	WEEP(5) = WEEP(5) + 1.
20	GO TO 40
30	WEEP(5) = 0.0
	DIMENSION WEEP(1000)
40	:
	:

Now, you write DIMENSION statements for the following variables.

I—500 elements
LOVE—350 elements
FORTRN—557 elements

- - - - - - - - - - - - - - - - - - - -

	DIMENSION I(500)
	DIMENSION LOVE(350)
	DIMENSION FORTRN(557)

Or you may combine all three in one DIMENSION statement (see frame 15).

	DIMENSION I(500), LOVE(350), FORTRN(557)

14. What is wrong with the following program segments?

(a)

```
      DIMENSION A(10), B(-4:10)
      A(11) = 2.
      B(-2:1) = A(7) + 3.
```

(b)

```
      HENRY(10) = 5.
      HENRY(10) = HENRY(10) * 6.
      DIMENSN HENRY(10)
```

- - - - - - - - - - - - - - - - - - - -

(a) The DIMENSION statement has only allocated storage area for ten elements. A reference to A(11) will produce unpredictable results, depending on whether the compiler catches this error before the program is executed. The element B(-2:1) is incorrect. The colon (:) is only used to declare subscript ranges. In this case only a single integer between -4 and 10 is allowed as a subscript.

(b) DIMENSN—what's this? The DIMENSION statement must be spelled correctly and must precede the first reference to an element of the array.

15. The basic form of a DIMENSION statement has two parts.

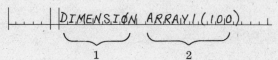

```
      DIMENSION ARRAY1(100),
```

$$\underbrace{\hspace{3em}}_{1}\quad\underbrace{\hspace{3em}}_{2}$$

As you can see, the first part consists of the word DIMENSION. The second part consists of an array name followed by the maximum number of elements in the array. If there are two or more arrays, you can write a DIMENSION statement for each array.

```
      DIMENSION ARRAY1(100)
      DIMENSION ARRAY2(-20:200)
      DIMENSION ARRAY3(3000)
```

Or you can use one DIMENSION statement with a comma separating the specifications for each array.

```
      DIMENSION ARRAY1(100), ARRAY2(-20:200),
     -    ARRAY3(3000)
```

If you are DIMENSIONing many arrays and you require more than one line you can separate the specifications into two or more DIMENSION statements or use a continuation statement line. The continued statement can start at any column after column 6, but for convenience we have indented the variable name E in our example on the next page.

```
     DIMENSIØN A(15),, B(25),, C(0:38,),, D(4756)
   -            E(-50:-25),,F(6758)
```

Point out the bugs in the following DIMENSION statements.

(a)
```
     DIMENSIØN SPEED(10),, SPEED(20)
```

(b)
```
     DIMENSEN BØY(100), GIRL(150:20)
```

(c)
```
     DIMENSIØN THIS(5),, IS(30) TRICKY(100),,
```

- - - - - - - - - - - - - - - - - -

(a) You can only DIMENSION an array once.
(b) Three things: Spell DIMENSION correctly. Use a comma to separate specifications for the arrays. Reverse the lower and upper bounds of GIRL.

```
     DIMENSIØN BØY(100),, GIRL(20:1150)
```

(c) Two things here also: There should be a comma following the specifications for the second array and there should not be a comma following the specifications for the last.

```
     DIMENSIØN THIS(5),, IS(30),, TRICKY(100)
```

One-Dimensional Array—An Illustrative Program

16. The program which follows illustrates many ways of using arrays. The program is to perform the following functions.

(1) Set up a list containing ten valid inventory numbers—INVNUM.
(2) Read a transaction record from device #9, containing both an item code (ITEMCD) and quantity sold (IQTY). A blank item code indicates that the total for each item code is to be printed since there are no more transaction cards. Remember, blanks are interpreted as zeros.
(3) Look up the item code in the list of valid inventory numbers. If a matching valid inventory number is not located, the invalid transaction is printed; otherwise, the quantity is accumulated for that particular inventory number.

The flowchart for the program appears on the next page. It is divided into two parts, the second containing the logic of the valid inventory number check.

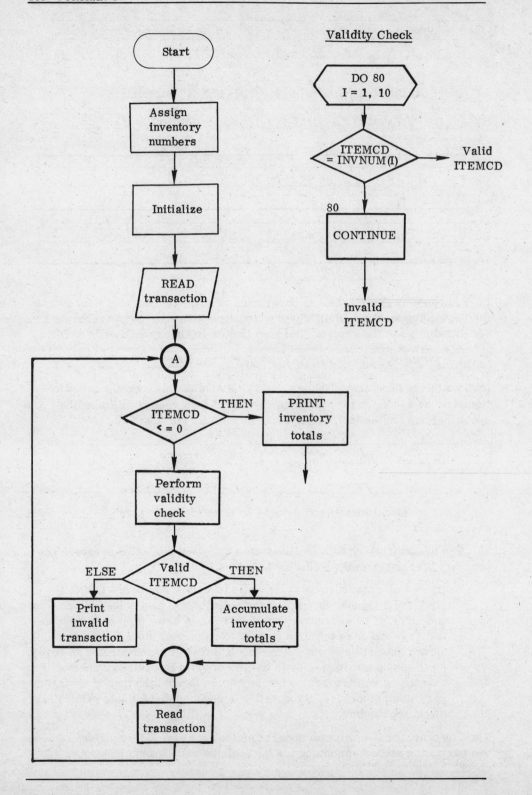

Here is a program that will perform the logic flow of the flowchart.

```
       DIMENSIØN INVNUM(10), ITØTAL(10)
C  ASSIGN VALID INVENTØRY NUMBERS
       INVNUM(1) = 325
       INVNUM(2) = 1426
       :
       :
       INVNUM(10) = 6897
C  INITIALIZE TØTAL ØF EACH ITEM TØ ZERØ
       DØ 20 I = 1, 10
           ITØTAL(I) = 0
20     CØNTINUE
C  READ TRANSACTIØN CARD
40     READ (9, 1000) ITEMCD, IQTY
C  TEST FØR LAST TRANSACTIØN
       IF (ITEMCD .LE. 0) GØ TØ 200
C  TEST FØR VALID INVENTØRY NUMBER
60     DØ 80 I = 1, 10
           IF (INVNUM(I) .EQ. ITEMCD) GØ TØ 100
80     CØNTINUE
C  PRINT ØUT INVALID TRANSACTIØN
       WRITE (6, 1020) ITEMCD, IQTY
       GØ TØ 120
C  ACCUMULATE QUANTITY FØR INVENTØRY NUMBER
100    ITØTAL(I) = ITØTAL(I) + IQTY
C  READ TRANSACTIØN
120    READ (9, 1000) ITEMCD, IQTY
       GØ TØ 40
C  PRINT TØTAL FØR EACH INVENTØRY NUMBER
200    DØ 220 I = 1, 10
           WRITE (6, 1040) INVNUM(I), ITØTAL(I)
220    CØNTINUE
       :
       :
       STØP
       END
```

Let's see how well you understand this program.

(a) What is the purpose of this program segment?

```
      DO  20  I  =  1,  10
      ITOTAL( I)  =  0
20    CONTINUE
```

(b) What would happen if a negative item code were read from the transaction card? _____

(c) Why would you want to print out invalid transactions? _____

(d) How many different arrays did this program use? _____

- - - - - - - - - - - - - - - - - -

(a) Most modern computers do not automatically clear storage at the onset of execution. In a supermarket, the checkout register has to be cleared of all previous transactions. Otherwise, totals of preceding transactions would be reflected in your grocery bill. In the same manner, the DO loop sets the accumulator ITOTAL(I) for each inventory number I equal to zero. If you skip this step, you probably will not get the correct results.

(b) The statement IF (ITEMCD . LE. 0) GO TO 200 will cause a branch to statement 200 (that part of the program which prints out the total for each inventory number), just as though the card had a blank ITEMCD field.

(c) A poorly planned program ignores invalid transactions; well planned programs report invalid transactions as exception items so you can follow up and correct the transactions when appropriate.

(d) This program uses two different arrays, but in the next frame we will show you how to combine these two arrays into one array.

Multi-Dimensional Array

17. A list of data is called a one-dimensional array, vector, or list. For convenience, data sometimes is arranged in a tabular form using rows and columns which we call a table, matrix, or two-dimensional array. Other arrangements of data are common and they are known as multi-dimensional arrays. Here are some examples.

This is a list of ten items.

INVNUM(1) INVNUM(2) INVNUM(3) . . . INVNUM(10)

On the next page is a table of twenty elements.

	Column 1	Column 2	Column 3	•••	Column 10
Row 1	ITABLE(1, 1)	ITABLE(1, 2)	ITABLE(1, 3)	•••	ITABLE(1, 10)
Row 2	ITABLE(2, 1)	ITABLE(2, 2)	ITABLE(2, 3)	•••	ITABLE(2, 10)

This is a three-dimensional array of thirty elements. It can represent commissions of three salesmen (columns) in five territories (rows) during a period of two years (planes).

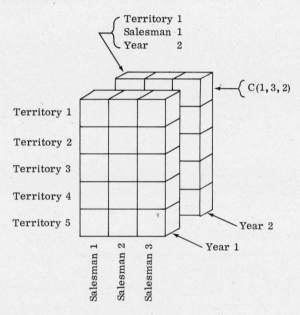

(a) The table above has _____ rows and _____ columns for a total of _____ elements.

(b) A list is also called a _____.

(c) A table is also called a _____.

(d) The three-dimensional array above has _____ rows, _____ columns, and _____ planes for a total of _____ elements.

- - - - - - - - - - - - - - - - - -

(a) two, ten, 20 (2 x 10 = 20); (b) vector or one-dimensional array; (c) matrix or two-dimensional array; (d) five, three, two, 30 (5 x 3 x 2 = 30)

18. FORTRAN provides that an array may have up to seven, or more subscripts or dimensions), depending upon the compiler you are using. Each subscript is separated by a comma.

DIMENSION ARRAY1(30, 50), LIST(100), ARRAY2(5, 5, 2), ITABLE(2, 10)
:
:
ANSWER = ARRAY1(5, N + 15) * LIST(3 * N)
LIST(1) = ITABLE(1, 4)

The subscripts for multi-dimensional arrays are subject to the rules we gave you in frames 5, 6, 7, and 12.

How many dimensions do each of the following arrays have?

(a)   INVNUM(I) _____

(b)   ITABLE(ITYPE, INDEX) _____

(c)   KLUTZ(3, N + 15, 3 * ITEM) _____

- - - - - - - - - - - - - - - - - -

(a) one dimension; (b) two dimensions; (c) three dimensions, even though two of the subscripts are expressions (refer to frame 7 if you missed this one)

19. In frame 13 you learned that the DIMENSION statement tells the compiler to allocate storage for each array according to its number of elements. The number of elements in an array is the product obtained from multiplying together the number of elements in each dimension of the array. If the lower bound of an array subscript is not equal to 1, you must be very careful counting the elements in each dimension of the array. As an example, an array with a subscript lower bound of -15 and an upper bound of 5 would have 21 elements in that dimension. In a one-dimensional array there is only one dimension (that is, the list or vector indicated by one subscript). The statement DIMENSION INVNUM(10) tells the compiler to allocate storage for the ten-element array INVNUM.

In two-dimensional arrays there are two dimensions. The first is called <u>row</u> and the second is known as <u>column</u>. The two-dimensional array is known as a table or matrix. A matrix always has two subscripts. The first corresponds to the number of elements in a column (or to the number of row); the second corresponds to the number of elements in a row (or to the number of columns). Refer to frame 17 for a visual representation of a table. The statement

DIMENSION ITABLE(2, 10)

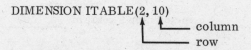
column
row

tells the compiler that the array ITABLE will have twenty elements, arranged in two rows and ten columns.

In three dimensions there are three subscripts. The array can be visualized as a box. A good example is found in frame 17. Arrays of four dimensions and higher cannot be visualized. The general rule is: Each dimension has a subscript, the subscripts must be separated by commas, and each subscript represents the number of elements in this dimension.

(a) How many elements does the array MULTIC contain? _____

   DIMENSION MULTIC(10, 6, 3, 2)

(b) The array TRAFIC has 36 elements. Complete the DIMENSION statement for the array TRAFIC.

   DIMENSION TRAFIC(3, 3, _____)

- - - - - - - - - - - - - - - - - - -

(a) 360 elements (10 x 6 x 3 x 2 = 360); (b) DIMENSION TRAFIC(3, 3, 4) (because 3 x 3 x 4 = 36)

20. The statement DIMENSION ABLE(3, 3) tells the compiler to reserve nine elements. The array ABLE can be visualized as shown below.

	Columns		
	1	2	3
Rows 1	ABLE(1, 1)	ABLE(1, 2)	ABLE(1, 3)
Rows 2	ABLE(2, 1)	ABLE(2, 2)	ABLE(2, 3)
Rows 3	ABLE(3, 1)	ABLE(3, 2)	ABLE(3, 3)

If we refer to the array element ABLE(3, 1), for example, ABLE(3, 1) = 14.759, we are referring to the element located in row 3, column 1 in the array ABLE.

ABLE(3, 1)

In which row and column do each of these array elements fall?

		Row	Column
ABLE(1, 3)	(a)	_____	_____
ABLE(3, 3)	(b)	_____	_____
ABLE(2, 3)	(c)	_____	_____

- - - - - - - - - - - - - - - - - - -

(a) 1, 3; (b) 3, 3; (c) 2, 3

How an Array is Stored in Memory

21. The FORTRAN compiler always internally converts multi-dimensional arrays (two or more subscripts) into scalar arrays (one dimension). The elements of a multi-dimensional array are stored in scalar fashion—the leftmost subscript varies the most rapidly and the rightmost varies the least rapidly. Here is an example using the two-dimensional array DIMENSION BOX(3, 2). Although we visualize the array BOX as:

$$BOX(1, 1) \quad BOX(1, 2)$$
$$BOX(2, 1) \quad BOX(2, 2)$$
$$BOX(3, 1) \quad BOX(3, 2)$$

the FORTRAN compiler converts it to a scalar array in storage.

$$BOX(1, 1)$$
$$BOX(2, 1)$$
$$BOX(3, 1)$$
$$BOX(1, 2)$$
$$BOX(2, 2)$$
$$BOX(3, 2)$$

It is important to realize how Fortran stores elements in an array. In Chapter 9 we will show you how to automatically read and write all of the elements of the array by simply mentioning its name. As you will see, Fortran can store data values during input in the order that the array is stored in memory.

As you can see, the first three elements of the array came from column

_____, whereas the next three elements of the array came from

_____. Using the rule we stated above, the array is stored so that the

_____ subscript varies least rapidly, whereas the _____

varies most rapidly.

- - - - - - - - - - - - - - - - - - -

1; 2; rightmost; leftmost

22. Applying the same rule to a three-dimensional array, DIMENSION CUBE(4, 4, 4), the FORTRAN compiler would allocate storage so that the elements of the array CUBE would be arranged in storage as follows.

CUBE(1, 1, 1)	1st element
CUBE(2, 1, 1)	2nd element
CUBE(3, 1, 1)	3rd element
CUBE(4, 1, 1)	4th element
CUBE(1, 2, 1)	5th element
CUBE(2, 2, 1)	6th element
CUBE(3, 2, 1)	7th element
CUBE(4, 2, 1)	8th element
CUBE(1, 3, 1)	9th element
CUBE(2, 3, 1)	10th element
CUBE(3, 3, 1)	11th element
CUBE(4, 3, 1)	12th element
CUBE(1, 4, 1)	13th element
CUBE(2, 4, 1)	14th element
CUBE(3, 4, 1)	15th element
CUBE(4, 4, 1)	16th element
CUBE(1, 1, 2)	17th element

CUBE(2, 1, 2)	18th element
CUBE(3, 1, 2)	19th element
CUBE(4, 1, 2)	20th element
CUBE(1, 2, 2)	21st element
CUBE(2, 2, 2)	22nd element
CUBE(3, 2, 2)	23rd element
CUBE(4, 2, 2)	24th element
CUBE(1, 3, 2)	25th element
⋮	⋮
CUBE(1, 4, 2)	29th element
⋮	⋮
CUBE(1, 1, 3)	33rd element
⋮	⋮
CUBE(1, 1, 4)	49th element
⋮	⋮
CUBE(3, 4, 4)	63rd element
CUBE(4, 4, 4)	64th element

Whew! That was a lot of work. Now you do one. Plot the arrangement of the two arrays as defined below. We have left space for your representation.

DIMENSION SQUARE(3, 3), CUBE(2, 2, 2)

SQUARE(1, 1)	CUBE(1, 1, 1)
SQUARE(2, 1)	CUBE(2, 1, 1)
SQUARE(3, 1)	CUBE(1, 2, 1)
SQUARE(1, 2)	CUBE(2, 2, 1)
SQUARE(2, 2)	CUBE(1, 1, 2)
SQUARE(3, 2)	CUBE(2, 1, 2)
SQUARE(1, 3)	CUBE(1, 2, 2)
SQUARE(2, 3)	CUBE(2, 2, 2)
SQUARE(3, 3)	

Use of Arrays—Illustrative Programs

23. Remember the inventory problem in frame 16? If necessary, review how
we used two one-dimensional arrays to store valid product number and quantity, respectively. Now that we have covered two-dimensional arrays, we
will rewrite the inventory problem using only one array.

The product number and its corresponding quantity can be visualized as
a specific column in a table containing ten columns and two rows. The first
row represents product numbers and the second row represents quantities,
so the element that stores the product number is immediately followed by an
element that stores the quantity of that product. Let's set up the table using
an array named INFO.

	1st product	2nd product	. . .	10th product
Product numbers	INFO(1, 1)	INFO(1, 2)	. . .	INFO(1, 10)
Quantities	INFO(2, 1)	INFO(2, 2)	. . .	INFO(2, 10)

Write two assignment statements to assign the product number 370 and
quantity 4,350 to the seventh product.

- - - - - - - - - - - - - - - - - -

INFO(1, 7) = 370
INFO(2, 7) = 4350
Hope you left out the comma in 4,350.

24. The products of frame 23 are manufactured and kept in stock at five different geographical locations. These five factory facilities ship to fifteen
distributors (who are concerned with the distribution within their geographical
territory). The method of shipment to a specific distributor is by a trucking
company owned by the manufacturer's brother-in-law. The traffic manager
of the manufacturer (another brother-in-law) calculated the shipping cost per
pound between each factory location and every distributor.

Distributors

1	2	3	4	5	6	7	8	9	10	11	12	13	14	15

Factories

1	2	3	4	5

Their programmer, in turn, incorporated this shipping data into the company's sales and invoicing program by means of an array. Using a two-dimensional array, write a DIMENSION statement to define the array TRANS, for which each element will contain the cost of transportation between a specific factory location and corresponding distributor.

- - - - - - - - - - - - - - - - - - -

There are two correct statements.
DIMENSION TRANS(5, 15)
                     ┌── number of distributors
                     └── number of factories
or
DIMENSION TRANS(15, 5)

25. Continuing the saga of the last frame, the manufacturer's daughter married a recent business graduate of the University of Hardknox. Without permission of his father-in-law, he calculated the transportation costs between the factories and the distributors for two other methods of shipment: independent trucking and United Parcel Service. Furthermore, in return for some favors, the programmer incorporated shipping information into the sales and invoicing program (by expanding the dimensions of the array TRANS) so that the program selected the least expensive method of shipment between the origin point and destination.

Write the DIMENSION statement to define TRANS so that the first subscript indicates the number of factories, the second indicates the number of distributors, and the last indicates the number of shipping methods. How many elements does TRANS have? _____

- - - - - - - - - - - - - - - - - - -

DIMENSION TRANS(5, 15, 3)
TRANS has 225 elements (5 x 15 x 3 = 225)

26. For the three-dimensional array TRANS, the first subscript indicates the factory number and the second indicates the distributor. If we want the various

costs for transportation between factory number 2 and distributor number 8, what elements of TRANS would the program have to examine?

TRANS(2,_____, 1)

TRANS(_____, 8,_____)

TRANS(_____,_____,_____)

- - - - - - - - - - - - - - - - - -

	Shipping method	
TRANS(2, 8, 1)	1	brother-in-law
TRANS(2, 8, 2)	2	independent trucker
TRANS(2, 8, 3)	3	United Parcel Service

27. The programmer very carefully designs her program so that the shipment should be made, if possible, at the least cost. However, if the cost of shipping by method 2 is equal to method 3, shipment would be made by method 3 (United Parcel Service) in order to avoid antagonizing the brother-in-law. Here is the flowchart for that segment of the program.

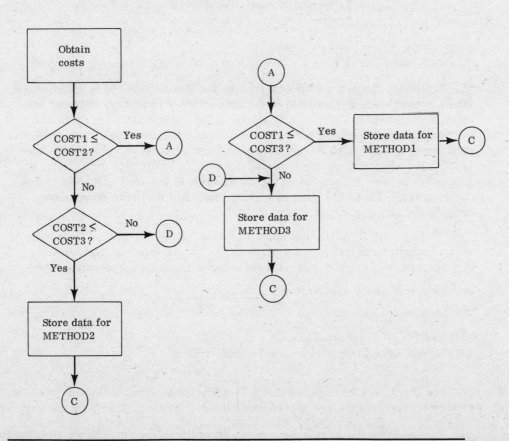

Okay, super-programmers, code a program segment corresponding to the flowchart.

- - - - - - - - - - - - - - - - - - - -

Here is one possible solution.

```
C   OBTAIN COMPARISON COSTS
        FIRST = TRANS(IFACT, IDISTR, 1)
        SECOND = TRANS(IFACT, IDISTR, 2)
        THIRD = TRANS(IFACT, IDISTR, 3)
C   COMPARE FIRST AND SECOND COSTS
        IF (FIRST - SECOND) 10, 10, 20
C   FIRST ≤ SECOND. COMPARE FIRST AND THIRD
10      IF (FIRST - THIRD) 11, 11, 12
C   FIRST ≤ THIRD. PREFER FIRST
11      METHOD = 1
        COST = FIRST
        GO TO 50
C   THIRD < FIRST (AND ≤ SECOND)
12      METHOD = 3
        COST = THIRD
        GO TO 50
C   SECOND < FIRST. COMPARE SECOND AND THIRD
20      IF (SECOND - THIRD) 21, 12, 12
C   SECOND < THIRD
21      METHOD = 2
        COST = SECOND
50      CONTINUE
```

Notice we used arithmetic IF statements. We could just as well have used logical IF statements. For example, statement number 10 could have been coded as IF (THIRD .GT. FIRST) GO TO 12. Take your choice.

28. A little bit of structured flowcharting would simplify the flowcharting and programming of frame 27.

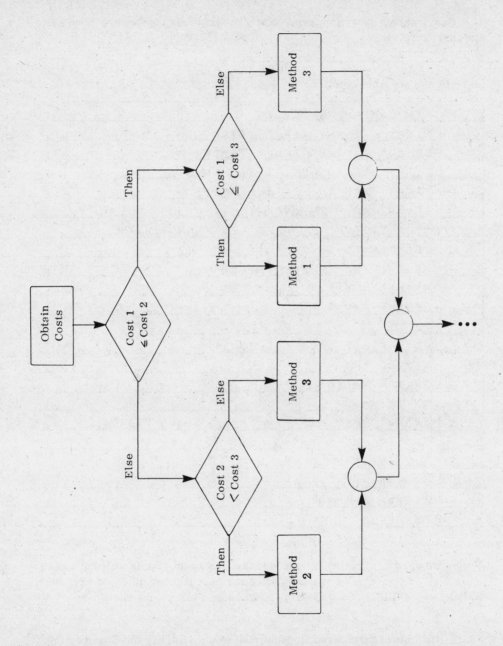

Frankly, this really looks much more organized than the flowchart in frame 27. Okay, super programmer, write some FORTRAN coding for this chart using the IF-ELSE programming statements

- - - - - - - - - - - - - - - - - -

Here is our program segment

```
IF (CØST1 .LE. CØST2) THEN
    IF (CØST1 .LE. CØST3) THEN
        METHØD = 1
        CØST = FIRST
    ELSE
        METHØD = 3
        CØST = THIRD
    END IF
ELSE IF (CØST2 .LT. CØST3) THEN
    METHØD = 2
    CØST = SECØND
ELSE
    METHØD = 3
    CØST = THIRD
END IF
```

The program is a lot easier to understand written this way!

29. If you don't know what matrix algebra is, skip to frame 30. Let us write a program which multiplies two 2x2 matrices. Some review might be helpful at this point. If two matrices A and B are multiplied, then the third matrix C is obtained in the following manner.

$$[C] = [A][B] = \begin{bmatrix} A_{11} & A_{12} \\ A_{21} & A_{22} \end{bmatrix} \begin{bmatrix} B_{11} & B_{12} \\ B_{21} & B_{22} \end{bmatrix}$$

$$\begin{bmatrix} C_{11} & C_{12} \\ C_{21} & C_{22} \end{bmatrix} = \begin{bmatrix} \overbrace{A_{11}B_{11} + A_{12}B_{21}}^{C_{11}} & \overbrace{A_{11}B_{12} + A_{12}B_{22}}^{C_{12}} \\ \underbrace{A_{21}B_{11} + A_{22}B_{21}}_{C_{21}} & \underbrace{A_{21}B_{12} + A_{22}B_{22}}_{C_{22}} \end{bmatrix}$$

Thus, to obtain the first element

$$C_{11} \leftarrow \text{1st column}$$
$$\phantom{C_{11}} \leftarrow \text{1st row}$$

multiply element by element of the first row of A by the first column of B and add the corresponding terms (i. e., $A_{11}B_{11} + A_{12}B_{21}$).

To get C_{21}, multiply the _____ row of A by the _____ column of B.

If you like, try writing a program that multiplies two 2x2 matrices. Our program is shown below the answer dashes.

- - - - - - - - - - - - - - - - - - - -

second; first

```
C  MATRIX MULTIPLICATION
      DIMENSION A(2,2), B(2,2), C(2,2)
      :
      DO 30 I = 1, 2
      DO 20 J = 1, 2
      C(I,J) = 0
      DO 10 K = 1, 2
      C(I,J) = A(I,K) * B(K,J)
10    CONTINUE
20    CONTINUE
30    CONTINUE
      :
```

Why did we set $C(I, J)$ equal to 0? Because we wanted to initialize this counter or accumulator so that it would only add the corresponding products of elements in rows and columns.

30. The administration of the University of Large Classes decided to reduce the workload of their faculty. As a first step they asked the computer center to provide a program which would calculate the average grade of 100 students at the end of each semester. The program was written to read punched cards. Each grade was punched on a separate card. The computer center provided the following program, show on the next page.

However, the professors quickly found that the program did not run (execute) correctly. The administration was heavily criticized for this failure. The faculty council decided to hire an independent consultant to find a solution. It was found that the original program was written to accommodate

```
C  THIS PROGRAM CALCULATES AND PRINTS AVERAGE OF
C     100 GRADES
      DIMENSION GRADE(100)
C  READ GRADES
      DO 10 I = 1, 100
         READ (5, 100) GRADE(I)
100   FORMAT (F5.1)
10    CONTINUE
      SUM = 0.0
C  ADD GRADES AND CALCULATE AVERAGE AND PRINT RESULT
      DO 20 J = 1, 100
         SUM = SUM + GRADE(J)
20    CONTINUE
      AVE = SUM / 100.0
      WRITE (6, 100) AVE
      :
      :
```

exactly 100 students, but the class size really varied from 10 to 250 students. (In any given semester none of the classes exceeded 250 students.)

In what ways could you modify this program so that the faculty may obtain their class averages? Write a corrected program.

- - - - - - - - - - - - - - - - - -

(1) Change the DIMENSION statement variable subscript from 100 to 250.
(2) Each instructor must precede his data (grade) deck with a card giving the number of students enrolled in his class.
(3) This card is read first and the information obtained is used to determine the limit of the DO loop.

```
C  THIS PROGRAM CALCULATES AND PRINTS THE AVERAGE
C     OF 250 GRADES
      DIMENSION GRADE(250)
      READ (5, 101) NCLASS
101   FORMAT (I3)
      DO 10 I = 1, NCLASS
         READ (5, 200) GRADE(I)
200   FORMAT (F5.1)
10    CONTINUE
      SUM = 0.0
```

(continued on next page)

```
      DO 20 I = 1, NCLASS
         SUM = SUM + GRADE(I)
20    CONTINUE
      SUM = SUM / NCLASS
      WRITE (6, 300) SUM
300   FORMAT (' ', 'THE AVERAGE IS ', F5.1)
      :
```

31. The professors at the University of Large Classes complained that they were overburdened with work when, in addition to their normal duties, they had to calculate the final grade of each of their students. The consultant, in return for free tuition, agreed to modify the program (shown in frame 29) to provide the average grade for each student for classes ranging up to 250 students. It was agreed that each instructor would provide information on four tests each semester. The student number (an integer from 1 to 250) and grades on four tests would be entered on a punched card as shown below.

Student number	Student grades			
	TEST1	TEST2	TEST3	TEST4
XXX	XXX.X	XXX.X	XXX.X	XXX.X
999 99	999 99	999 99	999 99	999 99	9999999999999999999999999
1 2 3	4 5	6 7 8 9 10	11 12 13 14 15	16 17 18 19 20	21 22 23 24 25	26 27 28 29 30 31 32 33 34 35 36 37 38 39 40 41 42 43 44 45

Since the grades would be posted, the program would print each student's identifying number and grade average.

Look at the program on the next page and then answer the questions that follow.

(a) What information does the statement READ (5, 100) NOSDNT provide after it is executed? _____

(b) What is the function of the student identifying number stored in the variable N by this statement?

   READ (5, 200) N, T1(N), T2(N), T3(N), T4(N)

_____

- - - - - - - - - - - - - - - - - - - -

(a) The first card in the data deck provides information on the number of students in the class.

(b) As soon as the student identifying number is read into the variable N (for example, N=135) the student grades are entered into the 135th location of each test array (that is, T1(135), T2(135), T3(135), T4(135) for each test taken by student number 135). The arrangement eliminates the necessity to sort the student cards into identifying number sequence before running the program.

```
C  THIS PROGRAM CALCULATES STUDENT GRADE AVERAGE
C     IN 4 TESTS
      DIMENSION T1(250), T2(250), T3(250),
     -    T4(250), AVE(250)
C  T1, T2, T3, AND T4 - TEST GRADES FOR 4 TESTS
      READ (5,101) NOSDNT
101   FORMAT (I3)
      DO 10 I = 1, NOSDNT
      READ (5,201) N, T1(N), T2(N), T3(N), T4(N)
201   FORMAT (I3, 2X, 4F5.1)
10    CONTINUE
      DO 20 I = 1, NOSDNT
      AVE(I) = (T1(I)+T2(I)+T3(I)+T4(I))/4.0
      WRITE (6,300) I, AVE(I)
300   FORMAT (' ', I3, 10X, F5.1)
20    CONTINUE
      :
```

32. The "Arf and Woof" Dog Food Company wants to computerize its inventory control. They want a program that stores a list of product numbers in an array LIST of size 100 and stores the quantity of each product number in each of its 20 warehouses in an array INVENT (two-dimensional) of maximum bounds 100 and 20. (INVENT(I, J) would represent the quantity of the product number corresponding to the index I in LIST in factory J.)

A typical order comes in by way of punched card with the format:

columns 1-5	Buyer number (an integer)—NUMBUY
columns 6-10	Product number (up to a four-digit integer—IPRDNO
columns 11-12	Factory (warehouse) number (a two-digit integer)— IFACT
columns 13-20	Number of items requested—NOITEM
columns 21-80	Blank

Write a program that will read in an order card as described above. If the product number does not correspond to a product number stored in LIST print out an error message along with the information on the data card. If there is an insufficient inventory at the factory requested, print out the information on the data card following the literal BACK ORDERED. If there is sufficient inventory to fill the order print out the information on the card followed by the literal ORDER FILLED and subtract the quantity of the order from the factory it was filled from. Assume a blank data card follows the last data card to indicate that no more data cards are present (implies all data fields are equal to zero). Assume that the arrays LIST and INVENT have been initialized for you.

- - - - - - - - - - - - - - - - - - - -

```
C  SOLUTION TO FRAME 32
       DIMENSION LIST(100), INVENT(100,20)
       :
C  READ DATA CARD
       READ (5,100) NUMBUY, IPRDNO, IFACT, NOITEM
100    FORMAT (I5, I5, I2, I8)
C  TEST FOR LAST CARD
150    IF (NUMBUY .LE. 0) GO TO 1000
C  TEST FOR SUBSCRIPT THAT REFERS TO IPRDNO
       DO 200 I = 1, 100
          IF (IPRDNO .EQ. LIST(I)) GO TO 225
200    CONTINUE
C  IPRDNO DOES NOT CORRESPOND TO ELEMENT OF LIST
       WRITE (6,201) NUMBUY, IPRDNO, IFACT, NOITEM
201    FORMAT (' ', 'NO PRODUCT NUMBER EXISTS ',
      -    I5, 2X, I5, 2X, I2, 5X, I8)
       GO TO 325
C  ACCESS CORRECT ELEMENT OF INVENT
225    IF (NOITEM .LE. INVENT(I,IFACT)) GO TO 300
C  BACK ORDER TRANSACTION
       WRITE (6,250) NUMBUY, IPRDNO, IFACT, NOITEM
250    FORMAT (' BACK ORDERED ', 2(I5, 2X), I2,
      -    5X, I8)
       GO TO 325
C  FILL ORDER
300    INVENT(I,IFACT) = INVENT(I,IFACT) - NOITEM
       WRITE (6,301) NUMBUY, IPRDNO, IFACT, NOITEM
301    FORMAT (' ', 2(I5, 2X), I2, 5X, I8, 5X,
      -    ' ORDER FILLED ')
C  READ NEXT DATA CARD
325    READ (5, 101) NUMBUY, IPRODNO, IFACT,
      -    NOITEM
       GO TO 150
1000   STOP
       END
```

33. Sometimes it is necessary to convert a date in the form month, day to the number of the day in the year. As an example, March 14 would be (in a non-leap year) the 73rd day. We get this number by adding the number of days in January (31) and February (28) and the 14 days in March. We would like you to write a program which will allow you to enter a date in the form month, day, and then would print the day of the year. The program should then request a new date. A date of 0,0 for month and day should stop the program. We will give you a hint. You can set up an array called MONTH which will have twelve elements and initialize MONTH(I) to the number of days in the year that have already passed. As an example, MONTH (1), indicating January, would have the value 0. MONTH (2) would have the value of 31, the 31 days that have passed since the beginning of the year before you get to the second month. MONTH (3) would have the value 59. Thus, as you can see, if we want to define the number of days until March 14, we would look for the third element in the array which would have the value 59 and add the number of days in the current month 14 to get 73. It's really easy.

- - - - - - - - - - - - - - - - - - - -

```
C  SOLUTION TO FRAME 33
       DIMENSION MONTH(12)
C  INITIALIZE ARRAY MONTH
       MONTH(1)=0
       MONTH(2)=31
       MONTH(3)=59
       ...
       ...
       MONTH(12)=334
C  READ IN DATE FROM DEVICE 11
       READ(11,100) MON, NDAY
100    FORMAT(.......)
120    IF (MON .LE. 0) GO TO 200
       NUMDAY = MONTH(MON) + NDAY
       WRITE (10, 150) MON, NDAY, NUMDAY
150    FORMAT(' DATE ', I2, '/', I2, ' IS DAY # ', I4)
       READ (11,100) MON, NDAY
       GO TO 120
200    STOP
       END
```

See, we said it was easy. To make the program give correct results you should also check if MON is less than 13. Most processors will (or should) give an error message if the subscript of an array has over-reached its bounds.

Self-Test

1. Identify the invalid subscripts.

_____ (a) YEAR(I * 1974)   _____ (f) A((10-10)*I)

_____ (b) FAT(OLD(LADY))   _____ (g) WINNER(3 * LUCK)

_____ (c) A(3 * K + 1.)   _____ (h) EXPORT(IMPORT+5)

_____ (d) 1A(SAVE+YOUR*SOUL)   _____ (i) MONA(LISA)

_____ (e) A(-10)

2. Point out the bugs in the following DIMENSION statements.

(a) DIMENSION INSIDE(1000) JOB(100)

_____

(b) DMENSION A(10,20,30), B(70,35), C(-10,8)

_____

(c) DIMENSION DAILY(10,10), NEWS(10,5,3), DAILY(10,5), NEWS(10)

_____

(d) PLEASE(100,10), LOOK(2,3,4,5), ERROR(10), DIMENSION

_____

3. DIMENSION A(10), B(5,3), C(0:7,8,-10:10)

In this statement, how many elements are reserved for the arrays A, B,

C, and D, respectively? _____

4. Write the order of elements in storage for the array ORDER(3,2).

DIMENSION ORDER(3,2)

5. Fishing Expedition

Problem statement: Assume you have a one-dimensional array of 500 three-digit integers arranged in a random order. Write a program to perform the following tasks.

(1) Find the average.
(2) Find the number of values greater than the average.

    (3) Find the number of values between 200–300 inclusive.

    (4) Find the subscript of the first integer larger than 500.

Output: Print the following:

    (1) AVERAGE IS   XXX.XX

    (2) NUMBER OF INTEGERS GREATER THAN THE AVERAGE IS XXX

    (3) NUMBER OF VALUES BETWEEN 200–300 IS   XXX

    (4) SUBSCRIPT OF THE FIRST INTEGER LARGER THAN 500 IS XXX

6. The health clinic of the University of Nancago wanted to obtain the following information about its students: average height, weight, and waist measurements. The computer center provided the height, weight, and waist measurement in inches, pounds, and inches, respectively—one card for each student. Write a program which would obtain this information. Assume that 1000 students were registered at that time. The input is as described below.

7. Write a short program to convert a day number in a year to its corresponding month and day values. Yes, this is the opposite conversion from that in frame 33. The input is a day number and the output is the date in the form month/day. Hint! an array MONTH should have stored in the element MONTH(I) the number of days in the year including the month I.

Answers to Self-Test

1. The following are invalid:

(b) OLD is not an integer variable. A subscript must be integer.

(c) 3+K+1. is real.

(d) Two errors: 1A is not a valid variable name; the expression subscript is not an integer expression.

(frames 5–7 and 12)

2. All are incorrect.

(a) Missing comma; should be DIMENSION INSIDE (1000), JOB(100).

(b) Incorrect spelling of DIMENSION, and C(–10, 8) is not correct. It should be C(–10:8).

(c) Array names must be unique; we used DAILY and NEWS twice.

(d) The key word DIMENSION must precede the array definitions.

(frames 12–15)

3. for A, 10 elements; for B, 15 elements (3 x 5); for C, 1,344 elements (8 x 8 x 21); (frames 18–19)

4.
ORDER(1, 1)   ORDER(1, 2)
ORDER(2, 1)   ORDER(2, 2)
ORDER(3, 1)   ORDER(3, 2)   (frame 21)

5.

```
C   SØLUTIØN TØ PRØBLEM 5
        DIMENSIØN NUMBER(500)
        . . .
        . . .
        . . .
        . . .
C   CØMPUTE AVERAGE
        NSUM = 0
        DØ 200 I = 1, 500
            NSUM = NSUM + NUMBER(I)
200     CØNTINUE
        AVERAG = NSUM / 500.
C   CØMPUTE NUMBER ØF VALUES GREATER THAN AVERAGE,
C        NUMBER ØF VALUES BETWEEN 200 AND 300 INCLUSIVE
C        AND SUBSCRIPT ØF FIRST INTEGER > 500
        KØUNT = 0
        INDEX = 0
        NUMVAL = 0
        DØ 300 I = 1, 500
            IF (NUMBER(I) .GT. AVERG) KØUNT=KØUNT+1
C   INDEX IS SET TØ FIRST SUBSCRIPT WHEN VALUE 7500
C   TEST TØ SEE IF INDEX HAS BEEN SET
250         IF (INDEX .GT. 0) GØ TØ 275
260         IF (NUMBER(I) .GT. 500) INDEX = I
C   TEST TØ SEE IF NUMBER(I) IS BETWEEN 200 AND 300
275         IF (NUMBER(I) .GE. 200 .AND. NUMBER(I)
     -          .LE. 300) NUMVAL = NUMVAL + 1
300     CØNTINUE
```

(continued on next page)

```
C  PRINT RESULTS
      WRITE (6,601) AVERAG, KOUNT, NUMVAL, INDEX
601   FORMAT ('1', ' AVERAGE IS ', F6.2 // ' ',
     -  'NUMBER OF INTEGERS GREATER THAN THE'
     -  ' AVERAGE IS ', I3 // ' ', 'NUMBER OF'
     -  ' VALUES BETWEEN 200-300 IS ', I3 //
     -  ' ', 'SUBSCRIPT OF FIRST INTEGER'
     -  ' LARGER THAN 500 ', I4)
      STOP
      END
```

(frames 16, 27, 30, 31)

6.

```
C  SOLUTION TO PROBLEM 6 IN SELF-TEST
C  PROGRAM FINDS AVERAGE HEIGHT, WEIGHT, AND WAIST
C  FOR STUDENTS AT UNIVERSITY OF NANCAGO
C  LAST DATA CARD IS BLANK-ASSUME ZEROS
      DIMENSION AVSIZE(1001, 3)
C  READ MEASUREMENTS AND INITIALIZE AVSIZE(1001, 1)
C  AVSIZE(1001, 2), AVSIZE(1001, 3)
      DO 20 I = 1, 1000
         READ (5,101) AVSIZE(I,1), AVSIZE(I,2)
     -      AVSIZE(I,3)
101      FORMAT (2F5.1, F2.0)
20    CONTINUE
C  ACCUMULATE HEIGHT, WEIGHT, AND WAIST
      DO 40 J = 1, 3
         DO 30 I = 1, 1000
            AVSIZE(1001, J) = AVSIZE(1001, J) +
     -         AVSIZE(I, J)
30       CONTINUE
40    CONTINUE
C  CALCULATE AVERAGE HEIGHT, WEIGHT, AND WAIST
      DO 50 J = 1, 3
         AVSIZE(1001, J) = AVSIZE(1001, J)/1000.0
50    CONTINUE
      WRITE (6, 201) AVSIZE(1001, 1), AVSIZE(1001, 2),
     -      AVSIZE(1001, 3)
```

(continued on next page)

```
201    FØRMAT (' ', 'AVERAGE HEIGHT ', F5.1//
   -      ' AVERAGE WEIGHT ', F5.1/ ' AVERAGE'
   -      ' WAIST ', F4.1)
       STØP
       END
```

(frames 30–31)

7.

```
C SØLUTION TØ PRØBLEM 7 ØF SELF TEST
       DIMENSIØN MØNTH (12)
C INITIALIZE MØNTH ARRAY
       MØNTH(1)=31
       MØNTH(2)=59
       MØNTH(3)=90
       ...
       MØNTH(12)=365
C READ IN DAY NUMBER
       READ (11,120) NUMDAY
120    FØRMAT(......)
150    IF (NUMDAY .LE. 0) GØ TØ 200
C FIND MØNTH WHEN MØNTH(I) .GE. NUMDAY
       DO 160 I= 1, 12
       IF (MØNTH(I) .GE. NUMDAY) GØ TØ 180
160    CØNTINUE
C      ERROR NUMDAY >365
       ....
180    MØN = I
       IF (I.EQ.1) NDAY= NUMDAY
       IF (I.GT.1) NDAY= NUMDAY - MØNTH(I-1)
       WRITE (11, 200) NUMDAY, MØN, NDAY
200    FØRMAT (' DAY # ', I4, 'IS ', I2, '/', I2
C GET NEXT DAY NUMBER
       READ (11,120) NUMDAY
       GØ TØ 150
200    STØP
       END
```

(frame 33)

CHAPTER EIGHT
More on Variables

You can drink beer or whiskey to get the same high. However, you may have to drink a lot of beer to attain the "high" gotten by drinking, say, eight ounces of whiskey (especially on an empty stomach). This same fact of life occurs in FORTRAN programming.

As we noted in Chapter Six, there are hard ways of writing programs and there are statements which simplify your writing efforts. In this chapter, we will emphasize the use of various types of variables (numerical and non-numerical) in programming. We will also simplify some of your initialization statements. In particular you will learn to:

- use a modified scientific notation to express real constants;

- get "additional accuracy" in your answers by using double precision variables;

- use character variables;

- use logical variables;

- use an IMPLICIT statement to specify the type of a variable;

- initialize program variables by using the DATA statement;

- use the EQUIVALENCE statement to form correspondences between variables and arrays.

E Notation

1. The FORTRAN E notation allows us to store and do arithmetic with very small or very large real numbers. As you will see, computers are limited with respect to the total number of digits in a real or integer constant (usually seven to fifteen digits). The use of the E notation allows us to overcome this problem (somewhat) when using real constants.

As you know, a real constant is a number written with a decimal point. So far we have expressed real constants in the following way.

Method 1: A number with a decimal point. For example, 573.34 is a real constant. 57334 is not a real constant; it is an integer constant.

But FORTRAN also allows us to express real constants in a second way.

Method 2: A real constant can also be written as a number multiplied by some power of 10. That is, 573.34 can be expressed as: .57334 x 10^3.

We call this method scientific notation—which you may remember from algebra. * The scientific notation has three basic parts: the mantissa, the base, and the exponent.

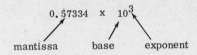

In the FORTRAN language we write

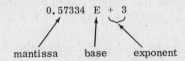

where E implies a base of ten. For this reason, we call this the E notation.

(a) Identify the mantissa, base, and exponent of the real constant

   37.12 E + 04.

(b) Which of the following real constants are written in the E notation?

_____ 360.   _____ 25. E + 03

_____ 25   _____ .31 E –05

- - - - - - - - - - - - - - - - - -

(a) In 37.12 E + 04, 37.12 is the mantissa, E is the base, and + 04 is the exponent.
(b) The real constants 25. E + 03 and .31 E –05 are written in the E notation. If you are familiar with scientific notation you may skip to the question found in frame 6.

2. Complete the following table.

---

*A good review can be found in Background Math for a Computer World 2nd Ed. by Ruth Ashley, another Self-Teaching Guide published by John Wiley & Sons, 1980.

Scientific notation		E notation
-5.243×10^5		$-5.243E+05$
6.372×10^{34}	(a) _____	
$-.714 \times 10^{14}$	(b) _____	
(c) _____		$83.21E-05$
(d) _____		$-.3141E+9$
$-.0134 \times 10^0$	(e) _____	
(f) _____		$-85.31426E+23$

- - - - - - - - - - - - - - - - - -

(a) $6.372E+34$; (b) $-.714E-14$; (c) 83.21×10^{-5}; (d) $-.3141 \times 10^9$;
(e) $-.0134E+0$; (f) -85.31426×10^{23}

3. The E notation consists of the mantissa (a real or integer constant) followed by the letter E and a signed or unsigned one- or two-digit integer constant (some computers allow three or more digits) as an exponent.

$$23 \, E -12 \qquad 1.6 \, E +8 \qquad -.19784 \, E \, 13$$

For both mantissa and exponent, a negative sign must be written when a negative quantity is indicated, whereas a positive sign is optional because it is implied.

A great deal of variation is permitted when writing constants in the E notation. Here are some examples.

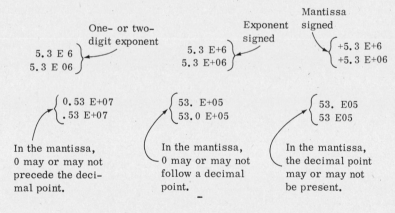

Rewrite these real constants using E notation.

(a) 3.6×10^{-7} _____   (c) -33.33×10^4 _____

(b) $55. \times 10^3$ _____   (d) $-.56 \times 10^{-6}$ _____

- - - - - - - - - - - - - - - - -

(a) $3.6E-7$; (b) $55.E3$; (c) $-33.33E4$; (d) $-.56E-6$. If your answers were different from these, check yours against the permitted variations.

4. Why learn and use a new and more complex notation instead of a simple notation? The next few frames will answer this question.

FORTRAN generally uses "one computer word" (sometimes called a full word) to store a real value. This imposes a limit on the size of the value the computer will store (just as in a desk calculator). The word size varies among computer systems, so computers vary as to the size of a value they can accommodate in storage. For illustration purposes we will use a word length of 32 bits (4 bytes) which is common to many computers.

A real value, whether written in method 1 or method 2 notation (frame 1), will appear in storage in a normalized form. That is, the value is stored in the E notation with a special twist: the decimal point always appears to the left of the leftmost nonzero digit. As a result, the mantissa is always a frac-tional value between 0 and 1. Examples:

Real value	Un-normalized E notation	(stored in) Normalized E notation
538.78 $\longrightarrow$	538.78 E 0 $\longrightarrow$	.53878E+03
359.801 $\longrightarrow$	359.801E0 $\longrightarrow$	.359801E+03

Which of the following real values are in normalized E notation?

_____ (a) 3.71E03   _____ (c) 2.39E-07

_____ (b) .2110E+02   _____ (d) .71E02

- - - - - - - - - - - - - - - - - -

Choices (b) and (d) are the real values in normalized E notation since the decimal point appears in the mantissa to the left of the leftmost nonzero digit.

5. You may ask, "How do I, and the computer, normalize an E value?" Here's the secret formula that has been handed down through the generations and revealed to us by our faithful high school teachers: If you move the deci-mal point one position to the left, increase the value of the exponent by one; two positions to the left, increase the value of the exponent by two; and for $\underline{n}$ positions to the left, increase the value of the exponent by $\underline{n}$. Likewise, if you move the decimal point one position to the right, decrease the value of the exponent by one; for two positions, by two; and for $\underline{n}$ positions, by $\underline{n}$.

Normalize the following E values.

(a) 102.32E2 _____

(b) 0.0031E1 _____

(c) 0.0045E-5 _____

(d) -53.42E-7 _____

- - - - - - - - - - - - - - - - - -

(a) .10232E5, since
102.32E2 $\longrightarrow$ 102.32 x 10^2 $\longrightarrow$ 102.32 x 10^{2+3} $\longrightarrow$ .10232 x 10^5 $\longrightarrow$ .10232E5
left(3)

(b) .31E-1, since
.0031E1 $\longrightarrow$ .00.31 x 10^{1-2} $\longrightarrow$ .31 x 10^{-1} $\longrightarrow$ .31E-1
right(2)

(c) .45E-7, since
0.0045E-5 $\longrightarrow$ 0.0045 x 10^{-5} $\longrightarrow$ .00.45 x 10^{-5-2} $\longrightarrow$ .45 x 10^{-7} $\longrightarrow$ .45E-7
right(2)

(d) -.5342E-5, since
-53.42E-7 $\longrightarrow$ -53.42 x 10^{-7} $\longrightarrow$ -.53.42 x 10^{-7+2} $\longrightarrow$ -.5342 x 10^{-5} $\longrightarrow$ -.5342E-5
left(2)

6.   The computer performs the normalization process on all real un-normalized values. Let's look at some more illustrations.

171.2 is a real value
$10^0 = 1$
So 171.2 $\longrightarrow$ 171.2 x 10^0 $\longrightarrow$ .171.2 x 10^{0+3} $\longrightarrow$ .1712 x 10^3 $\longrightarrow$
left(3)
$\longrightarrow$ .1712E03

Now you write the following real constants in the normalized E notation.

(a)   321.29 _____

(b)   0.0000012345 _____

- - - - - - - - - - - - - - - - - -

(a) .32129E+03
(b) 0.00000.12345 x 10^{0-5} $\longrightarrow$ .12345 x 10^{-5} $\longrightarrow$ .12345E-05
right(5)

If you did not get these examples correct, review frames 1 through 5 before you go on.

7.   Actually, a real value is stored in a computer word in three parts—the sign, the exponent, and the mantissa. The decimal point is assumed but never stored since the constant is stored in normalized E notation and the location of the decimal point is in front of the mantissa.

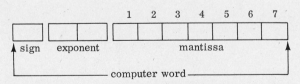

This word permits two decimal digits for the exponents and approximately seven decimal digits for the mantissa. (It is approximate—not exact—since the mantissa and exponent use a specified number of binary and not decimal digits.) Because of the word size, real values that can be stored in our 32-bit word computer must be in the range of approximately 10^{-75} through 10^{+75}.

The catch is that the mantissa can accommodate only seven decimal digits (called the significant digits). So, although 10000000000.0 can be stored as .1E11 and 0.000000000001 can be stored as .1E-11, the number 1234567.89 cannot be stored exactly as written. Only the first seven (most significant) digits will be stored.

> .1234567E07   Some compilers will discard or truncate the last two digits in the mantissa.

> .1234568E07   Some computers will round to the seventh digit in the mantissa and discard the rest.

In the examples above the number of digits exceeded seven, but the number of digits stored (the significant digits) did not exceed seven, even though the range or the magnitude of the numbers exceeded seven digits.

As you see, the computer's word size determines the number of "significant digits." This is not to imply that the digits "lost" are not significant, but there has to be a cutoff somewhere. Real constants are also called single precision constants.

For example, the number 1234567.E55 represents a very large number. In fact, the number has 62 decimal digits even though the number of significant digits in the mantissa consists of only seven; that is, the precision is seven.

Here are some questions. (See, we did not forget!)

(a) By using our 32-bit word size computer, what is the largest real value that can be represented in storage? _____ What is the smallest? _____ (In this case largest and smallest refer to the magnitude, an unsigned value.)

(b) How would the dollar amount 375889582.57 written as a real value appear in storage? _____

(c) Which of the following constants are in incorrect E notation?

_____   756.35F0115   _____   -21.2E34

- - - - - - - - - - - - - - - - - - -

(a) The largest number is 1×10^{75}. The smallest number is 1×10^{-75}.

(b) .3758895E09 or .3758896E09, depending on the computer you used. The computer has cheated us by $82.57 since it can only store seven significant digits.

(c) 756.35F0115 The letter F is not valid.

8.   What is the value of the FORTRAN E notation? The exponent part in the E notation lets us "sneak" in a value greater in magnitude than could be

expressed simply by seven decimal digits. Therefore, in applications which manipulate very large or very small values (usually scientific applications) you will want to use the E notation.

Here's a tricky question. Is there any difference between 1.0E2 and

10**2? _____

- - - - - - - - - - - - - - - - - - -

Yes, there is a big difference. The value 1.0E2 defines the value of 100. that is stored in some storage location. Whereas, 10**2 is a FORTRAN command to compute a value.

Double Precision Constants

9.   What if your boss insists that you store in the computer the real value 123456789. (which has more than seven digits) without truncation? Don't give up. Most FORTRAN compilers accept <u>double precision</u> or <u>D notation</u> values. This notation allows you to store real values up to sixteen (yes, 16) significant decimal digits in length so that our precision is now increased up to approximately sixteen decimal digits.

Internally, the computer uses two consecutive memory words to store such a real value, hence the name double precision.

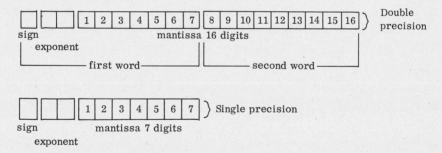

A double precision value is represented and used roughly as a real value but has a larger mantissa—at least twice as many significant digits as in single precision. The exponent, however, has the same range as for numbers written in E notation. You're probably anxious to see some examples.

12345678910111.21 D 0   .31415925635 D +1

7.317493D+30   -17.831457632941D-38

Generally, double precision values may be written only one way: as a real value expressed in the E notation, except the letter E is interchanged with the letter D. An example is 12345.6789D-30. Check your computer's FORTRAN manual since the allowable number of digits in the mantissa and exponent may vary among different computers.

Some compilers recognize a real number written with eight to sixteen decimal digits without the letter D as a double precision value. Check your computer's FORTRAN manual also for this useful feature.

Using everything you've learned so far, identify the invalid real values and explain why they are invalid.

(a)   3.72 _____

(b)   3.72E+ _____

(c)   5.68E79 _____

(d)   5,678.321E+22 _____

(e)   0.321E2.2 _____

(f)   .3724D22 _____

(g)   852.672D3,750.1 _____

- - - - - - - - - - - - - - - - - -

(a) Valid.
(b) Invalid. It must have a one- or two-digit exponent.
(c) Invalid. The exponent, 79, exceeds the permissible range of the value. It is important to remember that by using double precision values, only the number of significant digits is increased, not the magnitude of the value allowed.
(d) Invalid. No commas are allowed in a mantissa.
(e) Invalid. The exponent cannot have a decimal point. It must be an integer constant.
(f) Valid.
(g) Invalid. First the exponent cannot exceed two digits (sometimes three). Second, the exponent must be an integer constant, Finally, exponents cannot contain commas.

10. In frame 7 we stated that precision refers to the number of significant digits in the mantissa, and in frame 9 we said for double precision up to sixteen significant digits are allowed, However using our word size double precision, like single precision, can only accommodate values in the range of approximately 10^{-75} through 10^{+75}. For example, 12345.67D+105 would be prohibited but 12345.67D+60 is okay.

(a)   What is the maximum value for a double precision constant?

(b)   Which of these double precision constants is illegal in our word size? −3.1235D−17 or .31624517D+3217 _____

- - - - - - - - - - - - - - - - - -

(a) about 10^{75}

(b) .31624517D+3217 is an illegal double precision constant since the exponent is too large (greater than +75).

11. Represent the following constants as double precision constants.

(a) $-3.27145839 \times 10^{15}$ _____

(b) $-.00146735246 \times 10^{-4}$ _____

(c) 3.612×10^{-18} _____

- - - - - - - - - - - - - - - - - -

(a) -3.27145839D+15, or -3.27145839D15

(b) -.00146735246D-4

(c) 3.612D-18

Double Precision Variables

12. Please do not get the idea that double precision variables and constants are only used for scientific computations. A glance at the loan repayment program in frame **19** of Chapter One will show its use in a commercial program. Double precision variables and constants were used in this program because if the loan amount was $10,000,257.37 then the "lower order digits" (257.37) would suffer some truncation due to the word size of the computer. However, by using double precision arithmetic for the computations and then truncating rounded values of the double precision constants, errors were eliminated.

Programmers frequently use double precision constants and variables to guard against the effects of truncation or rounding errors which will occur in lengthy arithmetic computations. Let's look at some examples. Assume all real variables only store seven significant digits in the mantissa.

FORTRAN statements   Manual calculation

| A = 1.234567. |
| B = .4444444 |
| C = A + B |

```
       1234567.
  +        0.4444444
       1234567.4444444
```

What will be stored in the variable C? 1234567. The digits .4444444 were truncated because the variable C can accommodate only the first seven significant decimal digits. This error resulted because the value in variable B was very small as compared to the value in variable A. The effect of such an error can grow, as the example on the next page shows.

```
       D = 1234567.
       E = .4999999
       DO 10 I = 1, 1234567
       D = D + E
10     CONTINUE
```

After we have repeated the addition of E to D 1234567 times, the final result of D is 1234567., since D + E = 1234567.4999999 is stored in D as 1234567. Thus, at each loop we have lost about .5. After 1,234,567 loops we have lost approximately 1,234,567 x .5 (or 1,234,567 / 2). This is approximately a 50 percent error. However, if D were a double precision variable, no error would have occurred since up to sixteen significant digits would be stored.

Thus, to avoid losing significant digits by truncation errors, you should

use _____ constants and variables.

- - - - - - - - - - - - - - - - - -

double precision

13. We must tell the compiler which variables are to be double precision variables. This is done simply by writing

```
       DOUBLE PRECISION
```

followed by a list of variable names (array names are also allowed). For example, to denote VAR1 and TEMP3 as double precision variables write

```
       DOUBLE PRECISION VAR1, TEMP3
```

To indicate a list COST of size 100 and a variable TKO are to be double precision, we write

```
       DOUBLE PRECISION COST(100), TKO
```

Remember, you can only double precision <u>real</u> variables. You cannot use a DOUBLE PRECISION statement for an integer variable.

DOUBLE PRECISION statements can be continued. Many DOUBLE PRECISION statements can appear in a program.

Write DOUBLE PRECISION statements for the following sets of variables.

(a) Variables A, F2, and a two-dimensional array B of maximum dimensions 50 and 20

(b) A list FLOW of maximum dimension 350 and a three-dimensional array CUBE of maximum dimensions 100, 100, 3

- - - - - - - - - - - - - - - - - - -

(a)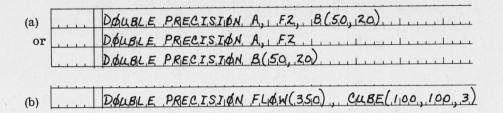

or

(b)

14. The FORTRAN compiler, when evaluating an arithmetic expression containing double precision constants or variables and single precision real constants or variables, will generate instructions to convert all single precision values to double precision by adding appropriate zeros (padding). The final result of the evaluation is a double precision value. Here is an example (DOUBLE is a double precision variable).

Converted to double precision

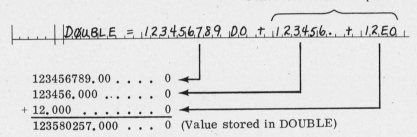

```
123456789.00 . . . . 0
123456.000 . . . . . 0
+ 12.000 . . . . . . . 0
123580257.000 . . . 0   (Value stored in DOUBLE)
```

The following table shows the relationship between real and double precision values when they are combined in an arithmetic expression.

		Second variable or constant	
		Real	Double precision
First variable or constant	Single precision (real or SP)	SP	DP
	Double precision (DP)	DP	DP

You can interpret this table as follows.

Let DSING be a double precision variable. Then the mode of the result of the expression S1 * DSING is double precision. You look on the first row of the table (since S1 is real) and column 2 of the table (since DSING is double precision). The box in which the row and column meet (the upper right box) is DP, or double precision. This is the mode of the expression.

The variables BIG and SUPER shown below are in double precision mode. What mode is the result of the expression on the right-hand side of the assignment statement? _____

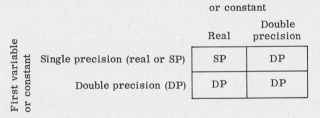

Double precision (BIG/STUFF) will result in a double precision value. REALLY + (BIG/STUFF) will also result in a double precision value which will be stored in the variable SUPER.)

15. Here is a program segment. The variable DOUBLE is in double precision mode. What is the value in the variable INBANK? _____

	`DOUBLE = 1202`
	`YOUR = 5.0`
	`MONEY = 3`
	`INBANK = DOUBLE + YOUR - MONEY`

- - - - - - - - - - - - - - - -

```
 DOUBLE = 1200.00 . . . . . 0
+YOUR   =    5.00 . . . . . 0
-MONEY  =    3.00 . . . . . 0
              1202.   (truncated)
```

The value in the variable INBANK is 1202 because INBANK is an integer variable.

16. Write a program segment which:

   specifies B as a double precision variable;
   stores the constants 4.325E2, -5.247D4 in the variables A and B respectively;
   computes the algebraic expression AB and stores the result in the variable F1.

   What value will be stored in F1? _____

- - - - - - - - - - - - - - - -

	`DOUBLE PRECISION B`
	`A = 4.325 E2`
	`B = -5.247 D4`
	`F1 = A * B`

-22.69327E6 will be stored in F1, since 4.325E2 x -5.247D4 = -22.693275D6. The digit 5 is truncated since F1 is single precision.

Character Variables

17. In frame 37 of Chapter Five you learned how to use character variables to store, input and output alphanumeric data in a convenient manner. In the next eleven frames you will learn powerful techniques for manipulating character variables. But first a little review. By writing

CHARACTER*60 INPUT, BARBLE

you declare two character variables INPUT and BARBLE which can contain up to 60 characters each.

Write a FORTRAN statement(s) which declares BIG and SMALL as character variables containing 132 and 80 characters respectively.

- - - - - - - - - - - - - - - - - - - -

      CHARACTER*132   BIG
      CHARACTER*80   SMALL

You must <u>use</u> two FORTRAN statements. Don't be nervous, now we will make it a little easier to do.

18. A more compact way of writing the answer to frame 17 is to use the single FORTRAN statement
    (a)   CHARACTER*132   BIG, SMALL*80
or (b)   CHARACTER*80   SMALL, BIG*132

As you see, in a), when the variable name SMALL is followed by a *, the FORTRAN compiler takes the number following the *, 80 in this case, to be the number of characters that SMALL can store. This overrides the declared length (132) at the beginning of the statement.

The statement   CHARACTER A, B, C

declares A, B, and C to be character variables which can store one character each.

In case you were wondering, yes, you can have arrays of character variables.

      CHARACTER*30   INVNUM(100)
or   CHARACTER INVNUM(100)*30

declares a 100 element array INVNUM with each element of the array able to store up to 30 characters. Since there was no length after the word CHARACTER in the second statement, a length of one is implied. That is why it is necessary to use *30 after the array name.

Write one FORTRAN statement declaring the following character variables:

WAT   containing 30 characters
FIV   an array of 200 elements with each array element con-
          taining 60 characters
FLAG1   containing one character
FLAG2   containing one character
DESCR   an array of 50 elements containing 30 characters each

- - - - - - - - - - - - - - - - - - - -

There are a lot of possible answers. Here are some.

    CHARACTER*30 WAT, FIV (200)*60, FLAG1*1, FLAG2*1, DESCR(50)
or CHARACTER WAT*30, FIV (200)*60, FLAG1, FLAG2, DESCR(50)*30

19. Suppose you are writing a program in which the user may either input
the words END or STOP to signal to the program that there is no more data
to be entered. What do you do? Well, you can write

```
      CHARACTER*80 INPUT
      . . .
      . . .
      READ (5, 70) INPUT
70    FORMAT (A80)
      IF (INPUT .EQ. 'END') GO TO 300
      IF (INPUT .EQ. 'STOP') GO TO 300
         . . .
```

The first logical IF statement compares the data stored in INPUT to the character string 'END'. Notice that apostrophes (') were used to signify the word
END is a character string and not a variable name. Whoa, you say, INPUT
has up to 80 characters and the word 'END' only has three characters. Is
that a valid comparison? Yes! In a comparison between two character
strings of unequal length, the shorter string is filled (padded) on the right by
blanks until the strings are of equal length. Since you remember Chapter Six
vividly, you have noted by this point that both logical IF statements could
have been combined into one statement

    IF (INPUT .EQ. 'END' .OR. INPUT .EQ. 'STOP') GO TO 300

Write the FORTRAN statements necessary to READ, from device number 11,
a character string from positions 1 to 6 of a record to be stored in STATUS
(length 6) and an integer value from positions 7 to 12 to be stored in LEVEL.
If the value of STATUS is 'FULL' or the value of STATUS is 'READY' and
LEVEL is less than 100 branch to the statement numbered 300.

- - - - - - - - - - - - - - - - - - - -

```
    CHARACTER*6 STATUS
    ...
    ...
    READ(11,80) STATUS, LEVEL
80  FORMAT(A6, I6)
    IF(STATUS .EQ. 'FULL' .OR.
    (STATUS .EQ. 'READY' .AND. LEVEL .LT. 100)) GO TO 300
```

20. Suppose you want to move the data from the seventh to the eleventh character of the CHARACTER string WYLBUR into a variable FIVE. All you have to do is to write the character assignment statement

    FIVE = WYLBUR (7:11)

The notation (7:11) specifies the beginning (7) and the end (11) positions of a substring of WYLBUR. The statement

    WHOSE (3:7) = FIRST (5:9)

would move the data from positions five through nine of FIRST to positions three to seven of WHOSE. The statement

    TRUCK (3:6) = LETTER (12:20)

only moves enough characters to fill positions three to six of TRUCK since the receiving field width can only accept four characters.

The statement
    PAD (5:13) = SNAP (6:8)

copies the data in SNAP to positions five to seven of PAD. Positions eight to thirteen are now filled with blanks.

If there is no (:) specification for a character variable, the compiler assumes, by default, that you want the complete character variable as defined in the the CHARACTER statement. So, if you write

    CHARACTER*8 TREE, OF*4, LIFE*10
    . . .
    . . .
    TREE = LIFE(2:9)

then positions one to eight of TREE are filled with the data stored in positions two to nine of LIFE.

Write FORTRAN statements to:
a) store the data in positions 4 to 9 of ARISM into positions K1 to K2 of PLAGIA
b) store the data in positions I to L of NMOS in the character variable ECL
c) branch to the statement numbered 500 if the data stored in positions one to three of LINPUT is 'END'

- - - - - - - - - - - - - - - - -

a) PLAGIA (K1:K2) = ARISM (4:9)
b) ECL = NMOS (I:L)
c) IF (LINPUT (1:3) .EQ. 'END') GO TO 500

Take a short break, this is heady stuff!

21. In this frame you will learn how to operate on character strings with the concatenation operator. The operator is written as two slashes (//) and is used to "sew" together character strings. First, an example. Let A, B and C (character variables) contain 'PAUL', 'GEORGE' and 'JOHN' respectively. The value of the data stored in A after the statement

    A (1:8)=B (1:5)//C (1:3)

is executed is 'GEORGJOH'. 'PAUL' has disappeared from A.

There is a rule in FORTRAN 77 that says you cannot have a character assignment in which the positions referenced on the left hand side of the assignment also appear on the right hand side of the statement. This means

    B (1:1)=B (2:2)

is allowed, but

    A (1:3)=A (2:3)//A (1:1)

is not allowed. As a practical matter, this is very reasonable since A (2:3) is moved into the first two position of A (A (1:2)). Thus, appending A (1:1) might cause an erroneous situation to occur since a question could arise about which A (1:1) is referred to. Was is the original A (1:1) or the modified A (1:1)?

What is the value of the concatenations:

a) 'HE'//'HAW'
b) 'HAW'//'HE'
c) A='BEST', B='HAVE' and C='NOT', A (1:3)//B (1:1)//C (3:3)=?

- - - - - - - - - - - - - - - - - - -

a) 'HEHAW'
b) 'HAWHE'
c) 'BESHT'

22. There are four FORTRAN functions which help you to manipulate characters strings. Here is the first.

To determine if one character string is a substring (contained in) of another string you use the INDEX function. Here's an example:

    INDEX('BANANAS', 'NA') = 3

since the position of the first occurrence of 'NA' occurs in 'BANANAS' at the third character of 'BANANAS'. However,

    INDEX('AUDIO', 'V') = 0

since 'V' does not appear in 'AUDIO'.

Complete the table.

	A	B	INDEX(A, B)
a)	'UNCLE'	'UN'	
b)	'YOSEMITE'	'E'	
c)	'GERGEOUS'	'GEO'	
d)	'TURGID'	'RUG'	

- - - - - - - - - - - - - - - - - -

a) 1
b) 4, the first E is the one that is counted.
c) 4
d) 0, since 'RUG' never appears in 'TURGID'

23. The string function LEN tells you how many characters are actually stored in a character string or variable. Let's look at these examples.

LEN('ABC') = 3
If A = '' (null)   ,   LEN(A) = 0

As you can see, the LEN function is used to measure the length of the data stored in a character variable. By using the statements

CHARACTER*20 CASH
. . . .
. . . . .
CASH = '123,456.35'
I = LEN(CASH)

the value of I is 10 since all of the characters in CASH are counted. We will use the LEN function in the next frame to control the number of iterations in a DO loop.

What is the value of I after the following statements are executed?

```
CHARACTER*8 MUDDY, MURKY, WATERS
. . .
. . .
MURKY = 'TURGID'
WATERS = 'PCB'
MUDDY(1:4) = MURKY
MUDDY(5:8) = WATERS(3:8)
I = LEN(MUDDY)
```

I = 5 since:
            MUDDY(1:4) = 'TURG'
            MUDDY(5:8) = 'Bbbb'
so LEN(MUDDY) = 5.

24. The last two string functions are the ICHAR and CHAR functions. These functions convert a single character to an integer value and vice versa. In frame 4 of Chapter Zero, we mentioned that every character is represented as a number in a computer. The numbers may differ depending upon the internal representation code of a machine. This internal number sequence is the key to the method by which characters are compared. The computer compares the internal representation number of a character and not the actual character. The ICHAR function converts a character to its internal representing number. Thus, if the digits 0, 1, 2, ... are internally represented as 48, 49, 50, ..., then ICHAR('8') = 56 and ICHAR('6') = 54.

On some machines letters are internally represented by higher numbers than those of digits. On other machines letters are internally represented by lower numbers than digits are. However, on all machines a blank is represented by a number which always is less than all digit or letter numbers. You should check your FORTRAN manual to find out what your machine does. (This is also called the collating sequence.).

The CHAR function converts an integer to its equivalent character. By using the numbers given above CHAR(51) = '3'. The CHAR function can be used in interactive programs to produce nice-looking screens on CRT terminals, flash warnings, ring a bell in the terminal, and so on. If you are using a CRT terminal for your input and output, a look at the terminal manual will tell you what characters control the CRT terminal options.

Let us assume that 'A', 'B', 'C', ... are represented internally by 65, 66, 67 .... Please complete the table:

	A	ICHAR(A)	N	CHAR(N)
a)	'F'		52	
b)		69	78	

- - - - - - - - - - - - - - - - - - -

	A	ICHAR(A)	N	CHAR(N)
a)	'F'	70	52	'4'
b)	'E'	69	78	'N'

25. We have a little application for you using the LEN and ICHAR functions. Sometimes, when a terminal is used for input you cannot depend on the fact that the operator will always enter data in the correct record positions or that the data entered is, say, all numeric.

In this program segment below, a number is to be input into the variable LINPUT. If all of the characters are numeric the value of the number is stored in N. If one of the characters is not numeric the program will branch to the statement numbered 500 and a message error will be printed.

```
        CHARACTER*80 LINPUT
        ...
        ...
100     READ(11, 110) LINPUT
110     FORMAT(A80)
C       IF NOTHING IS ENTERED BRANCH TO 400.
        IF(LEN(LINPUT).) .EQ. 0) GO TO 400
C       DATA IN INPUT
130     N = 0
C       TEST ALL CHARACTERS ENTERED
        DO 200 I=1, LEN(LINPUT)
150     IF(.NOT.(LINPUT(I:I) .GE. 'A' .AND.
            LINPUT(I:I) .LE. 'Z')) GO TO 500
C       ADD DIGIT TO NUMBER STORED IN N AFTER SUBTRACTING 48
C       FROM THE RESULT OF ICHAR
170     N = 10*N + (ICHAR(LINPUT(I:I)) - 48)
200     CONTINUE
        ...
C       ERROR MESSAGE
500     WRITE(6, 510) LINPUT(I:I)
510     FORMAT('**ERROR, ',A1,' IS NOT NUMERIC')
```

What changes would be required if the data in LINPUT is to be only alphabetic (with no spaces) and you wanted an error message printed if a non-
alphabetic character is found?

- - - - - - - - - - - - - - - - -

The statements numbered 130 and 170 should be deleted. The statement
numbered 150 should be changed to

```
150     IF(.NOT.(LINPUT(I:I) .GE. 'A' .AND.
            LINPUT(I:I) .LE. 'Z')) GO TO 500
```

and the work NUMERIC should be changed no ALPHABETIC in the FORMAT
statement (510).

26. So far we have been explicitly writing the number of characters to be
either input or output from a character variable by writing a number after

the A format specification. Take a quick look at statements 110 and 510 in the last frame. Now that you're back we will show how the compiler can work for you

The specification A80 in the FORMAT statement (110) was not really necessary. It would have been enough to write

110   FORMAT(A)

The compiler will notice the absence of a field length and create a length (80) from the declaration for LINPUT in the CHARACTER statement. The compiler will do this for both input and output.

If a data record contains 'ABC.......Z012...9', what will be stored by the READ statement in the program

	CHARACTER*10 KING, KØNG*4, LIVES*12	
	...	
	...	
	READ (11, 110) KING, KØNG, LIVES	
110	FØRMAT(A, 4X, A, 3X, A)	

KING = 'ABCDEFGHIJ'
KONG = 'OPQR'
LIVES = 'VWXYZ01234'

27. By specifying the number of characters to be input or output, you are in control of what is happening. Remember, you are supposed to be in control of the machine and not vice versa.

In the following examples, assume that AB is a variable defined as CHARACTER*10. Furthermore, assume that the data record to be input contains the string 'ABCDEFGHIJKL'.

The length specified by the format code determines the number of characters to be transferred. On input, if the size of the character variable is greater than the number of characters to be transferred, the data is completely transferred and is padded on the right with blanks to fill the character variable.

Format	Variable AB
A8	'ABCDEFGHℓℓ'

If the size of the character variable is less than the number of characters to be transferred on input, only the rightmost characters of the input data are stored in the variable.

Format	Variable AB
A12	'CDEFGHIJKL'

On output, if the size of the character variable is greater than the number of characters to be transferred, only the leftmost characters in the variable are transferred.

Format	Variable AB	output
A8	'ABCDEFGHIJ'	'ABCDEFGH'

If the size of the character variable is less than the number of characters to be transferred, the entire string is transferred and is padded on the left with blanks.

Format	Variable AB	output
A12	'ABCDEFGHIJ'	'ƁƁABCDEFGHIJ'

For both input and output, if both the size of the character variable and the number of characters to be transferred are equal, all the data is transferred.

a) If a data record contains the string 'ABCD....Z012....9', what will the following program segment store in TOUGH, STUFF, and THIS?

```
       CHARACTER*8 TOUGH, STUFF*4, THIS*6
       ...
       ...
       READ (11, 110) TOUGH, STUFF, THIS
110.   FORMAT (A, 2X, A3, A8)
```

b) If TOUGH = 'CHILDREN', STUFF = 'ARE', and THIS = 'SWEET' what will be written by

```
       WRITE(12, 210) TOUGH, STUFF, THIS
210.   FORMAT (1X, A, A2, A8)
```

- - - - - - - - - - - - - - - - - -

a) TOUGH = 'ABCDEFGH', STUFF = 'KLMb', THIS = 'PQRSTU'
b) CHILDRENARbbSWEETb will be printed

Type Statements

28. A type statement is a nonexecutable FORTRAN statement designed to convey the mode and storage requirements of variables to the compiler. During the compilation the compiler utilizes type statement information to allocate storage of proper size and mode. The general form of a type statement is shown below.

```
type  list
```

"Type" can be one of the following names:
       DOUBLE PRECISION
       REAL
       INTEGER
       LOGICAL
       CHARACTER
       COMPLEX (not discussed in this Self-Teaching Guide)

"List" consists of variable (subscripted or unsubscripted) names separated by commas. A variable is called declared if its name is found in a list of a type statement. You should check your FORTRAN manual to see which type statements (if any) are available on your computer. Some examples:

```
DOUBLE PRECISION A, STACK(40)
```

This statement declares A and a list STACK of dimension 40 to be double precision.

```
REAL IJKLMN, I(20, 15), NETPAY
```

This statement declares as real variables IJKLMN, an array I of maximum dimensions 20 and 15, and NETPAY.

```
INTEGER ATOH(10, 10, 10), HOURS, OTOZ(15, 20)
```

This statement declares a three-dimensional array ATOH of maximum dimensions 10, 10, 10, HOURS, and a two-dimensional array OTOZ of maximum dimensions 15 and 20 as integer variables.

```
LOGICAL SWITCH, CODE, LIGHT
```

This statement declares the variables SWITCH, CODE, and LIGHT as logical variables—variables having true or false values.

The type statement is available in ANS FORTRAN compilers but is not included in ANS BASIC FORTRAN compilers. Some computer manufacturers have extended their BASIC FORTRAN compilers to accept some or all of the type statements. If you are using a BASIC FORTRAN compiler, check your computer's FORTRAN manual. It is good programming practice to place all type statements at the beginning of the program and this will satisfy all compilers.

Code a type statement which tells the compiler to reserve a double word for the variables BIG, FAT, and DIGITS.

- - - - - - - - - - - - - - - - - -

```
DØUBLE PRECISIØN BIG, FAT, DIGITS
```

29. By using type statements, you may even reserve storage for arrays and thereby avoid having to describe these variables in a DIMENSION statement. The rules of Chapter Seven for the DIMENSION statement also apply here. However, if you use both a type statement and a DIMENSION statement for an array, you only have to mention the array name (not its dimensions) in the type statement.

Thus to code a type statement to reserve a double word for the variables BALANC (a two-dimensional array with maximum bounds 100 and 3) and ROUND, we would write

```
      DIMENSIØN BALANC(100, 3)
      DØUBLE PRECISIØN BALANC, RØUND
or    DØUBLE PRECISIØN BALANC(100, 3), RØUND
```

Write a type statement(s) to declare as logical variables BIT, a two-dimensional array TRUTAB (of maximum dimensions 3 and 3), and MANUAL.

- - - - - - - - - - - - - - - - - -

```
      DIMENSIØN TRUTAB(3, 3)
      LØGICAL BIT, TRUTAB, MANUAL
or    LØGICAL BIT, TRUTAB(3, 3), MANUAL
```

30. In frame 7 of Chapter Two, we discussed the procedure for naming variables. Generally, the compiler assumes as integer variables only those variables whose names start with any one of the letters IJKLMN and it considers the other variable names as representing real variables. However, occasions do arise when we wish to override this assumption (sometimes called a default).

As an example, the electrical engineer uses "I" for current, which is a real quantity (to the engineer). The variable TIME is frequently measured in seconds—but in integer quantities. Overriding the default assumption is easily accomplished by using type statements. For instance, if we write

```
      REAL LENGTH, I, J, K, SPEED(50, 100)
      INTEGER HØURS, TIME(500), NØ
or    DIMENSIØN TIME(500), SPEED(50, 100)
      REAL LENGTH, I, J, K, SPEED
      INTEGER HØURS, TIME, NØ
```

the compiler will now assume HOURS and TIME are in integer mode and LENGTH, I, J, and K are real mode. The variables NO and SPEED could have been omitted from the respective INTEGER and REAL statements because the compiler would otherwise use the first letter to identify their types.

The INTEGER and REAL statements are frequently used to correct errors in variable naming. For example, if the name NAVY were accidently used to store real values it would be much easier to list NAVY in a REAL statement than to try to change every statement containing this variable.

For the following type statements, identify the mode of each of the variables listed below as either real, integer, or double precision.

```
DOUBLE PRECISION A, B
REAL IT, IS, LATE, AT, NIGHT(500)
INTEGER TRY, THIS(50), CANDY
```

(a) TRY _____   (f) IS _____

(b) A _____   (g) B _____

(c) CANDY _____   (h) NIGHT _____

(d) IT _____   (i) OWL _____

(e) THIS _____   (j) LIGHT _____

- - - - - - - - - - - - - - - - - -

(a) integer; (b) double precision; (c) integer; (d) real; (e) integer; (f) real; (g) double precision; (h) real; (i) real; (j) integer

31. Write type statements declaring the type of these variables.

(a) TIME, BASEHR, ROOT (a list of 200 elements), and LIMIT—to be integer type

(b) MASS, SPEED, MOMNTM, and BOOR—to be real type

(c) ERRMIN and ABSERR—to be logical type

- - - - - - - - - - - - - - - - - -

(a)
```
INTEGER TIME, BASEHR, ROOT(200), LIMIT
```
or
```
DIMENSION ROOT(200)
INTEGER TIME, BASEHR, ROOT, LIMIT
```

In both of these, the listing of the variable LIMIT (with its preceding comma) is optional, since the compiler will already assume it is integer type.

(b)
```
REAL MASS, SPEED, MOMNTM, BOOR
```

(c)
```
LOGICAL ERRMIN, ABSERR
```

32. A numerical variable can assume many numerical values (but only one at a time!). In contrast, a logical variable can assume either of two values—true or false. Logical variables are used in problems where the expected answer is in the form yes/no or true/false.

All logical variables must be declared in a type statement. FORTRAN has two logical constants which are formally written:

.TRUE.	The periods are required so the compiler can recognize
	that these are logical constants and not variable names
.FALSE.	TRUE and FALSE.

By using the type statement

```
      DIMENSIØN A(100), X(2,3)
      LØGICAL YES, A, X
```

or, if more convenient,

```
      LØGICAL YES, A(100), X(2,3)
```

the logical variables YES, A(1), A(2), . . . A(100), X(1,1), . . . X(2,3) can have either of two values—true or false. These values can be stored in the variables by use of assignment statements, such as

```
      A(1) = .TRUE.
      YES = .FALSE.
```

where A(1) is given the value true and YES the value false.

(a) Write a statement to define as logical variables: USE, A, TYPE, STATE(100), and MENT(3, 10, 2).

(b) What is the value of the logical variable SOUR in this program segment?

```
      LØGICAL SØUR
      SØUR = .TRUE.
```

- - - - - - - - - - - - - - - - - - -

(a)
```
      LØGICAL USE, A, TYPE, STATE(100), MENT(3,10,2)
```
or
```
      DIMENSIØN STATE(100), MENT(3,10,2)
      LØGICAL USE, A, TYPE, STATE, MENT
```

(b) true

Logical Assignment Statements

33. We're going to introduce some work-saving techniques to use with logical expressions. Review frames 28–46 of Chapter Six first if you need to before we go on.

We formed a logical expression by combining the relational operators (.GT., .GE., .LT., .LE., .EQ., .NE.) and logical operators (.AND., .OR., .NOT.) with numerical constants and/or variables. The only time you may use two logical operators in sequence is when the second operator is .NOT..

Thus, assuming A, B, and C are logical variables, A .AND. .NOT. B is a valid logical expression; however, A .OR. (B .NOT. .OR. C) is not a valid logical expression.

If A, B, C, and D are logical variables, identify the errors in these logical expressions.

(a) A .NOT B _____

(b) C .NOT. .AND. D _____

(c) A .AND. OR. B _____

(d) .AND. D _____

- - - - - - - - - - - - - - - - - - - -

(a) Should be A .NOT. B (with a period after .NOT.).
(b) Two logical operators cannot appear in sequence unless the second operator is .NOT.. Thus, C .AND. .NOT. D would be correct.
(c) You cannot have .AND. .OR. B in sequence. (Only .NOT. is allowed as a second operator in a sequence.)
(d) .AND. must be preceded by and followed by a logical expression, a logical variable, or a logical constant.

34. A logical assignment statement looks and functions like the arithmetic assignment statement discussed in frame 22 of Chapter Two.

logical variable = logical expression, variable, or constant

a single variable   to be evaluated
name declared in   as true or false
a logical type
statement

The numbered statements on the next page are examples of logical assignment statements.

```
        LØGICAL DUMPY, SHØRT, FAT, YØUNG, ØLD,
      -    NØDATE, HAIRY
20      DUMPY = .FALSE.
40      YØUNG = MYAGE .LE. 30
60      ØLD = .NØT. YØUNG
80      IF (SHØRT .AND. FAT) DUMPY = .TRUE.
100     NØDATE = DUMPY .AND. ØLD
```

(a) What logical value is stored in the variable name HMMM by this program segment? _____

```
        LØGICAL HMMM
        :
        I = 13
        K = 24
        HMMM = (I .GT. K) .ØR. (I .GT. (K-10))
```

(b) Which of the following numbered statements are invalid logical assignment statements? _____

```
        INTEGER M
        LØGICAL A, B, C, D, E, F, G
        I = 15
        J = 25
        M = 13
        S = -17.3
        P = 52.6
10      A = P .GT. H
20      B = P + H
30      C = .ØR. A
40      D = .NØT. B
50      E = (C .AND. .NØT. B) .ØR. .FALSE.
60      M = .TRUE.
70      F = .TRUE. .AND. .FALSE.
80      G = B .ØR. .NØT. S
```

(a) You guessed it.   HMMM has the logical value false because

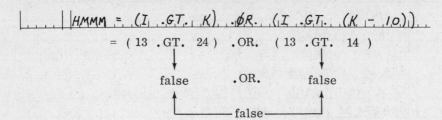

$$= (13 \ .GT. \ \ 24) \ .OR. \ \ (13 \ .GT. \ \ 14)$$

$$\text{false} \qquad .OR. \qquad \text{false}$$

$$\text{false}$$

(b) 20—invalid (+ is not a logical operator, therefore P + H is not a valid logical expression.)

30—invalid (? .OR. A—something is missing.)

60—invalid (M must be declared in a logical type statement.)

80—invalid (S is not a logical variable because it was not declared in a logical type statement.)

The statement numbered 70 is correct.   Don't let the wording fool you. The value of F will be false.

35 . Suppose we want to determine if two logical variables LVAR1 and LVAR2 are both true.   Unfortunately, we cannot write

```
      IF (LVAR1 .EQ. LVAR2) ANSWER = .TRUE.
```

since the relational operator .EQ. is only used to compare numerical values. What we do is create a logical statement which is true only if both of the variables LVAR1 and LVAR2 are true and then test this statement with a logical IF statement.   Such a statement (assuming TEMP is a logical variable) is

```
      TEMP = LVAR1 .AND. LVAR2
```

How does this statement work?   If LVAR1 and LVAR2 are both true, then the value true is assigned to TEMP.   However, if one of the variables is false, the value assigned to TEMP will be false.   Sometimes it is necessary to use the logical operator . NOT. to change a false value to a true value.

Assuming LAVR1, LAVAR, and TEMP are logical variables, write a logical assignment statement which assigns to TEMP the value true only if LAVR1 is true and LAVAR is false.

- - - - - - - - - - - - - - - -

```
      TEMP = LAVR1 .AND. .NOT. LAVAR
```

36. The logical assignment statement

```
      TEMP = (LVAR1 .AND. LVAR2) .OR. (.NOT.
    - LVAR1 .AND. .NOT. LVAR2)
```

assigns the value true to TEMP only if both LVAR1 and LVAR2 have the same logical value simultaneously (both are true or false at the same time). Let's see why.

If LVAR1 and LVAR2 are both true, then LVAR1 .AND. LVAR2 is also true. Thus TEMP has the value true because "true .OR. true" and "true .OR. false" both have the logical value true.

If LVAR1 and LVAR2 are both false, LVAR1 .AND. LVAR2 is false, but .NOT. LVAR1 and .NOT. LVAR2 are both true. Thus, .NOT. LVAR1 .AND. .NOT. LVAR2 is true. So, again TEMP is assigned the value true.

What if LVAR1 is true and LVAR2 is false? Then we would want to assign a value of false to TEMP. Go ahead and check it out yourself—the value assigned to TEMP will be false.

The logical assignment, then, uses the operator .AND. to join together logical variables which are to be true simultaneously; the .OR. operator to join logical expressions, one of which could be false while the other is true; and the use of the .NOT. operator to switch false values to true values and vice versa.

Write a logical assignment statement which assigns a value of true to a logical variable SWITCH only if a logical variable LVAR1 is true or if LVAR1 is false at the same time as a logical variable LVARA is false.

- - - - - - - - - - - - - - - - - -

```
        SWITCH = LVAR1 .OR. (.NOT. LVAR1 .AND.
       -        .NOT. LVARA)
```

37. Logical variables and expressions are used for purposes of making decisions based on the truth value of the variables. In a complex program branches are made depending on conditions of variables which may change throughout the program. As an example:

```
        LOGICAL L1, L2, L3, L4, L5
        :
        L1 = K .GT. 13 .AND. .NOT. B .GT. F**3
        L2 = E * B .GE. EC .AND. L4
        J = 1
        F2 = -13.
20      IF (.NOT. (L1 .OR. L2)) GO TO 200
        J = 2
        F2 = -F2 * F2 + F**3
40      IF (.NOT. (L1 .AND. L2)) GO TO 300
        J = 3
        L2 = .TRUE.
70      GO TO 400
        :
```

The example shows the use of logical variables in a rather fancy structure. If L1 and L2 are both false the program will branch to the statement numbered 200. If only one of L1 or L2 is false the program will branch to the statement numbered 300.

Complete the following program segment by writing logical IF statements so that if L1 is true and L2 is false the program will branch to the statement numbered 350, and if L1 is false and L2 is true the program will branch to the statement numbered 400.

```
      LOGICAL L1, L2
```

- - - - - - - - - - - - - - - - -

```
      LOGICAL L1, L2
       :
      IF (L1 .AND. .NOT. L2) GO TO 350
      IF (.NOT. L1 .AND. L2) GO TO 400
```

IMPLICIT Statement

38. All FORTRAN 77 compilers allow you to use an IMPLICIT statement. If your computer does not allow you to use an implicit type statement, GO TO frame 39. You're still here? Wonderful.

In frames 28–32 we discussed the form and usage of the type statement. We said every logical, character, and double precision variable must be declared in a type statement, whereas a type statement can be used to declare an integer or real variable whenever it is convenient or necessary to do so. Hence, these type statements are sometimes called explicit type statements.

In large programs where hundreds of variables are used, the explicit type statement is very inconvenient. The programmer must list each variable and must make certain that no variable remains unaccounted for, because an omitted variable could ca;use serious program errors.

FORTRAN provides us with a versatile type statement called the implicit statement. Only one such statement is allowed in a program and it must be the first statement in the program. This statement can be continued up to 19 lines. An example:

```
      IMPLICIT LOGICAL(L), INTEGER(A-C), REAL(Z),
     -CHARACTER*80 (F-H)
```

This statement causes every variable name starting with an L to be logical; with A, B, and C to be integer; and with Z to be real. Those variables starting with letters not mentioned in the IMPLICIT statement will take on their normal modes unless otherwise specified in an explicit type statement.

An implicit statement can be changed by an explicit statement, as shown below.

```
     |IMPLICIT REAL(A-Ø, X-Z)
     |DØUBLE PRECISIØN ABE, INN, ZEBRA
```

The DOUBLE PRECISION statement declares that ABE, INN, and ZEBRA are to be double precision variables and not real variables as specified in the IMPLICIT statement.

(a) Write an IMPLICIT statement such that all variables starting with the letters J through P and S through W are logical variables and all variables starting with the letters A through F are integer variables.

(b) Write an IMPLICIT statement which declares all variables which start with the letters A through I are integer, those with V to Z are character variables of length 20, but the variables BOY and CIGAR are real and FUN is logical (that is, you may need some explicit type statements).

- - - - - - - - - - - - - - - - - - - -

(a)
```
     |IMPLICIT LØGICAL(J-P, S-W), INTEGER(A-F)
```
(b)
```
     |IMPLICIT INTEGER(A-I), CHARACTER(V-Z)
     |LØGICAL FUN
     |REAL BØY, CIGAR
```

DATA Statement

39. Tired of writing a lot of statements initializing variables at the beginning of your programs? Well, cheer up, there is hope for you. The data statement comes to the rescue. Here's how.

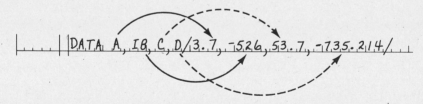

```
     |DATA A, IB, C, D/3.7, -526, 53.7, -735.214/
```

This automatically takes the place of the following statements.

```
     |A = 3.7
     |IB = -526
     |C = 53.7
     |D = -735.214
```

The / separates the variable names from the data values.

Write a DATA statement to perform the variable initializations performed by these statements.

```
      AI = -17.3
      IB = 34
```

- - - - - - - - - - - - - - - - - -

```
      DATA AI, IB/-17.3, 34/
```

40. If P and SING are logical variables and F is a list of four elements, these statements

```
      DATA A, P / - 3.7, .FALSE. /, F (3), SING /
     -  6.2, .TRUE. /, F (1) / 15.2 /
```

Note commas

take the place of the following assignment (initialization) statements.

```
      A = -3.7
      P = .FALSE.
      F(3) = 6.2
      SING = .TRUE.
      F(1) = 15.2
```

Notice the placement of a comma after the / following the data values. The two data statements below do the same work.

```
      DATA A, P, F(3), SING, F(1) /, -3.7, .FALSE.,
     -  6.2, .TRUE., 15.2 /
      DATA A / -3.7 /, P / .FALSE. /, F(3) / 6.2 /,
     -  SING / .TRUE. /, F(1) / 15.2 /
```

You must be careful when using data statements that the data values are in the correct mode for the variables they are initializing. We highly recommend that you use data statements to initialize variables because they will decrease program execution time. Furthermore, the data statement gives you extra documentation and makes it easier for you to locate and change the values used for initialization of program variables.

Write a DATA statement to eliminate the assignment statements on the next page.

```
      DIMENSION B(3)
      LOGICAL PING, PONG
      REAL LOCUST
      INTEGER STALAG
      STALAG = 17
      FLASH = -15.8
      B(3) = 5.7
      PONG = .TRUE.
      PING = .FALSE.
      B(1) = 2.3
      B(2) = -7.5
```

- - - - - - - - - - - - - - - - - -

```
      DATA STALAG /17/, FLASH, B(1), B(2), B(3) /
     -  -15.8, 2.3, -7.5, 5.7 /, PING, PONG /
     -  .FALSE., .TRUE. /
```

There are many other answers, of course, which are equivalent to this DATA statement. In this case, we grouped constants by mode. Some programmers prefer to use this style. It makes no difference and is sometimes useful for debugging purposes.

41. The data statement may also be used to initialize character variables and arrays easily. Here are two examples.

```
      DATA GRADE1, GRADE2 /'A','B'/
      DATA ARRAY1 /15*0./
```

In the first case, two character variables GRADE1 and GRADE2 have been initialized with 'A' and 'B' respectively. In the second DATA statement an array with at least 15 elements has had the first 15 elements initialized to 0.

But now a question. Write a DATA statement to initialize GOOGOL with the string 'BIG' and an array TABLE of 400 elements with the value 100.

- - - - - - - - - - - - - - - - - -

```
DATA GØØGØL / 'BIG' /, TABLE /400*0. /
DATA GØØGØL, TABLE / 'BIG', 400*0. /
```

or some other combination equivalent to these.

Equivalence Statement

42. If "to err is human," then programmers are very human. Say you used
the names GROSPY and GRSPAY in different places of the same program to
mean the same variable. To tell the compiler "I made a little mistake,"
simply include the statement

```
        EQUIVALENCE (GRØSPY, GRSPAY)
```

before any executable statements in your program. The group of two or more
variables being equivalenced must be enclosed within a set of parentheses,
each variable separated from the other by a comma. Additional groups of
variables may be equivalenced in the same statement by using a comma to
separate the groups. Equivalence statements can be continued.

The equivalence statement will not cause the compiler to change any
variable names for you. However, the compiler allocates the identical memory area for both GROSPY and GRSPAY, so referring to one variable also
refers to the other variable. Thus, the assignment statement GROSPY =
315.74 causes GRSPAY to have the value 315.74, since GROSPY occupies
the same memory location as GRSPAY.

Write a statement(s) equivalencing the variables I and KNOW, and equivalencing EASY, AS, and PI.

- - - - - - - - - - - - - - - - - -

```
        EQUIVALENCE (I, KNØW)
        EQUIVALENCE (EASY, AS, PI)
```

The above statements are "equivalent" to this statement.

```
        EQUIVALENCE (I, KNØW), (EASY, AS, PI)
```

43. The equivalence statement also can create an implied equivalence between arrays. This is done by noting which elements of two (or more) arrays
are in correspondence. The equivalence statement will allocate identical
memory areas for these elements. This feature may allow you to write programs which use more memory than your computer has. If you use two or
more arrays in your program, but never more than one at a time, you can
equivalence these arrays to conserve memory locations. However, character variables can only be equivalenced to character variables.

Since array elements are stored in adjoining memory locations, the rest of the arrays (whose storage areas overlap) will automatically be equivalenced. This is called an implied equivalence.

These statements imply the equivalences shown below. (Check our diagram.)

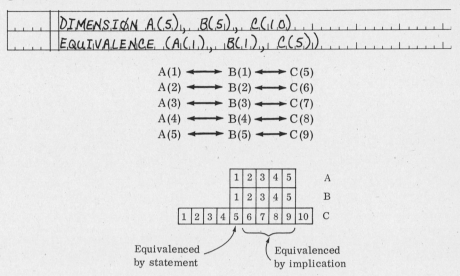

```
       DIMENSIØN A(5), B(5), C(10)
       EQUIVALENCE (A(1), B(1), C(5))
```

```
A(1) ←→ B(1) ←→ C(5)
A(2) ←→ B(2) ←→ C(6)
A(3) ←→ B(3) ←→ C(7)
A(4) ←→ B(4) ←→ C(8)
A(5) ←→ B(5) ←→ C(9)
```

1	2	3	4	5						A
1	2	3	4	5						B

| 1 | 2 | 3 | 4 | 5 | 6 | 7 | 8 | 9 | 10 | C |

Equivalenced by statement   Equivalenced by implication

These statements imply the equivalences shown below.

```
       DIMENSIØN A(10), B(2,4)
       EQUIVALENCE (A(3), B(1,1))
```

A	1	2	3	4	5	6	7	8	9	10
B			1,1	2,1	1,2	2,2	1,3	2,3	1,4	2,4

```
A(3)  ←→  B(1, 1)
A(4)  ←→  B(2, 1)
A(5)  ←→  B(1, 2)
A(6)  ←→  B(2, 2)
A(7)  ←→  B(1, 3)
A(8)  ←→  B(2, 3)
A(9)  ←→  B(1, 4)
A(10) ←→  B(2, 4)
```

You may have noticed that the elements of the array B conformed to the FORTRAN rule that the leftmost dimension changes most rapidly—which is the identical rule for storage of the array elements in the computer's memory.

Write an EQUIVALENCE statement(s) to indicate that SLOW and POKE "share" the same memory location. There is an implied equivalence between twenty-element array OUTPAY and ten-element array AMTPD where the elements OUTPAY(3) and AMTPD(1) are the same; and OUTPAY(2) is equivalent to OMONEY.

- - - - - - - - - - - - - - - - - -

```
      DIMENSION OUTPAY(20), AMTPD(10)
      EQUIVALENCE (SLOW, POKE), (OUTPAY(3),
     -   AMTPD(1)), (OMONEY, OUTPAY(2))
```

Self-Test

For the purposes of this Self-Test, assume you are working with a computer which has seven significant decimal places in single precision mode and sixteen significant decimal places in double precision mode, where the magnitude of real constants can vary from 10^{-75} through 10^{+75}.

1. Match as many entries from column B to column A as you can.

Column A

_____ (a) normalized E notation

_____ (b) scientific notation

_____ (c) normalized scientific notation

_____ (d) double precision constant

_____ (e) logical constant

Column B

(1) 312564178932.517D0
(2) TRUE
(3) 517E17
(4) -315.57×10^{14}
(5) $-.314 \times 10^{36}$
(6) .31524E-73

2. Normalize: 317.516E-12 _____

3. What are the values stored in ONEWRD, ABE, and BABE by this program segment? _____

```
      DOUBLE PRECISION ABE, BABE
      ABE = 315624.789345341,8 D0 -317.5289E-3
     -   +57.24963
      ONEWRD = ABE
      BABE = ONEWRD
```

4. Write a FORTRAN statement to allocate memory area for a double precision array CIBE of dimension 100, 100, 2.

5. Write a FORTRAN statement to declare FOX and E as character variables of length 8 and 12 respectively, and WOLF as an array of dimension 500 which can store 20 characters in each element.

6. Write a FORTRAN statement which will compare the characters in positions ten to twelve of INVNO with '999' and branch to the statement number 600 if the comparison is true.

7. By using the declaration

        CHARACTER COMM, DOT, D9*3, D2*2, FIELD*9

and the assignments

           D9 = '999'
           D2 = '99'
           COMM = ','
           DOT = '.'

what is stored in FIELD by the statement

    FIELD = D2//COMM//D9//DOT//D2

8. If the characters 'A', through 'Z' are represented internally as $65, 66, \ldots,$ what is the value of N if

    N = LEN('EBCDIC')*INDEX('BRAUER', 'R') + ICHAR('L')

9. What will the output look like from the program segment below

```
        CHARACTER N1*6, N2*7
        . . .
        . . .
        N1 = 'JOYOF'
        N2 = 'FORTRAN'
        WRITE(12, 210) N1(1:3), N1(4:5), N2
210     FORMAT (1X, A4, A2, A6)
        . . . .
```

10. What is wrong with the following FORTRAN statements?

(a)
```
        LOGCAL SWITCH(10)
```

(b)
```
      EQUIVALENCE AMOUNT(3), PAYROL OLDREC(3)
```

(c)
```
      REAL MONEY, INTEGER HOURS, OTRATE
```

(d)
```
      NEVER = MORE .OR. (NOT. QUO AND TETHE .NOT.
     -    .AND. RAVEN)
```

(e)
```
      LOGICAL A, SWITCH
      DATA A, SWITCH, / .TRUE. , 5.7 / B / 8.3 /
```

(f) If you skipped the material on the implicit statement, go to problem **11.**
```
      IMPLICIT (A-I) REAL, INTEGER (H, L-S),
     -    LOGICAL (T-Z), CHARACTER* 30 (JK)
```

11. What is the logical value stored in RESULT by the following program segment? _____

```
      LOGICAL RESULT, L, K
      REAL LENGTH
      DATA RADIUS, LENGTH, HEIGHT / 3., 10., 30. /
      AREA = 3. * RADIUS * RADIUS
      L = AREA .GT. 12.
      VOLUME = 2. * AREA + 2. * 3. * HEIGHT * LENGTH
      K = VOLUME .LE. 2000.
      RESULT = L .AND. .NOT. K
```

12. What does the following program segment do? _____

```
      LOGICAL KEY(20), ANSWER(20), TEMP
      INTEGER SCORE
C  READ DATA INTO ENTIRE ARRAY - KEY
      READ (5,102) KEY
C  READ DATA INTO ENTIRE ARRAY - ANSWER
200   READ (5,102) ANSWER
      SCORE = 0
C  COMPARE KEY AND ANSWER ELEMENT BY ELEMENT, FIRST
C  PART OF TEMP IS TRUE ONLY IF KEY AND ANSWER
C  ARE BOTH TRUE. SECOND PART IS TRUE ONLY IF
C  KEY AND ANSWER ARE BOTH FALSE.
      DO 300 I = 1, 20

      TEMP = (KEY(I) .AND. ANSWER(I)) .OR. .NOT.
     -    (KEY(I) .OR. ANSWER(I))
      IF (TEMP) SCORE = SCORE + 5
300   CONTINUE
C  WRITE SCORE
      WRITE (6,401) SCORE
401   FORMAT (1X, I4)
      GO TO 200
       :
```

13. Write a DATA statement to replace the following assignment statements.

```
      F(1) = -.732
      GELT = 3.24E14
      SWITCH = .FALSE.
      SENSE(1) = .TRUE.
      I3 = -18
```

14. A surveyor wishes to compute the area of various circles very accurately. Since the area of a circle is given by Area = πr^2, where r is the circle's radius, he wishes to use the value 3.1415926536 for π and will do his computations in double precision. The area will be truncated to single precision. Write a program which will read in a value of the radius (assumed to be a real value) from columns 1-7 of a card in F7.2 format, compute the area in double precision, truncate this value to single precision, and print the values of the radius and the area. Assume the radius is not greater than 1000. A negative value for the radius will cause the program to stop.

15. Write DIMENSION and EQUIVALENCE statements to set up the following equivalences.

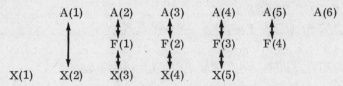

16. Write a **logical** assignment statement assigning the value true to a logical variable L if the value of a logical variable F1 is true and K (a variable) is greater than 5, or if a logical variable F2 is true and F1 is false.

Answers to Self-Test

1.   (a) 6 (frame 4); (b) 5 and 4 (frame 1); (c) 5 (frames 1, 4); (d) 1 (frame 9); (e) nothing (Number (2) is incorrect since TRUE is not a logical constant. However, .TRUE. is a logical constant.) **(frames 5, 6, 9, 32)**

2. $317.516E-12 \longrightarrow 317.516 \times 10^{-12} \longrightarrow .317.516 \times 10^{-12+3} \longrightarrow .317516 \times 10^{-9}$
$\longrightarrow .317516E-9$ (frames 5, 6)

3.
$$
\begin{array}{r}
ABE = 315624.7893453418 \\
- \qquad .3175289 \\
+ \qquad 57.24963 \\
\hline
315681.7214464418 \longrightarrow .3156817214464418D+6
\end{array}
$$

Thus, ABE has the value .3156817214464418D+6, and ONEWRD has the value .3156817E+6 (a simple truncation to one computer word). BABE has the value .3156817000000000D+6, since this assignment simply adds (pads) the necessary places to create a double word with zeros. (frames 14, 15)

4.

	DØUBLE PRECISIØN CIBE(100, 100, 2)
or	DIMENSIØN CIBE(100, 100, 2)
	DØUBLE PRECISIØN CIBE

(frames 13, 29)

5.   CHARACTER*8 FOX, E*12, WOLF(500)*20
or some variation of this statement.   (frame 18)

6.   IF(INVNO(10:12) .EQ. '999') GO TO 600
Did you forget the apostrophe's around the 999? If you did, you are wrong since you cannot compare a character string to a number since they are different data types.   (frames 19-20)

7.   FIELD = '99,999.99' (frame 21)

8. N = LEN('EBCDIC')*INDEX('BRAUER','R') + ICHAR('L')
    N =   6   *   2   + 76 = 88
                                         (frames 22-24)

9. 'bJOYOFbFORTRA' . Did we fool you? You should have noticed
that even though N1(1:3) specifies three characters, the A4 format puts a
blank before the data. (frame 27)

10.

(a) | | | | | |LØGICAL SWITCH(10)| | | | | | | | | | | | | | | |

Notice the missing letter in LOGICAL. (frame 28)

(b) | | | | | |EQUIVALENCE (AMØUNT(3), PAYRØL, ØLDREC(3),)

Notice the parentheses we've added before the first and after the last variables, and the commas. (frame 42)

(c) Your answer depends on how you interpret the question. If you considered
the statement as a REAL statement, then INTEGER is not a valid FORTRAN
variable name (too long) and a comma is missing after the name INTEGER.
If you considered this statement a "run-on" statement, then your answer
should be, "There should be two statements." (frame 30)

| | | | | |REAL MØNEY| | | | | | | | | | | | | | | | | | | | | |
| | | | | |INTEGER HØURS, ØRATE| | | | | | | | | | | | | |

(d) | | | | | |NEVER = MØRE .ØR. (.NØT. QUØ .AND. TETHE
     | | | | - | | | |.AND. .NØT. RAVEN)| | | | | | | | | | | |

Notice on the first line that we have written .NOT. and .AND. with periods
preceding them. In the second line, two operators cannot appear in sequence
unless the second is .NOT.. (frame 33)

(e) The statement should have no comma after SWITCH and is missing a
comma after 5.7/. There is an assignment error: SWITCH is logical.

| | | | | |DATA A, SWITCH / .TRUE., 5.7 /, B / 8.3 /| | |

(frames 39-40)

(f) | | | | | |IMPLICIT REAL(A-I), INTEGER(L-S),| | | | | | |
     | | | | - | | |LØGICAL(T-Z), CHARACTER (JI-K)| | | | | |

REAL must precede the range in letters. We took out the H in the integer
specification since it would conflict with the real specification. You should
have resolved this conflict somehow only a single letter can appear, not two
letters in the character type.   (frame 38)

11. AREA = 3. * 3. * 3. = 27., thus L = AREA .GT. 12. is true. (frame 23)
VOLUME = 2. * 27. + 2. * 3. * 30. * 10. = 54. + 1800. = 1854., thus K =
VOLUME .LE. 2000. is true. (frame 34)
RESULT = L .AND. .NOT. K = true .AND. .NOT. true = true .AND. false
= false. (frame 35)

12. This is a segment of a program which scores a twenty-question true-false
test. You will see the rest of this program in Chapter Nine. This is what
the program does.

> The program reads in an answer key (KEY). The program then reads
> in a set of answers. After equating SCORE to zero, each answer is
> matched to a corresponding key entry. If the answer is correct, 5 is
> added to the score. After all of the questions have been checked, the
> value of SCORE is printed and the program branches to the statement
> which reads in the answers of the next test.

(frame 36)

13.

```
       DATA F(1), GELT / -.732, 3.24E14 /, SWITCH,
     -   SENSE(1) / .FALSE., .TRUE. /, I3 / -18 /
```

(frame 40)

14.

```
       DOUBLE PRECISION PI
       DATA PI / 3.141592653600 /
C  READ IN RADIUS
100    READ (5,101) RADIUS
101    FORMAT (F7.2)
C  CHECK TO DETERMINE IF RADIUS < 0
       IF (RADIUS) 400, 150, 150
C  COMPUTE AREA AND PRINT RADIUS AND AREA
150    AREA = PI * RADIUS * RADIUS
       WRITE (6,301) RADIUS, AREA
301    FORMAT (' RADIUS= ', F15.7, ' AREA=', F15.7)
       GO TO 100
400    STOP
       END
```

(frame 16)

15.

```
       DIMENSION A(6), F(4), X(5)
       EQUIVALENCE (A(2), F(1), X(3))
```

This last EQUIVALENCE statement can also be replaced by

```
       EQUIVALENCE (F(1), A(2)), (A(1), X(2))
```

(frame 43)

16.

```
       L = (F1 .AND. K .GT. 5) .OR. (F2 .AND.
     -     .NOT. F1)
```

(frame 36)

CHAPTER NINE
Advanced Input and Output

As a cow without an udder is not a "whole cow," esoteric variable types—double precision and logical—without corresponding means to input and output data stored in them are "incomplete" variables. In this chapter you will learn powerful techniques for input and output which should simplify program coding and produce a more efficient machine code.

In particular you will learn how to input and output data using:

- speedy array input and output;

- implied DO's for array data;

- E and D format codes for data written in E or D notation;

- a P ("place") format to shift the decimal point in printed output;

- an L (logical) format code for logical (true/false) data.

And for those of you who have access to FORTRAN 77, you will also learn how to use

- list-directed input and output to eliminate the requirements of format statements, and to simplify keyboard data on input;

- character format specification;

- expressions in output statements;

- an internal file to transform data;

- the PRINT statement.

Array Input and Output

1. Much programming activity hinges on I/O (input and output). The following frames discuss the use of subscripted variables for input and output. The concepts are the same for both, so whenever input or output is mentioned here, the concept applies equally to each operation.

You have learned that a READ statement usually has a list of variables to be read and a WRITE statement lists the variables to be printed (described in Chapter Four). In Chapter Seven you learned that a subscripted variable is similar to an unsubscripted variable if the former is identified by a subscript, such as NELI(10). The FORMAT statement (also discussed in Chapters Three and Five) describes the type, form, and arrangement of the information in the record.

We now introduce you to a marvelous new technique that will allow you to write just a simple READ statement to read in an entire array. FORTRAN provides that if you specify only the array name (without subscripts) in a READ or WRITE statement, the entire array will be read or written in the same order in which the elements are stored (described in Chapter Seven).

If you are paid by the number of FORTRAN lines you produce, by all means use the long method, but you may be executed along with the program! (Among other reasons, FORTRAN will cause many system subroutines, which we'll discuss in Chapter Ten, to be executed for each array variable specified in your I/O list.)

Rewrite each I/O statement below using the marvelous new method.

(a)
```
DIMENSION A(4), B(2)
READ (5, 100) A(1), A(2), A(3), A(4), B(1),
   B(2)
```

(b)
```
DIMENSION C(2,3), D(2)
WRITE (6, 101) C(1,1), C(2,1), C(1,2), C(2,2),
   C(1,3), C(2,3), D(1), D(2)
```

(c)
```
DIMENSION E(2,2,3)
READ (5, 201) E(1,1,1), E(2,1,1), E(1,2,1),
   E(2,2,1), E(1,1,2), E(2,1,2), E(1,2,2),
   E(2,2,2), E(1,1,3), E(2,1,3), E(1,2,3),
   E(2,2,3), F
```

- - - - - - - - - - - - - - - - - -

(a) READ (5, 100) A, B
(b) WRITE (6, 101) C, D
(c) READ (5, 201) E, F
Note: The array dimensions still must be specified in either a DIMENSION statement or type statement (REAL, INTEGER, or LOGICAL).

2.   When handling entire arrays for I/O, FORTRAN writes or reads the data values in the same sequence that the array elements are allocated and arranged in memory. For example, for a vector array, the elements are referenced starting with subscript 1 and proceeding to the largest subscript defined for the array in the DIMENSION statement. For arrays with two or more dimensions, the elements are referenced as follows.

The first subscript varies the most rapidly. That is, the first subscript varies through its entire range before the second subscript is incremented, and the second varies through its range before the third is incremented, and so on. The last subscript varies the least rapidly.

If the entire array is not required or a different sequence of elements is desired, reference to array name alone will give you the wrong results. We will handle that problem in frame 5.

In the array below enter the values read, and then show the output written by the following segment.

```
        DIMENSION JOSH(5, 3)
        READ (5, 100), JOSH
        WRITE (6, 200), JOSH
100     FORMAT (15I2)
200     FORMAT ('bARRAYbJOSH', /, ('b', 6I4)))
        STOP
        END
```

The data in the card:

										1	1	1	1	1	1	1	1	1	1	2	2	2	2	2	2	2	2	2	2	3	
1	2	3	4	5	6	7	8	9	0	1	2	3	4	5	6	7	8	9	0	1	2	3	4	5	6	7	8	9	0	Card columns
1	1	2	2	3	3	4	4	5	5	6	6	7	7	8	8	9	9	0	1	0	2	0	3	0	4	0	5	0	6	Card data

Array   Output lines

Columns (2nd subscript)

Rows (1st subscript)	1	2	3
1	11		
2	22		
3			
4			
5			

line 1
line 2
line 3
line 4
line 5
line 6

- - - - - - - - - - - - - - - - - -

	1	2	3
1	11	66	2
2	22	77	3
3	33	88	4
4	44	99	5
5	55	1	6

line 1 ARRAY JOSH
line 2   11 22 33 44 55 66
line 3   77 88 99   1   2   3
line 4   4   5   6
line 5
line 6

In case you've forgotten, the array elements are actually stored internally as a vector, as shown below.

Subscript	1,1	2,1	3,1	4,1	5,1	1,2	2,2	3,2	4,2	5,2	1,3	2,3	3,3	4,3	5,3
Element value	11	22	33	44	55	66	77	88	99	1	2	3	4	5	6

3.   When you specify an array name in an I/O list, the computer continues to read or write using the specifications contained within the FORMAT statement, repeating them if necessary (as described in Chapter Five).   Compare these two program segments.   Note that method 1 will cause all ten values of the array to be read from one <u>record</u> because the FORMAT specifies 10F3.2.

Method 1

```
        DIMENSIØN CUTE(10)
        READ (5, 301) CUTE
301     FØRMAT (10F3.2)
```

In method 2, the READ statement reads only one element of the array at a time, even though the FORMAT statement is the same as above.   Consequently, <u>ten separate records</u> must be read to satisfy the DO loop.

Method 2

```
        DIMENSIØN CUTE(10)
        DØ 20 J = 1, 10
        READ (5, 301) CUTE(J)
301     FØRMAT (10F3.2)
20      CØNTINUE
```

(a)   How many records will be written? _____

```
        DIMENSIØN LEMØN(19)
        WRITE (18, 500,11) LEMØN
500,11  FØRMAT (20I4)
```

(b)   How many records will be read? _____

```
        DIMENSIØN APPLE(19)
        READ (5, 400,11) APPLE
400,11  FØRMAT (3F8.4)
```

- - - - - - - - - - - - - - - - - -

(a) One record, since the FORMAT statement specifies that each record can contain up to twenty values (we needed only nineteen).
(b) Seven records (six records containing three values each and one value from the seventh record).
If you had problems with these, review the material in Chapter Five.

4.   The array PRICES has 100 elements.

(a)   Write a program segment to read in all the values of PRICES from the
card reader (unit 5).   Each card is punched in the format below.

```
|  1        6 | 7          12 | 13          18 |
|  x x x x . x | x x x x . x | x x x x . x |
```

(b)   How many records will the program segment read? _____

- - - - - - - - - - - - - - - - - - -

(a)
```
          READ (5, 1001) PRICES
 1001    FORMAT (3F6.1)
```

(b)   34 (33 records with 3 values each and 1 record for the 100th value).

Comparison of Array Input/Output Methods

Specifying each element

WRITE (3, 111) A(1), A(2),..., A(50)
Certain I/O subroutines will be
invoked for each variable in the
I/O list; consequently, they will
be invoked 50 times because 50
variables are listed.

WRITE (3,121) A(9), A(11), A(49)
The above demonstrates that
less than all of the array elements can be input or output.

WRITE (3,131) A(50), A(49), A(1)
Enumeration of the specific
array elements permits input
or output of the elements in
any order.

```
       DO 100 KOUNT = 1, 25
 100  WRITE (3, 141) A(KOUNT),
   -     A(KOUNT + 25)
 141  FORMAT (3F8. 2, 2X, 2F6. 1)
```
The DO loop execution and the
FORMAT statement control how
many records will be processed;
in this example, the WRITE statement will be executed 25 times,
(continued)

Specifying the array name

WRITE (3, 111) A
Because only one variable, an
array name, is contained in the
list, the I/O routines are invoked
once; this method is more efficient
to I/O the entire array as stored.

WRITE (3, 121) A
Specifying the array name causes
the entire array to be input or
output.

WRITE (3, 131) A
Specification of the array name
causes input or output of the array
elements in the sequence in which
they are contained in storage.

WRITE (3, 141) A
Only the FORMAT statement determines how many records will
be written; the FORMAT statement
141 provides for 5 variables in
each record, so that 10 records
(continued)

causing 25 records to be written. This example also illustrates that the DO determines the sequence of the elements to be processed.

will be written (50 divided by 5). In contrast, each element is processed in the sequence in which it is stored.

Implied DO Loop

5. The following program segment uses a DO loop to read values into specific elements of an array.

```
      | DØ 2000 K = 4, 16, 4
      | READ (5, 801) BØXES(K)
2000  | CØNTINUE
```

Using the concept above, write a program segment which will write elements 1, 7, 13, and 19 of the array JONES. It is unnecessary for you to write the FORMAT statement; just use statement number 4051.

- - - - - - - - - - - - - - - - - -

```
      | DØ 2001 JUMP = 1, 19, 6
      | WRITE (6, 4051) JØNES(JUMP)
2001  | CØNTINUE
```

6. The implied DO loop provides an alternate method of accomplishing I/O in comparison to the DO loop in frame 5. Look at this example.

```
      | WRITE (6, 4051) (JØNES(JUMP), JUMP = 1, 19, 6)
```

In effect, the DO statement is incorporated in the I/O list, but the word DO and the statement number defining the range of the DO loop are omitted. Instead, the set of parentheses containing the implied DO loop determines the range of the loop.

The questions below relate to our implied DO loop example. You may refer to Chapter Six if you've forgotten the finer points of the DO statement.

(a) The variable JUMP corresponds to the DO-variable in a DO statement. What will be its initial value? _____

(b) By what value will the DO-variable JUMP be incremented?

(c) How many values of JONES will be written? _____

- - - - - - - - - - - - - - - - - -

(a) 1; (b) 6; (c) 4 values will be read: JONES(1), JONES(7), JONES(13), and JONES(19)

7. The parentheses containing the implied DO loop define the range of the implied DO loop. More than one variable may be contained within the set of parentheses, and it is not necessary that each be the element of an array (that is, subscripted). For instance, this statement

```
1    7
     READ (5,94011) (ALPHA, BETA(I),  I = 27,3,-3)
```

will read a value into ALPHA, then BETA (27), followed by ALPHA again. The next value would be read into which element of BETA? _____

- - - - - - - - - - - - - - - - - - -

The 24th element. You're right—not many programming applications require placing a single (scalar) variable within the range of the implied DO.

8. Write a program segment which will write the even-numbered elements of the arrays BIG and LITTLE. Have the segment write only those in the first twenty elements of each array. Use one implied DO loop.

- - - - - - - - - - - - - - - - - - -

```
      WRITE (6,1101) (BIG(J), LITTLE(J), J = 2, 20, 2)
```

9. In the same manner as the DO statement, the parameters of the implied DO loop may be variables and/or constants, such as in these two examples.

```
      READ (5, 1101) (OUT(KK), KK = 4, LT, 2)
      WRITE (8, 9011) (OUT(J), J = J1, J2)
```

In the first example, the terminal parameter is the variable LT, whereas in the second example, both the initializing and terminal parameters are variables. Note that the incrementation variable (or constant) was omitted from the second statement; when it's omitted, the compiler assumes it has the value of 1—just like the DO statement.

You may read any of the parameters in the same statement containing the implied DO loop, provided that such is done before the loop is encountered.

```
      READ (5, 2011) M, N, (X(JK), JK = N, M)
```

Write a READ statement to read in certain elements of the array SHOES; use an implied DO loop, obtaining the values of the parameters from the elements read earlier in the same READ statement.

- - - - - - - - - - - - - - - - - - -

```
      READ (5, 2011), I, J, K, (SHOES(L), L = I, J, K)
```

Your answer is correct if you first read in the values of the three parameters using integer variables. The parentheses containing the implied DO must be separate from the three parameters read in.

10. If you don't have access to a FORTRAN 77 compiler, skip to frame 11. FORTRAN 77 provides that the DO-variable may be either a real or an integer variable. Since the subscript in an array element must be integer type, you must convert the value of a real DO-variable which you wish to use as a subscript. The FORTRAN library function IFIX (discussed in Appendix B) gives you the integer value of a real variable. It does this by truncating the decimal portion of the real value. No rounding takes place. To illustrate how IFIX functions,

```
 1      7
        I = 1. 8
```

the variable I will have the value 1; likewise, ARRAY(IFIX(1. 8)) references the element ARRAY(1). Similarly, in this example,

```
 1      7
        PHIL = ALAN(IFIX(7/2))
```

PHIL takes on the value of the array element ALAN(3).

Now, what elements will be written using the WRITE statement below?

```
 1      7
        WRITE(6, 2012) (CHILD(IFIX(A)), A=13. 6, 10. 3, -1. 2)
```

- - - - - - - - - - - - - - - - - - - -

The implied DO loop will take three trips, and these elements will be written: CHILD(13), CHILD(12), and CHILD(11), in that order.

11. You may also nest implied DO loops. These two examples obtain equivalent results.

Explicit DO

```
        DO 100, J2 = K2, L2
           DO 99, J1 = K1, L1, M1
              READ (6, 911), A(J1, J2)
99         CONTINUE
100     CONTINUE
```

```
     READ (6,911), ((A(J1, J2), J1 = K1, L1, M1),
    -   J2 = K2, L2).
```

When using the implied DO, remember to use sets of parentheses to separate each level of the nesting.

READ (6,911) ((A(J1, J2), J1 = K1, L1, M1), J2 = K2, L2)

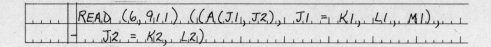

innermost loop
(varies most frequently)

outermost loop
(varies least frequently)

Write a program segment to write certain elements of the three-dimensional array CUBE. The first subscript is to have the values 1 through 4 in increments of 1; the second subscript varies from 2 through 6 in increments of 2; and the third subscript varies from 1 to 2. Vary the first subscript most frequently.

- - - - - - - - - - - - - - - - -

Be sure that you specified three levels of implied DO's, as in our answer.

```
     WRITE (8,141), (((CUBE(I1, I2, I3), I1 = 1, 4),
    -   I2 = 2, 6, 2), I3 = 1, 2)
```

12. Here's one example of using the implied DO which may suggest other uses in your program applications. In this instance, we would like to print a table which displays the values in the even-numbered columns in each row of the array ROSES, which is a 3 by 4 array. Here's how we did it. First the report.

```
                          Column
                          2      4
               Row 1     x. x   x. x
               Row 2     x. x   x. x
               Row 3     x. x   x. x
```

Then the program segment.

```
        WRITE (8,5241) (I, (ROSES(I,J), J = 2,4,2),
      -   I = 1,3)
5241  FORMAT (' ', 7X, 'COLUMN'/ '0', 7X, '2',
      -   4X, '4'/ ('0ROW', I2, F3.1, 1X, F3.1)
```

Write a program segment to write the value of the elements of the matrix array AUTOS which has 36 elements (6 by 6); the segment is to write 6 elements to a line, with each line numbered. Here's a sample line of output.

```
Line 1    xxx. xx   xxx. xx   xxx. xx   xxx. xx   xx. xx   xx.
```

- - - - - - - - - - - - - - - - - -

```
        WRITE (6,7811) (I, (AUTOS(I,J), J = 1,6),
      -   I = 1,6)
7811  FORMAT ('0LINE', I2, 4F8.2, F7.2, F5.0)
```

Summary of Implied DO Loop

Here's a general form of the implied DO.

$$\text{READ (or WRITE) (5,10091) } \underbrace{(X, \; G(N),}_{1} \; \underbrace{N = M, L, K)}_{2}$$
$$\underbrace{}_{3}$$

1. One or more variables, subscripted or unsubscripted, are contained within the READ or WRITE list, separated by a comma from the implied DO loop.

    If the DO-variable is of REAL type, you must use the FORTRAN library function IFIX to obtain the DO-variable's INTEGER value for use in indexing an array element.
2. The implied DO loop (or statement) is identical in form and function to the DO statement, except that it does not require the word DO and a statement number.
3. Each level of the implied DO must be within a set of parentheses so that the compiler can define the range of the implied DO.

E and D Format Specification for Output

13. In Chapter Eight you learned how the D and E notation differ from decimal notation. For you to input or output the value of a single or double precision variable using the E or D notation, you must use the corresponding E or D format specification. The E format specification has the following general form.

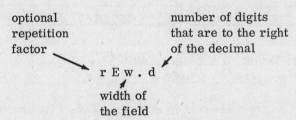

optional repetition factor

number of digits that are to the right of the decimal

r E w . d

width of the field

For example, the specification 3E10.4 can be interpreted as follows:

- The repetition factor means that 3E10.4 is the same as E10.4, E10.4, E10.4.
- The letter E tells the computer that this is E format and the value of a real variable is to be interpreted.
- 10 indicates the width of the field, including all signs, digits, decimal point, and letter E.
- 4 indicates how many digits are to be to the right of the decimal.

To illustrate:

Value expressed in E notation	E format specification
+0.231951E+03	E13.6 or 1E13.6
.231951E+03	E11.6
−.232E+03	E9.3

(a) In the first example, how wide is the field? _____

(b) In the second example, how many digits are to the right of the decimal?

_____

(c) For the third example, could we use E8.3 instead of E9.3? _____

- - - - - - - - - - - - - - - - - - -

(a) 13 (count the underlined characters: <u>+0.231951E+03</u>)

(b) 6 (.<u>231951</u>E03)

(c) No, because the field width is 9; 8 is not adequate. Count the characters including the minus sign: −.232E+03. However, for input you could specify as little as E6.3, which we'll cover in frame 16.

14. In an <u>output</u> format statement, your E specification should provide a field width that considers the following.

optional leading blank spaces;

optional sign if the value will always be positive (otherwise, you must provide one position for a sign);

optional zero;

decimal point;

at least one digit to the right of the decimal;

letter E;

sign of the exponent;

two-digit exponent (determined by your FORTRAN compiler).

For each value expressed in E notation below, write the applicable E format specification for output ($\emptyset$ indicates a blank).

Value as it is to appear in E notation		E format specification
$-0.456E-09$	(a)	_____
$\emptyset\emptyset0.37E+10$	(b)	_____
$\emptyset0.371E+10$	(c)	_____
$-0.371E+10$	(d)	_____
$.99999E-50$	(e)	_____

- - - - - - - - - - - - - - - - - - - -

(a) E10.3; (b) E10.2; (c) E10.3; (d) E10.3; (e) E10.5

15. As a rule of thumb, the field width should be equal to 6 plus the number of digits to appear to the right of the decimal. This provides enough width for a minus sign should the output value be negative; it also provides for a two-digit exponent. Let's examine what happens with various specifications.

Value stored in computer	E format specification	Output	Comment
$+.876 \times 10^{-23}$	E10.3	$\emptyset0.876E-23$	blank prints in sign position
$+.876 \times 10^{-23}$	E11.3	$\emptyset\emptyset0.876E-23$	additional leading blank
$+.876 \times 10^{-23}$	E9.3	$0.876E-23$	no leading blanks
$+.876 \times 10^{-23}$	E8.3	$.876E-23$	zero truncated
$+.876 \times 10^{-23}$	E7.3	********* (depends on your compiler)	insufficient field width
$-.876 \times 10^{-23}$	E9.3	$-.876E-23$	sign prints in leading zero position
$-.876 \times 10^{-23}$	E8.3	*********	insufficient field width

What will be the output for each of the following stored values using the indicated E format specifications?

Value stored in computer	E format specification		Output
$+.1234 \times 10^0$	E10.4	(a)	_____
$+.1234 \times 10^0$	E9.3	(b)	_____
$+.1234 \times 10^0$	E8.3	(c)	_____
$-.75643 \times 10^{-71}$	E15.3	(d)	_____

- - - - - - - - - - - - - - - - - - - -

(a) 0.1234E+00; (b) 0.123E+00; (c) .123E+00; (d) ƀƀƀƀƀ-0.756E-71

16. The E format statement will cause rounding on output in the same manner as the F format specification.

All of the discussion pertaining to the E format equally applies to the D format. The D format is used for double precision variables so that it is possible to output more than seven significant (and meaningful) digits. Your FORTRAN manual will specify the precision available for real and double precision variables.

For each of the stored values, write the appropriate output for the indicated format specification.

Value stored in computer	Format specification		Output
$-.31116785 \times 10^1$	D10.4	(a)	_____
$-.31116795 \times 10^1$	D12.4	(b)	_____
$-.31116795 \times 10^1$	F12.7	(c)	_____
$+.71149 \times 10^{10}$	E10.4	(d)	_____

- - - - - - - - - - - - - - - - - - - -

(a) -.3112D+01; (b) ƀ-0.3112D+01; (c) ƀƀ-3.1116795; (d) 0.7115E+10

E and D Format Specification for Input

17. When using the E format specification for <u>input</u>, the computer is not so rigid in its requirements with respect to field width. Here's what happens.

- All blanks are converted to zeros (we'll show you how this can cause you problems).
- The plus sign is optional. The minus sign is required.
- You need one or more digits.

- The decimal point is optional. The computer will insert a decimal point if you omitted it by acting in accordance to your E format specification (the computer will count "d" digits to the left of the exponent, if you included one in your input, and then insert the decimal point). If you include a decimal, it overrides the E format specification. Exponents are optional. They are preceded by either the letter E and/or a sign.

Examine each of the examples below and note how the above rules were applied.

E format specification	Input to computer	Stored in computer	Comment
E10.3	␢␢4␢.1E+10	$+.401 \times 10^{12}$	input treated as 40.1E+10
E10.3	␢␢␢4.215␢␢	$+.4215 \times 10^{1}$	no exponent
E10.3	␢␢␢4134E04	$+.4134 \times 10^{5}$	computer inserted decimal three digits to the left of exponent, treating input as 4.134E04
E10.3	␢␢4134E04␢	$+.4134 \times 10^{41}$	exponent is treated as E040 or E40
E10.3	␢4134E+04␢	$+.4134 \times 10^{41}$	
E10.3	␢4134+04␢␢	?	depends upon compiler, since the exponent is treated as E400 which may be beyond the acceptable range
E10.3	378.98␢␢␢␢	$+.37898 \times 10^{3}$	
E10.3	␢␢␢2␢9761␢	$+.209761 \times 10^{4}$	input treated as 2097.610

The rules for the D format specification are the same as those for the E, except that they apply to double precision variables.

Since all blanks are treated as zeros, it's best to right-justify all input data to avoid potential problems.

The following program segment reads some values from a punched card. Indicate in the space on the next page both the decimal and normalized value for each variable.

```
        DOUBLE PRECISION A, B(2), C
        READ (5,39101) A, B, C, X, Y, Z
39101   FORMAT (D8.3, 2D12.1, 2X, D10.5, 3E8.4)
```

Here's the card image.

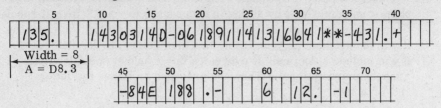

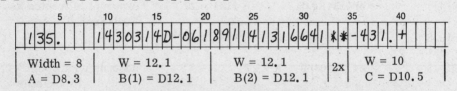

(Hint: Mark the fields on the card image above.) We did the first one for you.

Variable name	Decimal value	Normalized value
A	135. x 10^0	+.135 x 10^3

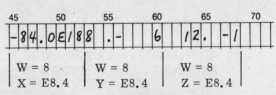

Variable name	Decimal value	Normalized value
B(1)	143031.4 x 10^{-61}	+.1430314 x 10^{-55}
B(2)	89114131664.1 x 10^0	+.891141316641 x 10^{11}
C	-431. x 10^0	-.431 x 10^3
X	-84. x 10^{18}	-.84 x 10^{20}
Y	80. x 10^{-6}	+.8 x 10^{-4}
Z	12. x 10^{-1}	+.12 x 10^1

18. Using the values stored in **frame 17** above, what will be printed by the following program segment?

```
        WRITE (8,39,1,1,1) A,, B,, C,, X,, Y,, Z
39,1,1,1 FORMAT (1X,, D.7..2,, 2D.12..5,, D.11..5,, 2F.6..2,, E.11..4,)
```

(Hint: Mark off the fields.)

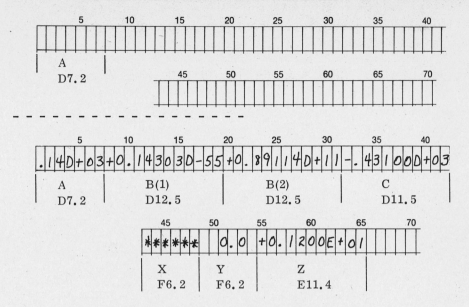

The Scale Factor (P Format Specification)

19. One of your programming applications may require you to shift the decimal point to the left or right during either operation of input or output. One possibility is for you to multiply or divide the value by some power of ten after reading it in or before printing it out. These three situations illustrate the concept.

1. A variable called PCNT has the stored decimal value of .075, but we would like to print 7.5% on our report.
2. A scientist was unhappy because his computer reported normalized numbers because of the D and E format specifications. He wanted two digits to appear to the left of the decimal, such as -91.137E+07 rather than -0.91137E+09.
3. Each morning a department store supplies its buyers with flash sales reports (that is, reports that show thousands of dollars), but sales are recorded in dollars and cents. The buyers want 34987.13 to appear as 35.0 on the report.

The P format specification (or <u>scale factor</u>) comes to our rescue. Its general form is <u>n</u>P where <u>n</u> is either a signed or unsigned integer. The scale factor is used as a <u>prefix</u> to either a D, E, or F format specification, and it remains in effect for the entire FORMAT statement until it is cancelled by another P specification or a OP specification. We'll show you some examples.

These two FORMAT statements operate identically.

```
10091  FØRMAT (3PF5.2, D10.4, E7.1)
10091  FØRMAT (3PF5.2, 3PD10.4, 3PE7.1)
```

0P causes cancellation of the scale factor, until another appears later in the same FORMAT statement.

```
10092  FORMAT (-2PE10.5, F4.1, 2D10.7, 0PD10.6,
     -        F4.1)
10092  FORMAT (-2PE10.5, -2PF4.1, -2P2D10.7,
     -        0PD10.6, F4.1)
```

The table below summarizes the operation of the scale factor during input and output.

Value of n in nP	Effect on input	Effect on output
positive	divides by 10^n	multiplies by 10^n
zero	cancels scale factor	cancels scale factor
negative	multiplies by 10^{-n}	divides by 10^{-n}

To illustrate:

Input data	Format	Internally stored	Output data
ҌҌҌҌҌ18	2PF8.2	$+.18 \times 10^{-2}$ (.0018)	ҌҌҌҌ.18
ҌҌҌҌҌ18	-2PF8.2	$+.18 \times 10^2$ (18.00)	ҌҌҌҌ.18
278.98ҌҌҌҌ	2PE10.2	$+.27898 \times 10^1$ (2.7898)	+27.90E-01
-Ҍ4134D04b	-1PD10.2	$-.4134 \times 10^{43}$	Ҍ-0.04D+44

Note that in all cases of input, the value actually stored is different from the original input data. For output, however, only the output data for the F format specification is actually a different value, whereas for the D and E format, only the presentation is different, but the displayed value is the same as that stored in the computer, rounded if required.

Fill in the missing items in the table below.

	Input data	Format specification		Normalized value stored in computer		Output data
(a)	_____	2PF10.0	(b)	_____		128000000.
(c)	_____	0PE10.4	(d)	_____		0.6041E-01
	ҌҌҌҌ-9431.	1PD10.4	(e)	_____	(f)	_____
	ҌҌҌ-.13294	(g) _____		$-.13294 \times 10^{-2}$		ҌҌҌҌҌ-.133
	ҌҌ141Ҍ-ҌҌ1	-1PE10.4	(h)	_____	(i)	_____

(a) +128000000 or 128000000.;   (b) +.128 x 10^7;   (c) $\cancel{bb}$6.041-2 is one possible answer;   (d) +.6041 x 10^{-1};   (e) -.9431 x 10^3;   (f) -9.431D+02;   (g) 2PF10.3;   (h) +.141 x 10^0;   (i) 0.0141E+01

Refer to your computer installation's FORTRAN manual for additional discussion.

20. Sometimes you are not quite sure how big the exponent in a floating point computation may become. This is possible in scientific computation. Generally, in commercial computations you should know how large numbers may become. The exponent may be greater (in absolute value) than 999. What do you do now? FORTRAN 77 comes to your rescue with a variation on the E format code. As an example, the format E12.3E4 tells the compiler to allow an exponent, in absolute value, of 9999 (10**4-1). Upon output 25.3E5367 will be printed as

$$0.253E+5369$$

By using the format code E13.3E5, the output will be printed as

$$0.253E+05369$$

In this case the E5 specification forced five digits to be printed. This variation of the E format code has no effect when used for input of data.

Write a suitable E format code sufficient to print the numbers

a)   57.3 X 10^{99}

b)   .024 X 10^{-3241}

- - - - - - - - - - - - - - - - - -

a) E11.3E3

b) E11.2E4

L Format Code

21. In Chapter Eight, **problem 12 of the Self-Test** discussed a program to grade a true/false answer quiz. We would have to input the correct answers to the test to an array (say, KEY) and the examination taker's answer to an array (say, ANSWER). How do we input logical values into the computer? We use an L format **code**   The data value of a logical variable is either T or F (representing true and false respectively). Look at this example.

```
      LOGICAL NU
      :
      READ (5, 100) NU
100   FORMAT (L4)
      :
```

These statements will input a logical value of true for the variable NU in each instance.

Card	Columns
1	TRUE
2	ƀTRU
3	ƀƀTR
4	ƀƀƀT
5	TALK

Notice the letter T, possibly preceded by blanks and followed either by blanks or other characters. Now if the first non-blank letter were F, the logical value of the variable NU would be false. The 4 in the L4 format code simply indicates the field width.

If the correct answers (T's or F's) to our twenty-question true/false test and the examination taker's answers are placed in twenty consecutive card columns starting with column 25, write a READ statement and FORMAT statement to input the logical data (assume columns 1-24 are to be skipped).

```
      LOGICAL KEY(20), ANSWER(20)



```

- - - - - - - - - - - - - - - - -

```
      READ (5, 100) KEY
      :
      READ (5, 100) ANSWER
100   FORMAT (24X, 20L1)
```

22. To output logical data is very simple. These statements cause the printing of the following output line.

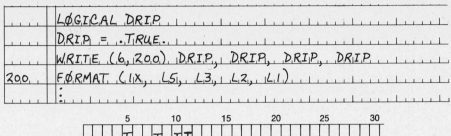

```
       LØGICAL DRIP
       DRIP = .TRUE.
       WRITE (6, 200) DRIP, DRIP, DRIP, DRIP
200    FØRMAT (1X, L5, L3, L2, L1)
       :
```

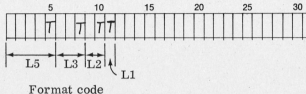

Format code

The letter T is right-adjusted in each output field. If the variable DRIP is assigned the logical value .FALSE., a letter F will replace each T shown above.

What output line does the following program print?

```
       LØGICAL TIRED, ØF, THIS
       TIRED = .TRUE.
       ØF = .FALSE.
       THIS = TIRED .AND. .NØT. ØF
       WRITE (6, 300) TIRED, ØF, THIS
300    FØRMAT (1X, L3, L4, L3)
```

23. Here is our program to grade a twenty-question true/false test. We assumed the following:

(1) The punched card with the correct answers contains the literal CORRECT ANSWERS punched somewhere in the first twenty columns and the correct answers consecutively punched starting in column 21.
(2) The test-taker's name is punched in the first twenty columns of a card.

(3) The answers (T's or F's) are punched consecutively in columns 21 through 40.

(4) Each correct answer is worth five points.

```
      INTEGER SCORE
      CHARACTER NAME*20
      LOGICAL ANSWER(20), KEY(20), TEMP
C READ CORRECT ANSWERS
      READ (5,1001) NAME, KEY
1001  FORMAT (A20, 20L1)
      WRITE (6,2002) NAME, KEY
2002  FORMAT ('1', A20, 20(1X, L1), 10X, 'SCORE')
C READ TEST ANSWERS
200   READ (5,1001) NAME, ANSWER
      IF(NAME(1:30).EQ.'END') GO TO 4000
C RESET SCORE TO ZERO
      SCORE = 0
C COMPARISON OF TEST ANSWERS WITH CORRECT ANSWERS
      DO 300 I = 1, 20
C IF TEST ANSWER CORRECT, FIVE IS ADDED TO SCORE
      TEMP = (KEY(I) .AND. ANSWER(I)) .OR. .NOT.
     -     (KEY(I) .OR. ANSWER(I))
      IF (TEMP) SCORE = SCORE + 5
300   CONTINUE
C WRITE NAME, ANSWER, AND SCORE
      WRITE (6,3001) NAME, ANSWER, SCORE
3001  FORMAT ('0', A20, 20(1X, L1), 11X, I4)
C BRANCH TO READ NEXT TEST-ANSWER CARD
      GO TO 200
4000  STOP
      END
```

This program can be easily modified to score any number of questions. Modify the program so that fifty questions can be graded (two points for each correct answer).

– – – – – – – – – – – – – – – – – –

```
1      5 6 7   10      15      20      25      30      35      40
      INTEGER SCORE
      CHARACTER NAME*20
      LOGICAL ANSWER(50), KEY(50), TEMP          ◄────┐
      READ (5,1001) NAME, KEY                          │
1001  FORMAT (A20, 50L1)                         ◄────┤
      WRITE (6,2002) NAME, KEY                         │
2002  FORMAT ('1', A20, 50(1X, L1),              ◄────┤
     -     10X, 'SCORE')                               │
      IF (NAME(1:3).EQ.'END') GO TO 4000               │
200   READ (5,1001) NAME, ANSWER                       │
      SCORE = 0                                  ◄────┤
      DO 300 K = 1, 50                           ◄────┤
      IF (TEMP)                                        │
     -        SCORE = SCORE + 2                         │
300   CONTINUE                                         │
      WRITE (6,3001) NAME, ANSWER, SCORE         ◄────┘
3001  FORMAT ('0', A20, 50(1X, L1), 1X, I4)
      GO TO 200
4000  STOP
      END
```

Statements which were changed

24. Here is another application of logical expressions and the input of logical
variables. Suppose you are the data processing expert at "There's Someone
for Everyone" Marriage Arrangement Bureau. You have information on
punched cards as follows.

Card column	Information
1-20	name
21	income (T if over $20,000; otherwise F)
22	age (F if over 35; otherwise T)
23	hair color (T if brown; otherwise F)

You have to write a program to find those people who are either over 35 years
old and have an income over $20,000/yr, or who are under 35 years old and
do not have brown hair. Such a program will contain the logical assignment
statement: MATCH = (.NOT. AGE .AND. INCOME) .OR. (AGE .AND. NOT.
HAIR), which will have the logical value true if and only if the above conditions are satisfied. Now there is only one thing missing—the program. So
just don't sit there, write it. Make sure you provide for printing the names
of the individuals which satisfy the conditions we specified. Use ZZZZ for a
name to indicate the last card. Be sure to fill in T's and F's for this card.

- - - - - - - - - - - - - - - - - - - -

How did you do it? Here's our program.

```
C  PROGRAM: MATCH
      CHARACTER NAME*20
      LOGICAL INCOME, AGE, HAIR
10    READ (5,100) NAME, INCOME, AGE, HAIR
100   FORMAT (A20, 3L1)
C  TEST FOR LAST CARD
105   IF NAME(1:4).EQ.'ZZZZ') GO TO 300
C  TEST FOR MATCH AND WRITE NAME IF SUCCESS
      IF ((.NOT. AGE .AND. INCOME) .OR. (AGE
     -     .AND. .NOT. HAIR)) WRITE (6,101) NAME
101   FORMAT ('0', A20)
      READ(5,100) NAME, INCOME, AGE, HAIR
      GO TO 105
C  END OF JOB
300   STOP
      END
```

Frames 25 through 35 apply only to FORTRAN 77. If you wish, you may skip to the Self-Test on page 387.

List-Directed Input

25. On occasion you will have a FORTRAN application that requires you to input data from a terminal keyboard (or punched card); in this instance you won't want to be bothered by having to enter your data in the rigorous format specified by a FORMAT statement. For example, if a field is specified as F10.3, ordinarily you would enter a total of 10 character positions—a lot of work, especially if your input consisted of less than 10 characters on the average for that field.

Instead, you would want to enter each input value, and then separate it from the next by, say, a comma or a space (or both), to improve readability and possibly save keystrokes. FORTRAN 77 comes to your rescue. Look closely at the following statement.

```
1     7
      READ (5,*) ALAN, JANET, AMY, DONNA, WENDY
```

Note how the asterisk replaces the FORMAT statement number. The asterisk instructs the compiler to compile your program so that it does not use a FORMAT statement. In its place, your program will accept each data value according to the type and sequence of the variables appearing in the READ statement's input list. Furthermore, your program will look for either a space or comma (both are acceptable) between data values. Consequently, embedded spaced within numeric values are prohibited and will not be converted to zeros.

Using the illustrative READ statement above, we could enter the following on our terminal keyboard (with spaces and commas as shown),

39.9, 36, 11, 7, 1

and our variables would be assigned the following values.

variable	value
ALAN	39.9
JANET	36 (If JANET were REAL type, the value would be 36.)
AMY	11.
DONNA	7.
WENDY	5.

What values would be assigned to the variables in the READ statement above is we keyed in these values?

2   7   11,   36,   39

- - - - - - - - - - - - - - - - - -

variable	value	
ALAN	2.	Remember: one or more spaces can be
JANET	7	interpreted as a separator as well as a
AMY	11.	comma between data values. There can
DONNA	36.	also be one or more spaces before and/or
WENDY	39.	after each comma.

26. The input unit specifier is optional when using a list-directed input statement. If you omit it, though, the input will take place on a unit that is predefined according to your computer installation. (You'll have to check what device is the default, such as a terminal keyboard or a card reader.) In the example below, note how the asterisk now becomes part of the input list since it need not be enclosed within parentheses.

READ*, ALAN, JANET, AMY, DONNA, WENDY

Let's assume the terminal keyboard is the default input device. Write a list-directed input statement to obtain entries from the keyboard to assign the following values to the variables listed below.

variable	value
PHIL	40.
RITA	39.
MIKE	12
ANDREW	10.
MATT	7

- - - - - - - - - - - - - - - - - -

READ*, PHIL, RITA, MIKE, ANDREW, MATT

27. If your input consists of a character constant rather than numeric as in our previous two frames, enclose the character constant within single quotes like this: 'THIS IS AN EXAMPLE OF A CHARACTER CONSTANT'. With character constants, you can have embedded blanks. What would the CHAR-ACTER variable JOSH have as its value if we typed '44' in response to the statement below?

READ*, JOSH

- - - - - - - - - - - - - - - - - -

44 Note that the apostrophes are not part of the string; they merely show the beginning and end of the string at the time of input. Furthermore, 44 is a character string and not a numeric value.

28. At the time of data entry, a <u>null value</u> is defined as having no characters between successive value separators, no characters preceding the first value separator in the first record read by a list-directed input statement, or by using R* (which we describe in frame 31). A null value has no effect on the input item, that is, the item retains the value it had before the list-directed READ was executed. The variables below have the following values.

variables	values	variable type
ALPHA	31.6	REAL
BETA	20.1	REAL
CHARS	'FRESH'	CHARACTER*5
DELTA	.0005	REAL

READ (5,*) ALPHA, BETA, CHARS, DELTA

Using the list-directed input statement above, what value will each variable have after execution of the READ statement if we key in the following values?

21.34, , 'DITTO' , .8734

- - - - - - - - - - - - - - - - - -

variables	values	
ALPHA	21.34	Note how BETA retains its value of 20.1.
BETA	20.1.	
CHARS	'DITTO'	
DELTA	.8734	

29. As you can see, the null value is useful for retaining a variable's value. It saves you keystrokes because you don't have to reenter a variable's value even though the variable is in the input list.

What values would you key in to achieve the following results? (Hint: be lazy and save keystrokes.)

	values of variables	
variables	before READ	after READ
A	1.267453	56.789021
B	2.9	61.38
PI	3.14159	3.14159
STRING	'THIS IS NUTS'	'THIS IS NUTS'

- - - - - - - - - - - - - - - - - -

One answer is: 56.789021, 61.38,,,   Note how the last two commas cause null values to be entered for the last two variables.

30. The slash represented as / is another useful separator. When you use the slash as a value separator in a list-directed input sequence, the presence of the slash terminates execution of the input statement, while the remaining values (to be read) are treated as null values.

Refer to the previous frame. How would you answer the question now? (Hint: use a slash and save at least two keystrokes.)

- - - - - - - - - - - - - - - - - - -

56.789021,61.38/   In this instance we left no space between the values, just a comma, to save keystrokes.

31. Sometimes you will want to consecutively repeat a constant (or null value) when entering data for a list-directed input statement. FORTRAN 77 makes it possible for you to use a <u>repetition factor,</u> followed by an asterisk, immediately followed by the value you want replicated (including a blank or comma if the value is to be null). Look at this example.

7*3 is the same as entering 3, 3, 3, 3, 3, 3, 3

The same rule applies to character constants.

10*'TIMES' is the same as

'TIME' 'TIME' 'TIME' 'TIME' 'TIME' 'TIME' 4*'TIME'.

You can repeat a null value by placing either a comma or space immediately following the repetition factor and asterisk. Suppose we want to READ in new values only for the fifth, ninth and tenth values for a list-directed READ which has 12 variables in the input list. Here is how our input data might look.

4*,   28.6,   3*,   2*'NINTH AND TENTH VALUES ARE THE SAME'/

first four   fifth   sixth to   ninth and tenth values   terminates
values   value   eighth values   input

What would you keyboard (or punch into a card) to assign 'HELP' to the
first variable, 28.981 to the sixth variable, 28.981 to the seventh variable,
and 'END' to the tenth variable, with all other variables retaining their values?
Assume there are 25 variables in the input list.

- - - - - - - - - - - - - - - - - - -

'HELP',4*,2*28.981,2*,'END'/   or 'HELP' 4* 2*28.981 2* 'END'/

Summary of List-Directed Input

This is the general form when specifying the input unit.

> READ (dsrn, *) input list

The asterisk indicates list-directed input, rather than the use of a FORMAT
statement. Use the general form below when using the default input unit.

> READ *, input list

A separator must appear between adjacent input values. There are two
separators.

- one or more space between adjacent values: value1 value2 value3

- one comma, with one or more optional spaces before and/or after the
  comma, between adjacent values: value1, value2, value3

Both type may be used intermixed: value1 value2, value3

A variable in the input list will retain its value if a null value is encountered during input. There are two methods of null input.

- use a comma separator (as defined above) in place of the value:

  > , value2,,value4 value5

- terminate the input data with a slash; each variable in the input list
  for which no value was entered will retain its original value:

  > value1 value2 , , value4 /

The fifth and remaining variables, if any, in the input list would retain
their values.

A repetition factor may be used to input two or more consecutive values
that are the same, including null values. The general form appears below.

> R*value
> 1   2

1. The repetition factor is an unsigned integer constant, immediately
   followed by an asterisk.
2. The value to be repeated immediately follows the asterisk. This
   value may be either a numeric or character constant, or a null
   value (by using a space or comma in place of the value).

List-Directed Output

32. List-directed output is quite similar to list-directed input.

WRITE (6, *) THIS, IS, A, SAMPLE

is an example of a list-directed output statement. On output, each output constant will be formatted by the computer processor according to the type of variable to which it relates in the output list. Furthermore, each output record begins with a blank character to provide carriage control when the output is printed.

Depending upon your compiler, output values will be either separated by commas or spaces, but probably not both. If required, the processor will generate a new record when a numeric constant will not completely fit on one line; rather than split the constant, it will place it entirely on the next line.

As to character constants, unlike list-directed input, character constants at output time do not have apostrophes enclosing the value; however, an apostrophe may be defined as part of the internal character string itself, as in

WENDY'S BALL

Furthermore, on output the processor will insert a blank character for carriage control at the beginning of a record, including when a character constant carries over from one line to another (because it is too long to fit on one line).

Depending upon your compiler, the processor may print a repetition factor when two or more successive values are identical...or it may print the value for each variable separately. Check your installation FORTRAN manual for the specifics.

Finally, slashes and null values are not produced by list-directed output. Unlike saving you keystrokes on input, the computer has to earn its keep, and so it must print everything on output, including the initial blank in each record for carriage control. When using list-directed output,

(a) will a blank appear embedded within a numeric constant?

(b) if a numeric constant won't fit completely on one line, because many other constants appear on the same line, what will the processor do with it?

(c) when do apostrophes appear in the output of character constants?

(d) what will the processor do if a character constant does not completely fit on one line?

- - - - - - - - - - - - - - - - - - - -

(a) No, numeric constants never have embedded blanks; (b) the processor will not print a partial numeric constant on one line, but will print the entire numeric constant on the next line; (c) apostrophes only appear during output of a character constant when the apostrophes are actually part of the constant itself; (d) the processor will continue the character constant on the next line, inserting a blank as the first character for the purpose of carriage control during printing.

Character Format Specification

33. FORTRAN 77 eliminates the requirement for a FORMAT statement separate and apart from its related input/output statement. It's now possible to include the format specification within the input/output statement.

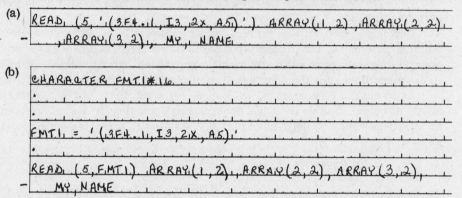

(a)
```
READ (5,'(3F4.1,I3,2X,A5)') ARRAY(1,2),ARRAY(2,2),
     ,ARRAY(3,2), MY, NAME
```

(b)
```
CHARACTER FMT1*16

FMT1 = '(3F4.1,I3,2X,A5)'

READ (5,FMT1) ARRAY(1,2),ARRAY(2,2), ARRAY(3,2),
     MY, NAME
```

Both examples have one thing in common: character format specification. Example (a) uses a character constant as the format specifier; this is acceptable for all FORTRAN 77 compilers. On the other hand, example (b) illustrates the use of a character variable which contains the character format specification; this may be either a scalar, array name, or an array element. Check your installation's FORTRAN 77 manual for this option's acceptability. (See chapter eleven's discussion of Object time FORMAT statements.)

Look carefully and you will note that both examples will achieve the same end result. Rewrite the statements below so that the WRITE statement contains a character string format specifier instead of the FORMAT statement number.

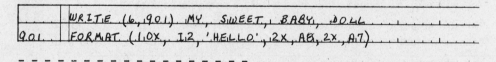

```
     WRITE (6,901) MY, SWEET, BABY, DOLL
901  FORMAT (10X, I2, 'HELLO', 2X, A8, 2X, A7)
```

- - - - - - - - - - - - - - - - - - - -

WRITE (6,'(10X,I2,"HELLO",2X,A8,2X,A7)') MY, SWEET, BABY, DOLL

Don't forget the parentheses; also, the double apostrophes are required because that's the only way you'll get the internal apostrophes to be part of the character constant.

Expressions in an Output List

34. FORTRAN 77 permits the use of expressions in the output list, including function references (which we won't cover in this Chapter). Look at this example.

```
1     7
          WRITE (6,902) A/B,C
902       FORMAT(F.4,2X,F5.1)
```

During execution, the result of the division of A divided by B will be output, followed by the output of D. This means that it is not necessary to establish variables for the sole purpose of printing out an intermediate value which is not used for any other purpose within the program.

Rewrite the statement sequence below so that a minimum number of variables are required in the program.

```
1   7
         TIRES = 4
         SPARE = 1
         FLAT = 1
         USABLE = TIRES + SPARE - FLAT
         WRITE (8,905) USABLE
```

- - - - - - - - - - - - - - - - - - -

You guessed it! WRITE (8,905) TIRES + SPARE - FLAT

INTERNAL FILES

35. On occassion, the programmer needs to transform data from one form to another, much like the practice of an alchemist. In the past, the programmer could write the data out to disk and then read it back, using a different format to achieve a change in the data's form. FORTRAN 77 recognized this need and gave us internal files for this purpose.

An internal file takes the form of a character variable (array, array element, scalar, or substring). The data transformation can be accomplished as follows:

(a) WRITE the initial data form to the internal file, and then

(b) READ the data in its new form from the internal file.

Here is the general form of the input/output statement using an internal file.

```
READ
  or        (fname,  format)      list
WRITE
   1        2    3     4   5        6
```

where
1. The word WRITE assigns the initial data form to the internal file specified by fname (although you could also use an assignment statement). The word READ is used to obtain the data in its desired form from the internal file.
2. Left parenthesis.
3. The name of the internal file, followed by a comma. The internal file must be of CHARACTER type, although it may be a scalar variable, an array, an array element, or a substring.
4. The format specifier applicable to the WRITE or READ statement.
5. The right parenthesis.
6. The applicable output or input list.

The following program segment shows some of the inherent beauty of the internal file.

```
        CHARACTER CODE*1, DATA*20
        .
        .
        READ (7,'(A1,A20)'), CODE, DATA
        IF (CODE .EQ. '$') THEN
            READ (DATA,'(F8.2)') SALARY
        ELSE IF (CODE .EQ. 'Y') THEN
            READ (DATA,908) YEAR
        ELSE
            READ (DATA,'(20)') NAME
        END IF
        .
        .
908     FORMAT (I4)
```

Assuming the following input records, what values would the variables be assigned using the above program segment?

	record layout 1 2	variables	values
Record 1	$ 23140.00	NAME	
Record 2	N HOFFBERG, AMY	YEAR	
Record 3	Y 1984	SALARY	

- - - - - - - - - - - - - - - - - -

variables	values
NAME	HOFFBERG, AMY
YEAR	1984
SALARY	23140.00

Print Statement

36. The PRINT statement is used in the identical way as you would a WRITE statement. Its basic purpose is to assign different default units to the PRINT and WRITE statements. For example, a WRITE statement might direct its output to a CRT screen, whereas the PRINT statement would direct its output to a line printer. The actual device assignment will depend upon your computer installation. Check your installation manual.

What differentiates the PRINT from the WRITE statement?

- - - - - - - - - - - - - - - - - - - -

Although they operate identically, they may have different default device assignments. This makes it possible for you to have output on either of two devices without specifying the unit numbers within your program.

Self-Test

1. The following statements use the implied DO loop. Some are written incorrectly. Your mission is to find and correct (debug) the errors. Rewrite the ones which are incorrect.

(a) READ (5,100) STG(I), I = 1, 20

(b) WRITE (6,100) (TRICKY (A) A = 2, 7, 4)   (Hint: A is a REAL variable)

(c) READ (5,300) (FRAME7(M,N), M, N = 2, 10, 3)

(d) WRITE (6,40) (COMMA(I,J,K) I = 1, 7) J = 1, 10) K = 20, 3, -1)

(e) WRITE (6,500) (CORECT(I,10), I = 1, 500)

(f) WRITE (5,600) (LEMON, CAR(LEMON,J), LEMON = 1, 17)

2. Write the shortest possible READ and FORMAT statements to read values into the two-dimensional array NOEASY(5,10) (i.e., 5 x 10 = 50 elements). The punched card has 50 one-digit consecutive values.

3. On the next page are values punched on four cards and a short program.

(a) What numbers would be stored and in which elements of the array when the READ statement is executed? _____

(b) What output would be produced by the WRITE statement? _____

	5		10		15	
1 1	2 2	3 3	4 4	5 5		Card 1
6 6	7 7	8 8	9 9	1 0		Card 2
1 0	1 1	1 2	1 2	1 3		Card 3
1 3	1 4	1 5	1 6	1 7		Card 4

```
      DIMENSIØN A(5,4)
      READ (5,100) ((A(I,J), I = 1,4), J = 1,3)
100   FØRMAT (5(I2, 1X))
      WRITE (6,200) (A(I,3), I = 1,3)
200   FØRMAT (' ', 3(I2, 1X))
      STØP
      END
```

4. Use an implied DO loop to complete the following.

(a) Write a READ statement for reading the following variables: $A(1,1)$, $A(1,5)$, $A(1,9)$, $A(1,13)$, $A(1,17)$.

(b) Code a WRITE statement to write the values $B(1,1)$, $B(2,1)$, $B(1,2)$, $B(2,2)$, $B(1,3)$, and $B(2,3)$.

5. What will be printed when the program below is executed?

```
      A = -132.44
      B = 3331.0.22
      C = 1.0001234
      WRITE (6,100) A, B, C
100   FØRMAT (' ', E15.5, 3X, E8.2, 3X, E11.4)
      STØP
      END
```

6. What value will be stored when the program segment below is executed?

```
          11111111112     Card
123456789 01234567890     columns
 bb123467E12
```

```
      READ (5,100) X
100   FØRMAT (2X, E9.5)
```

7. Write READ and FORMAT statements to read the double precision value punched on a card as follows.

$$1111\,1111112$$
$$\underline{1234567890123\,4567890}\qquad \text{Card columns}$$
$$\text{bbb}123456789\text{D}-05\qquad \text{Card value}$$

Use the variable name DOUBLE; assume the decimal point is between digits 5 and 6.

8. Write a WRITE statement to print the value .123456789D+06. Use the variable name DOUBLE.

9. What value will be printed by the following program segment?

	X = -1234.33	
	WRITE (6,100) X	
100	FØRMAT (' ', 1PE13.5)	

10. What would the program below print? _____

	LØGICAL SNØW
	SNØW = .TRUE.
	IF (SNØW .AND. .TRUE.) WRITE (6,101) SNØW
101	FØRMAT (' ', L10)
	STØP
	END

11. The variable TABLE is specified in the statement DIMENSION TABLE(2,3). Using the FORMAT statement

        11 FORMAT (6F7.2)

prepare a WRITE statement to output the element values of TABLE as specified below.

(a) TABLE(1,1), TABLE(1,2), TABLE(1,3), TABLE(2,1), TABLE(2,2), TABLE(2,3)

(b) TABLE(1,1), TABLE(2,1), TABLE(1,2), TABLE(2,2), TABLE(1,3), TABLE(2,3)

(c) TABLE(1,1), TABLE(2,1), TABLE(1,3), TABLE(2,3)

12. Think about this problem very carefully. Using an implied DO loop, prepare the WRITE and FORMAT statements to print a list of the <u>odd</u> integer values from 7 through 31. Print up to four values per line, skipping a line between each printed line.

13. The double precision variable QT has the value 93167493.48. Write appropriate output statements to do the following.

(a) Print on the printer: SALES FOR THE YEAR WERE xx.x MILLION DOLLARS AND xxxxxx.xx DOLLARS WERE OVER BUDGET. (Note: The computer uses the value of QT as sales and calculates the amount over budget by subtracting 93000000. from the value of QT and storing the value in DIFF.)

(b) Print on the printer: THE SUN IS xx.xxxxxD+xx MILES FROM THE EARTH. (Note: The computer uses the value of QT as the distance.)

14. The variable RATIO has the value .0125. Write appropriate statements to output the following on the printer: THE TENANT OCCUPIES x.xx PERCENT OF THE BUILDING.

15. (a) Develop a list-directed input statement to read the values of INVNUM, CSTNUM, ITMNUM, PRICE, and QTY. Use unit 5 for input.

(b) Rewrite your answer to (a) using the default input unit.

(c) How would you keyboard the values below for each of the variables in your answer to either (a) or (b) above?

variable	value
INVNUM	94361
CSTNUM	A431
ITMNUM	P64-3
PRICE	87.95
QTY	4

16. These constants will cause trouble if they are used for a list-directed input statement. Why?

(a) 6.4, ABCD

(b) 2*34/56

17. Rewrite the keyboard input below, using repetition factors, for use with a list-directed input statement.

1 2 2 2,, 'ABC' 'ABC',,,3

18. Rewrite these statements, using a character string/format specifier as part of the input/output statement.

(a)

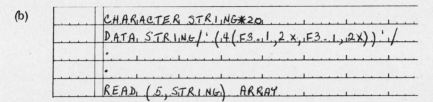

```
         WRITE (8,943) ARRAY
943      FORMAT (4(F3.1,2X,F3.1,2X))
```

(b)

```
         CHARACTER STRING*20
         DATA STRING/'(4(F3.1,2X,F3.1,2X))'/
         .
         .
         READ (5,STRING) ARRAY
```

19. Using the program segment below, what will be printed on unit 8?

```
    A = 3.1
    B = 6.9
    WRITE (8,'1X, F4.1') A + B / 2
```

20. What is the value of GOLD after executing statement 11111?

```
        CHARACTER LEAD (10)*1, GOLD*10
        MONEY = 10000
        WRITE (LEAD, '(I10)') MONEY
        DO KOUNT = 1,9
            IF (LEAD(KOUNT) .EQ. ' ') THEN
                LEAD(KOUNT) = '*'
            ELSE
                GOTO 11111
            END IF
        CONTINUE
11111   READ (LEAD, '(A10)') GOLD
```

Answers to Self-Test

1. (a) Did you get it? Parentheses were missing around the implied DO loop. READ (5,100) (STG(I), I = 1, 20)
    (b) A comma should appear before the index A. Use the library function IFIX if the DO-variable is a subscript. WRITE (6,100) (TRICKY(IFIX(A)), A = 2,7,4)
    (c) Implied DO loops must be properly nested. Each index (i.e., M and N here) must have an initial value and a final value (an increment is optional). Possible answer is: READ (5,300) ((FRAME7(M,N), M = 2, 10, 3), N = 3, 7, 2)

(d) Commas should appear before the indexes I, J, and K. WRITE (6,400)
(COMMA(I,J,K), I = 1, 7), J = 1, 10), K = 20,3,-1)
(e) This one is correct. The statement writes the tenth column of a
two-dimensional array CORECT.
(f) No error.
(frames 6-10)

2.   READ (5,100) NOEASY
     100 FORMAT (50I1)   (frame 3)

3. (a) The READ statement did not affect certain elements of the array,
which we have designated by inserting a "?" as the value for each. The
actual value of each such array element is whatever value it had prior
to the execution of the READ statement. See our diagram of the stored
numbers on the next page.

11	22	33	44	?	55	66	77	88	?	Value
A(1,1)	A(2,1)	A(3,1)	A(4,1)	A(5,1)	A(1,2)	A(2,2)	A(3,2)	A(4,2)	A(5,2)	Element

99	10	10	11	?	?	?	?	?	?
A(1,3)	A(2,3)	A(3,3)	A(4,3)	A(5,3)	A(1,4)	A(2,4)	A(3,4)	A(4,4)	A(5,4)

(b)

```
        5       10      15      20      25      30      35      40
 |9|9| |1|0| |1|0| | | | | | | | | | | | | | | | | | | | | | | | | |
```

(frames 4-8)

4. (a) READ (5,100) (A(1,M), M = 1, 17, 4)
   (b) WRITE (6,200) (B(M,N), M = 1, 2), N = 1, 3)
   (frame 8)

5.
```
        5       10      15      20      25      30      35      40
 | | | |-|0|.|1|3|2|4|4|E|+|0|3| | | |0|.|3|3|E|+|0|5| | | |0|.|1|2|3|4|E|-|0|3|
```

(frames 13-15)

6. 1.23467E12 or .123467E+13 (normalized) (frame 17)
7.   READ (5,100) DOUBLE
     100 FORMAT (D16.4)   (frame 17)
8.   WRITE (6,100) DOUBLE
     100 FORMAT (' ', D16.9) or 100 FORMAT (' ', D15.9) or
     100 FORMAT (' ', D14.9) (frame 18)
9. ᑯ-1.23433E+03 (frame 19)
10. ᑯᑯᑯᑯᑯᑯᑯᑯᑯT (frame 21)
11.

(a)
```
 . . . .  |WRITE (6,11), ((TABLE(K,L), L = 1,3), K = 1,2)
```

(frames 6, 11)

(b)
```
 . . . .  |WRITE (7,11) TABLE . . . . . . . . . . . . . .
```

(frame 1)

(c)
```
      WRITE (8,11) ((TABLE(I,J), I = 1,2),
    -    J = 1,3,2)
```
(frames 6, 11)

12.
```
      WRITE (8,21) (NUMBER, NUMBER = 7,31,2)
   21 FORMAT ('0', I2, 3X, I2, 3X, I2, 3X, I2, 3X)
```
(frame 6)

13.

(a)
```
      WRITE (8,41) QT, DIFF
   41 FORMAT (' SALES FOR THE YEAR WERE', -6PF5.1,
    -   ' MILLION DOLLARS AND', 0PF10.2/
    -   ' DOLLARS WERE OVER BUDGET.')
```
(frame 19)

(b)
```
      WRITE (8,51) QT
   51 FORMAT (' THE SUN IS', 2PD13.5, ' MILES FROM',
    -   ' THE EARTH.')
```
(frame 19)

14.
```
      WRITE (8,61) RATIO
   61 FORMAT (' THE TENANT OCCUPIES', 2PF5.2,
    -   ' PERCENT OF THE BUILDING.')
```
(frame 19)

15. (a) READ (5,*) INVNUM, CSTNUM, ITMNUM, PRICE, QTY
    (frame 25)
    (b) READ *, INVNUM, CSTNUM, ITMNUM, PRICE, QTY
    (frame 26)
    (c) 94361 'A431' 'P64-3' 87.95 4 (You may insert a comma between
    adjacent values. (frame 27)

16. (a) A character constant must be enclosed within a pair of parentheses
    like this: 'ABCD'.   (frame 27)
    (b) The slash terminates the input; the digits 5 and 6 would be lost.
    (frame 30)

17. 1 3*2,, 2*'ABC' 2*3 is one possible answer. (frame 31)

18. (a) WRITE (8,'(4(F3.1,2X,F3.1,2X))') ARRAY (frame 33)
    (b) READ (5,'(4(F3.1,2X,F3.1,2X))') ARRAY (frame 33)

19. The output would appear as

$$\frac{1}{}$$
ØØ3.1   Two records are printed because the format state-
ØØ3.5   ment provides only for one record.

(frame 34)

20. GOLD has the value *****10000. This concept is useful in applications
where you want to replace a blank with another character, such as in printing
dollar amounts on checks.   (frame 35)

CHAPTER TEN
Subprogram Chow Mein

Chow Mein is a mixture, and so is Chapter Ten—a mixture of ways you can make your programs more effective and at the same time save yourself valuable programming effort. In the first part of the chapter, you will learn about:

- statement functions—the use of program segments that other program segments can bring into operation;

- function and subroutine subprograms—program segments which you can compile independently of any main program in which you might use them.

Since computers generally have a limitation on how much memory is available for program execution, the second half of Chapter Ten deals with:

- COMMON area—which is the storage of data in memory in such a way that main programs and subprograms can share the same memory locations for data values.

Statement Functions

1. If someone has written a program segment that we could easily use without modification, we could save the time and effort we would otherwise need to write and test the segment. Makes sense, doesn't it? Furthermore, if a particular programming operation is to be carried out at several points within a program, we would use less memory if that program segment did not have to appear in each of those places in the program, especially if the operation is long.

FORTRAN has provided us with the capability to use a program segment at any point in a program without repeating the coding of that segment. There are three kinds of segments that you can use: statement functions, function subprograms, and subroutine subprograms. We will now discuss the first: statement functions.

This is the general form of the statement function definition.

1		5	6	7		10		15		20		25		30		35		40		45		50

```
      a = b
```

Ah, yes. It does look like an assignment statement. The letter a represents the name of the statement function, and when referred to (called) elsewhere in the program it will return a value calculated by b to the program. The letter b represents an expression inside of the program which calculates the value that is returned to the calling statement of the program.

To give you a better idea of what a statement function looks like, here is one which we will use in subsequent frames.

```
      YDIST (A, B, C) = -16.*C*C + B*C + A
```
         └────a────┘   └────────b────────┘

It is used in the following program.

```
      DATA TIME/ -.5/
C  STATEMENT FUNCTION
      YDIST(A, B, C) = -16. * C * C + B * C + A
C  PROGRAM STARTS EXECUTING NOW
      READ (5, 51) S0, V0
51    FORMAT (2F10.3)
      WRITE (6, 61) S0, V0
61    FORMAT ('1', 5X, 'FLIGHT OF OBJECT WITH INITIAL'
     -     'HEIGHT= ', F11.3, ' AND INITIAL VELOCITY= ',
     -     F11.3)
      WRITE (6, 71)
71    FORMAT ('0', 5X, 'TIME', 15X, 'HEIGHT')
75    TIME = TIME + .5
C  CALL TO YDIST STATEMENT FUNCTION
80    H = YDIST(S0, V0, TIME)
      WRITE (6, 101) TIME, H
101   FORMAT (1X, 5X, F9.1, 13X, F10.2)
      IF (H) 300, 350, 75
300   TIME = TIME - .25
C  CALL TO YDIST STATEMENT FUNCTION
310   H = YDIST(S0, V0, TIME)
      WRITE (6, 321) TIME, H
```

(continued on next page)

```
321    FØRMAT (1X, 5X, F10.2, 12X, F10.2/'+', 50X,
   -     'REPRESENTS HEIGHT 1/4 SECØND BEFØRE LAST
   -     'TIME')
350    WRITE (6, 351)
351    FØRMAT (/// 30X, 'FLIGHT ØVER')
       STØP
       END
```

The name of the statement function is YDIST. Its purpose is to calculate a vertical distance of an object thrown vertically, given (in statements 80 and 310) the values for A, B, and C which correspond to an initial height SO, an initial velocity VO, and a value for time TIME.

This statement function, as all other statement functions, has three parts.

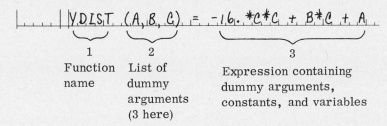

```
      YDIST (A, B, C) = -16.*C*C + B*C + A
```

1	2	3
Function name	List of dummy arguments (3 here)	Expression containing dummy arguments, constants, and variables

Statement functions have three parts, as shown above. What are they?

_____

- - - - - - - - - - - - - - - - - -

a function name; a list of dummy arguments (see frame 6); and an expression containing the dummy arguments, variables, and constants.

2. The statement function returns a value to the program statement which is called the function segment. This value can be real, integer, or logical, depending upon how the function is defined. The first character of the statement function name determines the type of function that it is (if you do not specify the name of the function in a type statement). This statement function would return a real value.

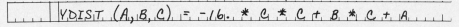

```
      YDIST (A, B, C) = -16.* C * C + B * C + A
```

On the other hand, if we specified YDIST in an integer type statement, YDIST would return an integer value, as shown below.

```
      INTEGER YDIST
```

The rules covered in frames 5-7 of Chapter Two for naming a variable also apply to naming a statement function. Which of these statement function names are invalid and why?

(a) ROUND _____

(b) SQUARE _____

(c) 123456 _____

(d) FUNCTION _____

(e) 9ROOMS _____

- -

(c) The first character of the statement function name must be alphabetic, not numeric; the name A12345 would be okay.
(d) A statement function name is limited to six characters or less; shortening the name to FUNCTI would be okay, as long as you did not use the name earlier in the program as a variable.
(e) The first character of the statement function name must be alphabetic.

3. Here are several lines of FORTRAN coding, many of them statement functions. Determine the type of value to be returned by each function.

```
REAL INC, DEC
INTEGER AMOUNT
LOGICAL SWITCH
    :
INDEX (A, B) = 2. * A + 3. * B
AMOUNT (I, A) = (137.7 * (I + 40.0/A)) /
-    (A + (2 * I))
INC (A, B, C) = A + B + C + AMOUNT (3, A) - DEC
SWITCH (A, I) = (A .GT. 200.) .OR. (I .LT.
-    10.0)
```

Function name	Type	
AMOUNT	(a)	_____
INC	(b)	_____
SWITCH	(c)	_____
INDEX	(d)	_____

- - - - - - - - - - - - - - - - - - -

(a) integer; (b) real; (c) logical; (d) integer

4. For each of the following functions, write a statement function (and a type statement, if necessary) to specify the mode of the value returned by the function.

(a) $M(MO, V) = \dfrac{MO}{\sqrt{1 - \left(\dfrac{V}{2.99776 \times 10^8}\right)^2}}$ (M is real.)

(b) $SINE(X) = X - \dfrac{X^3}{6} + \dfrac{X^5}{120}$ (SINE is real.)

(c) $OVTIME(HOURS, RATE) = (RATE)(HOURS)(FACTOR)$

(d) $IDOTJ(I1, I2, J1, J2) = (I1)(J1) + (I2)(J2)$

- - - - - - - - - - - - - - - - - -

(a) `REAL M`
     `M(MØ, V) = MØ/ ((1. - (V/2.99776E8)**2)**.5`
(b) `SINE(X) = X - X**3/6. + X**5/120.`
(c) `ØVTIME(HØURS, RATE) = RATE * HØURS * FACTØR`
(d) `IDØTJ(I1, I2, J1, J2) = I1 * J1 + I2 * J2`

Dummy Arguments and Variables

5.

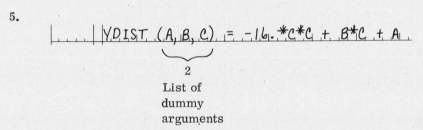

`YDIST (A, B, C) = -16.*C*C + B*C + A`

2

List of
dummy
arguments

The second part of a statement function is a list of "dummy arguments." These arguments are dummy variables. The values given in a function call such as

`80    H = YDIST (SØ, VØ, TIME)`
or `310    H = YDIST (SØ, VØ, TIME)`

are substituted for these dummy variables when the statement function name (YDIST) is found. That is, when the statement numbered 80 (or 310) is executed, the following substitutions occur: SO for A, VO for B, and TIME for C. Thus, YDIST (A, B, C) is computed as YDIST (SO, VO, TIME), which is equal to -16. * TIME * TIME + VO * TIME + SO.

As an example, if SO = 100., VO = 600., and TIME = 3., what would be stored in H after execution of this statement? _____

```
80      H = YDIST (SØ, VØ, TIME)
```

- - - - - - - - - - - - - - - - - -

1756, since YDIST (100., 600., 3.) = -16. * 3. * 3. + 600. * 3. + 100. = -144. + 1800. + 100. = 1756. (or 1756)

6. For each argument passed to the function (or subprogram) there is a corresponding dummy argument in the function (or subprogram) definition. This dummy argument corresponds from left to right in mode of the argument (that is, integer, real) and number of arguments.

When defining a statement function name, one or more dummy arguments are enclosed within a set of parentheses which immediately follow the function name. If there is more than one dummy argument, you must separate each such argument from the other by using a comma.

```
        ØVTIME (HØURS, RATE) = RATE * HØURS * FACTØR
```

Statement function name   Two dummy arguments   Expression which defines the operations to take place when the statement function is used

Remember, a dummy argument is a variable which is given a value when the function is invoked (called and executed). A dummy argument does not have a value unless the function is being executed, nor does it have any relationship to any variable used elsewhere in the program by the same name. So you may use any variable name for a dummy argument, as long as you specify its type (if necessary, in a type statement).

The statement on the right side of the equal sign defines the operations that are to take place when the statement function is called. In our case, each of the variables appearing to the right of the equal sign is a dummy variable.

```
        YDIST (A, B, C) = -16. * C * C + B * C + A
```

The computation depends only on the values of these dummy variables.

However, statement functions may be defined where the expression part of the statement function contains variable names which are not dummy variables. An example of such a statement function is

```
        ØVTIME (HØURS, RATE) = RATE * HØURS * FACTØR
```

In this case, when the function OVTIME is invoked, the value of FACTOR is whatever value is stored in the variable name FACTOR at that point in the program execution.

To illustrate the meaning of the term "dummy variable," when a statement function is invoked, a variable name is put into a one-to-one correspondence with a dummy variable and the value stored in this variable is used in the evaluation of the statement function expression. However, those variables appearing in the expression part of the statement function which are not dummy variables take their values directly from their variable names when the function is executed.

Remember that the dummy arguments serve the purpose of telling the compiler how the expression is to be evaluated at the time of execution. However, the actual values are supplied by the calling statement for evaluation of the expression. You see, a statement function is only activated when one of your program statements invokes (calls) it. The rules for variable type also apply to dummy variables. After the statement function has been executed, the dummy variables become undefined.

How do dummy variables in the argument list of a statement function differ from other variables used elsewhere in the same program?

_____

_____

- - - - - - - - - - - - - - - - - - - -

The dummy variable does not have a value until the point at which the statement function is executed; it then has the value only while the function is being executed, after which point the dummy variable is undefined.

7. Let's invoke this statement function in a program.

| | | | | | | ∅V.T.IME (H∅U.RS., RAT.E)₁ = RAT.E *. H∅U.RS₁ *. F.AC.T∅R | |

Here's the program.

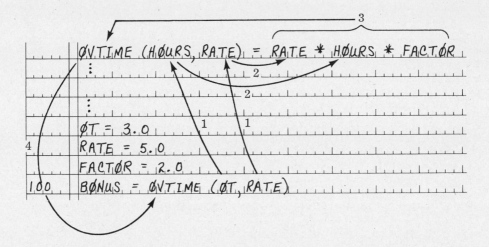

Statement 100 instructs the computer that we wish to evaluate the statement function OVTIME, previously defined at the beginning of the program. Statement 100 also instructs the computer to use the values of OT and RATE when evaluating the function.

Did you notice that the statement function definition used the value of OT and not HOURS? HOURS was only a dummy argument which indicated to the compiler that a real type variable was to be used a certain way in the calculation, with the actual variable to be specified at the time of execution.

In contrast, because FACTOR was not a dummy variable, the calculation of OVTIME used the actual value of FACTOR at the time of execution.

Now here's another program segment using our statement function OVTIME.

```
      OVTIME (HOURS, RATE) = RATE * HOURS * FACTOR
      :
50    READ (5,100) RATE, HOURS, FACTOR
      OT = HOURS - 40.
C     INITIALIZE BONUS TO 0
      BONUS = 0.0
C     COMPUTATION OF BONUS IF OT GREATER THAN 0
      IF (OT .GT. 0.0) BONUS = OVTIME (OT, RATE)
C     COMPUTATION OF GROSS PAY
      GROSPY = RATE * 40. + BONUS
```

Calculate the resulting value of BONUS for each set of values read by our program.

	RATE	HOURS	FACTOR	OT	BONUS
card 1	3.75	42.0	1.	2.0	7.5
card 2	3.75	46.0	2.	(a)	
card 3	6.00	50.0	1.	(b)	
card 4	5.50	41.25	1.	(c)	

- - - - - - - - - - - - - - - - - -

(a) 6.00, 45.000; (b) 10.00, 60.000; (c) 1.25, 6.875

8. The right side of a statement function definition may also contain other statement functions that you've previously defined. That is, writing

		`RØUND (A, B) = IRØUND (A, B) / 10.**B`

without defining the statement function IROUND is incorrect. However,

		`IRØUND (F, G) = F * 10.**G + .5`
		`RØUND (A, B) = IRØUND (A, B) / 10.**B`

is correct.

Which of the following are correct or incorrect, and why?

(a)
10		`IRØUND (AMØUNT) = AMØUNT + .5`
20		`RØUND (AMØUNT) = IRØUND (AMØUNT)`
		:
30		`AMØUNT = RØUND (AMØUNT)`

(b)
40		`SUMMIT (A, B, C, D) = A + B + C + D + E(I)`
		:
50		`PEAK = SUMMIT (W, X, Y, Z)`

(c)
60		`LIQUØR (DRINK) = (MALT - BARLEY + WATER) *`
	-	`DRINK`
		:
70		`QUARTS = LIQUØR (DRINK(NUMBER))/BØTTLE`

- - - - - - - - - - - - - - - - - - - -

(a) All of the statements are correct. Note that the statement numbered 20 uses one statement function as part of its definition. FORTRAN permits the use of one or more statement functions previously defined as part of a definition. In our example, the function ROUND as we've defined it takes a real variable and converts its value to integer type after rounding it to the nearest whole number, and it then converts the value back to a real type number with no digits to the right of the decimal. By illustration of our two statement function definitions, WEIGHT would be printed with a value of 165.00. (See our program segment on the next page.)

. . . . .	IROUND (AMOUNT) = AMOUNT + .5
. . . . .	ROUND (AMOUNT) = IROUND (AMOUNT)
. . . . .	WEIGHT = 165.34
. . . . .	WEIGHT = ROUND (WEIGHT)
. . . . .	WRITE (6, 100) WEIGHT
100	FORMAT (1X, F6.2)

(b) This is correct.

(c) Both are correct; here we've illustrated the use of a subscripted variable in substitution for a dummy variable at execution time.

9.   We saw that the number and type of variables in the dummy argument list must correspond from left to right with the arguments that appear in the FORTRAN statement which later invokes this function.

. . . . .	OVTIME (HOURS, RATE) = RATE * HOURS * FACTOR
. . . . .	:
. . . . .	BONUS = OVTIME (OT, RATE)

But is the following correct? If it isn't, why not?

. . . . .	XAVIER (NO, NEVER, MAYBE) = NO/MAYBE + NEVER
. . . . .	:
. . . . .	BUSY = XAVIER (YES, PERHAPS, MAYBE)

- - - - - - - - - - - - - - - - - -

NO cannot mean YES and NEVER cannot mean PERHAPS because integer variables do not correspond to real type variables (that is, the arguments must agree in mode as well as in number). Oh yes, we almost forgot—the variable name PERHAPS is too long for FORTRAN.

10. One last rule for statement functions: The statement function definition must come before any executable statements in your program. Some compilers permit exceptions to this rule; but in any event, the statement function name cannot be used prior to its definition, except in a type statement.

Now it's your turn to do some work. Write an integer statement function definition that will calculate the average of six values; the first two items to be averaged are integer variables and the remaining four are real. The result should be rounded to the nearest whole number (integer).

- - - - - - - - - - - - - - - - - -

```
IAVG (I, J, A, B, C, D) = (I+J+A+B+C+D)/6. + .5
```

11. Next, write a program segment to calculate the average of the following six items. Use your function definition from frame 10. Store the answer in the real variable RESULT.

```
NUM1 = 37
NUM2 = 13
AMT3 = 3.6
AMT4 = 3.4
AMT5 = 10.9
AMT6 = 11.9
```

- - - - - - - - - - - - - - - - - -

We've presented two possible answers. In our first, we've used the variable names as arguments when invoking the function.

```
RESULT = IAVG (NUM1, NUM2, AMT3, AMT4, AMT5,
       AMT6)
```

At the other extreme, our second example illustrates how we can substitute actual values as arguments when invoking the function.

```
RESULT = IAVG (37, 13, 3.6, 3.4, 10.9, 11.9)
```

Our second statement is rarely used (unless the programmer is rather lazy) because it would probably be easier to simply compute the value of the statement function by hand and assign it to RESULT.

12. What's the value of MYAVG? _____

```
INTEGER WEIGHT
IAVG (I, J, A, B, C, D) = (I + J + A + B + C + D)
      /6. + .5
WEIGHT = 125.6
AGE = 33
INDEX = 1973
MYAVG = IAVG (WEIGHT, INDEX, 15. 4, AGE, AGE+1, 6.)
```

- - - - - - - - - - - - - - - - - -

The integer value 365 is the value of MYAVG, obtained after truncation of WEIGHT and IAVG. The expression AGE + 1 is evaluated as 34. (33. + 1) prior to its substitution as an argument. In fact, any expression can be used as an argument as long as it is evaluated prior to the actual execution of the function in which it is used.

Function Subprograms

13. Statement functions do have some limitations: We are unable to define a function with more than one statement and the statement function computes and returns only one value, even though we may need to calculate and return more than one. So the designers of FORTRAN gave us <u>function subprograms</u> and <u>subroutine subprograms</u>, both of which remove those restrictions. The statement function must be compiled as a part of the program in which it is invoked; in contrast, subprograms can be compiled separately from the programs in which they are used. These separate compilations give us a rather free hand since the variables used within subprograms are completely independent of those in other subprograms or the main (calling) program even though the names given to the variable are the same.

Subprograms can also communicate with the calling programs by passing data from one to the other through either an argument list or by common memory locations (which we will discuss later).

The function subprogram consists of four parts, which we've illustrated in this example.

```
1       FUNCTION ØVTIME (X, R)
        IF (R .GT. 3.5) FACTØR = 1.
2       IF (R .LE. 3.5) FACTØR = 2.
3       ØVTIME = X * R * FACTØR
4       RETURN
        END
```

1. The first line of the function subprogram states that the program segment following is a function. The word FUNCTION is followed by the name of the function subprogram, along with one or more dummy arguments separated by commas and all enclosed within a set of parentheses.

2. This section contains any and all of the FORTRAN statements that you've learned thus far. For example, specification statements indicating DIMENSION, REAL, or INTEGER may appear, followed by the program statements.

3. At some point within the function subprogram, the subprogram must contain a FORTRAN statement that gives the name of the function subprogram a value, either by assignment or by reading a variable.

4. The program sequence must be followed by the words RETURN and END. The END statement signals the compiler that this is

the end of the statement sequence to be compiled for the function subprogram. The word RETURN instructs the computer to return to the main (calling) program. A subprogram may have more than one RETURN statement. The RETURN statement before an END statement is optional.

We've repeated our function subprogram below, along with a main program that invokes the subprogram to calculate the value of BONUS. Note that we have deleted the second IF statement in the function subprogram. However, we left the assignment statement. This program is more efficient because the computer executes fewer instructions.

```
READ (1, 235) RATE, ØTHRS                 ⎫ Main
BØNUS = ØVTIME (ØTHRS, RATE)              ⎬ program
WRITE (6, 236) RATE, ØTHRS, BØNUS        ⎭
```

Function subprogram
```
FUNCTIØN ØVTIME (X, R)
FACTØR = 2.
IF (R .GT. 3.5) FACTØR = 1.
ØVTIME = X * R * FACTØR
RETURN
END
```

Try your hand at determining the values that the computer will write for the variable BONUS.

	RATE	OTHRS		BONUS
card 1	3.75	2.0		7.5
card 2	3.75	6.0	(a)	_____
card 3	6.00	10.0	(b)	_____
card 4	2.25	10.0	(c)	_____
card 5	2.00	1.5	(d)	_____

- - - - - - - - - - - - - - - - - -

(a) 22.5; (b) 60.0; (c) 45.0; (d) 6.0

14. Neither the statement function nor the function subprogram can call themselves, although they may call other functions or subprograms. Let's see if you can identify the similar and the different characteristics of the statement function and function subprogram. On the next page, place an X in the appropriate column(s) to specify whether that characteristic is applicable.

Characteristic		Statement function	Function subprogram
first line must state FUNCTION	(a)	____	____
one or more dummy arguments are required	(b)	____	____
can contain one or more statements in the function definition	(c)	____	____
only one statement can define the function	(d)	____	____
RETURN statement is required	(e)	____	____
END statement is required	(f)	____	____
may contain specification statements such as DIMENSION, INTEGER, REAL	(g)	____	____
calculates a value that is associated with the function name	(h)	____	____
arguments in the invoking statement must correspond in mode and number to the dummy arguments	(i)	____	____

- - - - - - - - - - - - - - - - - -

	Statement function	Function subprogram	
(a)		X	
(b)	X	X	
(c)		X	
(d)	X		
(e)		X	if not immediately before an END statement
(f)		X	
(g)		X	
(h)	X	X	
(i)	X	X	

15. Below we've listed a number of function subprogram first lines. And wouldn't you know it—some of them are wrong. Rewrite the incorrect ones.

(a) `FUNCTION SINE(DEGREE)`

(b) `SINE(DEGREE) FUNCTION`

(c) `(DEGREE) SINEFUNCTION`

(d) `FUNCTION (DEGREE) SINE`

- - - - - - - - - - - - - - - -

All except choice (a) must be written as:

`FUNCTION SINE(DEGREE)`

16. Specify whether the function is either integer or real.

_____ (a)   `FUNCTION SINE(DEGREE)`

_____ (b)   `FUNCTION ASINE(IDEG)`

_____ (c)   `FUNCTION NAME(FIRST, MIDDLE, LAST)`

- - - - - - - - - - - - - - - - - -

(a) real; (b) real; (c) integer. Remember that the first letter of the function subprogram name determines the type of the function, except when you use the method shown in the next frame.

17. If you don't want the first letter of the function subprogram name to determine the mode of the subprogram, you can specify the type immediately before the word FUNCTION.

or   `LOGICAL FUNCTION SWITCH (ON, OFF)`
or   `INTEGER FUNCTION BABY (MOMMA, DADDY)`
or   `DOUBLE PRECISION FUNCTION BIGYUM (CASH, MAZUMA)`
or   `REAL FUNCTION IMAGE (INSIDE, OUT, AND, DOWN)`
or   `CHARACTER*8 ALCHEMY (LEAD, TO, GOLD)`

(a) How does FORTRAN usually determine the mode or type of the value to be returned by a function subprogram? _____

(b) How can we change the mode of the function subprogram without changing the name of the function subprogram? _____

- - - - - - - - - - - - - - - - - -

(a) The initial letter of the function subprogram name determines the mode of the subprogram value that will be returned to the calling program.
(b) However, by using words REAL, INTEGER, DOUBLE PRECISION, CHARACTER, or LOGICAL in front of the word FUNCTION, you can specify explicitly what kind of value is to be returned.

18. The function subprogram can have its own specification statements (such as DIMENSION and type) because the variables are local to the subprogram.
    Look at our example on the next page. The function subprogram calculates the average of the values contained in a 15-element array VALUES. In our example we've illustrated the use of a DIMENSION statement in the function subprogram as well as the use of an array as a dummy argument.

```
      REAL FUNCTION MEAN (VALUES)
      DIMENSION VALUES(15)
      SUM = 0.
      DO 1 INDEX = 1, 15
      SUM = SUM + VALUES (INDEX)
1     CONTINUE
      MEAN = SUM / 15.
      RETURN
      END
```

Subscripted variables and arrays may be used as arguments in both function subprograms and subroutine subprograms. However, if you use a subscripted variable or array as a dummy argument, the array size that you've used in your subprogram must be no larger than the array size you used in your calling program. You can use a smaller array size in the subprogram, but not a larger array size.

Put on your thinking cap and write a function subprogram to determine whether the value of a real variable is either greater than zero, or equal to or less than zero. If greater, return the value of true; otherwise, return the value of false. Name your function subprogram SWITCH.

- - - - - - - - - - - - - - - - - - -

```
      LOGICAL FUNCTION SWITCH (NUMBER)
      REAL NUMBER
      IF (NUMBER) 10, 10, 20
C EQUAL TO OR LESS THAN ZERO
10    SWITCH = .FALSE.
      RETURN
C GREATER THAN ZERO
20    SWITCH = .TRUE.
      RETURN
      END
```

A super-programmer might do it this way.

```
      LOGICAL FUNCTION SWITCH (NUMBER)
      REAL NUMBER
C LOGICALLY TEST VALUE OF NUMBER
      SWITCH = NUMBER .GT. 0.0
      RETURN
      END
```

19. You, too, can be a super-programmer. Rewrite the solution in frame 18 as a statement function instead of a function subprogram.

- - - - - - - - - - - - - - - - - - - -

```
      LOGICAL SWITCH
      SWITCH (A) = A .GT. 0.0
```

We can invoke this statement function by using the logical IF statement shown below to create a very powerful set of instructions.

```
      IF (SWITCH (NUMBER)) GO TO 37
```

20. When calling a function subprogram in your main program, the rule of naming variables applies to the name of the function. So, if you've specified in your function that its mode is not determined by its first letter, you will have to include the name of the function in a specification type statement in your calling program. Here's how we call a function subprogram from a main program.

```
      DIMENSION AMTS(15)
      REAL MEAN
      ANSWER = MEAN (AMTS)
```
⟵ Calling statement

     Yes, it's just like using the statement function that we covered in frames 1 through 12, except that the function subprogram can contain many statements. In effect, it is a program in itself, and it can return through its argument list more than one value to the calling program.

     As with statement functions, we must specify in the calling program that the name of the function subprogram INDEX is real because that is how the name is defined in the subprogram. Look at our example on the next page; the function subprogram is indented beneath the main program.

```
      REAL INDEX
      :
      IF (INDEX (ALPHA, BETA, CHARS) - 37.089)
     -    100, 105, 117
      :
      END
```

```
      REAL FUNCTION INDEX (A, B, C)
      :
      RETURN
      END
```

The following programs call a function.   Correct the first line of the function subprogram, if required.

(a)
```
      INTEGER ROUND
      INDEX = ROUND (SUM)
      PRICE = PRICES (INDEX)
      :
      END
```

```
      FUNCTION ROUND (S)
      ROUND = S + .5
      RETURN
      END
```

(b)
```
      REAL MATRIX (30, 13)
      UNITY = INVERT (MATRIX)
      :
      END
```

```
      FUNCTION INVERT (ARRAY)
      DIMENSION ARRAY (30, 13)
      :
      INVERT = ARRAY (I, J)
      RETURN
      END
```

(a) The main program specified that the value to be returned by ROUND is to be integer, so the function subprogram ROUND must be of integer mode. But, by default, the variable name ROUND is real because it begins with the letter R, so we must rewrite the first line of the function subprogram as

```
      INTEGER FUNCTION ROUND (S)
```

(b) No change is required. In this case, INVERT converts a real value to an integer value in the function subprogram. This value is converted to a real value in the calling program.

21. Our program segment below calls three function subprograms. Write the applicable specification type statements for these function subprograms, if necessary.

```
C  COLD IS TO RETURN A LOGICAL VALUE
C  TEMP AND INDEX ARE TO RETURN REAL VALUES
      A1 = COLD (TEMP)
      T3 = INDEX (B3)
      S = TEMP (I)
```

- - - - - - - - - - - - - - - - -

```
      REAL INDEX
      LOGICAL COLD, A1
```

22. In frame 20 we used an array when calling the function subprogram. Subscripted variables or array names may be used when calling a function subprogram, and subscripted variables can be used when calling a statement function—but all must be done with care.

For example, as we noted in frame 18, when using an array name in the calling program, be sure that the array corresponding in the subprogram is specified exactly the same as to both type and dimensions. Otherwise, you may not obtain the results you expected. In this example, our main program calls a function subprogram.

```
      REAL MATRIX(30, 13)
      :
      UNITY = INVERT (MATRIX, INDEX(I), I5)
      :
```

```
      FUNCTION INVERT (ARRAY, IBEGIN, IEND)
      DIMENSION ARRAY(30, 13)
      :
```

Notice that the function subprogram has a similar argument list in type, dimension, and number of variables.

We cannot present here the many other ways that you can use arrays in subprograms. Instead, we recommend that you refer to your computer installation's FORTRAN manual to determine what other techniques are available.

Below we've written some specification statements followed by a statement that calls the function subprogram THEEND. It's your mission to write the first line of the function subprogram and whatever specification statements would be required for the function subprogram to operate properly.

```
        REAL INPUT (20)
        LOGICAL THEEND
        IRECNO = 10
1       IF (THEEND (INPUT, IRECNO, 5)) GO TO 20
        :
        WRITE (6, 2) INPUT, IRECNO
2       FORMAT ('0', 20A4, 12X, I4)
        GO TO 1
20      STOP
        END
```

You'll need these specification statements.

```
        LOGICAL FUNCTION THEEND (IN, IREC, IDSNR)
        REAL IN (20)
```

23. You'll find this problem more interesting if we show you the entire function subprogram. Try to figure out what it does.

```
        REAL IN(20), TEST
        LOGICAL FUNCTION THEEND (IN, IREC, IDSNR)
        DATA TEST/ 4HEOJ/
C    READ RECORD
        READ (IDSNR, 100) IN
100     FORMAT (20A4)
C    TEST FOR END OF JOB
        IF (IN(1) .EQ. TEST) GO TO 200
```

(continued on next page)

```
C   NØT END ØF JØB
         IREC = IREC + 1
         THEEND = .FALSE.
         RETURN
C   END ØF JØB
200      THEEND = .TRUE.
         RETURN
         END
```

- - - - - - - - - - - - - - - - - -

This subprogram reads file IDSNR to input an array IN. If IN(1) contains the literal EOJ, control branches to the statement numbered 200 which sets THEEND equal to true and returns control to the main program (which will stop). On the other hand, if IN(1) doesn't contain the literal EOJ, IREC is incremented by one and THEEND is set to false. Control returns to the main program in which the array input is printed with the record number.

24. Look back at the answer to frame 20. Note that the function subprogram reads data into the array called INDEX. Subsequently, the main program uses that data because it was communicated to the main program through the argument list. So we have two ways in which a function subprogram can return values to the invoking program.

In your own words, explain the two methods by which a function subprogram can return values to a calling program. _____

_____

_____

- - - - - - - - - - - - - - - - - -

These are our own words . . . and we've listed them three ways.
   (1) assignment of a value to the function subprogram name, which is the usual method;
   (2) through the argument list;
   (3) COMMON. (Hey, now, if you thought of this one, you either have a fantastic memory or you cheated! We'll discuss COMMON soon.)

25. At this point we think a picture might be useful to illustrate how a main program can call a subprogram more than once. You can also call a statement function more than once, but we're not illustrating that. Here's our picture.

```
C  MAIN PROGRAM
         DIMENSION A(100), B(100)

25       READ (5, 200) A

50       SMALL = AMINIM(A)

125      WRITE (6, 201), SMALL, A

200      READ (5, 101) B

250      SMALL = AMINIM(B)

300      WRITE (6, 201) SMALL, B

350      STOP
         END
```

```
         FUNCTION AMINIM(C)
         DIMENSION C(100)
         AMINIM = C(1)
         DO 1 I = 2, 100
         IF (AMINIM .GT. C(I))
         AMINIM = C(I)
1        CONTINUE
         RETURN
         END
```

Which statements in the main program call the function AMINIM?

- - - - - - - - - - - - - - - - - - -

50, 250

26. On a separate sheet of paper, jot down the differences between a statement function and a function subprogram. Be sure to cover the following points.

- the number and type of results returned to the main or calling program;
- the relation of the variables within the function to those in the calling program;
- the complexity of the function, including the ability to perform logic;
- how and when it is compiled.

- - - - - - - - - - - - - - - - - - - -

Statement function	Function subprogram
Returns only one result; the mode (real, integer, logical) is determined by the specification of the function name.	Returns one result associated with the function name; the mode is determined by the first character of the function name unless the type appears before the word FUNCTION; also returns values in the argument list if the subprogram has changed them.
Variables in the function are the same as in the calling program, except for dummy variables which use the values of variables or constants supplied at time of execution.	Variables in the function are independent from those in the calling program, even if the names are identical; dummy variables assume values of variables or constants supplied at execution time.
Limited to one statement in definition, although this may include reference to other functions, although never to itself.	A program in itself, but cannot call itself.
Must be compiled with the main program; definition must usually appear before the executable statements in the program.	May be compiled separately; appears as a separate program.

27. How does a FORTRAN program know the difference between a statement function or function subprogram reference and an array name? An array name (and its size) must be mentioned in a dimension or type specification statement. A function subprogram name may be mentioned in a type specification statement if the function name is not sufficient to denote the function type. A statement function name (and definition) must be declared in a program.

What do you think would happen if you forgot to mention that the variable TABLE is a two-dimensional array and you referred to this variable in a program using this statement?

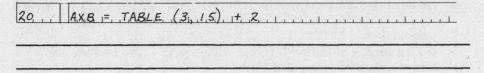

```
20      AXB = TABLE (3, 15) + 2
```

- - - - - - - - - - - - - - - - -

The compiler would assume TABLE is a function subprogram name, because TABLE was not mentioned in a dimension or type specification statement. Execution of the program would halt when this statement was executed as the computer searched its memory in vain for a function subprogram named TABLE.

Subroutine Subprograms

28. Now it's finally time to talk about <u>subroutine subprograms</u>. Subroutines are similar to function subprograms, but with one exception: no value is associated with the subroutine subprogram name. The subroutine can communicate values to the calling program by use of the argument list or common memory area. The subroutine can have its own specification statements, such as dimension or type statements because the variables in the subroutine are "local" to that subprogram.

Ah, yes, there is one other slight difference. Unlike both statement functions and function subprograms (in which we had only to name the function to invoke it), we must "call" (by actually using the word CALL) the subroutine subprogram to make it operative.

```
        CALL ATHOME (I, ABC, XYZ(IT))
```

To further illustrate, we've rewritten the example from frame 22 as a subroutine subprogram. In the earlier frame, UNITY was a function name. Look on the next page for our program.

By the way, a subroutine is named in the same fashion as you would name a variable. However, there is no value associated with the name, so don't worry about real, logical, character, or integer type specifications.

```
      REAL MATRIX (30, I3)
      :
      CALL SAMPLE (UNITY, MATRIX,
     -   INDEX(I), I5)
      :
      END
```

} Calling program

```
      SUBROUTINE SAMPLE (ANSWER,
     -   ARRAY, IBEGIN, IEND)
      DIMENSION ARRAY (30, I3)
      :
      ANSWER = IBEGIN+ARRAY (7,7)+IEND
      :
      RETURN
      END
```

Subroutine subprogram

(a)   Rewrite the function subprogram of frame 22 as a subroutine.

```
C  NOT END OF JOB
      IREC = IREC + I
      THEEND = .FALSE.
      RETURN
C  END OF JOB
200   THEEND = .TRUE.
```

(b)   Rewrite the statements of the main program of frame 22 so that the main program calls the subprogram and then tests the value of THEEND.

- - - - - - - - - - - - - - - - - - -

(a)
```
      SUBROUTINE INOUT (THEEND, IN, IREC, IDSNR)
      REAL IN(20), TEST
      LOGICAL THEEND
      DATA TEST/ 4HEOJ /
      READ (IDSNR, 100) IN
100   FORMAT (20A4)
      IF (IN(1) .EQ. TEST) GO TO 200
      IREC = IREC + I
      THEEND = .FALSE.
      RETURN
200   THEEND = .TRUE.
      RETURN
      END
```

(b)
```
      CALL INOUT (THEEND, INPUT, IRECNO, 5)
      IF (THEEND) GO TO 20
```

29. By definition, the subroutine subprogram does not have to return any value back to the main program. Likewise, you may also have a STOP statement in the subroutine, but don't try a STOP statement in a function subprogram unless you want your program to fail. The definition of a function subprogram requires it to return a value to the main program, so you cannot "quit" before then.

If you want your function subprogram to stop if the current value of a variable ISTOP is equal to 7, which of the following two sets of calling/function subprogram segments should you use? _____

Set 1
```
      FUNC = PACK (A, IN, -7)    ⎫ Main
                                 ⎭ program
```

Function subprogram
```
      FUNCTION PACK (X, ISTOP, IP)
      :
      PACK = ISTOP
      IF (ISTOP .EQ. 7)
        STOP
      RETURN
      END
```

Set 2
```
      FUNC = PACK (A, IN, -7)    ⎫
      IF (IN .EQ. 7)             ⎬ Main
        STOP                     ⎭ program
```

Function subprogram
```
      FUNCTION PACK (X, ISTOP, IP)
      :
      PACK = 15
      IF (ISTOP .EQ. 7) RETURN
      PACK = ISTOP
      RETURN
      END
```

- -

Set 2. A value of 7 for ISTOP will cause an immediate return to the main program which will test IN to see if it is 7 and then stop.

30. In programming practice today, the subroutine subprogram has found wider acceptance than the function subprogram because it is more versatile. In fact, many programmers think of the function subprogram as being only applicable to engineering and scientific problems. This question, however, will help you realize that the function subprogram can be quite versatile, given your imagination.

Since the full FORTRAN compiler permits logical variables, your objective is to write a logical function subprogram called TESTRD which does the following.

(1) Using data set DSRN, read a record into the 20-element array DATA. To input the decimal data into the array DATA, use this FORMAT statement

1	FØRMAT (20F4.0)

because the data is punched in columns 1 through 80 of each punched card.

(2) The last card is indicated by the negative number punched in the first four columns.

(3) The function name TESTRD is to have a value of false unless the last card is read, in which instance TESTRD is to have the value of true.

(4) The input data read by the function TESTRD will also be used by this invoking program.

```
         :
1000     IF (TESTRD (DATA, DSRN)) STØP
         DØ 1100 INDEX = 1, 20, 2
         DATA(I) = DATA(INDEX) + DATA(INDEX+1)
1100     CØNTINUE
         :
         GØ TØ 1000
         :
```

Now you write the statements for the function subprogram TESTRD.

- - - - - - - - - - - - - - - - - - -

```
      LOGICAL FUNCTION TESTRD (DATA, DSRN)
      DIMENSION DATA(20)
      INTEGER DSRN
      TESTRD = .FALSE.
      READ (DSRN, 1) DATA
      :
      IF (DATA(I) .LT. 0) TESTRD = .TRUE.
      RETURN
      END
```

EXTERNAL Statement

31. Pay very close attention now. FORTRAN provides that you may use the name of a function subprogram as one of the arguments in the argument list of both function subprograms and subroutine subprograms. Here's an example.

```
C   MAIN PROGRAM
100    B = TEMP (A, B, WARM, K)
200    C = TEMP (A, B, COLD, L)
```

```
      FUNCTION TEMP (X, Y, RANGE, J)
      :
500   SIMP = X + RANGE (J)
      :
      RETURN
      END
```

Our function subprogram TEMP is invoked by the statements numbered 100 and 200 in the main program. The function subprogram TEMP itself contains a reference to a <u>function</u> subprogram RANGE since RANGE is not mentioned in a DIMENSION or type statement (the variable J is not a subscript, but an argument of the function RANGE).

At the time of execution, when control reaches the statement numbered 100 the function name WARM is passed to the function TEMP by the dummy variable RANGE and so execution of the statement numbered 5000 proceeds as though the statement were

```
500   SIMP = X + WARM (J)
```

At the time of execution of the statement numbered 200 in the calling program, the function name COLD is substituted for RANGE. Execution of the statement numbered 500 proceeds as though the statement were

```
50,0,0 | SIMA = X + COLD (J)
```

For the passing of function subprogram references to occur, however, we must communicate to the compiler that we are passing a function name rather than a variable or array name (because to the compiler, it seems that WARM and COLD are variable names). It is for this reason that we use the EXTERNAL statement in our main (calling) program.

The EXTERNAL statement, if used, must appear in your specification statements, prior to any statement function definitions and executable program statements. For our program above, the EXTERNAL statement would look like this.

```
| EXTERNAL COLD, WARM
```

One or more function subprograms can be listed, each separated by a comma from the other. Mastering the use of the EXTERNAL statement is easier than it looks, so let's give it a try.

Write the EXTERNAL statement for our main program below which invokes a function subprogram, which in turn invokes the function specified in the argument list passed to it by the main program.

```
C MAIN PROGRAM
      DO 100 I = 1, 91
      IRAD = I/(180. * 3.14159)
      TABLE1(I) = TRIGON (IRAD, COSECT, I)
      TABLE2(I) = TRIGON (IRAD, SECANT, I)
      TABLE3(I) = TRIGON (IRAD, TANGNT, I)
100   CONTINUE
```

```
      FUNCTION TRIGON (J, FUNCT, K)
      :
      IF (K - 90) 20, 40, 20
20    TRIGON = FUNCT (J)
      RETURN
40    WRITE (6, 100)
100   FORMAT (' INFINITY')
      TRIGON = -50000.
      RETURN
      END
```

```
     |  EXTERNAL  COSECT,  SECANT,  TANGNT
```

We must tell the compiler that all of these function names will be passed to
the function TRIGON.

32. The postal regulations require that bulk rate mail be delivered to the
post office in a presorted sequence (by zip code) to facilitate distribution
of the mail. Large bulk mail houses go a step further, sorting the mailing
labels by street and name within zip code area. Consequently, the mail
houses (firms which prepare the mailing) maintain the lists in this presorted
sequence by assigning a file number using _recoded_ information consisting of
zip code, and part of the street and subscriber name. This coded information
sometimes appears as the first line of a mailing label. In this frame, you'll
see how we can use subroutines to perform the recoding, although in a simplified manner.

A large mail house maintains one 96-column punched card for each publication subscriber. Upon receiving a subscription order, the following information is punched and verified:

columns 1-5	sales code	
6-25	subscriber name (last name first)	
26-50	"	street
51-65	"	city
66-67	"	state abbreviation
68-72	"	zip code
73-80	blank (reserved for recoded information)	
81-84	magazine or publication code	
85-90	subscription commencement date	
91-96	"	expiration date

To minimize human error in keypunching and verification, the data to be
recoded and placed in columns 73 through 80 is handled by the computer.
The computer "calculates" this information and punches it into columns 73
through 80.

We've flowcharted our simplified recoding system on the next page.
Note that sales code 99999 indicates the last card.

The six-sided symbol ⟨⎯⎯⎯⟩ means a predefined process—in this
instance, a subroutine.

The main program:

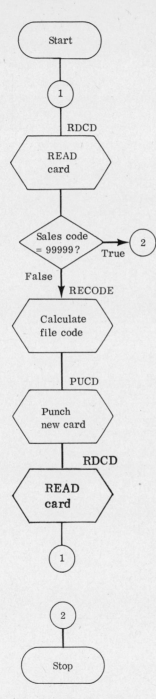

Subroutine to read card:

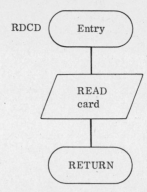

Subroutine to calculate recode:

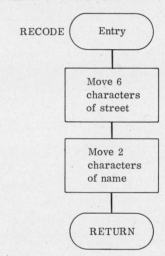

Subroutine to punch card:

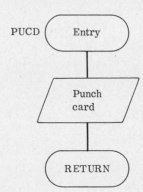

In the flowchart, notice how we printed the subroutine (1) at the top right of the symbol for a predefined process, and (2) to the left of the symbol indicating entry to the subroutine. This documentation technique makes it easy to refer from the main program flowchart to the flowchart for the applicable subroutine.

We've coded the main program below.

```
C   PROGRAM TO READ SUBSCRIPTION CARD, RECODE DATA,
C       AND PUNCH NEW CARD
        CHARACTER SDATA*91
        INTEGER SALECD
C   READ CARD
        CALL RDCD (SDATA, SALECD)
C   TEST FOR LAST CARD
5       IF (99999 .EQ. SALECD) GO TO 110
C   CALCULATE FILE CODE
        CALL RECODE (SDATA)
C   PUNCH NEW CARD
        CALL PUCD (SDATA, SALECD)
        CALL RDCD (SDATA, SALECD)
        GO TO 5
C   END OF JOB
10      STOP
        END
```

Note that we have used the character variable SDATA rather than individual variables. This enables us to refer to all of the elements by indicating the array name only during input, output, or as an argument in the argument list. However, because we must make a logical comparison of arithmetic data, we have an integer variable which will contain the sales code (refer to the card layout).

Now here's the subroutine RDCD which will further describe how we were able to use an array of real variables (SDATA) to contain integer and alphanumeric data.

```
C   SUBROUTINE TO READ NEW SUBSCRIBER CARD
        SUBROUTINE RDCD (SDATA, SALECD)
        CHARACTER SDATA*91
        INTEGER SALECD
C   READ CARD AND RETURN TO MAIN PROGRAM
        READ (5,100) SALECD, SDATA
100     FORMAT (I5,A91)
        RETURN
        END
```

Now it's your turn. Write subroutine PUCD to punch the new subscriber card, using device 7 as the card punch.

— — — — — — — — — — — — — — — — — —

Here's our version of subroutine PUCD.

```
C  SUBROUTINE TO PUNCH NEW CARD
       SUBROUTINE PUCD (SDATA, SALECD)
       CHARACTER SDATA*9
       INTEGER SALECD
C  PUNCH CARD AND RETURN TO MAIN PROGRAM
       WRITE (7, 100) SALECD, SDATA
100    FORMAT (I5, A9.1)
       RETURN
       END
```

33. In this frame we will explain the recoding process mentioned in frame 32. Afterwards, we will ask you to write subroutine RECODE.

If you refer back to the previous frame, you will recall that columns 73 through 80 are to contain file code information in the output card. The first six characters of the street field (columns 26 through 31) are to be duplicated in columns 73 through 78. The first two characters of the name field (columns 6 and 7) are to be duplicated in columns 79 and 80.

We now present in summary form the correspondence between the data on the cards, the FORMAT specifications, and the array elements containing the data.

Description	Columns	SDATA Position
name	6–25	SDATA (1:20)
first 2 characters	6–7	SDATA (1:2)
street	26–50	SDATA (21:45)
first 6 characters	26–31	SDATA (21:26)
recoded data	73–80	SDATA (68:75)
first 6 characters	73–78	SDATA (68:73)
last 2 characters	79–80	SDATA (74:75)

Use a FORTRAN coding sheet to write the subroutine RECODE which will duplicate information into elements SDATA (73) through SDATA (80) from certain of the other elements.

- - - - - - - - - - - - - - - - - -

Note the simplicity of moving the data by using the assignment statements.

C	SUBROUTINE TO RECORD DATA	
	SUBROUTINE RECODE (SDATA)	
	CHARACTER SDATA*91	
C	MOVE FIRST SIX CHARACTERS OF STREET - SDATA(21:26)	
C	ADD FIRST TWO CHARACTERS OF NAME - SDATA(1:2)	
	SDATA(68:75) =SDATA(21:26)//SDATA(1:2)	
	RETURN	
	END	

34. On a separate sheet of paper, write down the major differences between function subprograms and subroutine subprograms. (Hint: Discuss mode, method of invoking, and returned values.)

- - - - - - - - - - - - - - - - - -

Function subprograms

The mode is determined by the first letter of the function name, or by the type REAL, DOUBLE PRECISION, INTEGER, or LOGICAL appearing before the word FUNCTION.

Invoked by the appearance of its name (and arguments) within an expression.

A value must be given to the function name so it can return a value to the invoking program; the argument list can return additional values to the invoking program, if desired, as can the common memory area (frame 35).

Subroutine subprograms

The subroutine subprogram has no mode because no value is associated with its name.

Invoked by calling the subroutine (with a CALL statement).

Values are returned only through the argument list and/or common memory area (frame 35).

COMMON Statement

35. In addition to the argument list, the common memory area is the other method for a subprogram to communicate with a main or calling program.

Subprograms are able to share memory locations with main programs, and even other subprograms. We use the COMMON statement to allocate this common memory area.

The COMMON statement causes the compiler to allocate memory in contiguous memory locations for the variables specified followed the word COMMON.

```
C  MAIN PROGRAM
      REAL XYZ(30, 18), INDEX, ITSELF, NOHELP
      COMMON ABC, I, XYZ
      ABC = XYZ(7, 14)
```

```
C  SUBPROGRAM
      REAL FGH(30, 18)
      COMMON BCD, I, FGH
```

The COMMON statement is a specification statement and is thus not executable. The COMMON statement, when used, should appear after the type specification statements.

In our example above, we also used a COMMON statement in the subprogram, so that the variables listed would be assigned the memory locations in sequence as those variables specified by the COMMON statement in the main program. Thus, each pair (ABC and BCD; I and I, XYZ and FGH) share a common storage area.

If we used this COMMON statement in our subprogram, we would have a mess.

```
      COMMON FIRST, SECOND, THIRD, FOURTH
```

ABC would share the same memory location as FIRST. The variable I would share memory with the variable SECOND (but I is integer mode and SECOND is real mode). The first element of the array XYZ would be stored in the same location as the variable THIRD, whereas FOURTH would be stored in the same location as the second element of the array XYZ, or XYZ(2, 1).

So be careful when you use the COMMON statement. It is an effective way to save memory space when subprograms can use the same memory allocated for variables in the main program or other subprograms. But be sure to specify the variables in the same order and mode and dimension thoughout-unless you are trying for spectacular and unusual results.
It should be noted that most structured programming practitioners avoid the use of COMMON areas since they tend to lose visibility as to what data values are passed between subprograms.

Suppose you want the main program variables A, B, and C to share common memory locations with subprogram variables RITA, AJANET, and

SUSAN, respectively. Write appropriate COMMON statements for the main program and the subprogram.

- - - - - - - - - - - - - - - - - - -

```
C  MAIN PROGRAM STATEMENT
       COMMON A, B, C
C  SUBPROGRAM STATEMENT
       COMMON RITA, AJANET, SUSAN
```

36. There are no general rules on the specific order of variable names in a COMMON statement. No expressions of variable names are allowed.

Some programmers write the variables in a COMMON statement in an order such that the first variable is used by most subprograms, the second variable less often, and so on. Variables only used in one or two subprograms (except arrays) and which do not use much extra memory are better passed by an argument list than in a COMMON statement.

Which variables share the same memory locations?

```
C  MAIN PROGRAM
       DIMENSION A(2, 2), B(4)
       COMMON C, A, D
```

```
C  SUBPROGRAM
       SUBROUTINE QUEST
       DIMENSION S(2, 2), D(10)
       COMMON S, A, D
```

- - - - - - - - - - - - - - - - - -

Main program	Subprogram
C	S(1, 1)
A(1, 1)	S(2, 1)
A(2, 1)	S(1, 2)
A(1, 2)	S(2, 2)
A(2, 2)	A
D	D(1)

37. COMMON statements allow you, in certain cases, to eliminate a DIMENSION statement. As an example, the following statements

```
      DIMENSION F(10,15)
      COMMON A, F, D
```

can be replaced by a single statement.

```
      COMMON A, F(10,15), D
```

You cannot use this simple replacement technique when the variable <u>must</u> be specified in a type statement—logical, double precision, real, or integer. Whatever you do, don't dimension an array in a type, DIMENSION, <u>and</u> a COMMON statement. This is just not accepted by the compiler.

Rewrite the following statements to eliminate as many array declarations as possible from type statements.

```
      REAL ABC(30,20), INT(5)
      INTEGER I5(10), HOURS(7)
      LOGICAL SWITCH, SENSE(5)
      COMMON SWITCH, ABC, I5, HOURS, INT
```

- - - - - - - - - - - - - - - - - -

```
      REAL INT(5)
      INTEGER HOURS(7)
      LOGICAL SWITCH, SENSE(5)
      COMMON SWITCH, ABC(30,20), I5(10), HOURS, INT
```

38. Our examples below have broken some rules. Identify the mistakes.

```
C MAIN PROGRAM
      DIMENSION GIN(100), POKER(300)
      COMMON MOCHA, CHERRY, + PECAN, POKER
        :
      CALL CHILD (X, NO)
```

```
C  SUBPROGRAM
      SUBROUTINE CHILD (A, BAD)
      COMMON PEACH, CHERRY, + PECAN,
     -   POKER(300)
```

- - - - - - - - - - - - - - - - - -

First, the variable MOCHA in the calling program is a different mode from
the corresponding variable in the subprogram, PEACH. Second, CHERRY +
PECAN is an expression, and expressions are not allowed in a COMMON
statement. Finally, the second argument in the argument list of the CALL
in the main program, NO, does not agree with the second argument in the
list of the called subprogram, BAD, because the modes are different.

A Story: The Ice Cream Cone

A small but intelligent child walked into an ice cream store and
asked for a triple dipper cone of butter pecan, burgundy cherry,
and butterscotch vanilla. The counterman made up a cone and gave
it to the child.

The child cried, "That's not right! The butter pecan is on the
top and the butterscotch vanilla is on the bottom. I wanted the
butter pecan on the bottom, the burgundy cherry in the middle, and
the butterscotch vanilla on the top."

MORAL: Order is important in FORTRAN, too. The variables
in our argument lists and COMMON statements must agree.

Labeled COMMON Statement

39. In some programming applications, it may be useful to have more than
one common area; we can do this by using the <u>labeled</u> COMMON statement.
Select some name (up to six characters, the first of which must be alphabetic) and don't use the name of some variable (because you may confuse the
compiler). Just enclose this name within slashes after the word COMMON,
followed by the variables you want in that labeled common area.

```
      COMMON /FIRST/ VAR1, VAR2, ARRAY
```

Continuation lines are permissible.

Using labeled common memory area, rewrite the statements in the program segments on the next page so that no arguments are required in the
CALL statement or in the SUBROUTINE statement.

```
      SUBRØUTINE INØUT (THEEND, IN, IREC, IDSNR)
      REAL IN(20), TEST
      LØGICAL THEEND
      DATA TEST/'EØJ '/
      READ (IDSNR, 100) IN
C MAIN PRØGRAM
      IDSNR = 5
      CALL INPUT (THEEND, IN, IREC, IDSNR)
```

- - - - - - - - - - - - - - - -

Subroutine:

```
      SUBRØUTINE INØUT
      REAL IN(20), TEST
      LØGICAL THEEND
      DATA TEST/'EØJ '/
      CØMMØN /AREA1/ THEEND, IN, IREC, IDSNR
      READ (IDSNR, 100) IN
```

Main:

```
      CØMMØN /AREA1/ THEEND, INPUT, IRECNØ, IDSNR
      IDSNR = 5
      CALL INØUT
```

A subprogram without an argument list will generally execute more rapidly than a subprogram that has an argument list with many variables—which is one good reason for using the labeled COMMON statement. However, as we noted in frame 35, the passed values are more transparent.

40. In Appendix C we present various ideas for more effective programming. One is modularization of programs. Modular programming is the concept of breaking a program down into logically complete segments (such as subroutines) which are then compiled, tested, and debugged.

On the next page is part of a main program which reflects the application of modular programming philosophy. Each of the subprograms communicates information between the main program (and other subprograms) through the variables in the common storage area. Some of the variables, however, affect one or two subprograms only, and for that reason, are passed in the argument lists.

```
       INTEGER DATE(3), DSRNI, DSRNØ, STATUS, DATA(20)
       LØGICAL LAST
       CØMMØN DATA
C  INITIALIZE CØNSTANTS
       DATA DSRNI, DSRNØ /5, 8/, DATE /1, 1, 75/
C  READ INPUT RECØRD
1000   CALL INPUT (DSRNI, LAST)
C  CHECK FØR LAST RECØRD
       IF (LAST) GØ TØ 9000
C  CØMPARE DATE
       CALL DATECK (DATE, STATUS)
C  CHECK STATUS
       IF (STATUS) 2000, 3000, 4000
C  WRITE REPØRT LINE
2000   CALL ØUTPUT (DSRNØ)
       CALL INPUT (DSRNI, LAST)
       GØ TØ 1000
```

When the subroutine INPUT was first compiled, however, many errors were detected by the compiler.

```
       SUBRØUTINE INPUT (TEST, DSRN)
       DIMENSIØN ARRAY(20)
       INTEGER ARRAY(20)
       LØGICAL TEST
       CØMMØN ARRAY
C  READ A RECØRD
       READ (DSRN, 1000) ARRAY
1000   FØRMAT (20I4)
C  TEST FØR LAST RECØRD
       TEST = ARRAY(1) .LT. 0
       RETURN
       END
```

After correcting the syntax errors, it is possible for the program to compile properly, but that does not mean it will execute as you expect it to when invoked by the main program.

Identify those statements that must be modified so that the subroutine INPUT will properly communicate with the main program.   Then rewrite the subroutine INPUT so that it will properly compile and execute with the main program.

- - - - - - - - - - - - - - - - - - -

We've rewritten the subroutine INPUT as follows.

```
        SUBROUTINE INPUT (DSRN, TEST)
        INTEGER DSRN, ARRAY(20)
        LOGICAL TEST
        COMMON ARRAY
C  READ A RECORD
        READ (DSRN, 1000) ARRAY
1000    FORMAT (20I4)
C  TEST FOR LAST RECORD
        TEST = ARRAY(1) .LT. 0
        RETURN
        END
```

First, DSRN must be an integer variable, so we must specify it as such. Also, we don't need the DIMENSION statement because we've specified the array size in the INTEGER specification statement.

Block Data Subprograms

41. In frames **39 and 40** of Chapter Eight, we used the DATA statement to initialize values of variables. You can initialize variables in common memory by use of assignment statements, but generally not DATA statements. Variables in a labeled common area can be initialized by use of a block data subprogram. Your computer's FORTRAN manual is the place to look for this subprogram.

42. We mentioned that the parameter list in a function or subroutine subprogram is used to pass data values between a calling and called subprogram. These data values are not lost in the shift between subprograms. However, all of the other variables in a function or subroutine subprogram become undefined after a RETURN or END statement unless the variables are in COMMON areas. To enable variables in a subprogram to keep their values so that on the next call these values are available one must use the SAVE statement.

There are two forms of the SAVE statement. The first consists of the word SAVE and nothing else. This is a command to save all of the data values in the subprogram. The second form

        SAVE I, CASH, CLOTHE

will save only the values of I, CASH, and CLOTHE. By the use of this state-ment, those hardy souls who follow in your footsteps will be able to determine how you want the subprogram to execute.

Write a SAVE statement that will
(a) Save the values of the variables LOVE, THAT, and CALL in a subprogram
(b) Save the values of all the variables in a subprogram.

- - - - - - - - - - - - - - - - - - -

a) SAVE LOVE, THAT, CALL

b) SAVE

Library Functions

43. We stated earlier that one of the benefits of using functions and subrou-tines is that if someone else has written and tested them, and if they are ap-plicable to your programs, it will save you time to use them. Well, FOR-TRAN includes a number of built-in functions as part of the language. For your convenience, we have listed these functions in Appendix B.

If you have a FORTRAN 77 compiler there are two types of functions, generic and intrinsic. The functions available from pre-FORTRAN 77 compilers are intrinsic functions. When you use intrinsic functions you must be careful as to the type of the argument(s) of the function and the type of the result of the function. The FORTRAN 77 compiler allows the use of generic functions. Generic functions automatically take the proper form for various types of arguments. As an example, the intrinsic function DSQRT (the double pre-cision square root function) requires that the argument be double precision also. SQRT (the single precision square root function) requires that the argument be real, not double precision. The use of the generic function SQRT with a FORTRAN 77 compiler, allows the compiler to choose which function to use based on the type of the argument. The FORTRAN statement
      SSQ = SQRT (X)

will either compute the square root as double precision if X is double pre-cision or single precision if X is single precision.

The FORTRAN 77 compiler also has four types of conversion generic functions: INT, REAL, DBLE, and CMPLX (complex) whose arguments may be either integer, real, double precision, or complex. The argument of the function is converted to the type of the function. As an example
      X = REAL (J)
will convert the integer value of J to a real value.

As an example of an intrinsic function, suppose you want to select the minimum value of the variables I, J, and K; you could use the MINO function as follows.

```
      MINVAL = MINO (I, J, K)
```

How about turning to Appendix B now, to see what's available and how to add these to your programs!

44. When you use the intrinsic FORTRAN functions in your program your compiler will recognize them as intrinsic. However, you may want to run your program on another computer which does not have the same intrinsic functions. What can you do? Either use generic functions or, the next best thing is to use an INTRINSIC statement. The INTRINSIC statement doesn't create the missing functions but rather generates warnings during program compilation if the intrinsic functions do not exist in the compiler. To specify that you are using the intrinsic functions DINT, DATAN and DSQRT in your program you write

INTRINSIC DINT, DATAN, DSQRT

A function named in an INTRINSIC statement must not appear in an EXTERNAL statement.

Write a program statement naming the functions DCOS, DCOSH, and IDINT as intrinsic functions.

- -

INTRINSIC DCOS, DCOSH, IDINT

Self-Test

1. Each of the programming examples below is incorrect. Why?

(a)
```
      SUM (A, B, C) = A + B + C
      :
      ANSWER = SUM (MEN, AND, WOMEN)
      :
      ANSWER = SUM (15, 370, 87)
```

(b)
```
       BUMPS (A, B, C) = 2 * A + BRUISE
```

(c)
```
      :
      CALL ACAB (FIRST, SECOND)
      :
      END
      SUBROUTINE ACAB (DUMMY1, DUMMY2, DUMMY3)
      :
      ACAB = DUMMY1 + DUMMY2 + DUMMY3
      :
      RETURN
      END
```

(d)

```
      SMØKE = CIGAR (15)
      :
      END
      FUNCTIØN CIGAR (DØZENS)
      NUMBER = 12 * DØZENS
      RETURN
      END
```

2. We want you to become familiar with using some of the FORTRAN built-in functions, so you will have to refer to Appendix B to locate the applicable statement functions to solve this problem.

Let's suppose that a person has written a program which stores five values in the five-element array LEAKS.

(a) You are to write a statement function called ANSWER which is to calculate the square root of the sum of the largest and smallest values of the five values stored in the array.

(b) How would you use the function ANSWER to assign a value to the variable RESULT, using the values that are stored in the array LEAKS?

3. A main program written by a slightly inefficient programmer calls a function subprogram F1 by the following statement.

```
      ANS = F1 (K, A2, L4, S, ISØP, CLEAN, BREAK)
```

However, since K, A2, L4, and S are large arrays, his supervisor decides to rewrite the invoking statement and add a COMMON statement to transfer all of the variables to the function subprogram except one—BREAK. Your job will be to complete the necessary statements for the main program below and the subprogram on the next page.

```
C  MAIN PRØGRAM
      DIMENSIØN K(2000), A2(50, 20), S(200)
      LØGICAL L4(500)
      CØMMØN


      ANS =

```

```
C   SUBPROGRAM
    FUNCTION
    DIMENSION K(2000), A2(50, 20),
-      S(200)
    LOGICAL L4(500)
    COMMON


    FI =

    RETURN
    END
```

Problems 4 through 8 of this Self-Test refer to the following utility program to transfer information from 80-column cards to 96-column cards.

Problem statement: WRE Co. is replacing its 80-column punched card equipment with 96-column card devices; consequently, WRE must convert many of its files from 80-column cards to 96-column cards. The following problems concern only one of these files: the commission transactions. Each commission transaction requires two 80-column punched cards, but only one under the 96-column card system. The existing file is in ascending sequence on the transaction number and card code fields. The transaction numbers are consecutive with no missing numbers. A program must be written to read the 80-column commission transaction file, list each transaction number on the printer, and punch each transaction into a 96-column card. If a sequence error is detected or a transaction card is missing, a message to that effect will be printed, followed by a termination of the job. Otherwise, the total commission for each transaction is accumulated, as well as the total cards read and punched, and the totals are printed on a separate page at the end of the job. Separate subroutines for reading and punching cards and listing on the printer will be used. Transaction number 99999 indicates the last card.

Purpose of the problem: Write a main program and the subroutines to perform the major program operations.

Card input:

80-column cards—card 1

columns 1-5	transaction number
6	card number: 1
7-12	transaction date (YYMMDD)
13-15	salesman code
16-21	client code
22-27	next billing date (YYMMDD)
28-77	transaction description

80-column cards—card 2

columns 1-5	transaction number
6	card number: 2
7-14	commission amount (e.g., $100000.00 will be punched as 10000000)
15-22	commission received to date (punched in the same manner as commission amount)

Card output:

96-column cards

columns 1-5	transaction number
7-12	transaction date (YYMMDD)
13-15	salesman code
16-21	client code
22-71	transaction description
72-79	commission amount (punched in the same manner as on 80-column card)
80-87	commission received to date (punched in the same manner as commission amount)
88-93	next billing date (YYMMDD)

Printer layout: See Figure A.

Suggested test data: See Figure B.

Sample output using suggested test data: See Figure B.

After you have checked out your program, rearrange the data card input so as to force a sequence error when the program is run again. This will verify the sequence checking logic of your program.

Printer layout

Transaction listing

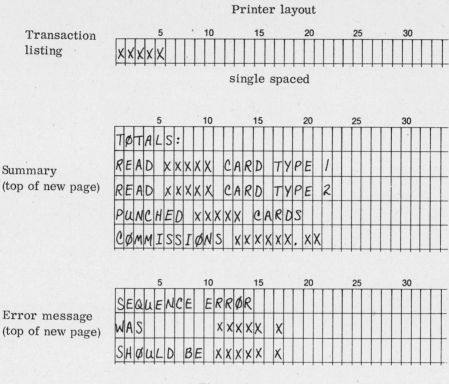

single spaced

Summary (top of new page)

Error message (top of new page)

Figure A

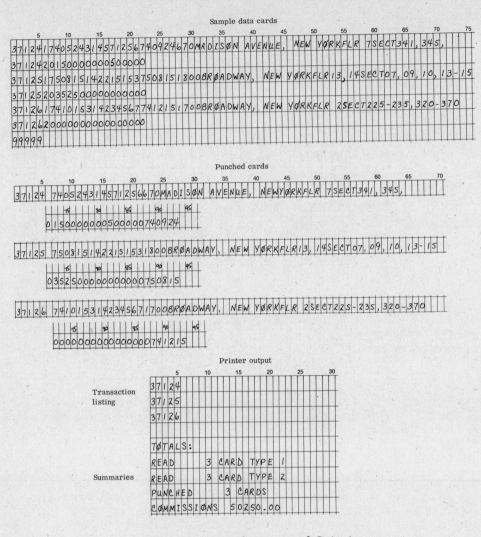

Figure B.   Sample Input and Output

4. Here is a flowchart to perform the transfer of this information from 80-column cards to 96-column cards. Subroutines are indicated with the symbol

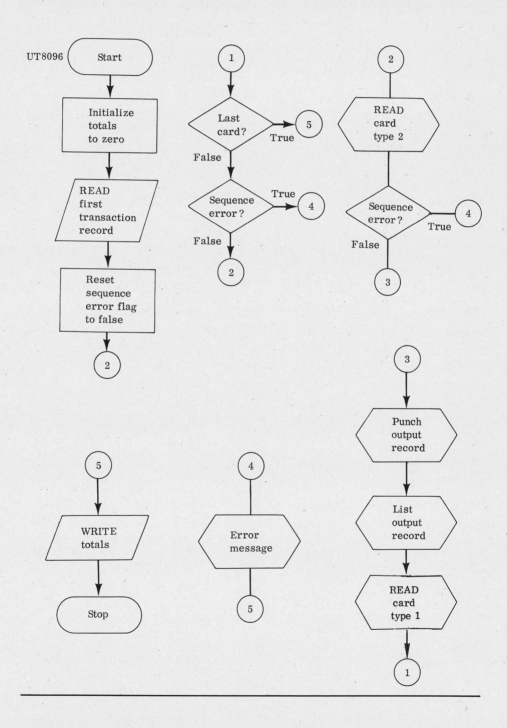

. Write a main program corresponding to the flowchart.

5. On a separate piece of paper, draw a flowchart for the punch subroutine and write a subprogram corresponding to your flowchart.

6. On another sheet of paper, draw a flowchart for the error message subprogram and write a subroutine corresponding to this flowchart.

7.   Here is a flowchart for the subprogram which reads the first card of the
pair.   Write a subroutine for this flowchart.

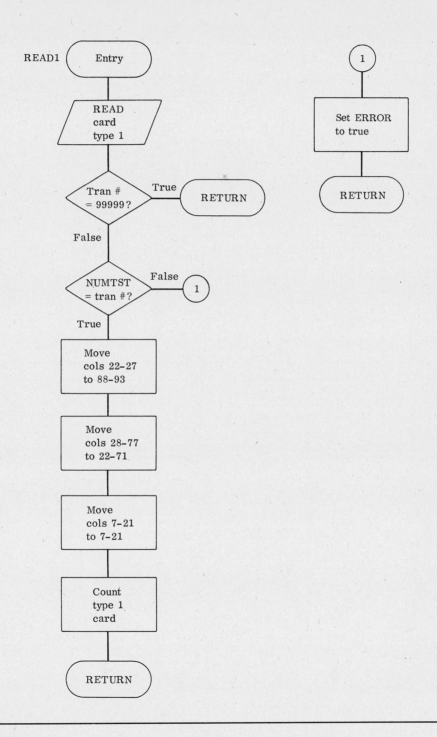

8.   Here is a flowchart for the subprogram which reads the second card of the pair. Write a subprogram for this flowchart.

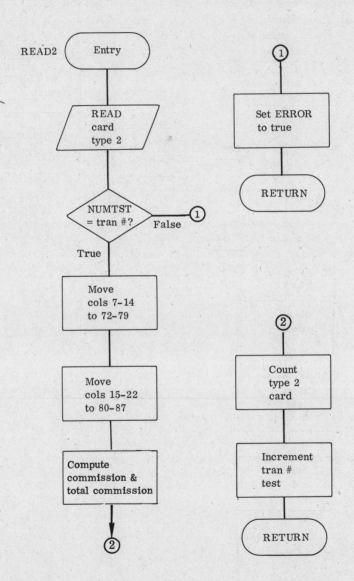

Answers to Self-Test

1.   (a) The dummy arguments of the statement function are real because they do not begin with the letters I through N.   Consequently, when invoking the statement function within the programming, the actual arguments must agree in mode, but in our two examples, integer constants or variables were passed as arguments, which will cause the function to malfunction (if it works at all). (frames 5-9)

(b) The variables B and C are designated as dummy arguments in the statement function definition, but are not utilized on the right side of the equal sign. Depending upon the compiler, the dummy arguments B and C may be ignored and the function will only consider the variable A.   (frames 5-9)

(c) A subroutine subprogram does not have to return a value to the invoking program; if it is desired to return a value, it is done through the argument list or the COMMON statement, but not by assigning some value to the subroutine name.   Don't confuse the compiler by using the subprogram name as a variable, unless you've used the EXTERNAL statement—and then use it properly.   (frame 28)

(d) A function subprogram must return a value to the invoking program by means of the function name, CIGAR, being assigned some value within the function itself.   The program will fail in execution because CIGAR was not given some value to return.   (frame 13)

2.

(a)
```
DIMENSION LEAKS(5)
ANSWER (I1, I2, I3, I4, I5) = SQRT (FLOAT
   (MAXO (I1, I2, I3, I4, I5) + MINO (I1, I2,
   I3, I4, I5)))
```

(b)
```
RESULT = ANSWER (LEAKS(1), LEAKS(2), LEAKS(3),
   LEAKS(4), LEAKS(5))
```

If you are using a FORTRAN 77 compiler, a) can be also written as

ANSWER (I1, I2, I3, I4, I5) = SQRT (REAL (MAX (I1, I2, I3, I4, I5) +

— MIN (I1, I2, I3, I4, I5)))

In this case we are using the generic functions REAL, MAX and MIN. (frames 8, 43)

3.

```
C  MAIN PROGRAM
      DIMENSION K(2000), A2(50, 20), S(200)
      LOGICAL L4(500)
      COMMON K, A2, L4, S, ISOP, CLEAN
      :
      ANS = F1 (BREAK)
      :
```

```
C  SUBPROGRAM
      FUNCTION F1 (BREAK)
      DIMENSION K(2000), A2(50, 20), S(200)
      LOGICAL L4(500)
      COMMON K, A2, L4, S, ISOP, CLEAN
      :
      F1 = ...
      :
      RETURN
      END
```

(frames 35-37)

Our answers to problems 4 through 8 follow. Your programs may be different from ours. To check your programs, you may want to try to run the program with some sample data. (If you do not have 96-column card equipment available, you may simulate the card punch by printing rather than punching the output.) Or you may have an experienced FORTRAN programmer check your work.

FORTRAN CODING FORM

Program	UT 8096			Punching Instructions		Page 1 of 4
Programmer		Date	Graphic	ØOI1IZU	Card Form #	Identification 73 — 80
			Punch	ANANANA		

FORTRAN STATEMENT

```
C PURPOSE: CONVERT COMMISSIONS FROM 80-COLUMN FORMAT TO 96-COLUMN FORMAT
      CHARACTER DATAIN*71, DATAØ1*87
      DIMENSION IDNUM(2)
      INTEGER TOTCOM, TOTRD1, TOTRD2, TOTPCH, START
      LOGICAL ERROR
      COMMON NUMTST, ERROR, IDNUM, TOTRD1, TOTRD2, TOTPCH, TOTCOM,
     1 START
      COMMON/DI1/DATAIN, DATAØ1
C VARIABLES:
C    TOTCOM-ACCUMULATED COMMISSIONS
C    TOTRD1 - TOTAL NUMBER 1 CARDS READ
C    TOTRD2 - TOTAL NUMBER 2 CARDS READ
C    TOTPCH - TOTAL CARDS PUNCHED
C INITIALIZE VARIABLES
      TOTCOM = 0
      TOTRD1 = 0
      TOTRD2 = 0
      TOTPCH = 0
C READ FIRST CARD
```

4.

FORTRAN CODING FORM

Program	UT8096		Punching Instructions		Card Form #	Page 2 of 4
Programmer		Date	Graphic	Punch		Identification 73 80

C FOR COMMENT

FORTRAN STATEMENT

```
      START = 1
      CALL READI
C  RESET ERROR INDICATOR FOR FIRST CARD, AND SAVE TRANSACTION NUMBER,
C  THEN READ SECOND CARD
      ERROR = .FALSE.
      START = 0
      NUMTST = IDNUM(1)
      GO TO 2
C  READ NEXT TRANSACTION - CARD TYPE 1
      CALL READI
C  CHECK FOR LAST CARD
1     IF (999999 .EQ. IDNUM(1)) GO TO 5
C  CHECK FOR SEQUENCE-NUMBER ERROR
      IF (.NOT. ERROR) GO TO 2
C  OUTPUT ERROR MESSAGE
      CALL ERRMSG (1)
      GO TO 5
C  READ CARD TYPE 2
2     CALL READ2
```

FORTRAN CODING FORM

Program	UT8096			Punching Instructions		Card Form #		Page 3 of 4
Programmer		Date		Graphic				Identification
				Punch				73 80

C FOR COMMENT STATEMENT NUMBER 1...5 6 7	FORTRAN STATEMENT 10 ... 80
C	CHECK FOR SEQUENCE-NUMBER ERROR
	IF (.NOT. ERROR) GO TO 3
C	OUTPUT ERROR MESSAGE
	CALL ERRMSG (2)
	GO TO 5
C	OUTPUT NEW RECORD
3	CALL PUNCH
C	LIST OUTPUT RECORD
	WRITE (6,41) IDNUM(1)
41	FORMAT ('0', I5)
C	READ CARD TYPE/CALL READ
	CALL READ
	GO TO 1
C	CONVERT COMMISSION TOTAL TO REAL VALUE
5	COMM = TOTCOM
	COMM = COMM/100.
C	END OF JOB - WRITE TOTALS
	WRITE (6,61) TOTRD1, TOTRD2, TOTPCH, COMM
61	FORMAT ('1TOTALS'//)

FORTRAN CODING FORM

Program	UT8096			Punching Instructions		Page 4 of 4
Programmer		Date		Graphic	Card Form #	Identification
				Punch		73 80

C FOR COMMENT

FORTRAN STATEMENT

```
      'ØREAD  ', I5, ' CARD TYPE 1'/
      'ØREAD  ', I5, ' CARD TYPE 2'/
      'ØPUNCHED ', I5, ' CARDS'/
      'ØCØMMISSIØNS ', F9.2)
      STØP
      END
```

(frames
28, 35–39)

5.

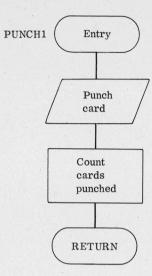

FORTRAN CODING FORM

Program	PUNCH1		Punching Instructions			Page 1 of 1
Programmer		Date	Graphic	Ø O I Z Z U	Card Form #	Identification
			Punch	A N A N A		73 80

FORTRAN STATEMENT

```
      SUBROUTINE PUNCH1
C  PURPOSE: PUNCH OUTPUT RECORD
      CHARACTER DATAIN*74, DATAOT*87
      DIMENSION IDNUM(2)
      INTEGER TOTCOM, TOTRD1, TOTRD2, TOTPCH, START
      LOGICAL ERROR
      COMMON NUMTST, ERROR, IDNUM, TOTRD1, TOTRD2, TOTPCH, TOTCOM,
     1  START
      COMMON/D1/ DATAIN, DATAOT
C  PUNCH OUTPUT RECORD
      WRITE (7,11) IDNUM(1), DATAOT
   11 FORMAT (I5, 1X, A87)
C  TOTALIZE CARDS PUNCHED
      TOTPCH = TOTPCH + 1
      RETURN
      END
```

(frames 35–39)

6.

ERRMSG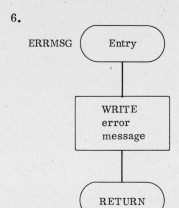

FORTRAN CODING FORM

Program   ERRMSG

Programmer   Date

Punching Instructions

Graphic   Card Form #

Punch

Page 1 of 1

Identification
73   80

FORTRAN STATEMENT

```
C  PURPØSE: ØUTPUT ERRØR TRANSACTIØN MESSAGE
   SUBRØUTINE ERRMSG (ITYPE)
   DIMENSIØM IDNUM(2)
   INTEGER TØTCØM, TØTRD1, TØTRD2, TØTPCH
   LØGICAL ERRØR
   CØMMØN, NUMTST, ERRØR, IDNUM
C  WRITE MESSAGE
   WRITE (8,11) IDNUM, NUMTST, ITYPE
11 FØRMAT ('SEQUENCE ERRØR', ' WAS', 7X, I5, IX, I1/
  1      ' SHØULD BE', I5, IX, I1)
   RETURN
   END
```

(frames 28, 35–39)

7.

FORTRAN CODING FORM

Program **READI**

Programmer _____   Date _____

Punching Instructions

Graphic | Ø | O | I | I | Z | 2 | ₵ |
Punch | A | N | A | N | A | A |

Card Form # _____

Page 1 of 2

Identification [73 ... 80]

```
C     SUBRØUTINE READI
C  PURPØSE: READ CØMMISSIØN CARD TYPE I
C          CHARACTER DATAIN*74, DATAØT*87
C          DIMENSIØN IDNUM(2)
C          INTEGER START
C  LØGICAL ERRØR
C          CØMMØN DATAIN, DATAØT, NUMTST, ERRØR, IDNUM, TØTRDI, TØTRD2,
C         1         TØTPCH, TØTCØM, START
C          CØMMØN/DI/DATAIN, DATAØT
C  READ CARD TYPE I
C          READ (5, II) IDNUM, DATAIN
C  II      FØRMAT (I5, II, 3A4, A3, A4, A2, I2A4, A2)
C  RETURN IF LAST CARD
C          IF (99999 .EQ. IDNUM(I)) RETURN
C  TEST FØR FIRST DATA CARD AND BRANCH TØ 2 IF TRUE CØNDITIØN
C          IF (START .EQ. I .AND. IDNUM(2) .EQ. I) GØ TØ 2
C  CHECK CARD SEQUENCE AND CARD TYPE
C          IF (NUMTST .EQ. IDNUM(I) .AND. I .EQ. IDNUM(2)) GØ TØ 2
C  SEQUENCE ERRØR
```

[10   15   20   25   30   35   40   45   50   55   60   65   70   72]

FORTRAN CODING FORM

Program READ1

Page 2 of 2

Punching Instructions		
Graphic		
Punch		

Card Form #

Identification (73–80)

```
      C FOR COMMENT
STATEMENT
NUMBER
1   5 6 7  10

        ERROR = .TRUE.
        RETURN
C       MOVE COLUMNS 9-21 TO 7-21
2       DATAOUT(1:15) = DATAIN(1:15)
C       MOVE COLUMNS 22-27 TO 188-193
        DATAOUT(16:21) = DATAIN(16:21)
C       MOVE COLUMNS 28-41 TO 22-71
        DATAOUT(16:41) = DATAIN(22:71)
C       INITIALIZE TYPE + CARD READ
        CONTROL = CCRD+1
        RETURN
        END
```

(frames
13, 28,
35–39)

FORTRAN CODING FORM

Program: READ 2
Programmer: ___ Date: ___

Punching Instructions

| Graphic | Ø | O | I | I | Z | Z | 4 |
| Punch | A | N | A | N | A | N | A |

Card Form # ___

Page 1 of 2
Identification 73—80

FORTRAN STATEMENT

```
C  PURPØSE: READ EMISSIØN CARD TYPE 2
   SUBRØUTINE READ2
   DIMENSIØN IDNUM(2)
   CHARACTER DATA1N*71, DATA1ØT*87
   INTEGER TØTCØM, TØTRD1, TØTRD2, TØTCØM, TCØM
   LØGICAL ERRØR
   CØMMØN NUMTST, ERRØR, IDNUM
   CØMMØN/D1/DATA1N, DATA1ØT
C  READ CARD TYPE 2
   READ (5,11) IDNUM, DATA1ØT(66:81)
11 FØRMAT (I5, 1X, A16)
C  CHECK CARD SEQUENCE AND CARD TYPE
   IF (NUMTST .EQ. IDNUM(1) .AND. 2 .EQ. IDNUM(2)) GØ TØ 2
C  SEQUENCE ERRØR
   ERRØR = .TRUE.
   RETURN
C  CØNVERT DATAØT(66:81) TØ EMISSIØN -TCØM
   CALL CNVRT (TCØM)
   TØTCØM=TØTCØM+TCØM
```

8.

FORTRAN CODING FORM

Program	READ2			Punching Instructions			Card Form #		Page 2 of 2
Programmer		Date		Graphic					Identification
				Punch					73 — 80

FORTRAN STATEMENT

```
C  INCREMENT TRANSACTION TEST NUMBER AND TOTALIZE CARD TYPE
      NUMTSI = NUMTSI + 1
      TOTRD2 = TOTRD2 + 1
      RETURN
      END
      SUBROUTINE COUNT(TCOM)
      CHARACTER DATAIN*71, DATAOT*87
      INTEGER TCOM
      COMMON /DI/ DATAIN, DATAOT
      TCOM = 0
      DO 110 I = 66,73
      TCOM = TCOM + ICHAR(DATAOT(I:I)) - 48
  110 CONTINUE
      RETURN
```

(frames
1, 28,
35-39
and frame 25
of Chapter
Eight)

CHAPTER ELEVEN
Specialized Input and Output

The concepts you will cover in this chapter are the frosting on the cake—and it's the frosting that makes the cake much better eating. You don't really have to learn this material—but if you do, you can be better than the FORTRAN programmer who hasn't had the exposure to these concepts (and many haven't).

You see, most of these advanced concepts are not taught during a first course in FORTRAN programming and rarely during the second course. However, these concepts are the ones that permit FORTRAN programmers to use FORTRAN so that it rivals COBOL and even PL/I for input/output speed, depending upon both the application and programmer's programming techniques.

In this chapter we will discuss object-time FORMAT statements which permit you to read in your FORMAT statements at program execution time rather than requiring you to compile them as part of the program.

Out there in the real world, the programmer is expected to work with magnetic tape and disk files in addition to punched cards, so we will cover:

- input and output techniques using tape and disk files, including discussion of sequential access and random access to records within a file;

- features that permit testing for errors during reading or writing records, and testing for the end of a file while reading a record.

Object-Time FORMAT Statements

1.   If you've forgotten what the A format specification is all about, reread Chapter Five, frames 35 and 36 to revive your memory. Let's first take a look at object-time (execution time) FORMAT statements. Way back when, one of the authors had to tabulate the answers to 60 questions contained in over 400 responses to a survey he had conducted. The author was very fortunate to have a computer available, but its compiler was limited. Each time the author wanted to relate the data in different card columns, he had

to change a FORMAT statement within the program and recompile the modified program—a very time consuming and inconvenient process.

The task would have been easier if the first card read by the program
contained information the program could then use as a FORMAT statement
for reading the remaining data cards. Today we have this feature: object-
time FORMAT statements, or the capability of reading one or more FORMAT
statements at object time to make your programs more flexible.

First, our program will require some statements to read in our FOR-
MAT statement(s) at object time. The FORMAT statement which is read in
must be punched on a data card. So we have provided the card which follows.

```
            11 111111 112 2222222 22 33333333 33444 44
123 45  78901 234567 890 1234567 89 01234567 89012 34   Punched card columns
(2X, F3. 1, 5X, I4,  2X, 2A4///7X, F3. 2, I3, F3. 2, A4)   Punched card characters
```

Now, we give you our program segment which contains a READ statement
that reads this FORMAT statement into the array we called FMT, which will
hold the FORMAT specifications in the form of alphanumeric data.

```
        | DIMENSION FMT(17)
        | READ (5,10001) FMT
10001   | FORMAT (17A4)
```

Notice that this array is at least as long as the FORMAT statement specifications we read in (that is, the number of characters in the punched card above
is 44). If each array element of the array FMT contains four bytes, then we
have room for 68 characters.

Assume that each element in an array contains four bytes. (Remember
that an unpunched card column—a blank, symbolized by b̸—is considered a
valid character.) The DIMENSION statement specifies that the array of 17
elements will store _____ characters (bytes). How many characters
will the READ statement read in? _____ What is the name of the array
that will contain the format data? _____

- - - - - - - - - - - - - - - - - - -

68; 68; FMT

2. To use the FORMAT statement data that we have stored in our array
FMT, we use the array name (without any subscript) in place of the statement number in our READ (or WRITE) statement.

```
        | READ (5,FMT) A1, ITEM1, B1, A2, ITEM2, A3, B2
```

Our READ (or WRITE) statement would then use the data stored (by the first
READ statement) in the array FMT as the FORMAT statement.

Before we proceed, let us glance at the sequence of events as reconstruct-
ed by our programming detective.

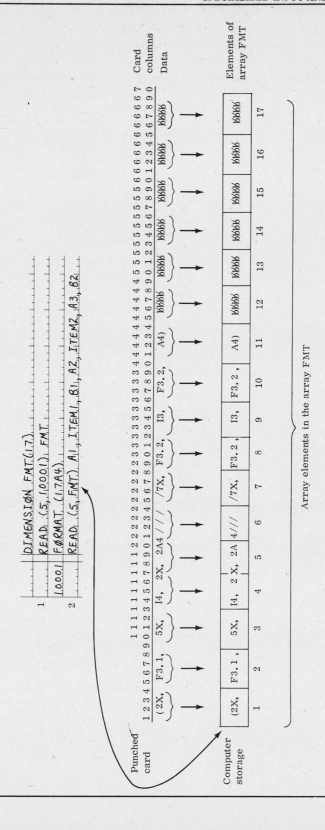

Simple, isn't it. Ah, but there's one more thing. The FORMAT statement that you read in using statement 1 above looks just like a FORMAT statement except that it has neither a statement number nor the word FORMAT punched on the data card. In other words, only the format specifications enclosed within a pair of parentheses are punched; these are subsequently read and stored in the array FMT.

If we were to read in a FORMAT statement at object time, which of the following do you think would be correct to read in using this program segment?

```
        DIMENSION FMT(17)
        READ (5,10001), FMT
10001   FORMAT (17A4)
```

```
              1 1 1 11111112
              1234567 8 9 0 1 2 34567890     Punched card columns
       (a)    15610bFORMATb( 2I 4)           Punched card characters
```

```
              1 1 1 11111112
              1234567 8 9 0 1 2 34567890     Punched card columns
       (b)    bbbbbFORMATb( 2I 4)            Punched card characters
```

```
              11111111112
              12345678901234567890           Punched card columns
       (c)    bbbbbb( 2I 4)                  Punched card characters
```

```
              11111111112
              12345678901234567890           Punched card columns
       (d)    ( 2I 4)                        Punched card characters
```

- - - - - - - - - - - - - - - - - - - -

Both (c) and (d) may be read in at object time since they contain the format specifications enclosed in a pair of parentheses. Note that the array FMT has more than enough room to accommodate the format specifications. In fact, the array FMT may accommodate up to 68 format specifications punched on a card. When statement 2 is executed it references the array FMT for the format specifications. For (c) the format specifications would be found in the second and third element of the array FMT. Statement 2 looks for the format specifications anywhere in the array FMT.

3.

```
14      READ (5,15) ITEM1, ITEM2
15      FORMAT (28X, I1, 34X, I1)
```

The above statement sequence appeared in the author's program. Write sufficient FORTRAN statements to enable the author to read in FORMAT statement data at object time instead, so that he does not have to recompile his program when changing the input column specifications. The longest FORMAT statement would contain 26 characters within the outer pair of

parentheses.   (Hint: Include two A positions for the outer right and left parentheses.)

- - - - - - - - - - - - - - - - -

Here's one possible answer.

```
C  DEFINE THE ARRAY TO STORE THE FORMAT STATEMENT
C      DATA
       DIMENSION FMTIN (7)
C  READ IN FORMAT STATEMENT DATA
       READ (5,100) FMTIN
100    FORMAT (7A4)
```

4.   Using the program from frame 3, what format data should be read in to
give us the effect of using at object time this FORMAT statement?

```
15     FORMAT (28X, I1, 34X, I1)
```

Write your answer here.

```
    5      10     15     20     25     30
| | | | | | | | | | | | | | | | | | | | | | | | | | | | | | |      Punched card columns
```

- - - - - - - - - - - - - - - - -

Your answer should be similar to the following. The format data may be contained anywhere from columns 1 through 28 because the array FMTIN has
seven elements (computer words) at four bytes each, giving a total of 28
character positions.

```
          11 111111112222222222 3
1234 5678901 2345678901234567890
(28X, I1, 34X, I1) ȸȸȸȸȸȸȸȸȸȸȸ
```

```
          11 1111111 122222222223
12345678901 2345678 901234567890
or ȸȸȸȸȸȸ (28X, I1, 34X, I1) ȸȸȸȸȸ
```

```
          11111111 1122222 222223
12345678901234567 8901234 567890
or ȸȸȸȸȸȸȸȸȸȸȸ (28X, I1, 34X, I1)
```

or any other arrangement, as long as the first 28 card columns are used

5. A program contains these statements.

```
     DIMENSION NAME(7), STREET(7), CITY(4)
     REAL NAME
     INTEGER ZIPCD
     WRITE (6,IMAGE) NAME, STREET, CITY, STATE,
    -   ZIPCD
```

The statements are used to print address labels. The variables have the following specifications.

| | | | To be printed | |
Variable	Type	Contains	on line	in columns (inclusive)
NAME	real	characters	1	1–25
STREET	real	characters	2	1–25
CITY	real	characters	3	1–15
STATE	real	characters	3	18–19
ZIPCD	integer	numbers	3	21–25

The output image might look like this.

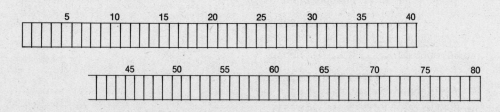

Assuming that a computer word is four bytes in length, what data would you read into the array IMAGE for use as an object-time FORMAT statement to write our label above? How many elements must the array IMAGE contain? _____

- - - - - - - - - - - - - - - - - - -

Here's one possible answer.

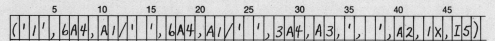

Because our format data contains a minimum of 48 characters, our array IMAGE must have at least 12 elements (12 x 4 = 48).

Object-time FORMAT statements are useful in many applications. Their usefulness is due to the very high cost involved in coding and delivering an operational FORTRAN program. Very often even a minor change in one part of a program might require many changes elsewhere in the same program. Also, many recompilations of this program might be necessary, increasing the programming costs considerably. The object-time FORMAT statement allows you to make changes in a FORMAT statement without having to recompile your program. Here are four applications.

(1) Suppose you want to print the labels of frame 5 starting at any print position other than print position 1. All you have to do is to change one data card and your job is done.

(2) Usually when reports are written, the date is printed in the heading at the top of each page. Such a date may be entered by use of an object-time FORMAT statement.

(3) When designing a standard statistical package, the program designer wants to write as general a package as possible to increase its marketability. In such a case, an object-time FORMAT statement is used by the program user to define the format of the user's input cards and output storage media.

(4) Commercial organizations are often interested in 100 or 1000 units as opposed to single or fractional units. This type of information may be extracted when an object-time FORMAT statement with the format code P is used. As you may remember, the P format is used to shift the decimal point on input or output when used with an F format.

Introduction to Tape and Disk Processing

Our previous discussion and examples have mostly concerned the input/output devices of card reader and punch, high speed printer, and console typewriter. Computer installations which process a large amount of data, even as little as 10,000 records in a processing run, would probably store data on a medium other than punched cards, such as magnetic tape or magnetic disk (sometimes spelled disc) because of the requirements of mass storage and processing speed.

These media can be written or read by the computer at very fast speeds in contrast to a card reader or punch or a high speed line printer, in the magnitude of 10,000 characters per second and above. Magnetic tape is similar to that used in your tape recorder except that it is wider (half an inch because it may be recorded with nine tracks) and thicker (to withstand repeated use). Reels of tape are usually 2,400 feet long, will accept recording densities in excess of 6,000 characters per inch, and cost about $15.00 each, depending upon quality, quantity, and guarantee.

Magnetic tape is a sequential processing medium (like cards); that is, you have to read through 25,999 records to get to the 26,000th record on a tape.

Because this can be cumbersome in some data processing applications, magnetic disk is available. Similar to a phonograph record in that you can begin anywhere you position the pickup arm, the disk has <u>random</u> access capability.

Disks can be classified as either of two categories: flexible disks or hard disks. Flexible disks are approximately 5 or 8 inches in diameter, looking somewhat like a 45 rpm record except that each disk is sealed in a square paper envelope with a hole in the center. The flexible disk is usually made of plastic material and is coated on one or both surfaces with a magnetic recording material. To distinguish it from hard disks, the computer industry refers to the flexible disk as the <u>floppy disk</u>. Each flexible disk will store from about 120,000 to 500,000 characters and upward, depending upon whether recording is on both surfaces as well as the number of recording tracks and characters per inch. Prices for such disks range from $2.75 to $8.00 each.

The hard disk is constructed as a metal base coated with a magnetic recording material and two or more may be stacked above each other like pancakes (with about a half-inch between each disk). Disks are also made singly and called cartridges because the single disk is enclosed within a cartridge. A single disk will hold from 2.5 million to 20 million characters, whereas a disk pack will hold over 1 billion characters, depending upon its construction and the recording density. The disk revolves on a spindle many times a second, so that a movable arm can position itself over the proper area on the disk surface and either write or read a record in a fraction of a second. A disk cartridge may cost as little as $85.00 and a disk pack may cost more than $500.00.

Tape and disk are two recording media which are not readable by humans but by machines. There may be no good reason for using FORMAT statements when originally recording the data and reading it back later using other FORTRAN programs. So FORTRAN allows you to omit the specification of a FORMAT statement number in your READ or WRITE statement when using tape or disk, which will significantly speed up execution of your program.

Input and Output without FORMAT Statements

6. Information is represented in the computer in a binary form. Whenever information is read in a coded form such as punched cards (Hollerith code) or written out in printed characters or other forms readable by humans, it must be converted to a binary form for storage input or to a character form for printing. This task is accomplished whenever a FORMAT statement is used along with a READ or WRITE statement(s). Each READ or WRITE statement that uses a FORMAT statement is compiled so that it calls numerous subroutines during execution of your program. These subroutines convert character (or coded) data from the original form to a binary form or vice versa whenever input or output is desired. That can use up a lot of execution time, especially in applications that have extensive input and/or output.

However, if we wish to write out some information into temporary storage (or external storage) for later rereading without ever printing or punching it, such as when we use magnetic tape or disk, we can do it by <u>not</u> specifying the FORMAT statement. This form of the READ or WRITE statement is the same as before, except that no statement number or FORMAT array name appears in the READ or WRITE statements. Here is an example.

```
      DIMENSION TENANT(800), PAYREC(120)
      :
      READ (3) TENANT
      :
      WRITE (10) PAYREC
```

Unformatted READ or WRITE statements substantially decrease the execution time of running a program that has a lot of tape or disk input/output, since the computer does not have to repeatedly convert data to or from binary form. Usually data which is written or read to or from a magnetic tape or disk to be retransmitted back to main storage or to another tape or disk is handled more efficiently with unformatted input and/or output statements.

(a) Write a READ statement to transfer data in binary form from device number 3 which represents a tape drive into storage variables PAY and DAY.

(b) Write a WRITE statement to write binary data from the variables GOOD, NIGHT, and CHARLY on a tape device number 10.

- - - - - - - - - - - - - - - - - -

(a)
```
      READ (3) PAY, DAY
```
(b)
```
      WRITE (10) GOOD, NIGHT, CHARLY
```

7. Under certain circumstances, unformatted input/output records will be shorter than formatted records. For example, the number in the card record below occupies ten card columns. However, in storage the same record might occupy one computer word, or four bytes (depending upon your computer).

1

$\underline{1234567890}$ Punched card columns

5656565656   Punched card data

This difference arises from the different ways the same information is represented in computer storage (binary) and on a punched card (Hollerith).

One of the authors wrote a program which reads and writes records 800 bytes (200 computer words) long on a magnetic disk. The program executes in a relatively short time because it does not use FORMAT statements. This application also conserves storage space on the disk.

In general, I/O without FORMAT statements would be applicable when records can be in binary form, and do not have to be readable by humans.

Under what circumstances do you think FORMAT statements would be required or advisable for I/O? _____

_____

_____

_____

- - - - - - - - - - - - - - - - - -

(1) when the input is not already in binary form—that is, when the input consists of alphanumeric characters (and spaces) such as data punched on a card; (2) when the output is to be readable by humans, such as information printed on a printing device.

As a matter of interest, magnetic tapes are often recorded on a computer of one kind and shipped to another computer center for further processing. However, the binary representation of data values may differ between models and brands of computers, so using formatted records for writing and reading tape would be a safe bet.

END and ERR Options

8.   FORTRAN 77 and a number of the extended 1966 FORTRAN compilers provide options to transfer control within the program to specific statements upon detecting a transmission error while reading or writing a record or the end of the file upon reading beyond the last record.   We call these options the ERR and END options, respectively.   The READ statement may contain either or both options, but the WRITE can only contain the ERR option.   The options usually appear in the input/output statement following the data set reference number (which we'll discuss soon) and FORMAT statement number. Your compiler will determine whether the order of appearance is critical. Program execution will terminate if either condition occurs unless you have specified the appropriate options.   Here are some examples.

(1)   READ (5, 23161, ERR=304, END=305) VAR1, VAR2, VAR3

(2)   READ (5, 23161, END=305, ERR=304) VAR1, VAR2, VAR3

(3)   WRITE (6, 98001, ERR=78111) VAR4, VAR5, VAR6

Examples (1) and (2) are identical in operation even though the order of the options is reversed (check your FORTRAN manual).   Upon detecting an error during reading, execution will next commence with statement 304.

(a)   In examples (1) and (2), to what statement will execution transfer if the end of the file is detected? _____

(b)   In example (2), if an error is detected while writing the record, to what statement will execution be transferred? _____   In example (3)?

_____

(c)   Complete this WRITE statement to write the variables NAME, BIRTH, and ID on data set 15, using FORMAT statement 60001, with execution transfer to statement 59001 upon detecting an error during writing.

```
      WRITE (15,
```

(d)   Complete this READ statement to read from data set 5 the variables A, B, C, and D using FORMAT statement 4891, with execution to transfer to statement 888 upon detecting the end of the file.

```
      READ (5,
```

(e) Rewrite the READ statement so that it <u>also</u> will transfer control to statement 999 if an error is detected during reading.

- - - - - - - - - - - - - - - - - - -

(a) 305

(b) for example (2), statement 304; for example (3), statement 78111

(c) WRITE (15, 60001, ERR=59001) NAME, BIRTH, ID

(d) READ (5, 4891, END=888) A, B, C, D

(e) READ (5, 4891, ERR=999, END=888) A, B, C, D

or READ (5, 4891, END=888, ERR=999) A, B, C, D

Tape Commands

9.   The READ and WRITE commands that you have learned so far are all applicable to processing magnetic tape.   There are three additional FORTRAN commands for tape processing.

ENDFILE dsrn
BACKSPACE dsrn
REWIND dsrn

We've used the letters dsrn to stand for data set reference number, or a device number.   As you already know, each device connected to the computer is given a one- or two-digit number, depending upon your computer, for use by your FORTRAN programs.   The computer uses the dsrn to identify a particular device.

Now, to indicate the end of a file recorded on magnetic tape, we use the ENDFILE command to cause the tape drive to record a file mark character on the tape following the last record of the file.   For example, to record a file mark on the tape mounted on dsrn 18, we would use the command ENDFILE 18.

Now, if you were to use the END option in your READ statement, execution would transfer to the statement indicated by the END option upon sensing this file mark (after reading the last record).

The backspace command causes the tape drive to backspace one record. If you wanted to backspace three records on dsrn 13, for example, you would issue the command three times in succession.

BACKSPACE 13
BACKSPACE 13
BACKSPACE 13

Upon finishing with a reel of magnetic tape, you may want to return to the beginning for additional processing or just to rewind it.   To cause the tape to rewind to the beginning of the reel (which is called the <u>load point</u>), use the REWIND command: REWIND 16 (for use with dsrn 16).

Prepare commands to do the following with the tape drive identified as dsrn 15.

(a) Write a file mark. _____

(b) Write two file marks. _____

(c) Backspace two records. _____

(d) Rewind. _____

- - - - - - - - - - - - - - - - - -

(a) ENDFILE 15
(b) ENDFILE 15
    ENDFILE 15
(c) BACKSPACE 15
    BACKSPACE 15
(d) REWIND 15

Summary of Optional Commands for Cards or Tape Usage

Command	Tape	Card
READ (5, 1002, END=I2, ERR=I3) DATA	X	X
READ (5, END=I2, ERR=I3) DATA	X	
WRITE (6, ERR=8I) DATA	X	
WRITE (6, 354) DATA	X	
BACKSPACE 7	X	
REWIND 9	X	
ENDFILE 28	X	

END and ERR are extensions of the FORTRAN compiler. Check your manual.

10. Let us now write programs to illustrate the concepts learned so far. The program segment which follows reads up to 10,000 employee wage records from a tape, dsrn 12. Each record is accumulated to obtain a running total. However, if the end of the file is reached before 10,000 records are read, the running total and the number of records read will be printed and the tape will be rewound.

Look at the program segment (on the next page), then modify it to check for reading error. If a reading error occurred, branch to statement 30 which prints the message READING ERROR OCCURRED, the running total, and the number of records read so far.

```
C    THIS PROGRAM ILLUSTRATES THE USE OF THE
C    END-OF-FILE END OPTION
     SUM = 0.0
     KOUNT = 0
10   READ (12, 101, END = 20) WAGE
101  FORMAT (F7.2)
     SUM = SUM + WAGE
     KOUNT = KOUNT + 1
     IF (KOUNT .LT. 10000) GO TO 10
20   WRITE (6, 201) KOUNT, SUM
201  FORMAT (' NUMBER OF RECORDS= ', I4, 5X,
    -    'RUNNING TOTAL IS ', F9.2)
40   REWIND 12
     STOP
     END
```

- - - - - - - - - - - - - - - - - -

```
     SUM = 0.0
     KOUNT = 0
10   READ (12, 101, ERR=30, END=20) WAGE
101  FORMAT (F7.2)
     SUM = SUM + WAGE
     KOUNT = KOUNT + 1
     IF (KOUNT .LT. 10000) GO TO 10
20   WRITE (6, 201) KOUNT, SUM
201  FORMAT (' NUMBER OF RECORDS= ', I4, 5X,
    -    'RUNNING TOTAL IS ', F9.2)
     GO TO 40
30   WRITE (6, 301) KOUNT, SUM
301  FORMAT (' READING ERROR OCCURRED', 5X,
    -    'NO OF RECORDS ', I4, 5X, 'SUM', 5X, F9.2)
40   REWIND 12
     STOP
     END
```

Disk Commands

11. The FORTRAN standard prior to 1977 had no provision for processing direct (random) access disk files. Many of these early compilers however, were extended by their developers to include features that gave the user the ability to process such files anyway. Almost every computer system today, from microcomputer to large mainframe, has disk processing; consequently, FORTRAN 77 includes direct access file processing features.

Before you program READs or WRITEs to a direct access file, it is a good idea to connect your input (or output) unit to a file. We do this with the OPEN statement, whose general form is below.

```
1       7
        OPEN (unit, FILE=fin, ACCESS='DIRECT', FORM=fm, RECL=rl)
```

Don't get excited because the command isn't that complicated.

- unit is an integer expression and stands for the data set reference number, in the same manner as card and tape (a one- or two-digit number, depending upon your installation).
- fin is a character expression and stands for the file name. The limited or subset version of FORTRAN 77 does not support this feature. If this specifier is omitted, the unit becomes connected to a processor-determined file.
- The ACCESS method specifies how the processor is to access the file. Your installation may support other methods besides 'DIRECT'.
- fm is a character expression which stands for FORMATTED or UNFORMATTED input or output. Some FORTRAN 77 compilers may not provide for this specifier.
- rl is an integer expression which specifies the length of each record to be processed with direct access.

FORM	Measure RECL in
FORMATTED	characters (Remember, formatted records may occupy more space than unformatted.)
UNFORMATTED	processor-dependent units, usually words, consisting of some even multiple of bytes, such as four, eight, etc.

This statement OPENs a direct access disk file.

```
1       7
        OPEN (10, FILE='MASTER', ACCESS='DIRECT', FORM=
              'UNFORMATTED', RECL=256)
```

(a)   This file will be accessed by using READ and WRITE statements that refer to unit _____.

(b)   The name of the file is _____.

(c)   All the records will be read and written (with/without) FORMAT statements.

(d)   Each record will be _____ characters in length.

- - - - - - - - - - - - - - - - - -

(a) 10; (b) 'MASTER'; (c) without FORMAT statements; (d) 256.

Note: Check your FORTRAN manual to determine how FORTRAN disk processing is implemented on your computer; review the specific programming requirements and commands.

12. The READ and WRITE statements for direct access differ from those for tape and card because we must indicate the relative position of the disk record that we are going to access. We indicate this record position by using a record specifier.

> READ
> or   (unit, format, REC=recno) list
> WRITE

- • unit is the data set reference number;
- • format is the FORMAT specifier, if applicable;
- • recno is a positive integer expression which is the number of the record to be read or written;
- • list is the input or output list of variables.

```
1    7
1    READ (11, REC=15) BLDG
2    READ (10, REC=INDEX) TENANT
3    READ (12, REC=NUM+5) BILL
```

In example 1, the value of the variable BLDG would be read from record 15 in the file connected to unit 11.

In example 2, the value of the variable TENANT would be read on unit 10 from the record number contained in the integer variable INDEX at the time this statement is executed. If the value of INDEX during execution time is 40, the 40th record is read.

In example 3, the value of the variable BILL is read from unit 12 from record NUM+5. If at execution time the value contained in the variable NUM is 10, the 15th record is read. In this last example, +5 is called a displacement.

(a)   Write a WRITE statement so that the value of the variable A would be written in the 45th record of the file connected to unit 25.

(b)   Write an OPEN statement and an associated READ statement for the following specifications: The unit number is 10; the file name is 'NAME. MASTER'; the number of characters per record is 124; the input and output statements use the FORMAT specifier contained within the character variable RECFMT; and the record number to be accessed is contained in the variable RECNO. A is the input variable.

- - - - - - - - - - - - - - - - - - - -

1	7

(a)   WRITE (25, REC=45) A

(b)   OPEN (10, FILE='NAME. MASTER', ACCESS='DIRECT', FORM=
             'FORMATTED', RECL=124)
             READ (10, RECFMT, REC=RECNO) A

Summary of Disk Commands

OPEN (unit, FILE=fin, ACCESS='DIRECT', FORM=fm, RECL=rl)

        optional   optional

READ (unit, format, REC=recno, ERR=sn1, END=sn2) list

        optional   optional   optional

WRITE (unit, format, REC=recno, ERR=sn1) list

        optional   optional

Self-Test

1. Write a program which will do the following.

    (1) Rewind a tape file before reading the tape.
    (2) Read up to 100 tape records, each containing three integers A(1), A(2), and A(3).
    (3) Calculate A(3) = A(1) + A(2) - A(3) for each tape record read.
    (4) Write the value of A(3) on a disk file for each record read.
    (5) Determine if there are less than 100 tape records and if so, write the number of the last record and the literal (message) IS THE LAST

RECORD on a printer. If there are 100 records the program will write on the printer the literal 100 RECORDS ON TAPE 3.

(6) If an error condition arises during tape reading the program will cause the literal ERROR IN TAPE 3 to be printed along with the record number at which the error occurred before stopping.

Input description: Each record on the magnetic tape (file 3) contains three integers (unformatted). There may be up to 100 records on the tape.

Output description: Disk file number 25. There will be 100 records possibly written. Each record is one computer word. No format is used for writing the disk file. **The record specifier is INDEX.**

2. Modify the program of problem 1 to include an object-time FORMAT statement for I/O. Assume the format data card for two formats has the following layout.

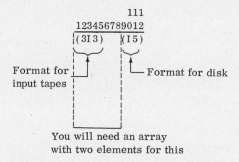

You will need an array
with two elements for this

Input description: The same as for problem 1. However, each tape record is formatted so each element of A is read in with format code I3.

Output description: The same as for problem 1. However, each record is formatted with format code I5.

3. Write a program to transfer records from tape to disk. The records are not formatted and are 100 words long. Use the END option. The tape drive is device 10 and the disk drive is device 9. Count the number of records transferred and print the total on the console (device 6) at the end of the job. **There are a maximum of 4,000 records. Use K9 as the record specifier and write the records sequentially. Rewind the tape at the end of the job.**

Answers to Self-Test

FORTRAN CODING FORM

Program PROBLEM/SOLUTION   Date

Punching Instructions

| Graphic | Φ | O | I | I | Z | U |
| Punch | A | A | A | A | A | A |

Card Form #

Page 1 of 2

Identification 73 — 80

C FOR COMMENT

FORTRAN STATEMENT

STATEMENT NUMBER

1.

```
C   SOLUTION TO PROBLEM 1
    INTEGER A(3)
    OPEN (25, ACCESS='DIRECT', FORM='UNFORMATTED', RECL=1)
C   REWIND TAPE FILE 3
    REWIND 3
C   SET RECORD SPECIFIER TO 1
    INDEX = 1
    DO 10 KOUNT = 1, 100, 1
C   READ TAPE RECORD AND CALCULATE A(3)
50  READ (3, END=110, ERR=150) A
    A(3) = A(1) + A(2) - A(3)
C   WRITE A(3) ON DISK FILE
    WRITE (25, REC=INDEX) A(3)
60
C   INCREMENT RECORD SPECIFIER
    INDEX = INDEX + 1
10  CONTINUE
C   EXACTLY 100 TAPE RECORDS WRITTEN  INDEX = 101
    WRITE (6, 101)
101 FORMAT ('1', 25X, '100 RECORDS ON TAPE 3')
    GO TO 200
```

FORTRAN CODING FORM

Program **PROBLEM 1 SOLUTION**

Programmer

Date

Punching Instructions

Graphic

Punch

Card Form #

Page 2 of 2

Identification
73   80

C FOR COMMENT

STATEMENT NUMBER		FORTRAN STATEMENT
1 5	6 7	
C		LESS THAN 1 DO TAPE RECORDS ON TAPE NUMBER = INDEX - 1
110		INDEX = INDEX - 1
		WRITE (6,121) INDEX
121		FORMAT ('1', I4, ' IS THE LAST RECORD WRITTEN')
		GO TO 200
C		ERROR DURING TAPE READ - RECORD NUMBER IS INDEX
150		WRITE (6,161) INDEX
161		FORMAT ('1', 25X, 'READ ERROR IN TAPE 3. RECORD NUMBER ', I4)
200		STOP
		END

(frames
10, 11, 12)

FORTRAN CODING FORM

Program	PRØBLEM 2 SØLUTIØN			Page 1 of 2

Punching Instructions

| Graphic | Ø | D | F | I | Z | Z | U | Card Form # |
| Punch | A | N | A | N | A | N | A | |

Identification 73 _____ 80

FORTRAN STATEMENT

```
C   SØLUTIØN TØ PRØBLEM 2
    INTEGER A(3)
    OPEN (25, ACCESS='DIRECT', FØRM='FØRMATTED', RECL=5)
    DIMENSIØN FMT1(2)
C   REWIND TAPE FILE
    REWIND 3
C   SET RECØRD SPECIFIER TØ 1
    INDEX = 1
    READ (5,21) FMT1, FMT2
    DØ 70 KØUNT = 1, 100, 1
21  FØRMAT (3A4)
C   READ TAPE RECØRD AND CALCULATE A(3)
50  READ (3, FMT1, END=110, ERR=150) A
    A(3) = A(1) + A(2) - A(3)
C   WRITE A(3) ØN DISK FILE
60  WRITE (25, FMT2, REC=INDEX) A(3)
C   INCREMENT RECØRD SPECIFIER
    INDEX = INDEX + 1
70  CØNTINUE
C   EXACTLY 100 TAPE RECØRDS WRITTEN  INDEX = 101
```

2.

FORTRAN CODING FORM

Program PRØBLEM 2 SØLUTIØN

Programmer _____ Date _____

Page 2 of 2

Punching Instructions

Graphic _____ Punch _____

Card Form # _____

Identification 73 ____ 80

STATEMENT NUMBER		FORTRAN STATEMENT
		WRITE (6,101)
101		FØRMAT ('1', 25X, '100 RECØRDS ØN TAPE 3')
		GØ TØ 200
C		LESS THAN 100 TAPE RECØRDS ØN TAPE NUMBER = INDEX - 1
110		INDEX = INDEX - 1
		WRITE (6,121) INDEX
121		FØRMAT ('1', I4, ' IS THE LAST RECØRD WRITTEN')
		GØ TØ 200
C		ERRØR DURING TAPE READ - RECØRD NUMBER IS INDEX
150		WRITE (6,161) INDEX
161		FØRMAT ('1', 25X, 'READ ERRØR IN TAPE 3. RECØRD NUMBER', I4)
200		STØP
		END

C FOR COMMENT

(frames 2, 3, 6, 7, 8, 12)

FORTRAN CODING FORM

Program PRØBLEM 3 SØLUTIØN		Punching Instructions			Page 1 of 1
Programmer	Date	Graphic	Ø O I I Z Z U	Card Form #	Identification
		Punch	A N A N A N A		73 80

FORTRAN STATEMENT

```
C   PROGRAM TO TRANSFER TAPE RECORDS TO DISK
    DIMENSION INFO(100)
C   DEFINE DISK FILE AND INITIALIZE POINTER
    OPEN (9,ACCESS='DIRECT',FORM='UNFORMATTED',RECL=100)
    K9=1
    REWIND 10
C   TRANSFER RECORD
50  READ (10,END=100) INFO
    WRITE (9,REC=K9)
    K9=K9+1
    GO TO 50
C   END OF JOB
100 K9=K9-1
    WRITE (6,101) K9
101 FORMAT (' ',I5,' RECORDS TRANSFERRED.')
    REWIND 10
    STOP
    END
```

(frames 9, 11, 12)

3.

APPENDIX A
Precision of Arithmetic Operations and Assignments

Determination of the Type of the Result of *, /, +, and - Operations

First operand →

	Second operand		
	Integer	Real	Double[1]
Integer	Integer	Real[2]	Double[2]
Real	Real[2]	Real	Double
Double	Double[2]	Double	Double

Examples

Real * Double → Double

Double + Integer → Double[2]

Real / Real → Real

Double - Double → Double

Determination of the Type of the Result of the ** Operation

First operand →

	Second operand		
	Integer	Real	Double
Integer	Integer	NA[3]	NA
Real	Real	Real[4]	Double[4]
Double	Double	Double[4]	Double[4]

Examples

Integer ** Real → NA

Real ** Integer → Real

Double ** Real → Double[4]

---

1 Double means Double Precision.

2 The FORTRAN standard did not provide for mixed modes prior to FORTRAN 77. However, most compilers correctly perform such computations. See your computer's FORTRAN manual to see what you can do.

3 NA means not allowed in pre-FORTRAN 77 compilers.

4 The first operand must not be negative in pre-FORTRAN 77 compiler.

Determination of the Result of the
Assignment Statement A = B

Type of A ⟶ Type of B   Assignment rule

Type of A	Type of B	Assignment rule
Integer	Integer	Assign
Real	Integer	Float and Assign
Double	Integer	Double Float and Assign
Integer	Real	Fix and Assign
Real	Real	Assign
Double	Real	Double evaluate and Assign
Integer	Double	Fix and Assign
Real	Double	Double evaluate and Real assign
Double	Double	Assign

Assign means to transmit the resulting value, without change to A.

Float means to transform the value to the form of a real value.

Double Float means to transform the value to the form of a double precision value, retaining in the process as much of the precision of the value as a double precision value can contain.

Fix means to truncate any fractional part of the value and transform that value to the form of an integer value.

Double evaluate means to evaluate the expression and Double Float.

Real assign means to transmit as much precision of the most significant part of the value as a real value can contain.

APPENDIX B
FORTRAN Library Functions

FORTRAN provides a number of built-in (also called <u>library</u>) mathematical functions which you can use at will in your programs.

Your program can invoke these functions in the same manner as it would invoke statement functions or function subprograms—by the appearance of the function name followed by an argument list. All rules for the variables in such an argument list are the same as those for statement functions and function subprograms except that the number of arguments must conform to the specified number found in this appendix.

The library functions are available for use in integer, real, and double precision arithmetic expressions. An intrinsic function which returns a double precision value usually has the letter D as the first letter of its name, with a few exceptions. As in the case of statement functions and function subprograms, the first character of the intrinsic function name usually determines the type of the function (integer, real, or double precision). You should use generic functions whenever possible. The FORTRAN library functions are found in the table on pages 486-490. Use the table as follows.

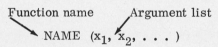

For example, to compute the real maximum of the four real variables A, B, C, and D, use the MAX or AMAXI functions.

```
      RESULT = AMAXI (A, B, C, D)
```

To compute the <u>positive</u> difference between the real values A and B (which may be zero if A is less than B), use the statement

```
      POSDIF = DIM (A, B)
```

Any function may be used with another function. For example, this statement will compute the square root of an integer variable NUMBER since, from the table, the argument of SQRT must be real.

```
      B = SQRT (REAL(NUMBER))
```

You would also use the REAL function to convert integer values for use in the logarithm, exponential, trigonometric, DIM functions, and so on. The effect of the REAL function used above is the same as

```
      A = NUMBER
      B = SQRT (A)
```

However, in this case, storage for A would be required, as opposed to simply using the REAL function. To computer the double precision cosine of a real argument RADIAN, you may use either of the two lines below.

```
      A = DCØS (DBLE(RADIAN))
      A = DBLE (CØS(RADIAN))
```

The functions listed in the table are standard on FORTRAN compilers. Each of the computer manufacturers may add additional library functions to their compilers to make your life easier. Therefore, check your computer's FORTRAN manual to see what goodies are waiting for you.

FORTRAN Library Functions

Intrinsic Function	Definition	Number of arguments	Generic Name	Intrinsic Name	Type of argument(s)	Type of function
Type conversion	Conversion to integer	1	INT	INT IFIX IDINT	Real Real Double	Integer Integer Integer
	Conversion to real	1	REAL	REAL FLOAT SNGL	Integer Integer Double	Real Real Real
	Conversion to double	1	DBLE	DBLE DBLE	Integer Real	Double Double
	Conversion to integer	1		ICHAR	Character	Integer
	Conversion to character	1		CHAR	Integer	Character
Truncation	Gives the sign of the argument times the largest integer which is less than or equal to the absolute value of the argument.	1 1 1	AINT	AINT IDINT	Real Double	Real Integer

Description	Definition	No. of args	Generic name	Specific name	Argument type	Function type
Nearest whole number	$\text{Int}(x+.5)$ if $x \geq 0$ $\text{Int}(x-.5)$ if $x < 0$	1	ANINT	ANINT DNINT	Real Double	Real Double
Nearest integer	$\text{Int}(x+.5)$ if $x \geq 0$ $\text{Int}(x-.5)$ if $x < 0$	1	NINT	NINT IDINT	Real Double	Integer Integer
Absolute value	$\|x\|$ The magnitude of a number without regard to its sign.	1 1 1	ABS	ABS IABS DABS	Real Integer Double	Real Integer Double
Exponential	e^x Raises e to the power of the argument x.	1 1	EXP	EXP DEXP	Real Double	Real Double
Natural logarithm	$\log_e(x)$, $x > 0$ Calculates the base e logarithm of the argument x.	1 1	LOG	ALOG DLOG	Real Double	Real Double
Common logarithm	$\log_{10}(x)$, $x > 0$ Calculates the base 10 logarithm of the argument x.	1 1	LOG10	ALOG10 DLOG10	Real Double	Real Double
Sine	$\sin(x)$ Calculates the sin of the argument x in radians.	1 1	SIN	SIN DSIN	Real Double	Real Double

					Type	Type
Cosine	$\cos(x)$ Calculates the cos of the argument x in radians.	1 1	COS	COS DCOS	Real Double	Real Double
Tangent	$\tan(x)$ Calculates the tan of the argument x in radians.	1	TAN	TAN DTAN	Real Double	Real Double
Arcsine	$\arcsin(a)$	1	ASIN	ASIN DASIN	Real Double	Real Double
Arccosine	$\arccos(a)$	1	ACOS	ACOS DACOS	Real Double	Real Double
Arctangent	$\arctan(x)$	1 1 2 2	ATAN ATAN2	ATAN DATAN ATAN2 DATAN2	Real Double Real Double	Real Double Real Double
	$\arctan(x_1/x_2)$, except when $(x_1, x_2) = 0.$					
Hyperbolic sine	$\sinh(x) = \dfrac{e^x - e^{-x}}{2}$	1	SINH	SINH DSINH	Real Double	Real Double
Hyperbolic cosine	$\cosh(x) = \dfrac{e^x + e^{-x}}{2}$	1	COSH	COSH DCOSH	Real Double	Real Double
Hyperbolic tangent	$\tanh(x) = \dfrac{e^x - e^{-x}}{e^x + e^{-x}}$	1	TANH	TANH DTANH	Real Double	Real Double

		No. of args	Generic name	Specific names	Type of argument	Type of function
Remaindering	The function AMOD (x_1, x_2), MOD(x_1, x_2), and DMOD(x_1, x_2) is defined as $x_1 - [x_1/x_2]\, x_2$, where $[x]$ is the largest integer$\leq x$, $(x \neq 0)$.	2 2 2	MOD	AMOD MOD DMOD	Real Integer Double	Real Integer Double
Transfer of sign	(sign of x_2) times $\lvert x_1 \rvert$	2	SIGN	SIGN ISIGN DSIGN	Real Integer Double	Real Integer Double
Positive of difference	$x_1 -$ Min(x_1, x_2) If argument 1 is $>$ argument 2 it determines the positive difference; otherwise the result is 0.	2 2	DIM	DIM IDIM	Real Integer	Real Integer
Maximum value	Max$(x_1, x_2, \ldots)$ Finds the largest value from the listed arguments.	2 or more 2 or more 2 or more 2 or more 2 or more	MAX	AMAX0 AMAX1 MAX0 MAX1 DMAX1	Integer Real Integer Real Double	Real Real Integer Integer Double
Minimum value	Min$(x_1, x_2, \ldots)$ Finds the smallest value from the listed arguments.	2 or more 2 or more 2 or more 2 or more 2 or more	MIN	AMIN0 AMIN1 MIN0 MIN1 DMIN1	Integer Real Integer Real Double	Real Real Integer Integer Double

		Number of arguments			Type of argument	Type of function
Length	Length of character string	1		LEN	Character	Integer
Index of a substring	Location of first occurrence of substring	2		INDEX	Character	Integer
Square root	$x^{1/2}$ or $\sqrt{x}$ Calculates the square root of the argument x.	1 1	SQRT	SQRT DSQRT	Real Double	Real Double

APPENDIX C
Some Ideas
for Better Programming

Arithmetic Statements

When squaring (or cubing) a variable, it is better to write A * A (instead of A**2) or A * A * A (instead of A**3) since execution speed is increased. The square root (library) function, SQRT, is more accurate and executes faster than the exponential function. Use SQRT (X) instead of X**(1/2) or X**0.5.

We mentioned (Chapter Two, frame 33) that usage of mixed mode expressions is "legal" for many compilers. Remember, however, a compiler will create extra machine language instructions to cause variable mode changes, and these statements increase execution time. Try to avoid mixing modes in arithmetic expressions as much as possible. Use B + (M + N + K) instead of B + M + N + K, since the former requires only one mixed mode operation while the latter requires three.

Decision Statements

When using the arithmetic IF statement, one of the statement numbers following the parenthetical expression should refer to the next executable statement following the IF statement. This eliminates unnecessary branching, which may make the program hard to read by someone else. Use

```
         IF (DISCR) 50, 100, 150
50       WRITE (6,1001)
1001     FORMAT (' COMPLEX')
         :
100      WRITE (6,1101)
         :
150      WRITE (6,1201)
         :
```

instead of

```
         IF (DISCR) 50, 100, 150
25       K = -5
         :
50       WRITE (6, 100, 1)
         :
100      WRITE (6, 110, 1)
         :
150      WRITE (6, 120, 1)
         :
```

When using the logical IF statement, you can sometimes avoid unnecessary branching by testing the negative of a condition.   As an example, if a group of statements are to be performed only if a condition is true, test the negative of the condition.   Use

```
         IF (.NØT. (N(I) .GT. N(K))) GØ TØ 100
         ITEMP = N(K)
         N(K) = N(I)
         N(I) = ITEMP
100      ...
```

instead of

```
         IF (N(I) .GT. N(K)) GØ TØ 200
         GØ TØ 100
200      ITEMP = N(K)
         N(K) = N(I)
         N(I) = ITEMP
100      ...
```

DO Loop Considerations

Only variables or functions which vary during execution of a DO loop should be included in the range of the DO.   Use

```
      SAVE(K) = B * ERRØR(F)
      NEXTK = K * ERRØR(SAVE(K))
      DØ 1000 I = 1, 100, 5
      INDEX(I) = NEXTK * I * I
1000  CØNTINUE
```

instead of

```
      DØ 1000 I = 1, 100, 5
      :
      SAVE(K) = B * ERRØR(F)
      NEXTK = K * ERRØR(SAVE(K))
      INDEX(I) = NEXTK * I * I
1000  CØNTINUE
```

Subscripted variables used in the range of a DO loop, for which the subscript does not vary in the range of the DO, should be avoided. In this case it would be necessary to perform a subscript calculation each time the range is executed. Use

```
      S = SAVE(K)
      DØ 1000 I = 1, 100, 5
      :
      NEXTK(I) = NUMBER(I)/S
      :
1000  CØNTINUE
      :
```

instead of

```
      DØ 1000 I = 1, 100, 5
      :
      NEXTK(I) = NUMBER(I)/SAVE(K)
      :
1000  CØNTINUE
      :
```

In the two examples above, you will note we used

```
      DØ 1000 I = 1, 1000, 5
```

to indicate the value I was to take on the values 1, 6, 11, 16, ..., 96. This method of specifying the value of the DO index variable is preferred to extensive calculations within the range of the DO. Use the following

```
        DØ 1000 I = 1, 100, 5
        INDEX(I) = NEXTK * I * I
1000    CØNTINUE
```

instead of

```
        DØ 1000 I = 1, 20
        INDEX(5*I-4) = NEXTK * (5*I-4) * (5*I-4)
1000    CØNTINUE
```

Read/Write Considerations

Unless you are required to output information in a special format, you should try to put as much information as possible on each output record. This reduces the number of lines written and reduces the execution time of a program. The same consideration given to inputting data will use less data cards. Use

```
        WRITE (6, 101) PHRØG, PHØØL
101     FØRMAT (2(10X, F12.7))
```

instead of

```
        WRITE (6, 102) PHRØG
        WRITE (6, 102) PHØØL
102     FØRMAT (10X, F12.7)
```

If you are outputting data on a non-print device, and you will not later cause the data to be written on a print device, you should use unformatted READ or WRITE statements. This decreases execution time significantly. Use

```
        WRITE (7) DREKLE
        :
        BACKSPACE 7
        READ (7) DREKLE
```

instead of

```
        WRITE (7, 202) DREKLE
        :
        BACKSPACE 7
        READ (7, 202) DREKLE
202     FØRMAT (10F12.7)
```

When reading or writing arrays you should use if possible in the list:
(1) the array name (unsubscripted) instead of an implied DO, and (2) implied
DO's instead of a DO loop. Both of these techniques will reduce execution
time (see Chapter Nine). Here are some examples. Use

	WRITE (6, 2001) ((T(I, J), J=1, 5), I=1, 5)
2001	FORMAT (2X, F7.3)

to decrease execution time, or

	WRITE (6, 3001) ((T(I, J), J=1, 5), I=1, 5)
3001	FORMAT (2X, 15(F7.3, 1X))

to decrease execution time and reduce the number of printed lines, instead of

	DO 200 I = 1, 5
	DO 100 J = 1, 5
	WRITE (6, 1001) T(I, J)
1001	FORMAT (2X, F7.3)
100	CONTINUE
200	CONTINUE

Use

	READ (5, 2001) T
2001	FORMAT (15(F7.3, 1X))

instead of

	READ (5, 2001) ((T(I, J), I=1, 5), J=1, 5)
2001	FORMAT (15(F7.3, 1X))

Index

MORE THAN A MILLION PEOPLE HAVE LEARNED TO PROGRAM, USE, AND ENJOY MICROCOMPUTERS WITH WILEY PAPERBACK GUIDES. LOOK FOR THEM ALL AT YOUR FAVORITE BOOKSHOP OR COMPUTER STORE:

ANS COBOL, 2nd ed., Ashley
Apple™ BASIC: Data File Programming, Finkel & Brown
Apple II™ Programming Exercises, Scanlon
8080/Z80 Assembly Language, Miller
6502 Assembly Language Programming, Fernandez, Tabler, & Ashley
ATARI® BASIC, Albrecht, Finkel & Brown
ATARI® Sound and Graphics, Moore, Lower, & Albrecht
Background Math for a Computer World, 2nd ed., Ashley
BASIC, 2nd ed., Albrecht, Finkel, & Brown
BASIC for Home Computers, Albrecht, Finkel, & Brown
BASIC for the Apple II™, Brown, Finkel, & Albrecht
BASIC Programmer's Guide to Pascal, Borgerson
Complete BASIC Dictionary, Adamis
Data File Programming in BASIC, Finkel & Brown
FAST BASIC: Beyond TRS-80™ BASIC, Gratzer
Flowcharting, Stern
FORTRAN IV, 2nd ed., Friedmann, Greenberg, & Hoffberg·
Fundamentals of Microcomputer Programming including Pascal, McGlynn
Golden Delicious Games for the Apple™ Computer, Franklin, Finkel, & Koltnow
How to Buy the Right Small Business Computer System, Smolin
Introduction to 8080/8085 Assembly Language Programming,
     Fernandez & Ashley
Introduction to Computer Music, Bateman
Introduction to Data Processing, 2nd ed., Harris
Job Control Language, Ashley & Fernandez
More Subroutine Sandwich, Grillo & Robertson
More TRS-80™ BASIC, Inman, Zamora, & Albrecht
Personal Computing, 2nd ed., McGlynn
Problem-Solving on the TRS-80 ™ Pocket Computer, Inman & Conlan
Structured COBOL, Ashley
Subroutine Sandwich, Grillo & Robertson
TRS-80™ BASIC, Albrecht, Inman & Zamora
TRS-80™ Color BASIC, Albrecht
TRS-80™ Means Business, Lewis
Useful Subroutines in BASIC, Adamis
Using CP/M, Fernandez & Ashley
Using the TRS-80™ Model III, Finkel & Bove
Using Programmable Calculators for Business, Hohenstein
Why Do You Need A Personal Computer?, Leventhal & Stafford